# Eight Essays

Published in the United States by Mill Creek Press.
Mill Creek Press is a registered trademark of Mill Creek Press, LLC.
www.millcreekpress.com

ISBN-13: 978-0-9982076-0-5

Printed in the United States of America on acid-free paper.

First Edition

## Preface:

This book contains eight essays. They have been prepared as part of an ongoing labor to recover and restore the work begun through Joseph Smith. The essays have been written between 2014 and 2019, the last one completed on January 1, 2019.

The first, *The Lost Piece of Silver*, was written to present at a conference in Centerville in 2018, but not given to the conference.

Next are four essays presented at the Sunstone Symposium between 2014 and 2018, *Cutting Down the Tree of Life*, *Was There an Original*, *Other Sheep Indeed*, and *Shattered Promises and Great Hope*. Although prepared as part of the summer Sunstone Symposium event, they were written with the larger objective in mind.

Next is an essay based on a talk given to the Bountiful, Utah fellowship, *The Holy Order*. This essay was in response to questions about the priesthood. It discusses the original "holy order after the order of the Son of God" that was first given to Adam in the beginning and handed down through generations until it was lost through apostasy.

The seventh essay is from a General Conference, *Our Divine Parents* and the final is *Problems in Restoration History*. These are a doctrinal exposition of topics those who will build Zion ought to understand.

The final essay is about challenges in restoration history. An Appendix accompanies that essay to illustrate for readers the difficulty with restoration source material.

Taken as a whole, these eight essays are stepping stones in the ongoing labor to recover and explain restoration ideas first declared by Joseph Smith.

Denver C. Snuffer, Jr.
Sandy, Utah January 1, 2019

Table of Contents:

## Chapter 1: The Lost Piece of Silver
© Denver C. Snuffer, Jr. 2018

Two months before Joseph and Hyrum were murdered, in Joseph Smith's final address to a general conference of his church, he said:

> You don't know me; you never knew my heart. No man knows my history. I cannot tell it: I shall never undertake it. I don't blame any one for not believing my history. If I had not experienced what I have, I would not have believed it myself. I never did harm any man since I was born in the world. My voice is always for peace. (April 7, 1844)

Almost every history and biography of Joseph Smith has been written based on what those present that day have provided to us. We also rely on the same people for the transcripts of Joseph Smith's journals and talks.

Although Joseph Smith did draft a replacement history for the one John Whitmer took with him when he was excommunicated, Joseph's statement on April 7th included even that account. He said, "I shall never undertake" providing for us his life's story.

Some believers today are descended from or related to Joseph Smith or his brother Hyrum. These individuals may have family reasons for thinking they understand Joseph. I began a serious examination of Joseph Smith's life when 19 years old. If God called that man as a prophet to restore a lost religion, his life merits every effort to try to uncover his lost history.

Although Joseph told us we do not know him, we still need to attempt to know that man. Our effort should spare no limit in examining every history, biography, journal, diary and record involving him. In four-and-a-half decades I've been diligent in trying to know him, to know his heart.

Christ told a parable about finding lost treasure that included this:

> W]hat woman having ten pieces of silver, if she lose one piece, does not light a candle, and sweep the house, and seek diligently until she find it? And when she has found it, she calls friends and

3

neighbors together saying, Rejoice with me, for I have found the piece which I had lost.[1]

We have lost something more valuable than a silver coin. We need to pursue Joseph: A candle needs to be lit. The house needs to be swept. Diligent searching is needed. Joseph's history is worth the effort required to understand him.

The despicable adulterer, self-proclaimed liar and disgraced former Nauvoo City mayor, John C. Bennett, told this fabulous (and to me amusing) yarn about Joseph:

> Few can doubt the profanity of many of the citizens of Nauvoo, and the Prophet Joe, in particular. Mr. Benjamin Avise, of Carthage, said that the first time he ever saw Joe and heard him speak, *he swore an oath*! Joe is notoriously profane, but he says God will not notice him in cursing the Damned Gentiles!
>
> All who are acquainted with the Prophet know that he gets most gloriously drunk, occasionally; but he says he only does this to try the faith of the Saints, and show them that he is fallible, like other men.[2]

I must confess, I read Bennett when I'm looking for a good laugh.

Contradicting Bennett was John D. Lee, the sacrificial man executed for the Mountain Meadows Massacre. Lee described Joseph Smith in these words:

> [O]n the whole there was something in his manner and appearance that was bewitching and winning; his countenance was that of a plain, honest man, full of benevolence and philanthropy and void of deceit or hypocrisy. He was resolute and firm of purpose,

---

[1] NC Luke 9:12. In this paper I cite to the new scriptures, the Old Covenants ("OC") containing the Joseph Smith Translation of the Old Testament, the New Covenants ("NC") containing the Joseph Smith Translation of the New Testament and the 1840 edited version of the Book of Mormon, and Teachings and Commandments ("T&C") containing the original texts of Joseph Smith revelations with additional letters, Lectures on Faith, and other revelations and instructions.

[2] John C. Bennett, *The History of the Saints, or, An Expose' of Joe Smith and Mormonism*, p.94.

4

strong as most men in physical power, and all who
saw were forced to admire him, as he then looked
and existed.[3]

Fawn Brodie, another biographer, explained what she thought of
him, writing:

The source of [Joseph's] power lay not in his
doctrine but in his person, and the rare quality of his
genius was not due to his reason but to his
imagination. He was a mythmaker of prodigious
talent. And after a hundred years the myths he
created are still an energizing force in the lives of a
million followers. The moving power of Mormonism
was a fable – one that few converts stopped to
question, for its meaning seemed profound and its
inspiration was contagious.[4]

That cynical assessment does not set right with me. Millions of
people are more likely moved by the content of doctrine than by a
personality. I think Fawn Brodie is completely mistaken, and for me it
IS his doctrine.

Yale professor of humanities, Harold Bloom, held a broader
view of Joseph Smith. He wrote:

The God of Joseph Smith is a daring revival of
the God of some of the Kabbalists and Gnostics,
prophetic sages who, like Smith himself, asserted
that they had returned to the true religion.
...Mormonism is a purely American Gnosis, for
which Joseph Smith was and is a far more crucial
figure than Jesus could be. Smith is not just 'a'
prophet, another prophet, but he is the essential
prophet of these latter days, leading into the end
time, whenever it comes.[5]

This seems to me to strike much closer to the truth.

BH Roberts made this attempt to explain Joseph:

But though a man of like passions with other
men, yet to Joseph Smith was given access to the

---

[3] John D. Lee, *Mormonism Unveiled, or, Life and Confessions of John D. Lee*, p. 81.

[4] Fawn Brodie, *No Man Knows My History*, p. ix

[5] Harold Bloom, *The American Religion* (New York: Simon & Schuster, 1992),
pp. 99, 123.

mind of Deity, through the revelations of God to him; and likewise to him was given a divine authority to declare that mind of God to the world. *Is that true?* And does what he announced, *ex cathedra*, as word of God, stand such tests of truth as men and time may apply to it? These are questions which most concern men in reference to this Prophet of our age; and that brings us to the consideration of this Prophet's work. ...

It is this work of Joseph Smith's, this promulgation of a New Dispensation of the Christian religion; the development of a priesthood; the organization of the wonderful system of ecclesiastical government—the church he founded; the announcement of physical and metaphysical principles dealing with the profoundest subjects of intellectual investigation and thought; and which, when they are finally arranged in proper order, will constitute a system of philosophy worthy of the enlightened age in which it was brought forth—it is this work, and the whole volume of it, that constitutes Joseph Smith's vindication before the world, and justifies his followers in believing that his life's work was a superhuman achievement; and hence there was in him a divine inspiration that wrought the work of his great though brief career; *the inspiration of the Almighty gave him understanding—He was a Prophet of God.*[6]

Indiana University professor Jan Shipps, author of *Mormonism: The Story of a New Religious Tradition*, and *Sojourner in the Promised Land: Forty Years Among the Mormons*, said of Joseph:

This is the key to understanding Joseph Smith and to understanding Mormonism, I am convinced: It is the literalness, the experiencing the same things that are described in the scriptures. Mormonism takes the scriptures and brings them into life. Literally recapitulates the scriptures. Now, if you get

---

[6] B. H. Roberts, in *A Comprehensive History of the Church*, 2:360-361; 411-412, emphasis in original.

that understanding of Joseph Smith's understanding of what was going on, then you begin to see that this could not have been just somebody making it up as he went along.

In concluding his biography of Joseph, Richard L. Bushman explained this of Joseph:

> Joseph's work was not about democracy but about knowledge, power, visions, and blessings. ...Joseph Smith himself did not take credit for his achievements. All he could speak of were his 'marvelous experiences.' Perhaps his signal trait was trust in his own inspiration. He knew he was no more than a rough stone cut from a Vermont hillside. He told one audience, 'he was but a man, ...a plain, untutored man; seeking what he should do to be saved.' But his revelations enabled him, as one scholar has said of the prophet, 'to do unaccustomed things.' It was his calling, as Joseph himself put it, to 'lay a foundation that will revolutionize the whole world.'[7]

If you haven't gathered already, I'll make it plain. Biographies of Joseph Smith are a cacophony of discordant voices advocating one, then another, contradictory explanation for that man. Joseph was an enigma, mischaracterized by followers and opponents alike. Searching through biographies and journals has not permitted me, and will not permit you, to uncover or adequately explain Joseph. In the short biography I wrote of him,[8] I used Joseph's words alone to explain him. I believe that he alone provides the best explanation of what was in his heart. In that book I explained the events that led to him composing his *Lectures on Faith*, replacement *History*, and *Letter from Liberty Jail*. Then Joseph's own voice was allowed to speak in those three documents. I chose those three documents because they are his longest personal compositions, other than the Book of Mormon.[9] But

---

[7] Richard Lyman Bushman, *Joseph Smith: Rough Stone Rolling*, (New York: Alfred A. Knoff, 2005), pp. 560-561.

[8] *A Man Without Doubt*, (Salt Lake: Mill Creek Press, 2016).

[9] In all three others contributed to the documents. However, Joseph supervised and controlled the content, and therefore they are a reliable way to understand his mind.

I accept Joseph's explanation that the Book of Mormon was not his, but the composition of others he only translated.

As we approach two centuries separating us from his death on June 27, 1844, it seems less likely each passing year that biographers will be able to understand the authentic Joseph, because they are looking in the wrong place. Joseph's voice can tell us more than all the biographers' fanciful reconstructions. Biographies are almost always projections by the writer of themselves upon their subject.[10]

I suggest we back into knowing Joseph, by looking at what Joseph thought of YOU. Then you can decide for yourself what was in the heart of a man who thought of you in these terms:

What follows are excerpts from the King Follett Discourse, what can be regarded as 'Joseph's Valedictory Address,' given two months prior to his murder:

> First, God himself, who sits enthroned in yonder heaven, is a man like one of you. That is the great secret. If the veil were rent today and you were to see the great God who holds this world in its orbit and upholds all things by his power, you would see him in the image and very form of a man; for Adam was created in the very fashion and image of God.

This concept remains revolutionary still. Unlike the theologians and divines of other religions, Joseph made you God's literal child. This exalted view of you does nothing to lower God, as critics have complained. Joseph did nothing to demean the Almighty with this

---

[10] *Mark Twain's Autobiography* correctly observes: "What a wee little part of a person's life are his acts and his words! His real life is led in his head and is known to none but himself. All day long, and every day, the mill of his brain is grinding, and his thoughts, not those other things, are his history. His acts and his words are merely the visible, thin crust of his world, with its scattered snow summits and its vacant wastes of water—and they are so trifling a part of his bulk! A mere skin enveloping it. The mass of him is hidden—it and its volcanic fires that toss and boil, and never rest, night nor day. These are his life, and they are not written, and cannot be written. Every day would make a whole book of eighty thousand words—three hundred and sixty-five books a year. Biographies are but the clothes and buttons of the man—the biography of the man himself cannot be written." (*Mark Twain's Autobiography*, with an introduction by Albert Bigelow Paine, 2 vols. (New York: Harper and Brothers, 1924), 1:[xviii].)

teaching. Instead he raised mankind to have exalted parentage. This was the real value of Joseph's teaching.

> ...Here, then, is eternal life—to know the only wise and true God. And you have got to learn how to be Gods yourselves—to be kings and priests to God, the same as all Gods have done—by going from a small degree to another, from grace to grace, from exaltation to exaltation, until you are able to sit in glory as do those who sit enthroned in everlasting power.

This mirrors the language of the May 6, 1833 revelation (D&C 93) describing Christ's ascent from grace to grace until He received the fullness.[11] Joseph believed that you are not dissimilar from Christ, only presently behind Him in progression. But Joseph believed that you are destined to continue that progression and eventually arrive at that same Divine destiny.

Here, too, Joseph suggests there are multiple stages of "exaltation" and that we are required to progress from "exaltation to exaltation" until we, like the Father and Son, are able to sit in "everlasting power."

There is no mere "heaven" and "hell." There are stages of development. There is a pathway that grows from a small degree to something more. It is incremental and is how all the Gods have done.

In this talk Joseph more fully explained theology of ascending up Jacob's Ladder to occupy the Throne of God.[12] Cycles of creation,

---

[11] T&C 93:3-4: "He was full of grace and truth, even the Spirit of Truth which came and dwelt in the flesh, and dwelt among us. And I, John, saw that he received not of the fullness at the first, but received grace for grace. And he received not of the fullness, at first, but continued from grace to grace, until he received a fullness. And thus he was called the Son of God, because he received not of the fullness at the first."

[12] This theological teaching had been around since 1832: D&C 69:13: "They are they who are priests and kings, who, having received of his fullness and of his Glory, are priests of the Most High after the order of Melchizedek, which was after the order of Enoch, which was after the order of the Only Begotten Son. Wherefore, as it is written, they are Gods, even the sons of God. Wherefore, all things are theirs, whether life or death, or things present or things to come, all are theirs and they are Christ's, and Christ is God's. And they shall overcome all things. Wherefore, let no man glory in man, but rather let them glory in God who shall subdue all enemies under his feet."

probation, and development have been, are, and will be underway across the universe, worlds without end.[13]

This means there are indeed Gods many, and Lords many, as Paul wrote to the Corinthians.[14] And that Christ will be a "King of kings" because there will be others advancing to become kings also.[15] Joseph saw the whole of humanity as part of a great family, the head of which was God the Father.

The greatness of the plan and the vastness of the eons involved were explained:

> … When you climb a ladder, you must begin at
> the bottom and go on until you learn the last principle;
> it will be a great while before you have learned the last.
> It is not all to be comprehended in this world; it is a
> great thing to learn salvation beyond the grave.

This changes and enlarges our understanding of God's plan for us. Mortality is just one stop along a very long pathway. Eternity is right here and now, and death will not interrupt the process of developing God's children into something far greater than we now see. It is "a great thing to learn salvation beyond the grave." We will all go on to labor elsewhere. We do not retire when we lay down our mortal bodies. Worlds without end will be required to develop us. We are not expected to, and cannot bridge the gulf between what we are at present and what Christ and the Father have attained, during the short life we experience here.

But God's work and glory is to bring to pass the immortality and eternal life of man. Therefore as one earth passes away, another has been organized for man to occupy.[16] This is God's work. This is our

---

[13]See, e.g., T&C 69:28: "…every man shall receive according to his own works and his own dominion, in the mansions which are prepared, and they shall be servants of the Most High, but where God and Christ dwell they cannot come, worlds without end."

[14] NC 1 Cor. 1:32.
[15] See, NC Rev. 6:12; 8:1.
[16] OC Gen. 1:7: "And as one earth shall pass away and the heavens thereof, even so shall another come. And there is no end to my works, neither my words. For behold, this is my work and my glory: to bring to pass the immortality and Eternal life of man."

opportunity. We are somewhere on that Ladder, and each of us is being added upon by what we experience in our present lives.

Joseph's teaching puts eternity right here. We are in one of the Father's mansions. We have obtained what we experience here and now by the past heed and diligence we gave to the truth while in an earlier cycle of creation. We will move along into yet another estate inheriting what we obtain from the heed and diligence we give now. "Whatever principle of intelligence we attain unto in this life, it will rise with us in the resurrection. And if a person gains more knowledge and intelligence in this life through his diligence and obedience than another, he will have so much the advantage in the world to come. There is a law, irrevocably decreed in Heaven before the foundations of the world, upon which all blessings are predicated, and when we obtain any blessing from God, it is by obedience to that law upon which it is predicated."[17]

God has laid this opportunity before us. And all are invited to receive:

> ... When we know how to come to him, he begins to unfold the heavens to us and tell us all about it. When we are ready to come to him, he is ready to come to us.

This is Joseph's God: A being who is as eager to embrace us as we ought to be eager to embrace Him. He has been and is now ready. WE are the ones who hold Him at a distance. The greatness of Joseph's perspective of God and the plan of salvation is hard to find words adequate to proclaim it in plain simplicity. It is glorious!

And again, Joseph declared:

> ... The mind of man is as immortal as God himself.

> ... Intelligence exists upon a self-existent principle; it is a spirit from age to age, and there is no creation about it. Moreover, all the spirits that God ever sent into the world are susceptible to enlargement. The first principles of man are self-existent with God. God found himself in the midst of spirits and glory, and because he was greater, he saw proper to institute laws whereby the rest could have the privilege of advancing like himself--that

---

[17] D&C 130:18-19.

they might have one glory upon another and all the knowledge, power, and glory necessary to save the world of spirits.

You and I are indeed "gods-in-embryo" because that sentient part of us that learns, understands and develops is akin to God Himself. Physical impairment does not limit our minds. Every spirit is capable of growth and development. Even the weakest soul to live in this world can be and is "added upon" by the mortal experience here.[18]

Joseph echoed the words in the Book of Mormon about God's judgment. It turns out that God does not actually judge us, we judge ourselves. God only establishes the standard against which we measure ourselves:

> ... A man is his own tormenter and his own condemner. Hence the saying, "They shall go into the lake that burns with fire and brimstone." The torment of the mind of man is as exquisite as a lake burning with fire and brimstone. So is the torment of man.

This repeats the Book of Mormon's description of that judgment all of us will face when this cycle of experience concludes:

> Yea, in that great day when ye shall be brought to stand before the Lamb of God, then will ye say that there is no God? Then will ye longer deny the Christ, or can ye behold the Lamb of God? Do ye suppose that ye shall dwell with him under a consciousness of your guilt? Do ye suppose that ye could be happy to dwell with that holy being when your souls are racked with a consciousness of guilt that ye have ever abused his laws? Behold, I say unto you that ye would be more miserable to dwell with a holy and a just God under a consciousness of your filthiness before him than ye would to dwell with the damned souls in hell. For behold, when ye shall be brought to see your nakedness before God, and also the glory of God, and the holiness of Jesus Christ, it

---

[18] See T&C 149: Abr. 6:2: "We will go down for there is space there, and we will take of these materials and we will make an earth whereon these may dwell. And we will prove them herewith to see if they will do all things whatsoever the Lord their God shall command them. And they who keep their first estate shall be added upon[.]"

will kindle a flame of unquenchable fire upon you.

O then ye unbelieving, turn ye unto the Lord.[19]

In this description God is not judging man. Man is reacting to the presence of God. It is mankind's own recognition of the standard of glory, holiness and purity embodied by Jesus Christ that causes our pain. We can, through the contrast, see clearly our own failures. We will be racked with guilt, not because God punishes us, but because we feel disappointment in what we failed to do. Think again about the opportunity you have in front of you. It is in your power to change all eternity: You can gain more knowledge and intelligence in this life through your diligence and obedience and in turn have so much the advantage in the world to come. That is up to you.

Joseph's unwavering voice spoke with the certainty befitting a prophet of God. As Hugh Nibley explained: "whereas every other major religious founder went through a mandatory period of uncertainty and self-doubt, there is in Joseph Smith's behavior never a moment of doubt or hesitation as to what is what."[20]

Joseph Smith was a great prophet, and a powerful teacher. We should not be distracted by all the rumors, innuendos and inconclusive speculation about him. Nor should we be discouraged by the contradictory accounts written of his life. He can best be understood by studying the material that came from him. His teachings lead to happiness in this life and glory in the world to come. They will bring anyone who will consider them closer to God.

---

[19] NC Mormon 4:6.

[20] Hugh Nibley, *Temple and Cosmos*, p. 422.

## Chapter 2: Cutting Down the Tree of Life
© 2014, Denver C. Snuffer, Jr.

There are four topics discussed in this paper: plural wives, ordination of black African men, pressure to ordain women, and same sex marriage. The history of changing LDS doctrine, past, present and the likely future, are illustrated using these four subjects to show doctrinal changes required to build a necessary bridge between LDS Mormonism[21] and the American public.

Religion moves through two stages. In the first, God interrupts history by revealing Himself to man. This is called "restoration," because it restores man to communion with God as in the Garden of Eden. In the second, man attempts to worship God according to His latest visit. The second stage is always marked by scarcity[22] and inadequacy. This is called "apostasy." Restoration begins the process, but apostasy always follows.

Abraham, Moses and Isaiah ascended the bridge to God's presence.[23] God descended the Celestial bridge to live with man through Jesus Christ. They all show God wants to restore us. But a restoration's witnesses leave only an echo of God's voice. Unless we remain with God, we lapse back into scarcity and apostasy.

Whether the echo is preserved through a family organization, as in ancient Israel, or churches,[24] as in Christianity,[25] some organization

---

[21] I refer to the Church of Jesus Christ of Latter-day Saints as "LDS Mormonism" or "the LDS Church." It is the most successful of the offshoots claiming Joseph Smith as a founder. I belonged to that denomination until 2013, when I was excommunicated for "apostasy" because I did not withdraw from publication the book *Passing the Heavenly Gift*, Mill Creek Press, (Salt Lake City, 2011).

[22] See, e.g., 1 Sam. 3: 1: "And the word of the Lord was precious in those days; there was on open vision." Omni 1; 11: "I know of no revelation save that which has been written, neither prophecy; wherefore, that which is sufficient is written."

[23] Each of them was the subject of an "ascension" text (*The Assumption of Moses, The Ascension of Isaiah,* and *The Apocalypse of Abraham*) as a testimony it is possible for man to ascend to God's presence.

[24] Contrary to the claims of "Restorationist" movement, out of which both Mormonism and the Stone-Campbell churches (both Sidney Rigdon and Parley Pratt belonged to this movement prior to their conversion to Mormonism), there was no single form of New Testament Christianity. The apostles left behind various churches, not a single organization. For a

during times of apostasy substitutes for God's presence. Unfortunately, organizations can only mimic God's involvement.[26]

Though Moses brought Joshua into abundance through direct contact with God,[27] Israel forfeited their opportunity to be there.[28] Abraham established a restored dynasty in Isaac,[29] Jacob[30] and Joseph.[31] Abraham's success was the greatest since Adam.[32] Apostasy is the rule, restoration the exception. Only the echo is heard in man's churches. It is a curious failure, since God declared His works and words never cease.[33]

God cannot submit to institutional control.[34] As faith is institutionalized, it becomes part of this world and necessarily influenced by cultural, social, legal and economic pressure. Those forces erode faith. Religious institutions are where the ideal comes into conflict with the less-than-ideal.

LDS Mormonism illustrates the dynamic.[35] Through compromises of its ideals we see the pattern unfolding in our lifetime.

---

discussion of this see S.S. Raymond E. Brown, *The Churches the Apostles Left Behind*, Paulest Press, (New Jersey, 1984).

[25] The New Testament word ("ekklesia") would be better rendered "assembly" or "congregation" rather than "church."

[26] If it is impossible to serve both God and mammon (Luke 16: 13), religions administering tithes and offerings seem invariably to hate the first and love the second.

[27] Exo. 24: 13-17.

[28] See D&C 84: 21-25; Exo. 20: 18-21.

[29] Gen. 26: 24.

[30] Gen. 28: 12-15.

[31] Gen. 37: 5-7, 9.

[32] Adam was able to hand down a living connection to God through eleven generations: Adam, Seth, Enos, Cainan, Mahalaleel, Jared, Enoch, Methuselah, Lamech, Noah, and Shem/Melchizedek. Abraham was second, with only half that number.

[33] Moses 1: 4.

[34] D&C 1: 31; D&C 38: 11-12.

[35] LDS leaders assert their status has not changed, and their version of Mormonism preserves the ideal, unchanged. However, two quotes illustrate the difference between its founding generation of leaders and today's. Oliver Cowdery admonished the first Quorum of Twelve their ordination as an Apostle was not complete until Christ visited and laid hands on them. (*DHC* 2:194-198.) This charge was dropped in 1911. In the 2014 Priesthood and Relief Society Manual, LDS Church President Joseph Fielding Smith is quoted, "I did not live in the days of our Savior; he has not come to me in

Religion has always frustrated good men. Churches fail to practice the ideal. This frustration produces reformers who reject the inevitability of scarcity and long for a return of a revelatory God. St. Francis lived the ideal inside the institutional church.[36] I was pleased when Pope Francis chose his Papal name, and then to follow St. Francis' example.

Martin Luther,[37] John Calvin, Roger Williams, John Wycliffe and other Protestant fathers thought the church too compromised, and sought God outside the predominating church body. They produced offspring churches, but failed to restore God's presence.

Joseph Smith claimed to have crossed the bridge to God's presence again. Some few, myself included, believe his claim. I regard him the equal of Abraham, Moses and Isaiah. But the various denominations claiming Joseph Smith as their founder again are afflicted by scarcity and struggle to cope with God's silence.

Man is born and then dies. In this world entropy overtakes everything, including religion. Faith does not hesitate between restoration and apostasy. There can be no stasis in religion. God's voice is heard anew when restoration is underway and scarcity ends.[38] But it returns as the influences of this world take over.

With time, all religious bodies confront the complex challenge of holding onto God's word. The ever-changing present causes cracks in every church. The church will try to patch the cracks. This leads to fractures, then defections. Former believers either lose faith in the religion altogether, or faith in the church. Without a restoration's abundance, pragmatic choices become first policy, then doctrine. God's silence does not curtail doctrine, but often compels it.

After nearly a millennium-and-a-half,[39] there was a great gulf between God's last revelation and Catholic doctrines. When

---

person. I have not beheld him. His Father and he have not felt it necessary to grant me such a great blessing as this. But it is not necessary." *Teachings of the Presidents of the Church: Joseph Fielding Smith*, (LDS Church, 2013) p. 49.

[36] Toward the end of his life, St. Francis said an angel visited him on September 14, 1224.

[37] Luther began as a reformer inside the Catholic Church, but ultimately became the father of the Lutheran Church.

[38] This is because God's voice is heard through the minister. See, John 10: 27.

[39] The 10th Century split between Eastern Orthodoxy and Roman Catholicism is not relevant to the point in this paper, and therefore not

Gutenberg's 1439 press and an increasingly literate population made it impossible for the Roman hierarchy to control information, Catholicism fractured. The Internet is to LDS Mormonism what Gutenberg's press was to Catholicism. It is no longer possible for the institution to control the narrative.[40]

Catholicism attempted to regain control in two ways. First, the "Dogs of God"[41] were unleashed to confront heresy and suppress dissent. After two-and-a-half centuries of pursuing this ill-advised course, the failure was recognized even in Rome.[42] Pope Paul III

---

considered.

[40] LDS Church Historian Marlin K. Jensen entertained questions at Utah State University. In response to a question about people leaving the church, he compared current events to the Kirtland Apostasy. A transcript and recording of that interview was posted on the Internet on a site titled "Simple Mormon Spectator" (www.simplemoremonspectator.blogspot.com). The site subsequently took it down putting up a notice, which read, in part: "This audio and commentary has been removed out of respect for friends, most especially Elder Jensen. This audio was not fulfilling the purpose I had hoped it would: of inspiring more good, respect, tolerance, and love in the church." Despite removing the material, a cached copy was posted on another site "New Mormon Apostasy" (www.newmormonapostasy.blogspot.com) where it presently remains available.

[41] This nickname for the Dominicans was used by historian James Reston, Jr. in the title to his 2005 book, *Dogs of God: Columbus, the Inquisition, and the Defeat of the Moors*, (Doubleday, New York). Saint Dominic founded the Order in 1216, through the approval of Pope Honorius III, to combat heresy. This order was responsible for later leading the Inquisition, an attempt to forcibly compel orthodoxy and convert Jews, Torquemada, a Dominican, was the First Grand Inquisitor.

[42] The outcome of this struggle was inevitable. Power has its limits that those in power seem to ignore. Throughout history, those in power lose their claim to legitimacy through their abuse. The theme is embedded in LDS scripture. D&C 121: 34-42. Therefore it would seem much easier for LDS Mormonism to avoid making Catholic mistakes, but the allure of power is blinding. As one writer recently put it: "'It has been said that most revolutions are not caused by revolutionaries in the first place, but by the stupidity and brutality of governments,' Sean MacStiofain, the provisional IRA's first chief of staff once said, looking back on those early years. 'Well, you had that to start with in [Northern Ireland], all right." Malcom Gladwell, *David and Goliath: Underdogs, Misfits, and the Art of Battling Giants*, Little, Brown and Company, New York, (2013), p. 204. "And when the law is applied in the absence of

reversed course and launched the Counter-Reformation. A new order called the Society of Jesus (Jesuits) was established at the Council of Trent to focus on needed reforms. The LDS Church is repeating the same miss-step. They are now attempting the first approach, to suppress dissent. The LDS Church's Correlation infrastructure has been put into place to protect doctrine and practice. An LDS group of "Dominicans," the Strengthening the Members Committee,[43] has been empowered to find and then remove perceived threats.[44] Ironically, the original targets of the Strengthening the Members Committee were fundamentalist groups advocating the practice of plural marriage. At one time this practice was the hallmark of orthodoxy for the LDS Church. The juxtaposition of first advocacy, followed by suppression of plural marriages, illustrates a passage from God's interruption of history by speaking to man, and man's effort to please a quiet and distant God by studied appeasement of the worldly forces of government and economics. From heaven's silence men conjure "doctrines" they attribute to God. Therefore plural marriage bespeaks the larger dynamic.

Because LDS Mormonism has been "correlated" a great deal of what it once was has been trimmed away. Not only doctrine, but also history has been forgotten or rejected. By reworking history, the LDS Church has managed to brand even those who believe in Joseph Smith, and accept the same scriptures, as nevertheless "apostate" if they challenge the newly correlated part-truths. Within LDS Mormonism a short memory is necessary to accept the history and doctrine now taught. Long memories get its members into trouble.

---

legitimacy, it does not produce obedience. It produces the opposite. It leads to backlash." *Id.*, at p. 222. Often it is the most reluctant who are drawn into battle with the powers wrongly seeking to control what is not their right to even influence, much less dictate, like the conscience of a man. Religion in particular is ill fitted to do more than give advice, letting men and women govern themselves.

[43] We await the arrival of LDS "Jesuits" still. Apparently significant damage must be first done to LDS Mormonism, as was the case with Catholicism, before the lessons of history can be learned anew. Sad experience will teach when nothing else will.

[44] The Counter-Reformation was Pope Paul III's effort to reform the church and deal with corrupt bishops, indulgences and financial abuses. Strengthening the Members Committee presently attempts to "reform" only targeted dissidents by compelling them to retract, obey or be cast away.

For LDS Mormonism, te Internet has become a bastion of unsettling or unwanted information. Some of it is inaccurate. The more effective challenges, however, come from on-line sources telling the truth. When the false narrative perpetuated by the institution[45] is confronted by truth, the institution loses. To deal with this, the on-line LDS Church is now trying "search engine optimization,"[46] meaning the LDS Church pays money to have their sites come up first on search engine result pages. This directs traffic to church approved sources.[47] LDS websites recount history designed to soothe the troubled Saint. It is not effective.[48] All an inquirer need do is press through the first page or so of LDS Church website referrals to locate other independent sources.

On their webpage "mormonchurch.org" the church states plural wives "was not mandatory and not required for salvation[.]"[49] This is both true (artfully using the term "salvation") and false. It is true that plural wives are not necessary for salvation according to LDS Mormonism. But, then again, neither is faith in Christ, repentance, baptism or a good life. All are "saved" in Mormon theology, other than sons of Perdition.[50] Therefore, this LDS Church on-line

---

[45] It doesn't matter if the false narrative misstates history or merely gives an incomplete account. The effect is the same. The institution breaks the trust of its followers, and cannot be repaired.

[46] This was the term LDS Church Historian Marlin Jensen used in his discussion at Utah State University. The Jensen interview is described in footnote 13, supra. The "search engine optimization" subject is discussed in the blog entry: mormon-chronicles.blogspot.com/2011/08/lds-church-and-search-engine.html.

[47] Additionally the church employs a form of on-line "astro-turf" by having paid employees or volunteer missionaries post to discussion groups and blogs to present the church's position or direct discussions to be favorable by posting more sympathetic contributions.

[48] The bureaucracy of the Church Office Building ("COB") has a lot of paid staff whose livelihoods are dependent upon such ill-advised experimentation. A former COB employee, Daymon Smith, wrote an amusing account of his tenure in this costly, inefficient and foolish system (*The Book of Mammon: A Book About A Book About the Corporation That Owns The Mormons*, CreateSpace Publisher, (2010)). It is a fictional account in order to avoid a violation of the "non-disclosure agreement" required of COB employees.

[49] See the LDS Church owned website www.mormonchurch.org/mormon-beliefs/mormon-polygamy.

[50] See, e.g., *Encyclopedia of Mormonism*, "Salvation," p. 1256; mormon.org/

assertion is true enough. But the LDS Church once claimed as a matter of doctrine plural wives was an absolute requirement for exaltation.[51] Therefore a reader lacking skill in LDS vocabulary will get the wrong impression, which appears to be purposeful in many church announcements.[52]

Marriage involving multiple wives was so secretive during Joseph Smith's life that his widow could deny it was actually practiced.[53] It was not until 1852 that the LDS Church publicly advocated belief in this form of marriage.[54] The announcement caused national outrage,

---

beliefs/plan-of-salvation has this explanation: "IMMORTALITY—ONE OF GOD'S GREATEST GIFTS: If you could have one wish, what would it be? Most of us would probably say we want to live forever. That's exactly what God gave to each of us when He sent His son, Jesus Christ, to earth to die for us and to atone for our sins. It's called resurrection and everyone born on earth, even wicked people, will receive this gift of immortality (1 Corinthians 15:22). On the third day after His Crucifixion, Jesus Christ became the first person to be resurrected. His spirit was reunited with His glorified, perfected body and He could no longer die. When Christ's friends went to visit His tomb, angels said, 'He is not here: for he is risen, as he said' (Matthew 28:6). 'WILL I GO TO HEAVEN?' Yes! God will judge all men fairly and reward them appropriately with a place within His kingdom."

[51] Exaltation means to become "like God" and inherit Celestial glory. See, e.g., D&C 76, D&C 132 and *Encyclopedia of Mormonism*, "Exaltation," p. 479.

[52] LDS Mormonism has employed evasive language throughout its history of public statements. That is too broad a topic to be addressed here. Language distinctions like "Celestial Marriage" allowed the church for years to deny the practice of "polygamy" for example. A series of recent press releases and editorials about church disciplinary councils likewise seeks to distance the hierarchy from responsibility for excommunications driven by the top of the LDS Church. The "truthfulness" of their announcements depends upon whether the necessary final act (which must be done locally) can be said to be outside of the hierarchy's control (even when the impetus for discipline originated and was sustained by constant pressure from above).

[53] "No such thing as polygamy, or spiritual wifery, was taught, publicly or privately, before my husband's death, that I have now, or ever had any knowledge of … He had no other wife but me; nor did he to my knowledge ever have." (*History of the Reorganized Church of Jesus Christ of Latter Day Saints*, Vol. 3, pp. 355-56.)

[54] The LDS canon of scripture added *Doctrine and Covenants* Section 132 (allowing plural wives) in 1876, and at the same time Section 101 (requiring

with Abraham Lincoln's upstart Republican Party denouncing it as one of the "twin relics of barbarism," the other being slavery.[55] Beginning with the Morrill Act signed by President Lincoln in 1862, the full weight of national ire was brought to bear against the LDS Church. The dispute lasted three decades before the church surrendered. The final victory was achieved through the draconian measures imposed on the institution by the Edmunds-Tucker Act. The act dis-incorporated the LDS Church and the Perpetual Emigrating Fund Company, giving their assets to the public schools of the territory. It mandated an oath denouncing polygamy to be taken before any person could vote, sit on a jury, or serve as a public official. It removed local judges (who were LDS) and replaced them with federally appointed judges (certain to be anti-polygamy). The act rearranged family law by requiring marriage licenses, disinherited illegitimate children, and abrogated the spousal privilege that prevented wives from testifying against their husbands in polygamy prosecution cases.

Although the LDS Church fought these laws through appeals to the US Supreme Court, they lost the fight. Faced with the dire prospect of remaining an outlaw organization, the church relented. The struggle and surrender inform LDS Church conduct in ways that remain part of the institution's psyche.[56]

We begin the story five years after Joseph Smith's death, when the doctrine of taking plural wives was first made public.[57] Wisely

---

only one wife) was deleted from their scripture. Section 101 stated, in part: "we declare that we believe, that one man should have one wife; and one woman, but one husband."

[55] The Republican platform adopted in Philadelphia in 1856 included this language: "It is the duty of Congress to prohibit in the territories those twin relics of barbarism, polygamy and slavery."

[56] For a discussion about law and social change, see Scott L. Cummings, *Empirical Studies of Law and Social Change: What is the Field? What are the Questions*, Wisconsin Law Review, 2013:171. In the article he discusses the whole approach of litigation as a shortcut tool to achieve societal change rather than through slower political processes. In the case of LDS Mormonism, both political will and litigation united to achieve change within the church.

[57] Dealing with this subject during Joseph Smith's lifetime is too complicated and adds too much to the discussion. From Fanny Alger in the early 1830's to John C. Bennett's activities in Nauvoo the history is too great to deal with cursorily and therefore I pass it over. The three volume series by Brian C.

Joseph deliberately limited the practice and kept it secret.[58] Personally, I believe plural wives should never have been publicly adopted[59] and preached by the LDS Church, and was never essential to "exaltation." Much of the content when preaching it publicly was based on advice Brigham Young received from a US Senator. To win protection under the First Amendment it was necessary to portray plural wives as essential to the religion, which it was not. But it was portrayed so as part of a strategy to win in the courts. When the LDS Church lost the fight, they were faced with the conundrum of undoing an oversold doctrine. However, this paper does not deal with those questions.[60]

President Brigham Young asserted the practice was constitutionally protected if it was a fundamental part of the Latter-day Saint religion. When he presided, Brigham Young made plural wives essential to the church.[61] He was encouraged in this view by an unnamed US Senator. He explained it was protected by:

---

Hales is the most recent and extensive effort to preserve the events. (*Joseph Smith's Polygamy, Volume 1: History, Joseph Smith's Polygamy, Volume 2: History* and *Joseph Smith's Polygamy, Volume 3: Theology* are published by Greg Kofford Books.)

[58] Young explained: "'But were you not persecuted for teaching that odious doctrine called polygamy?' No. We were planted in these valleys before it was publicly made known to the people. Only a few of Joseph Smith's intimate friends knew it previous to its being published to the world, which was several years after his death." *The Complete Discourses of Brigham Young*, Volume 4, p. 2044 (hereafter "*CDBY* 4:2044"), Smith-Pettit, (Salt Lake, 2009). "When we left Nauvoo did they drive us for polygamy? No. It was not publicly known of." *CDBY* 4:2259.

[59] Even in Joseph's day the full meaning and practical mechanics of sealing together families to effect salvation was elusive. The doctrinal basis did not roll out in a single revelation, but began perhaps as early as 1828 and continued periodically thereafter. Section 132 is an amalgamation, consisting of perhaps five or more different revelations spanning 1828 to 1843. Even with Section 132, there are questions and mechanics, which are not clarified, and it is not certain its contents were what originated from Joseph Smith. Joseph may well have practiced something very different from what Brigham Young adopted.

[60] Fundamentalist Mormons have more faithfully preserved observance of this faulty practice and therefore claim to be of superior purity than LDS Mormonism. However, I believe them to only be perpetuating an LDS mistake.

[61] Brigham Young's latest biographer writes: "Young also connected plural marriage with exaltation into the celestial kingdom." John G. Turner, *Brigham*

22

...the sacred liberty which the Constitution of our country guarantees unto us... The world have known, long ago, even in brother Joseph's days, that he had more wives than one. One of the senators in Congress knew it very well. Did he oppose it? No, but he has been our friend all the day long, especially upon that subject. He said pointedly to his friends, "If the United States do not adopt that very method—let them continue as they are now—pursue the precise course they are now pursuing, and it will come to this—that their generations will not live until they are 30 years old. They are going to destruction; disease is spreading so fast among the inhabitants of the United States, that they are born rotten with it, and in a few years they are gone." Said he, "Joseph has introduced the best plan for restoring and establishing strength and long life among men, of any man on earth; and the Mormons are a very good and virtuous people."

Many others are of the same mind, they are not ignorant of what we are doing in our social capacity. They have cried out, "Proclaim it." But it would not do, a few years ago; everything must come in its time, and there is a time to all things. I am now ready to proclaim it.[62]

The unidentified Senator was likely Steven A. Douglas, who had been elected to the Senate in 1846.[63] Mormon leaders defended the right to practice plural wives as constitutional,[64] and delivered

---

*Young, Pioneer Prophet*, p. 205, Harvard University (Cambridge, 2012).

[62] *CDBY* 1:582.

[63] Steven A. Douglas had a long association with LDS Mormonism, beginning in Illinois. He was among the delegation sent by Governor Ford to negotiate the departure from Nauvoo. The assignment was to persuade the Mormons to leave the state quickly and peacefully. See *Brigham Young— Pioneer Prophet*, supra, at p. 125.

[64] Three years later, while Congress was considering a resolution against polygamy, Young added an additional constitutional restraint on outlawing the practice: Such legislation would be ex post facto, and therefore invalid: "True we have more wives than one, and what of that? They have their scores of thousands of prostitutes, we have none. But polygamy they are

sermons for three decades to define the practice as a fundamental part of their religious beliefs. Young continually asserted it was both "wholesome" and constitutionally protected.[65]

Orson Pratt first announced why the church was confident of their right to engage in the practice. As the talk began, he declared:

> I think, if I am not mistaken, that the constitution gives the privilege to all the inhabitants of this country, of the free exercise of their religious notions, and the freedom of their faith, and the practice of it. Then, if it can be proven to a demonstration, that the Latter-day Saints have actually embraced, as a part and portion of their religion, the doctrine of plurality of wives, it is constitutional. And should there ever be laws enacted by this government to restrict them from the free exercise of this part of their religion, such laws must be unconstitutional.[66]

The preceding month President Brigham Young made a similar declaration: "There is not a single constitution of any single state,

---

unconstitutionally striving to prevent: when they will accomplish their object is not for me to say. They have already presented a resolution in Congress that no man, in any of the Territories of the United States, shall be allowed to have more than one wife, under penalty not exceeding five years imprisonment, and five hundred dollars fine. ...the Constitution of the United States forbids making an ex post facto law. The presenting of the resolution alluded to shows their feelings, they wish the Constitution out of existence, and there is no question but that they will get rid of it as quickly as they can, and that would be by ex post facto law, which the Constitution of the United States strictly forbids. ...If we introduce the practice of polygamy it is not their prerogative to meddle with it; ...it is not their prerogative to meddle with these affairs, for in so doing they would violate the Constitution." *CWBY* 2:1160-61.

[65] "In all the revelations God has given it does not infringe in the least upon the laws of our land, and when he reveals to Joseph Smith it is the privilege of a man to raise up posterity to the name of God, that a holy nation may rise and a royal priesthood a mighty kingdom may spring up before him, where is the constitutional laws against it? They are not to be found. It is just as wholesome a doctrine as any other wholesome doctrine promulgated by any Christians sect in this Government, and the constitution is bound to protect us." *CWBY* 3:1883.

[66] *Journal of Discourses*, Volume 1, p. 54, (hereafter "*JD* 1:54).

much less the constitution of the Federal Government, that hinders a man from having two wives; and I defy all the lawyers of the United States to prove the contrary."[67]

President Young frequently declared this practice was essential. He claimed his sermons were "as good Scripture as is couched in this Bible."[68] Taking him at his word, the following quotes show what the LDS Church believed during its second phase,[69] following Joseph Smith's death.

"Now if any of you will deny the plurality of wives, and continue to do so, I promise that you will be damned,"[70]

"The only men who become Gods, even the Sons of God, are those who enter into polygamy."[71]

Young preached it was monogamy that was a great evil, imposed by the Romans who, you will recall, were responsible for killing Peter and Paul. Romans were a band of robbers who imposed monogamy

---

[67] *CDBY* 1:552.

[68] *Journal of Discourses*, Vol. 9, p. 312, (hereafter *"JD* 9:312"). At another time Pres. Young declared: "I am here to answer. I shall be on hand to answer when I am called upon, for all the counsel and for all the instruction that I have given to this people. If there is an Elder here, or any member of this Church, called the Church of Jesus Christ of Latter-day Saints, who can bring up the first idea, the first sentence that I have delivered to the people as counsel that is wrong, I really wish they would do it; but they cannot do it, for the simple reason that I have never given counsel that is wrong; this is the reason." *JD* 16:161.

[69] I have previously broken LDS Church history into four phases, the second phase beginning at Joseph Smith's death and lasting until polygamy was abandoned. My position is set out in *Passing the Heavenly Gift*, (Mill Creek Press, 2012, Salt Lake City). The transition between these phases was not clean. The Manifesto ostensibly ending plural wives was issued in 1890, but a second "manifesto" was issued by letter from Pres. Joseph F. Smith in 1904. During the fourteen-year interim, plural marriages continued to be performed by church leaders in quiet. (See, *LDS Church Authority and New Plural Marriages, 1890-1904*, D. Michael Quinn, Dialogue: A Journal of Mormon Thought, Spring 1985, pp. 9-105.)

[70] *JD* 3:266.

[71] *JD* 11: 269. The LDS Church today denies this was ever a teaching: "Polygamy was openly practiced during the time of Brigham Young. It was not mandatory and not required for salvation, unlike the teachings of some modern offshoots." See www.mormonchurch.org/mormon-beliefs/ mormon -polygamy.

to further the Empire's lust for prostitution. But polygamy was, according to Young, the only religion practiced in heaven.[72]

This Roman imposed monogamy had at its foundation the objective of producing an excess of unmarried women. This, in turn, according to Young, was responsible for prostitution and whoredom throughout the Christian world.[73]

Young warned women they risked servitude in eternity if they objected to their husband taking plural wives in this life. They would serve those who live polygamy in this life and will be elevated into godhood in the afterlife.[74]

---

[72] "Monogamy, or restrictions by law to one wife, is no part of the economy of heaven among men. Such a system was commenced by the founders of the Roman empire. ...Rome became the mistress of the world, and introduced this order of monogamy wherever her sway was acknowledged. Thus this monogamic order of marriage, so esteemed by modern Christians as a holy sacrament and divine institution, is nothing but a system established by a set of robbers.... Why do we believe in and practice polygamy? Because the Lord introduced it to his servants in a revelation given to Joseph Smith, and the Lord's servants have always practiced it. "And is that religion popular in heaven?" it is the only popular religion there,..." *CWBY* 4:2031.

[73] "Since the founding of the Roman empire monogamy has prevailed more extensively than in times previous to that. The founders of that ancient empire were robbers and women stealers, and made laws favoring monogamy in consequence of the scarcity of women among them, and hence this monogamic system which now prevails throughout Christendom, and which had been so fruitful a source of prostitution and whoredom throughout all the Christian monogamic cities of the Old and New World, until rottenness and decay are at the root of their institutions both national and religious." (*JD* 11:128.)   In another talk Young declared: "Just ask yourselves, historians, when was monogamy introduced on to the face of the earth? When those buccaneers, who settled on the peninsula where Rome now stands, could not steal women enough to have two or three apiece, they passed a law that a man should have but one woman. And this started monogamy and the downfall of the plurality system. In the days of Jesus, Rome, having dominion over Jerusalem, they carried out the doctrine more or less. This was the rise, start and foundation of the doctrine of monogamy; and never till then was there a law passed, that we have any knowledge of, that a man should have but one wife." (*CWBY* 5:2582.)

[74] "But if the woman is determined to not enter into plural marriage, that woman, when she comes forth, will have the privilege of living in single blessedness through all eternity. Now sisters, do not say, 'I do not want a husband when I get up in the resurrection.' You do not know what you will

Even speaking against plural wives could imperil your eternal reward: "those who spoke against a Plurality of wives & in there [sic] feelings will not receive it will never inherit the Celestial Kingdom of God, for it has always been practiced there and always will be."[75]

Young even saw God's plural wives implied in Isaiah's description of the Lord: "The Scripture says that he, the Lord, came walking in the Temple, with his train;[76] I do not know who they were, unless his wives and children;..."[77]

This was as "Christian" a doctrine as Martin Luther's Reformation. According to Young, Martin Luther preached it as Biblical and true.[78] Polygamy, according to Young, should unite all who believe the Bible. In particular, all who oppose Rome should welcome its return.

---

want. If, in the resurrection, you really want to be single and alone and live forever and ever and be made servants, while others receive the higher order of intelligence, and are bringing worlds into existence, you can have the privilege. They who will be exalted cannot perform all the labor, they must have servants, and you can be servants to them." (JD 16:166.) The idea of servitude in eternity remains a Mormon expectation. Joseph Fielding Smith said in the April, 1968 General Conference: "[T]he Lord is going to make a great segregation after the resurrection of mankind, and many—in fact, the greater part of the inhabitants of this earth—will not be called the sons and daughters of God, but they will go into the next world to be servants." (*Conference Report*, April 1968, p. 11.)

[75] CWBY 5:2671, all as in original.
[76] Isaiah 6: 1: "...I saw also the Lord sitting upon a throne, high and lifted up, and his train filled the temple."
[77] JD 13:309.
[78] "The Protestant reformers believed the doctrine of polygamy. Philip, Landgrave of Hess, one of the principal lords and princes of Germany, wrote to the great reformer Martin Luther and his associate reformers, anxiously imploring them to grant unto him the privilege of marrying a second wife, while his first wife, the princess, was yet living. He urged that the practice was in accordance with the Bible, and not prohibited under the Christian dispensation. Upon the reception of this letter, Luther, who had denounced the Romish church for prohibiting the marriage of priests, and who favored polygamy, met in council with the principal Reformers to consult upon the letter which had been received from the Landgrave. They wrote him a lengthy letter in reply, approving this taking a second wife[.]" (CWBY 4:2281-82; citing to *History of the Variations of the Protestant Churches*, a book written by Jacques Benigne Bossuet, and printed by Richard Coyne Publisher to the Royal College of St. Patrick (Dublin, 1836).)

For Mormonism, it was an essential part of the "royal priesthood" advocated by Young: "the Lord instituted Polygamy to raise up a royal Priesthood a kingdom of Priest[s]. It is an institution of heaven."[79] Plurality of wives was obligatory, not optional. If you rejected it, you were damned.[80]

Young absolutely rejected the idea of surrendering to government pressure. Doing so would be surrender to the devil. Polygamy was God's command and could not be disobeyed.[81] Only God's law could save. Ideals governed, and anything less than the ideal would lead to damnation.

Young called out the hypocrisy of the society condemning the Saints. LDS women were wives and mothers. Congress was against that, but tolerated adultery and illegitimacy. Young replied, "I would say to Congress that if they will pass a law, making it death for any man to hold illicit intercourse with any woman but his lawful wife, we would meet them half way on that ground."[82] He went on to discuss Queen Victoria's approval of a bigamist son-in-law.[83] It was the

---

[79] *CDBY* 4: 2290.

[80] "I will now give you, in short, my opinion with regard to plural marriage. It is of God, and He has revealed it from the Heavens and made it obligatory upon the Saints in the last days. …It is obligatory upon me to tell them the truth, to teach them correct doctrine, and leave them to take their choice, whether they receive it and live by it, and be saved, or reject it and be damned." (*CDBY* 4: 2313.)

[81] "We are told that if we would give up polygamy—which we know to be a doctrine revealed from heaven and it is God and the world for it—but suppose this Church should give up this holy order of marriage, then would the devil, and all who are in league with him against the cause of God, rejoice that they had prevailed upon the Saints to refuse to obey one of the revelations and commandments of God to them." (*CDBY* 4: 2333-34.)

[82] *CWBY* 4: 2353.

[83] "A recent case occurred in Europe which illustrates this point. Prince Christian of Holstein, who has recently married one of the daughters of Victoria, Queen of England, has what is termed a morganatic wife in Germany, by whom he has several children, yet the first lady in Europe is not shocked by an alliance of this kind, no more than is the first society of this country by similar occurrences in the cities east. Men may do as they please with women, have numerous children by them, and take as many liberties with them as if they were wives, and yet not call them wives, and modern society smiles upon them. But whenever a man applies the sacred name of wife to the mother of his children, if he happen to have more than

inconsistency of society's reaction, a generation of adulterers who wanted to make polygamy illegal, which Brigham Young rightly condemned.[84]

This doctrine was essential for the faithful to practice. Mormonism held forth the promise man could become like God. But becoming gods in the afterlife demanded polygamy here and now. The only men who would qualify as "sons of God" were those whose quiver was filled with children[85] produced by multiple women bearing offspring for him.[86]

Brigham Young died August 29, 1877 and was succeeded by John Taylor. When Taylor took over LDS Church history was more the product of Young than Joseph Smith. Smith led the church for 14

---

one, then the world professes to be wonderfully shocked at the idea. What inconsistency!" (*Id.*, p. 2353-54.)

[84] Congress has distinguished itself by its inability to live up to standards it imposes on others, both in Brigham Young's day and ours.

[85] "Lo, children are an heritage of the Lord: and the fruit of the womb is his reward. As arrows are in the hand of a mighty man; so are children of the youth. Happy is the man that hath his quiver full of them; they shall not be ashamed, but they shall speak with the enemies in the gate." Psalms 127: 3-5.

[86] "I wish here to say to the Elders of Israel, and to all the members of this Church and kingdom, that it is in the hearts of many of them to wish that the doctrine of polygamy was not taught and practiced by us. It may be hard for many, and especially for the ladies, yet it is no harder for them than it is for the gentlemen. It is the word of the Lord, and I wish to say to you, and all the world, that if you desire with all your hearts to obtain the blessings which Abraham obtained, you will be polygamists at lest [sic] in your faith, or you will come short of enjoying the salvation and glory which Abraham has obtained. This is as true as that God lives. You who wish that there were no such thing in existence, if you have in your hearts to say: 'We will pass along in the Church without obeying or submitting to it in our faith or believing this order, because, for aught that we know, this community may be broken up yet, and we may have lucrative offices offered to us; we will not, therefore, be polygamists lest we should fain obtaining some earthly honor, character and office, etc,' –the man that has that in his heart, and will continue to persist in pursuing that policy, will come short of dwelling in the presence of the Father and the Son, in celestial glory. The only men who become Gods, even the Sons of God, are those who enter into polygamy. Others attain unto a glory and may even be permitted to come into the presence of the Father and the Son; but they cannot reign as kings in glory, because they had blessings offered unto them, and they refused to accept them." *CWBY* 4:2357.

29

years, Young for 33. The doctrine of plural wives had become public and essential under Young. Whatever price had to be paid,[87] the doctrine had been carved in stone as the necessary ideal.

As the president of the church, Taylor was just as emphatic about the necessity of plural wives to qualify for exaltation. He had a full quiver from nine wives[88] and who bore him thirty-four children. Taylor preached it was apostasy to oppose polygamy.[89]

Facing Federal prosecution under anti-polygamy legislation, Taylor spent years of his presidency in hiding. He wrote a revelation on September 27, 1886 confirming to his mind the necessity of complying with the practice of plural wives. The revelation does not mention "plural wives" but refers instead to "the New and Everlasting Covenant" which he, and Mormon fundamentalists, regard necessarily to include plural wives.[90] He died in exile, firmly defending the practice, and preaching its continuation.

---

[87] As Turner put it: "The church had managed to carve out a measure of sympathy from other Americans because of its forced expulsion from Illinois, but the open practice of polygamy made the narrative of the 'suffering Saints' viable no longer." *Brigham Young: Pioneer Prophet*, supra, p. 205.

[88] His wives included Leonora Cannon, Elizabeth Kaighin, Jane Ballantyne, Mary Ann Oakley, Sophia Whitaker, Harriet Whitaker, Margaret Young, and Josephine Elizabeth Roueche.

[89] "Where did this commandment come from in relation to polygamy? It also came from God...When this commandment was given, it was so far religious, and so far binding upon the Elders of this Church that it was told them if they were not prepared to enter into it, and to stem the torrent of opposition that would come in consequence of it, the keys of the kingdom would be taken from them. When I see any of our people, men or women, opposing a principle of this kind, I have years ago set them down as on the high road to apostasy, and I do today; I consider them apostates, and not interested in this Church and kingdom." *JD* 11:221.

[90] The text is as follows: "My son John: You have asked me concerning the New and Everlasting Covenant, and how far it is binding upon my people. Thus saith the Lord: All commandments that I give must be obeyed by those calling themselves by my name unless they are revoked by me or by my authority and how can I revoke an everlasting covenant. For I the Lord and everlasting and my covenants cannot be abrogated nor done away with; but they stand forever. Have I not given my word in great plainness on this subject? Yet have not great numbers of my people been negligent in the observance of my law and the keeping of my commandment, and yet have I borne with them these many years and this because of their weakness

Taylor was succeeded by Wilford Woodruff, likewise a full-quivered polygamist, having seven wives (or more)[91] and fathering thirty-three children. He was equally adamant about the indispensable practice of plural wives. Mormons would practice it "come life or death" he declared.[92]

Like Taylor before him, Woodruff wrote a revelation confirming polygamy was not to be abandoned.[93] The document was read to the Twelve on December 19, 1889 and Apostle Abraham H. Cannon recorded: "The word of the Lord was for us not to yield one particle

---

because of the perilous times. And furthermore, it is more pleasing to me that men should use their free agency in regard to these matters. Nevertheless I the Lord do not change and my word and my covenants and my laws do not. And as I have heretofore said by my servant Joseph all those who would enter into my glory must and shall obey my law. And have I not commanded men that if they were Abraham's seed and would enter into my glory they must do the works of Abraham. I have not revoked this law nor will I for it is everlasting and those who will enter into my glory must obey the conditions thereof, even so Amen." (A photocopy of the handwritten document is in possession of this author.)

[91] Phoebe Whittemore Carter, Mary Ann Jackson, Mary Meek Giles Webster, Emma Smoot Smith, Sarah Elinore Brown, Sarah Delight Stocking and Eudora Young Dunford. Post-Manifesto marriages were possible, but concealed, and therefore cannot be adequately confirmed from available records. Diaries make cryptic and ambiguous references I am not willing to use as clear enough proof to decide the matter.

[92] "If we were to do away with polygamy, it would only be one feather in the bird, one ordinance in the Church and kingdom. Do away with that, then we must do away with prophets and Apostles, with revelation and the gifts and graces of the Gospel, and finally give up our religion altogether and turn sectarians and do as the world does, then all would be right. We just can't do that, for God has commanded us to build up His kingdom and to bear our testimony to the nations of the earth, and we are going to do it, come life or come death. He has told us to do thus, and we shall obey Him in days to come as we have in days past." *JD* 13:165-66.

[93] In the November 24, 1899 revelation among other things Woodruff wrote: "If the Saints will hearken unto my voice, and the counsel of my Servants, the wicked shall not prevail. Let my servants, who officiate as your Counselors before the courts, make their pleadings as they are moved upon by the Holy Spirit, without any further pledges from the Priesthood, and they shall be justified." For a complete transcript, see *In the President's Office: The Diaries of L. John Nuttall, 1879-1892*, pp. 395-96 , Edited by Jedediah S. Rogers, Signature Books (Salt Lake City, 2007).

of that which He had revealed and established."[94] First Presidency Secretary John Nuttall recorded in his diary: "As I wrote at his dictation, I felt better all the time and when I completed I felt as light and joyous as it is possible to feel, for I was satisfied that Prest. Woodruff had received the word of the Lord."[95]

Despite heaven urging them to continue, both society and the US Government were pulling in the opposite direction. Legal setbacks continued to accumulate. *Reynolds v. United States*[96] upheld the Morrill Anti-Bigamy Act. The polygamist church leadership was guilty of a federal crime. *Davis v. Beason*[97] upheld the Idaho test oath designed to disqualify Mormons from jury duty and public office. *The Late Corporation of the Mormon Church v. United States*[98] upheld Federal seizure of LDS Church property. It was expected the government would take possession of all LDS Temples.

When *The Late Corporation of the Mormon Church* decision was announced on May 19, 1890, a member of the Twelve Apostles recorded the internal reaction:

> The U.S. Supreme Court today rendered one of the most important decisions of its existence. By the provisions of the Edmunds Tucker act the property of the Church was ordered escheated for the use of the schools. In pursuance of this provision some $750,000 worth of church property was seized and placed in the hands of a receiver. …Justice Bradley read the decision in which the law is upheld, and the property is confiscated. The principal ground for this unjust ruling is that the Church upholds polygamy, and doubtless uses this means for the promotion of its doctrine.[99]

---

[94] *Candid Insights of a Mormon Apostle: The Diaries of Abraham H. Cannon, 1889-1895*, p. 38, Edward Leo Lyman, editor, Signature Books (Salt Lake; 2010).

[95] *In the President's Office: The Diaries of L. John Nuttall, 1879-1892*, p. 393, Edited by Jedediah S. Rogers, Signature Books (Salt Lake City, 2007).

[96] 98 US 145 (1878).

[97] 133 US 333 (1890). This was a particularly clear loss for the LDS Church. In a 9-0 decision the opinion stated, "Few crimes are more pernicious to the best interests of society, and receive more general or more deserved punishment."

[98] 136 US 1 (1890).

[99] *Candid Insights of a Mormon Apostle: The Diaries of Abraham H. Cannon, 1889-*

Events unfolded quickly once the church lost its property. US Secretary of State, James G. Blaine prepared a document June 12th for the church's leaders to sign renouncing plural marriage. In the only existing document referring to a pre-Manifesto policy change (prepared two months prior to the Manifesto), Apostle Abraham H. Cannon's diary records on July 10th: "The resolution of the First Presidency of June 30/90 in regard to plural marriages was read. It is to the effect that none shall be permitted to occur even in Mexico unless the contracting parties, or at least the female, has resolved to remain in that country."[100]

The church's worst fears were confirmed August 26th when the former Federal receiver, Frank Dyer related the US would soon attempt "to confiscate the Logan, Manti and St. George temples on the grounds that they are not used for public worship."[101]

On September 24th Wilford Woodruff issued the press release now called the "Manifesto" in which he denied plural marriages were taking place. The LDS Church would continue to perform plural marriages until a second "Manifesto" was issued by President Joseph F. Smith in 1904.[102] Plural marriage began in the LDS Church in secret. It remained secret after the 1890 Manifesto, ultimately dying sometime after 1904. It is now denounced[103] and those who practice it are excommunicated.

Finally, the LDS Church was motivated by popular disapproval and federal legislation to abandon plural wives. In a Sacrament meeting of the First Presidency and Quorum of the Twelve, on April 2, 1891, President Woodruff defended the Manifesto by claiming he had been "inspired" by God to issue the document, but polygamy would yet be restored in the Church.[104]

---

1895, p. 95, Edward Leo Lyman, editor, Signature Books (Salt Lake; 2010).

[100] Id., p. 104.

[101] Id., p. 124.

[102] This topic has been discussed by others including D. Michael Quinn in *The Mormon Hierarchy: Extensions of Power*, Signature Books, (Salt Lake City, 1997), Richard Van Wagoner, *Mormon Polygamy: A History*, Signature Books, (Salt Lake City, 1989), and Drew Briney, *Apostles on Trial: Examining the Membership Trials of Apostles Taylor and Cowley*, Hindsight Publications, (Salt Lake, 2012), among many others.

[103] "Today, the practice of polygamy is strictly prohibited in the Church, as it has been for over a century." (LDS.org website, mormonnewsroom.org in the article titled "Polygamy.")

Resistance to the popular will reflected in federal legislation had proven impossible. The LDS Church would not have survived as a legal enterprise if their members could not vote, serve on juries, hold public office, and if their temples were taken, their property escheated to the government, and their officials jailed. If the church wanted to remain a corporate entity, possess property, and practice their religion, there was no other choice. Polygamy had to go. The church chose to keep its corporate status and property. It wanted to continue as it had developed. Likewise, today the LDS Church wants to retain its tax preference, and keep its considerable property. A recent acquisition of property in Florida resulted in one newspaper headline: *"Mormon Church purchases 2% of the state of Florida for half a billion dollars."*[105]

The likelihood of the LDS Church ever becoming embroiled in a similar collision of wills with the US government is improbable. As it did in the past, the church will find some way to bridge the gulf between its teachings and governmental ire. It has much more at stake today than the estimated $750,000 taken at the time of Edmunds-Tucker. It would lose more than that perhaps weekly if the church's tax-exempt status were now revoked. Today the LDS Church must be more nimble regarding public opinion than ever before because today it has more at risk than ever before.[106]

---

[104] "In the name of Jesus Christ I say that God has not forsaken the Presidency or Twelve. He inspired me to issue the manifesto and if he had not done so I should never have taken that course even though all ordinances for the living and the dead had ceased, and our temples had fallen into the hands of our enemies. The principle of plural marriage will yet be restored to this Church, but how or when I cannot say. God will hold this nation responsible for the wrongs done this people." *Candid Insights of a Mormon Apostle: The Diaries of Abraham H. Cannon, 1889-1895*, supra, p. 196.

[105] See, Home/USA/rt.com article dated November 8, 2013.

[106] NBC News estimated the LDS Church earns $7 billion annually from tithing and owns $35 billion in temples and meeting houses. *Mormon Church Earns 7 Billion A Year From Tithing Analysis Indicates*, Peter Henderson, NBC News.com, August 13, 2012. In addition to church property, the business holdings include the 14th largest radio chain in the US (Bonneville International), 228,000 acres in Nebraska, 51,600 acres in Oklahoma, 312,000 acres in Florida (Farmland Reserve, Inc. with a dba Deseret Cattle and Citrus), properties in Hawaii including pineapple orchards and the Polynesian Cultural center (Hawaii Reserves, Inc.), the largest nut production in the US (AgReserves, Inc.), and the over $2 billion City Creek Center in downtown Salt Lake City. Other retail/office and condominium

Another abandoned LDS doctrine involves the status of black Africans. While welcomed as members, blacks were denied ordination. Brigham Young propounded,[107] and other leaders echoed, teachings relegating black Africans to doctrinally inferior status.

Slavery in America began centuries before the United States was a nation. From the late 1400's African slaves[108] were transported to the Americas. By the end of the 19th Century there had been five times as many Africans in the Americas than Europeans. African slavery was a fact of life in the English colonies before the American Revolution. Once the US was independent, it had an economic infrastructure in which African slavery was a fact of life. Before considering or condemning the LDS Church's teachings, the larger social, legal and economic setting should be remembered. Context is everything. Allowing black membership, integrated congregations, and opposition to slavery shows early Mormonism was more racially tolerant then the nation at large.

In 1856 the Republican Party was formed, in part to oppose the spread of slavery into the western territories acquired through the Mexican-American war that ended in 1846.[109] In 1857, the US

---

development projects similar to City Creek are underway or planned for Philadelphia and Arizona. Newspaper Agency Corporation, Deseret Book, Zions Securities, Deseret Digital Media, Brigham Young University and divisions of the university in Hawaii and Idaho, as well as other investments managed by Deseret Management Corporation are all part of the church asset portfolio.

[107] There are certainly reasons to associate the ban on ordination to Joseph Smith, who was clearly against interracial marriage between whites and blacks. (See, *Teachings of the Prophet Joseph Smith*, p. 269, Deseret Book, Salt Lake City). However, during his lifetime there were ordinations of black church members. These included Elijah Able and Walker Lewis. But Zebedee Coltrin, who ordained Elijah Able, later claimed Joseph Smith had Elijah cease exercising priesthood authority. Two scriptures through Joseph Smith also add to the conclusion the ban originated at the time of Joseph Smith: Moses 7: 22 and Abraham 1: 27.

[108] Slavery was not limited to the African race, but included Europeans and Native Americans, as well. However, that issue is beyond the scope of this paper.

[109] This resulted in a Democratic Party reaction to woo Mormon votes, and many southern Democrats opposed the anti-polygamy legislation. See *Brigham Young—Mormon Pioneer*, supra, p. 247. It did not last, however, and a few years later the national popularity of suppressing polygamy resulted in

Supreme Court issued their *Dred Scott* decision.[110] The ruling established that blacks free or slave, have no citizenship rights and therefore no standing to sue in federal courts.

On January 16, 1852, Young explained to the Utah Territorial Legislature Africans were the "seed of Cain" and could not hold priesthood. He described them as black, uncouth, uncomely, disagreeable, wild, and unintelligent members of the human family. "[A]ny man having one drop of the seed of [Cain] ... in him cannot hold the priesthood and if no other Prophet ever spake it before I will say it now in the name of Jesus Christ I know it is true and others know it."[111]

The curse was not just to protect the right to priesthood; it was also to prevent intermarriage. Said Young, "If the white man who belongs to the chosen seed mixes his blood with the seed of Cain, the penalty, under the law of God, is death on the spot. This will always be so."[112]

The nation fought the Civil War to resolve the national debate on slavery. In 1863 Abraham Lincoln issued the Emancipation Proclamation (arguably an illegal and unconstitutional[113] decree) to begin the process. But slavery was only concluded by adoption of the 13th Amendment in 1865.[114] To make the 13th Amendment a

---

even the Democratic Party getting aboard. Id., at p. 268.

[110] *Dred Scott v. Sandford*, 60 U.S. 393.

[111] *JD* 7:290. He continued: "You see some classes of the human family that are black, uncouth, uncomely, disagreeable and low in their habits, wild, and seemingly deprived of nearly all the blessings of the intelligence that is generally bestowed upon mankind .... Cain slew his brother. Cain might have been killed, and that would have put a termination to that line of human beings. This was not to be, and the Lord put a mark upon him, which is the flat nose and black skin. Trace mankind down to after the flood, and then another curse is pronounced upon the same race—that they should be the 'servant of servants'; and they will be, until that curse is removed; and the Abolitionists cannot help it, nor in the least alter that decree." On the bright side, he did describe them as fellow members of the human family.

[112] *JD* 10: 104.

[113] The 5th Amendment to the Constitution prevented taking "property" (and slaves were regarded at the time as property) without "just compensation." There was debatable wartime authority under the constitutional war powers given the Commander-in-Chief.

[114] The Amendment reads, in relevant part: "Neither slavery nor involuntary servitude, except as punishment for crime whereof the party shall have been

restriction on State conduct, the 14th Amendment was likewise adopted. The 14th Amendment reads, in relevant part:

> No State shall make or enforce any law which shall abridge the privileges and immunities of citizens of the United States; nor shall any state deprive any person of life, liberty, or property, without due process of law; nor deny to any person within its jurisdiction the equal protection of the laws.

The post-Civil War constitutional amendments were only the beginning of the process to establish equality for former slaves and their descendants. Segregation in Post-Civil War America was legal, having been approved by the Supreme Court.[115]

Although Brigham Young's comments about racial intermarriage seem offensive in 2014, the United States had widespread laws making such marriages illegal. These were referred to as "Anti-Miscegenation" statutes. It was not until 1948 that California became the first state to strike down an anti-miscegenation statute.[116] The US Supreme Court did not decide the issue until 1967, finally making all State statutes against interracial marriages illegal.[117]

The Civil Rights movement, establishment of the NAACP,[118] Rosa Parks,[119] Martin Luther King[120] and the Civil Rights Acts[121] all were required to change the status of the descendants of former

---

duly convicted, shall exist within the United States, or any place subject to their jurisdiction."

[115] *Plessy v. Ferguson*, 163 U.S. 537 (1896).

[116] *Perez v. Sharp*, 198 P.2d 17 (Cal 1948).

[117] *Loving v. Virginia*, 388 U.S. 1 (1967).

[118] Founded in 1909.

[119] She refused to move to the back of a public transportation bus in Montgomery, Alabama on December 1, 1955 and was arrested for her refusal. Her act of defiance became a national symbol. Congress passed a resolution calling her "the first lady of civil rights" and "the mother of a freedom movement." (Public Law 106-26.)

[120] Martin Luther King became a national figure with the 1955 Montgomery Bus Boycott. He was awarded the Nobel Peace Prize in 1964 and slain in 1968 at age 39.

[121] One adopted in 1964 banned discrimination in employment practice and public accommodations, followed by the Voting Rights Act of 1965, then a second Civil Rights Act in 1968 that banned discrimination in housing.

slaves in the American culture. Notwithstanding these events, racial disharmony remains a persistent source of continuing antagonism in the United States.

While the Civil Rights Movement was gaining momentum, LDS Church leaders remained committed to preserve their racial teachings. Apostle Mark E. Peterson defended the church's position on race and priesthood in an address to BYU audience of Institute and Seminary teachers in 1954 at Brigham Young University. He said:

> The reason that one would lose his blessings by marrying a negro is due to the restriction placed upon them. "No person having the least particle of negro blood can hold the priesthood" (Brigham Young). It does not matter if they are one-sixth negro or one-hundred and sixth, the curse of no Priesthood is the same. If an individual who is entitled to the priesthood marries a negro, the Lord has decreed that only spirits who are not eligible for the priesthood will come to that marriage as children. To intermarry with a negro is to forfeit a "nation of priesthood holders."[122]

The question was so well settled that when LDS Church leader Bruce R. McConkie assembled an encyclopedic summary of Mormon beliefs titled *Mormon Doctrine*, he could state with authority the church's beliefs. Under the entry "Negroes" he summarized:

> The negroes are not equal with other races where the receipt of certain spiritual blessings are concerned, particularly the priesthood and the temple blessings that flow therefore, but this inequality is not of man's origin. It is the Lord's doing, is based on his eternal laws of justice, and grows out of the lack of spiritual valiance of those concerned in their first estate.[123]

However, clearly the legal trends were against discrimination. Institutional racial discrimination had been targeted by Civil Rights organizations for years. As would be expected, the LDS Church came to the attention of the NAACP, and efforts were made to negotiate for change. In 1963 the NAACP leadership attempted to meet with

---

[122] *Race Problems—As They Affect The Church*, copy available at lds-mormon.com/racism.shtml.
[123] *Mormon Doctrine*, "Negroes", p. 527-28, Deseret Book (Salt Lake City, 1966). My copy was in the 12th printing in 1973.

LDS Church leaders, but the church refused. A meeting took place two years later in 1965 when the LDS Church agreed to support civil rights legislation pending in the Utah legislature. They agreed to publish an editorial in the church-owned newspaper, the Deseret News. The church failed to keep the agreement. N. Eldon Tanner explained "We have decided to remain silent."[124]

By March 1965 the NAACP took more public means to pressure the LDS Church. They organized an anti-discrimination march in Salt Lake City to protest church policies. The next year the NAACP issued a statement criticizing the church, complaining it "maintained a rigid and continuous segregation stand" and has made "no effort to counteract the widespread discriminatory practices in education, in housing, in employment, and other areas of life."[125]

Although the institution was hesitating, its membership was increasingly willing to see more racial equality.[126] The culture was changing, and change began to exert pressure inside the LDS Church.[127]

---

[124] See, Glen W. Davidson, *Mormon Missionaries and the Race Question*, The Christian Century, September 29, 1965, pp. 1183-86.

[125] Deseret News, May 3, 1966.

[126] Newell G. Bringhurst and Darron T. Smith, *Black and Mormon*, pp. 94-97, University of Illinois Press (Urbana, 2004).

[127] In the 2014 Mormon History Association meeting there was a good deal of praise for the LDS Church's recent essay on the history of blacks and the priesthood. (See Tad Walch, *LDS Blacks, Scholars Cheer Church's Essay on Priesthood*, Deseret News June 8, 2014.) The collective relief from changing the position is palpable. Prior doctrinal teachings have been first reduced to "theories" and then condemned by "a crystal-clear disavowal of those theories." Now LDS Mormons get to join ranks with others in decrying racism, with little regard for their church's history or their ancestor's beliefs. BYU Professor Randy Bott was interviewed by the Washington Post and truthfully restated earlier teachings of the LDS Church: "Bott points to the Mormon holy text the Book of Abraham as suggesting that all of the descendants of Ham and Egypt were thus black and barred from the priesthood. ...church leaders suggested that the ban on blacks resulted from consequences of the 'conduct of spirits in the pre-mortal existence.' As a result, many Mormons believed that blacks were less valiant in the pre-Earth life, or fence sitters in the war between God and Satan. ...'God has always been discriminatory' when it comes to whom he grants the authority of the priesthood, says Bott, the BYU theologian." (Jason Horowitz, *The Genesis of a Church Stand on Race*, Washington Post, February 28, 2012.) The LDS Church responded less than a day later denouncing Bott: "Bott's comments, the church, said, 'absolutely do not represent the teachings and doctrines of The

In addition, Brigham Young University offered a visible target for protests. The University of Texas at El Paso (UTEP) was confronted with a protest by their track team: "After the assassination of Dr. Martin Luther King, black members of the track team approached their coach and expressed their desire not to compete against Brigham Young University in an upcoming meet. When the coach disregarded the athletes' complaint, the athletes boycotted the meet."[128] In 1969 members of the University of Wyoming football team intended to protest during a BYU football game by wearing black armbands. The protest was aborted when the university suspended the players, which in turn resulted in a lawsuit in Federal Court. One of the athletes testified "they were protesting against racial policies" referring to "the Mormon Church." Others likewise testified they intended to "protest the views of the Mormon Church."[129] Unlike the University of Wyoming, Stanford University's President Kenneth Pitzer suspended all athletic relations with BYU in November, 1969.[130] Legal pressure on this issue stirred memories of earlier conflicts with the Federal government.[131]

There were rumors the LDS Church faced a threat to remove its tax-exempt status. These rumors were denied by an LDS spokesman.[132]

---

Church of Jesus Christ of Latter-day Saints.' It went on to say that 'the church's position is clear—we believe all people are God's children and are equal in his eyes and in the church. We do not tolerate racism in any form.'" (Peggy Fletcher Stack, *Mormon Church Disputes BYU Prof's Remarks About Blacks*, Salt Lake Tribune, February 29, 2012.)

[128] Gil Fried & Michael Hiller, *ADR in Youth and Intercollegiate Athletics*, BYU Law Review, pp. 631-32, Vol. 1977, Issue 3.

[129] See *Williams v. Eaton*, 468 F2nd 1079 (10th Cir. 1972).

[130] James J. Kilpatric, *A Sturdy Discipline Serves Mormons Well*, December 11, 1969, Evening Independent.

[131] Outside the US there were legal challenges as well. In Costa Rica a lawsuit by a black lawyer sought to disenfranchise the church under the law of that country prohibiting racial discrimination by a church in its proselyting. The missionaries were using a "genealogical survey" as a technique to determine if the contact had African ancestry. (See Edward L. Kimball, *Spencer W. Kimball and the Revelation on Priesthood*, BYU Studies 47, no. 2, (2008), p. 42.

[132] "It's one thing to distort history, quite another to invent it. Kathy Erickson (Forum, March 11) claims that the federal government threatened The Church of Jesus Christ of Latter-day Saints with its tax-exempt status in 1978 because of the church's position regarding blacks and the priesthood. "We state categorically that the federal government made no such threat in

However, the issue of racial discrimination was before the US courts for years prior to the LDS announcement of a change in positions. Because of institutional opposition to interracial marriage, Bob Jones University only admitted black students if they were married. The IRS threatened to revoke their tax exemption in 1970. The university sued in 1971 and the US District Court granted an injunction against the IRS. The Fourth Circuit reversed for lack of jurisdiction, and the US Supreme Court affirmed. In 1975 the IRS notified the university their tax exemption was revoked. The university paid $21 and sued for a refund in US District Court. The IRS counterclaimed for $489,675.59 in back taxes. The case was pending in 1978 and decided by the District Court in December, six months after the LDS Church changed its policy.

The case was ultimately decided by the US Supreme Court allowing the IRS to revoke tax-exempt status because of racial discrimination.[133] A direct threat by the US Government would not have been unnecessary in the circumstances. At the time the case was pending in the US District Court it came to the attention of law students at BYU, including myself. When the case was finally argued, Rex E. Lee, my former law school Dean at BYU, was the US Solicitor General.[134] There is little doubt Lee was aware of the case and its

---

1978 or at any other time. The decision to extend the blessings of the priesthood to all worthy males had nothing to do with federal tax policy or any other secular law." Bruce L. Olsen, Public Affairs Department, The Church of Jesus Christ of Latter-day Saints, *Distorted History*, Salt Lake Tribune, April 5, 2001.

[133] *Bob Jones University v. US*, 461 U.S. 574 (1983). Bob Jones University prohibited interracial dating. The IRS revoked tax-exempt status because of this policy. The majority opinion read, in part: "The governmental interest at stake here is compelling. As discussed in Part II-B, supra, the Government has a fundamental, overriding interest in eradicating racial discrimination in education – discrimination that prevailed, with official approval, for the first 165 years of this Nation's constitutional history. That governmental interest substantially outweighs whatever burden denial of tax benefits places on petitioners' exercise of their religious beliefs. The interests asserted by petitioners cannot be accommodated with that compelling governmental interest, see *United States v. Lee*, supra, at and no 'less restrictive means,' see *Thomas v. Review Board of Indiana Employment Security Div.*, supra, at 718, are available to achieve the governmental interest."

[134] Rex E. Lee was the Dean while I attended the J. Reuben Clark Law School. He served as Dean until 1981, when President Reagan appointed

implications for BYU and ultimately the LDS Church. Former BYU President Dallin H. Oaks was on the Utah Supreme Court when *Bob Jones University* was decided.

The threat of taxation can ultimately destroy any institution, including the LDS Church, if the sovereign chooses to do so. Chief Justice John Marshall coined the truism: "The power to tax involves the power to destroy."[135]

Faced with the obvious national trend against institutional racism, and the memory of its past conflict with the US, the LDS Church changed its teaching June 8, 1978. Prior to this, efforts to make the change were unsuccessful because church leaders were unable to get approval from God. President Spencer W. Kimball turned the problem around. He wanted to make the change, pondered for months, had a growing conviction it would be a good thing to accomplish. He consulted carefully with the Twelve, taking their comments and seeking their advice. When the day came to decide the matter he did not pray to have Divine approval, instead he presumed it to be time for the change and asked to be clearly told not to proceed if the Lord objected.[136] Hearing no objection from the Twelve, his counselors or heaven, the change was adopted. It was implemented in 1978 and announced in Official Declaration 2, now part of the Doctrine & Covenants.[137]

---

him US Solicitor General. The *Bob Jones University* case was argued in October 1982. Rex Lee recused himself from arguing the case because of his prior involvement with BYU.

[135] *McCulloch v. Maryland*, 17 U.S. 327 (1819).

[136] See *Spencer W. Kimball and the Revelation on Priesthood*, BYU Studies 47, n0.2 (2008), pp. 54-56; in relevant part: "He had reached a decision after great struggle, and he wanted the Lord's confirmation, if it would come. They surrounded the altar in a prayer circle. President Kimball told the Lord at length that if extending the priesthood was not right, if the Lord did not want this change to come in the Church, he would fight the world's opposition."

[137] Interestingly the language of OD2 reflects the Civil Rights vocabulary, rather than scriptural terminology. The Declaration refers to lifting the ban "without regard to race or color." The scriptures refer to either "lineage" (Abr. 1: 27) or "seed" (Moses 7: 22) when the subjects of disqualification for priesthood, or inclusion are mentioned. The choice of language suggests the Civil Rights Movement was on the minds of the committee who drafted the declaration.

It is obvious the LDS Church could not admit forfeiting priesthood because African Americans are now ordained. It is equally obvious this change is incompatible with prior teaching. To bridge this gulf the church issued a press release titled *Race and the Church: All Are Alike Unto God*. The contradiction is accounted for by "the absence of direct revelation" to guide the earlier leaders. The return of scarcity is blamed: "The origins of priesthood availability are not entirely clear. Some explanations with respect to this matter were made in the absence of direct revelation and references to these explanations are sometimes cited in publications. These previous personal statements do not represent Church doctrine."[138] This describes the process. Scarcity forces the institution to substitute man's doctrinal innovations for God's voice. Restoration has ended and apostasy has begun.

In addition to now denigrating earlier prophets, seers and revelators for not having revelation to guide them, the LDS Church also unequivocally condemned them in a lengthy editorial on their lds.org website:

> Over time, Church leaders and members advanced many theories to explain the priesthood and temple restrictions. None of these explanations is accepted today as the official doctrine of the Church. …Today, the Church disavows the theories advanced in the past that black skin is a sign of divine disfavor or curse, or that it reflects actions in a premortal life; that mixed-race marriages are a sin; or that blacks or people of any other race or ethnicity are inferior in any way to anyone else. Church leaders today unequivocally condemn all racism, past and present, in any form.[139]

They attribute their earlier missteps to US history, including legal slavery when the LDS Church began. The conversion of Africans in Brazil had an effect on the timing. These black members donated to build a temple in Sao Paulo but would be barred from entry without a policy change.

Latter-day Saint history has surprisingly few teachings addressing homosexuality than recent events would suggest. There is a timeline

---

[138] Mormonnewsroom.org/article/race-church
[139] lds.org/topics/race-and-the-priesthood?lang=eng

published on the website "No More Strangers: LGBT Mormon Forum,"[140] which retells many of the events. The issue did not seem to emerge into direct and regular discussion until the 1950's.

As a matter of traditional LDS doctrine, homosexuality is sinful, requiring repentance by the homosexual. In Spencer W. Kimball's book *The Miracle of Forgiveness*, he wrote, "the seriousness of the sin of homosexuality is equal to or greater than that of fornication or adultery; and that *the Lord's Church will as readily take action to disfellowship or excommunicate the unrepentant practicing homosexual as it will the unrepentant fornicator or adulterer.*"[141]

In a chapter titled *Crime Against Nature*, Spencer Kimball called it "unnatural and wrong." He elaborated "All such deviations from normal, proper heterosexual relationships are not merely unnatural but wrong in the sight of God. Like adultery, incest and bestiality they carried the death penalty under the Mosaic law."[142]

A grim milestone was set in 1965 when five young Mormons, all homosexual and all counseled by Apostle Spencer W. Kimball for homosexual sin, committed suicide. All were in their early 20's. Three had recently returned from missionary service. All had been BYU students.[143] "Their continued education at BYU and their precious membership in the Mormon church were made contingent upon their complete repentance and their willingness to provide names of other gay people."[144]

---

[140] Seth Anderson, *Timeline of Mormon Thinking About Homosexuality*, Nomorestrangers.org, posted December 9, 2013, also posted at RationalFaiths.com. The article does not attempt to be exhaustive, but appears to be representative.

[141] *The Miracle of Forgiveness*, p. 81-82, Deseret Book, (Salt Lake City, 1969), italics in original.

[142] *Id.* at p. 79.

[143] In 1965 (the year of these suicides) BYU President Ernest Wilkinson gave a devotional talk in which he declared: "Nor do we intend to admit to our campus any homosexuals. If any of you has this tendency and have not completely abandoned it, may I suggest that you leave the University immediately after this assembly ...we do not want others on this campus to be contaminated by your presence." See Allie Rae Treharne, *History of BYU & Homosexuality*, thestudentreview.org/history-of-byu-homosexuality.

[144] Robert I. McQueen, *Outside the Temple Gates—The Gay Mormon*, The Advocate, August 13, 1975. See also *History of BYU & Homosexuality*, supra, which confirmed: "some students who were caught faced the ultimatum of providing names of other gay students or expulsion from school." (Citing

In the *Guide to the Scriptures* published by the LDS Church, there is a section titled "Sexual Immorality." This section includes a list of scriptures under the general description: "Willful participation in adultery, fornication, homosexuality, lesbianism, incest, or other unholy, unnatural, or impure sexual activity." What follows includes this statement and citation: "Homosexuality and other sex perversions are an abomination: Lev. 18: 22-23." Also, "In the last days men shall be without natural affection: 2 Tim. 3: 1-3."

In the United States there is a tidal wave of legal activity on homosexual rights underway. Since 2003 every state has either legalized same-sex marriage or adopted laws prohibiting it.

The Utah legislature is overwhelmingly LDS. In 1977 the Utah legislature amended Utah Code §30-1-2 to state marriages "between persons of the same sex" were "prohibited and declared void." In 2004 the Utah legislature passed Utah Code §30-1-4.1 which stated: "it is the policy of this state to recognize as marriage only the legal union of a man and a woman as provided in this chapter." It anticipated same-sex marriages in other states and nullified them in Utah.[145] Then, as a precaution against the rising tide of changing attitudes regarding same-sex marriage,[146] the legislature also adopted a proposed amendment to the Utah State Constitution. The amendment was put on the November 2, 2004 ballot and passed with approximately 66% of the vote favoring the amendment to Article I, §29, adding the following language: "Marriage consists only of the

---

Connell O'Donovan, *The Abominable and Detestable Crime Against Nature: A Revised History of Homosexuality and Mormonism, 1840-1980*, Signature Books, Salt Lake, 1994; now revised as of 2004 and available online at connellodonovan.com/abom.html.)

[145] "Except for the relationship of marriage between a man and a woman recognized pursuant to this chapter, this state will not recognize, enforce, or give legal effect to any law creating any legal status, rights, benefits, or duties that are substantially equivalent to those provided under Utah law to a man and woman because they are married."

[146] In 1998 36% of the US population believed sexual orientation could not be changed. By 2012 58% believed sexual orientation was unchangeable. In 2001 40% of the US believed homosexuality was acceptable. In 2013 59% believe it acceptable. (See, *Public Opinion Polls on Two Key LDB Questions*, religioustolerance.orghom_poll2htm.) In 1993 the Hawaii Supreme Court struck down the Hawaiian statute prohibiting same-sex marriage. In 1999 the Vermont Supreme Court held same-sex marriage was likewise constitutionally protected.

legal union between a man and a woman. No other domestic union, however denominated, may be recognized as a marriage or given the same or substantially equivalent effect."[147] This provision took effect January 1, 2005. It was declared unconstitutional in December 2013 by the US District Court,[148] and again in June 2014 by the 10th Circuit Court of Appeals.[149]

The year before this amendment to the Utah Constitution, the US Supreme Court invalidated Texas' criminalization of homosexual acts.[150] In Massachusetts the State Supreme Court ruled the state's constitution protected the right of same-sex couples to marry.[151] Utah's statutes and amendment to the state constitution was struck down in December of 2014.[152]

In California the issue of same-sex marriage was voted on in November 2008. The ballot fight was aided by the LDS Church providing both vocal support, and assisting with facilitating door-to-door campaign efforts. Before the vote was taken, church leaders David A. Bednar, Russell M. Ballard and Quentin L. Cook (of the Twelve Apostles) and Whitney Clayton (of the Seventy) broadcast video into California urging church members to be involved in supporting Proposition 8. When the vote was counted, the LDS effort has proven decisive and Proposition 8 passed. In a post-election statement the LDS church made this announcement: "The Church expresses deep appreciation for the hard work and dedication of the many Latter-day Saints and others who supported the coalitions in efforts regarding these amendments."[153]

Opposition to Proposition 8 in California resulted in an organized effort seeking to revoke the LDS Church's tax exempt

---

[147] Depending on how the Utah Supreme Court interpreted this language, it appears on the face of the bill to outlaw civil unions in Utah as well as marriage.

[148] *Kitchen, et. al. v Herbert, et. al.*, Case No. 2:13-cv-217, US District Court for the District of Utah, Memorandum Decision and Order filed December 20, 2013.

[149] *Kitchen, et. al. v. Herbert, et. al.*, Case No. 13-4178, Decision filed June 25, 2014.

[150] *Lawrence v. Texas*, 539 U.S. 558 (2003).

[151] *Goodridge v. Dep't of Pub. Health*, 798 N.E.2d 941 (2003).

[152] *Derek Kitchen, et. al., v. Gary R. Herbert, et. al.*, supra.

[153] See mormonnewsroom.org/article/church-responds-to-same-sex-marriage-votes, November 5, 2008.

status. A website was established to instruct those willing to protest on how to approach removing the 501c3 status of the church.[154] The protest focused on the IRC provision which limited favorable tax treatment to institutions "organized and operated exclusively for religious" purposes and in which "no part of the net earnings" are used nor "no substantial part of the activities of which is carrying on propaganda, or otherwise attempting to influence legislation."[155] The IRS has now agreed to investigate politically active churches.[156]

The LDS Church has been publicly softening its position on homosexuality since winning the Proposition 8 battle. The Boy Scouts change to accept homosexuals was immediately approved by the LDS Church[157] as a visible mea culpa.[158] This is also true of others involved with Proposition 8.[159] An LDS writer has advocated same-sex temple sealing in a popular Mormon journal.[160]

---

[154] See http://lds501c3.wordpress.com/

[155] The website quotes IRC §501c3.

[156] See Deseret News article, *The IRS agrees to investigate churches that preach politics after settling with atheist lobbying group*, July 31, 2014 at national.desnews.com/article/2016/The-IRS-agrees-to-investigate-churches-thatpreach-politics-after-settling-with-athies-lobbying.html

[157] *The Christian Post* reported the news with alarm (*LDS Church Accepts New Boy Scout Policy on Gay Members*, May 24, 2013).

[158] LDS Church owned Deseret News quoted church spokesman Michael R. Otterson in an article titled LDS Church Public Relations Official Writes About Scouting Decision for Washington Post, May 31, 2013, as saying: "'For the Church of Jesus Christ of Latter-day Saints, this was never about whether the BSA or local scout leaders should try to discern or categorize ill-defined and emerging sexual awareness of pre-pubescent boys and early pubescent young men who make up 90 percent of scouting. Sexual orientation has not previously been — and is not now — a disqualifying factor for boys who want to join Latter-day Saint scout troops. Rather, it has always about teaching moral behavior to *all* boys, and instilling the core values that are part of responsible adulthood,' according to Otterson."

[159] Expert witness David Blankenhorn recanted his view in a New York Times editorial on June 22, 2012 titled *How My View on Gay Marriage Changed*. He announced in the editorial: "I took a stand against gay marriage. But as a marriage advocate, the time has come for me to accept gay marriage and emphasize the good that it can do."

[160] See Taylor Petrey, *Toward a Post-Heterosexual Mormon Theology*, Dialogue: A Journal of Mormon Thought, Vol. 44, No. 4, December 8, 2011. In the 2011

The LDS Church is necessarily attentive to legal trends. Its existence was once hanging by the thinnest of threads because of laws targeting it. Lawyers are consistently among the highest leadership of the LDS Church.[161] At the time of writing this paper, the Quorum of Twelve includes lawyers Dallin H. Oaks, Quentin L. Cook, D. Todd Christofferson and Neil L. Anderson. The legal and social environment in which LDS Mormonism has evolved cannot be divorced from its evolving doctrine, because many changes were adaptations to this environment.

When Joseph Smith was alive, women had limited property rights. When married their property became their husband's under the common law doctrine of coverture. It was not until the 1840's that state legislatures in the United States first began to modify the common law by adopting statutes to protect women's property from their husbands and their husbands' creditors.

Women's right to vote in the US began in 1869 when Wyoming passing the first suffrage law. The following year women began to serve on Wyoming juries. In 1893 Colorado granted women the right to vote. In 1896 Idaho and Utah did likewise. Remember this as you consider how different a world you live in when it comes to women's place in society.

The National Organization for Women (NOW) was created in 1966 to pursue equal rights. They fought for the Equal Rights Amendment (ERA) to amend the constitution to add: "equality of rights under the law shall not be denied or abridged by the United States or any state on account of sex." The amendment died in 1982 because enough states failed to adopt it.

The ACLU announces on its website "Forty years ago, the American Civil Liberties Union (ACLU) board of directors determined that women's rights should be the organization's highest priority. Then-executive director Aryeh Neier, created the ACLU Women's Rights Project and named Ruth Bader Ginsburg as the first director. Since then, Ginsburg has become a justice on the United

---

Sunstone Symposium Brad Carmak presented a paper, *Why Mormonism can Abide Gay Marriage*, which is viewable on YouTube at: "youtube.com/watch?v=E1jDUcBKml0"

[161] At the time of changing the policy in 1978, the First Presidency and Quorum of the Twelve included lawyers Marion G. Romney, Howard W. Hunter and Bruce R. McConkie, as well as N. Eldon Tanner who, although not a lawyer, was a former legislator in Canada.

States Supreme Court, and the Women's Rights Project (WRP) has won many landmark court decisions, achieved significant legislative successes, and shifted public awareness and understanding of women's equality."[162]

Reproductive rights and the ability of women to access birth control was decided in 1965. Connecticut had a statute that prohibited any person from using "any drug, medicinal article or instrument for the purpose of preventing conception." The Supreme Court decided this kind of law violated the "right to marital privacy" and was therefore unconstitutional.[163] The effect was to change the nation's outlook on sexuality so radically that by 1967 the "Summer of Love" was underway in the San Francisco Haight-Ashbury district. Hunter S. Thompson wrote about it in *The New York Times Magazine* which helped attract widespread attention. Soon the national media was fascinated and began to report daily of events there. In June, 1967 the Monterey Pop Festival happened, with 60,000 people attending by the last day. If you were going to San Francisco at the time you needed to wear some flowers in your hair.[164] Sexual promiscuity seemed the perfect antidote for the relentless tension of the compulsory draft and service in the Vietnam War. Timothy Leary admonished us to "turn on, tune in, drop out" and become one with the movement. Sexual liberation proved alluring indeed.[165]

In the *Griswold* case, although the Bill of Rights does not mention privacy, Justice William O. Douglas wrote the right was found in the "penumbras" and "emanations" of the other rights enumerated. That innovation would produce another dramatic

---

[162] See, aclu.org/womens-rights.

[163] *Griswold v. Connecticut*, 381 U.S. 479 (1965).

[164] John Phillips penned the song *San Francisco (Be Sure to Wear Flowers in Your Hair)* that promoted both the Monterey Pop Festival and the movement in San Francisco generally.

[165] During the Summer of Love, LDS General Conference included a sermon stating: "In this day when modesty is thrust into the background, and chastity is considered an outmoded virtue, I appeal to parents especially, and to my fellow teachers, both in and out of the Church, to teach youth to keep their souls unmarred and unsullied from this and other debasing sins, the consequences of which will smite and haunt them intimately until their conscience is eared and their character becomes sordid." Gordon B. Hinckley, *Conference Report*, April 1967, p. 54.

emanation in Justice Blackmun's landmark abortion ruling eight years later.

In the newly found constitutional "penumbra" Justice Harry Blackmun found the right to privacy also gave women the right to an abortion. Writing for a 7-2 majority in *Roe V. Wade*,[166] he stated: "the right to privacy, whether it be founded in the Fourteenth Amendment's concept of personal liberty and restrictions upon state action, as we feel it is, or, as the district court determined, in the Ninth Amendment's reservation of rights to the people, is broad enough to encompass a woman's decision whether or not to terminate her pregnancy." At the time of the decision all states limited abortion, and the majority of the states prohibited abortion altogether. The dissenting opinion of Justices Byron White and William Rehnquist dissented, lamenting the majority exercised improvident and extravagant power to fashion a new constitutional right.[167]

Whether it was improvident or not, the culture of the United States has been shaped by *Roe v. Wade* from 1973 to the present. At present it is estimated over 60 million Americans do not live today, having been aborted. That holocaust was designed to target an unwanted population, and has worked as intended.[168]

---

[166] 410 U.S. 113 (1973).

[167] "I find nothing in the language or history of the Constitution to support the Court's judgment. The Court simply fashions and announces a new constitutional right for pregnant women and, with scarcely any reason or authority for its action, invests that right with sufficient substance to override most existing state abortion statutes. The upshot is that the people and the legislatures of the 50 States are constitutionally disentitled to weigh the relative importance of the continued existence and development of the fetus, on the one hand, against a spectrum of possible impacts on the woman, on the other hand. As an exercise of raw judicial power, the Court perhaps has authority to do what it does today; but, in my view, its judgment is an improvident and extravagant exercise of the power of judicial review that the Constitution extends to this Court." *Roe v. Wade*, dissent by Rhenquist, White.

[168] As Justice Ruth Bader Ginsburg explained in an interview with the New York Times: "Frankly I had thought that at the time *Roe* was decided there was concern about population growth and particularly growth in populations that we don't want to have too many of." (Emily Blazelon, *The Place of Women on the Court*, an interview published in the *New York Times* on July 7, 2009.)

In 1986 the US Supreme Court found that sexual harassment is a form of illegal job discrimination.[169]  In 1999 the Supreme Court ruled punitive damages for sex discrimination was permitted if the anti-discrimination law was violated with malice or indifference to the law, even if the conduct was not especially severe.[170]  In 2009 President Obama signed the Lily Ledbetter Fair Pay Restoration Act allowing victims of pay discrimination to file a complaint against employers within 180 days of their last paycheck, instead of within 180 days from the date of the first unfair paycheck.

In 2013 Defense Secretary Leon Panetta lifted the ban on women serving in combat roles, reversing a 1994 rule.

All these larger national events affected views of Latter-day Saints. From imposing short haircuts on missionaries[171] and BYU students,[172] warning about "hippies" and drug use,[173] advocating large

---

The results included effects which only recently have been noted by two economists: "Perhaps the most dramatic effect of legalized abortion, however, and one that would take years to reveal itself, was its impact on crime. In the early 1990's, just as the first cohort of children born after Roe v. Wade was hitting its late teens—the years during which young men enter their criminal prime—the rate of crime began to fall. What this cohort was missing, of course, were the children who stood the greatest chance of becoming criminals. And the crime rate continued to fall as an entire generation came of age minus the children whose mothers had not wanted to bring a child into the world. Legalized abortions led to less unwantedness; unwantedness leads to high crime, legalized abortion, therefore, led to less crime." Steven D. Levitt & Stephen J. Dubner, *Freakonomics*, William Morrow, New York (2009), pp. 139-140. See generally Chapter 4, *Where Have All the Criminals Gone*, pp. 115-145 for the statistical analysis supporting this conclusion.

[169] *Meritor Savings Bank v. Vinson*, 477 U.S. 57.

[170] *Kolstad v. American Dental Association*, 527 U.S. 526

[171] LDS standards are at "missionary.lds.org/dress-grooming/elder/grooming/hair/?lang=eng" and states: "Always maintain a conservative hairstyle. Keep your hair short and evenly tapered on the top, back, and sides. Sideburns should reach no lower than the middle of the ear."

[172] *BYU Honor Code*, "Dress and Grooming Standards," reads: "A clean and well-cared-for appearance should be maintained. Clothing is inappropriate when it is sleeveless, revealing, or form fitting. Shorts must be knee-length or longer. Hairstyles should be clean and neat, avoiding extreme styles or colors, and trimmed above the collar, leaving the ear uncovered. Sideburns should not extend below the earlobe or onto the cheek. If worn, moustaches

families and not artificially limiting births,[174] to denouncing rock and roll music,[175] the LDS Church has been reactionary, trying to slow

---

should be neatly trimmed and may not extend beyond or below the corners of the mouth. Men are expected to be clean-shaven; beards are not acceptable. Earrings and other body piercing are not acceptable. Shoes should be worn in all public campus areas."

[173] Here is an example from the Second Counselor in the First Presidency given in General Conference: "Just before conference a bishop called me from California to make an appointment to bring in a young man from his ward who was involved with hippies. He felt I might be able to help him. They came in just after conference. His long hair, dress and general appearance left no doubt that he was a hippie. I asked him to tell me his story. Briefly, this is what he said: 'I am a returned missionary, a married man, and I have a child; and here I am, a hippie, a drug addict, and I am guilty of many misdemeanors and even felonies. I am most unhappy. This is not what I want.' I asked him how it was that a man with his background ever got mixed up with these people. He said that one day when he was feeling despondent and discouraged, he decided that he wanted to be free, that he did not want to be bound by any traditions or Church restrictions in any way. He went out with some of these fellows in a spirit of rebellion, and then he said, 'Here I am. Instead of being free, I'm a slave.'" N. Eldon Tanner, *Conference Report*, April 1968, p. 109.

[174] See, e.g., Joseph F. Smith, *Gospel Doctrine*, Deseret Book (Salt Lake City) pp. 278-79: "I regret, I think it is a crying evil that there should exist a sentiment or a feeling among any members of the Church to curtail the birth of their children. I think that is a crime wherever it occurs, where husband and wife are in possession of health and vigor and are free from impurities that would be entailed upon their posterity. I believe that where people undertake to curtail or prevent the birth of their children that they are going to reap disappointment by and by. I have no hesitancy in saying that I believe that this is one of the greatest crimes of the world today, this evil practice."

[175] Boyd K. Packer, October 1973 General Conference talk, *Inspiring Music— Worthy Thoughts*, included this warning: "In our day music itself has been corrupted. Music can, by its tempo, by its beat, by its intensity, dull the spiritual sensitivity of men. Studies citing physiological effects from some of the extreme music of today neglect the most serious thing concerning it. Our youth have been brought up on a diet of music that is loud and fast, more intended to agitate than to pacify, more intended to excite than to calm. Even so, there is a breadth of it, some soft enough to be innocent and appealing to our youth, and that which is hard, and that is where the problem is. One of the signs of apostasy in the Christian churches today is the willingness of their ministers to compromise and introduce into what had

cultural changes.[176] Whether viewed as progress or decay, LDS leaders have fought against it.

The Ordain Women organization maintains a website (ordainwomen.org) in which Mormons are given a place to advocate change in LDS Church policy. They hope to end "gender inequality" by "calling attention to the need for the ordination of Mormon women to the priesthood." The public has responded with numerous profiles pleading for change by the LDS Church. The church responded through the Deseret News in an article March 17, 2014 titled *LDS Church: Aims of 'Ordain Women' Detract from Dialogue*. The article begins with this sentence: "A small activist women's organization is detracting from thoughtful discussions about women in The Church of Jesus Christ of Latter-day Saints, a church spokeswoman said Monday in a letter to the group." The article goes on to assert "LDS leaders are listening to women and responding. The recent changes you have seen, most notably the lowering of missionary age for sisters, serve as examples and were facilitated by

---

been, theretofore, the most sacred religious meetings the music of the drug and the hard rock culture. Such music has little virtue and it is repellent to the Spirit of God." Thomas S. Monson's October 1990 General Conference talk, *That We May Touch Heaven*, stated: "[M]usic can, by its tempo, beat, intensity, and lyrics, dully your spiritual sensitivity. You cannot afford to fill your minds with unworthy music."

[176] See, e.g., Richard G. Scott's April 2004 General Conference talk, *How to Live Well Amid Increasing Evil*, which said, in part, "You have a choice. You can wring your hands and be consumed with concern for the future or choose to use the counsel the Lord has given to live with peace and happiness in a world awash with evil. If you choose to concentrate on the dark side, this is what you will see. Much of the world is being engulfed in a rising river of degenerate filth, with the abandonment of virtue, righteousness, personal integrity, traditional marriage, and family life. Sodom and Gomorrah was the epitome of unholy life in the Old Testament. It was isolated then; now that condition is spread over the world. Satan skillfully manipulates the power of all types of media and communication. His success has greatly increased the extent and availability of such degrading and destructive influences worldwide. In the past some effort was required to seek out such evil. Now it saturates significant portions of virtually every corner of the world. We cannot dry up the mounting river of evil influences, for they result from the exercise of moral agency divinely granted by our Father. But we can and must, with clarity, warn of the consequences of getting close to its enticing, destructive current."

the input of many extraordinary LDS women around the world." It declares: "Ordaining women to the priesthood, as the letter says, is contrary both to church doctrine and the view of the vast majority of Latter-day Saints, especially women."[177]

The following month in General Conference, Apostle Dallin H. Oaks gave a talk titled: *The Keys and Authority of the Priesthood* in which he stated: "The Lord has directed that only men will be ordained to offices in the priesthood." He continued to add, however:

> We are not accustomed to speaking of women having the authority of the priesthood in their Church callings, but what other authority can it be? When a woman—young or old—is set apart to preach the gospel as a full-time missionary, she is given priesthood authority to perform a priesthood function. The same is true when a woman is set apart to function as an officer or teacher in a Church organization under the direction of one who holds the keys of the priesthood. Whoever functions in an office or calling received from one who holds priesthood keys exercises priesthood authority in performing her or his assigned duties.[178]

And so according to Oaks, women can use the authority of the priesthood, although not necessarily ordained. Extending this reasoning to its logical conclusion, women will one day be able to baptize with "authority" borrowed from a male key-holder. If institutional discrimination on the basis of sex ever threatens the LDS Church tax-exempt status, this seminal General Conference talk by a former Justice on the Utah Supreme Court can be the basis to permit the first female Bishop to serve, using authority borrowed from a male key-holder.

---

[177] Leaders in the Ordain Women movement have been threatened with excommunication. See Peggy Fletcher Stack, *Founder of Mormon Women's Group Threatened with Excommunication*, Salt Lake Tribune, June 11, 2014. History informs us the LDS Church will only move to accommodate social change when sufficient legal and economic pressure has been applied. Beforehand, posturing by the church's leadership to seem unmovable is to be expected.

[178] Dallin H. Oaks is a former editor for *Dialogue: A Journal of Mormon Thought*, which published the doctrinal explanation for sealing same-sex marriages.

LDS Mormonism claims Joseph Smith as its founder. Joseph thought his restoration would one day revolutionize the world. It was a "stone cut out of the mountain without hands" that would roll forth and grind to dust all other institutions.[179] Brigham Young thought one of the necessary obstacles needing grinding was the US Government.[180] However, LDS Church history is filled with the contrary process: The US culture has been grinding away at LDS Mormonism's peculiar doctrines, and pushing it to conform with national cultural changes. It is not difficult to foresee how the present legal and social environment will influence future position changes on women's rights and more open acceptance of homosexuality.

There are two possibilities to account for the LDS Church's history of compromise on their doctrine. The first possibility is these teachings, although once proclaimed to be fundamental, even necessary to obtain exaltation in the afterlife, were falsely portrayed in the first place. The Book of Mormon seems to support this view.[181] If this is so, then contrary to LDS past claims, no soul was ever damned by refusing to accept the doctrine of plural wives. Nor was God going to take away all priesthood from the church as soon as the church

---

[179] See, Daniel 2: 31-45; D&C 65: 2.

[180] As the US Army approached Utah territory to remove Brigham Young as Governor, he defiantly proclaimed: "You need have no fear but the fear to offend God. If you have any trembling in your hearts, or timid feelings with regard to our present situation, let me tell you one thing, which is as true as that the sun now shines, that whatever transpires with us, with our enemies, with the world here or there, will still more promote the kingdom of God on earth, and bring to a final end the kingdoms of this world. ...The world are determined to destroy the kingdom of God upon the earth; they wish to obliterate it. The kingdoms of darkness are determined to destroy this kingdom. In their feelings they are fighting against you and me, and do not know that they are contending against Jehovah. They have not the least idea of that, but think they are contending against the 'Mormons.' They are not contending against you and me—they are contending against the God of heaven." *CDBY* 3:1289-90.

[181] See 3 Ne. 11: 31-40 where Christ declares His "doctrine." The explanation has no mention of plural wives, priesthood or priesthood bans, nor homosexuality. It concluded with the warning, "whoso shall declare more or less than this, and establish it for my doctrine, the same cometh of evil." (*Id.* v. 40.) The LDS Church appears to have chosen this alternative by abandoning their earlier doctrinal positions and condemning those who advanced them.

attempted to ordain black African descendants. Nor has Almighty God banned women from the priesthood. Nor is homosexuality a serious moral offense before God. God's silence led the LDS Church to oversell these teachings and therefore they were, and are, free to "correct" them.

The other possibility is they got the doctrine right before, and by accommodating American legal and cultural demands LDS Mormonism has been cutting down the Tree of Life to build a wooden bridge. If this is the case, then popular will, federal legislation and the US Supreme Court will have more to say in the future about LDS Mormon doctrine than the church's "prophets, seers and revelators," just as they have exerted the primary influence after Joseph Smith and Brigham Young.

## Chapter 3: Was There An Original?
©2016 Denver C. Snuffer, Jr.

Mormonism is compelling. It began as a very big religion, but has diminished considerably over the years.[182] Joseph Smith asserted:

> The first and fundamental principle of our holy religion is, that we believe that we have a right to embrace all, and every item of truth, without limitation or without being circumscribed or prohibited by the creeds or superstitious notions of men, or by the dominations of one another, when that truth is clearly demonstrated to our minds, and we have the highest degree of evidence of the same.[183]

Everything true, lovely or of good report was intended to be part of original Mormonism.[184] Such a religion would be compelling indeed.

Joseph's original Mormonism was inclusive, not exclusive. All truth belonged to Mormonism, and it never pretended to have it all. Mormonism was the search for truth.[185] It included undiscovered truths, even unpleasant truths. It began as the search to discover "truth," without any regard for the reaction believers would have to something new.

To Joseph, Mormonism did not possess all truth. His religion was not based on conceit, but on humility—the willingness to continue to search, pray, study and hope for newly revealed additions. It was understood there was a great deal more to be discovered.[186]

---

[182] In *Passing the Heavenly Gift,* (Salt Lake City: Mill Creek Press, 2011) I explain the four developmental stages of Mormonism and how only the first was additive, each of the subsequent stages have been deductive.

[183] Letter from Joseph Smith to Isaac Galland, Mar. 22, 1839, Liberty Jail, Liberty, Missouri, published in *Times and Seasons*, Feb. 1840, pp. 53–54; spelling and grammar modernized.

[184] See *13th Article of Faith*, Pearl of Great Price.

[185] "[O]ne (of) the grand fundamental principles of Mormonism (is) to receive thruth (truth) let it come from where it may." (*JS Papers, Journals Vol. 3: May 1843-June 1844*, p. 55.)

[186] *The Articles of Faith* included these affirmations: "9 We believe all that God has revealed, all that He does now reveal, and we believe that He will yet reveal many great and important things pertaining to the Kingdom of

The claim that Mormonism was the "only true and living church" presumes its willingness to hear God's voice and receive new truth, not because it was already in possession of all truth. It was "living" during Joseph's life because it continued to grow and expand. Living organisms grow, dead ones decay.[187]

While Boyd K. Packer may have had a point in asserting, "Some things that are true are not very useful,"[188] as for the original Mormonism it would be more correct to state, 'All truth, (even if unpleasant and un-useful), belongs to Mormonism.' Packer failed to

---

God." "13 We believe... If there is anything virtuous, lovely, or of good report or praiseworthy, we seek after these things."

[187] "Growth" and "decay" should not be measured by numbers, but by the content of light. Measured by numbers alone, Mormonism has had a triumphant history (although its momentum is now likewise showing signs of decay). Measured by light, it has only dimmed since the passing of Joseph and Hyrum.

[188] *The Mantle is Far, Far Greater Than the Intellect*, CES Symposium on the Doctrine and Covenants, 22 August 1981, Brigham Young University, p. 3.

[189] See, e.g., John 14:23 and D&C 130:3; D&C 93:1. The full explanation of this quest for Mormonism is set out in my first book, *The Second Comforter: Conversing With the Lord Through the Veil*, (Salt Lake City: Mill Creek Press, 2006).

[190] Ether 3:13.

[191] That talk (*The Mantle is Far, Far Greater Than the Intellect*) by Boyd K. Packer has done greater damage, both short and long term, than anything Mormon opponents have written. It represents LDS leadership enshrining dishonest LDS history as a false virtue, and frames a fight the institution can never win.

[192] D. Michael Quinn, *J. Reuben Clark: The Church Years*, (Provo, Utah: Brigham Young University Press, 1983), p. 24.

[193] The futile search for antecedents to credit, from Solomon Spaulding to Soren Kierkegaard, is beyond the scope of this paper. As Harold Bloom said, "The God of Joseph Smith is a daring revival of the God of some of the Kabbalists and Gnostics, prophetic sages who, like Smith himself, asserted that they had returned to the true religion....Mormonism is a purely American Gnosis, for which Joseph Smith was and is a far more crucial figure than Jesus could be. Smith is not just 'a' prophet, another prophet, but he is the essential prophet of these latter days, leading into the end time, whenever it comes." (*The American Religion*, (New York: Simon & Schuster, 1992), pp. 99, 123.)

acknowledge that enlightenment does not bring immediate contentment. Packer did not clarify to what end truth needed to be "useful." Because the original end of Mormonism was not to merely preserve institutional loyalty, but to teach mankind to converse with the Lord through the veil preliminary to entering into His presence; then to enter into His presence,[189] thereby to be redeemed from the fall.[190] But we must all concede that Packer is quite right that truth that destroys idolatry is never "useful" for the idol.[191]

The present fracturing of Mormonism is because it has lost sight of the original inclusiveness. The opposite of the Packer standard is the one suggested by J. Reuben Clark, "If we have the truth, it cannot be harmed by investigation. If we have not the truth, it ought to be harmed."[192] Between the approaches of J. Reuben Clark and Boyd K. Packer, the LDS version of Mormonism departed from an inclusive truth to an exclusive truth, becoming intolerant, arrogant, and consequently much smaller.

At its inception, Mormonism revived the original relevance of religion: mankind wants big picture answers from the God who created us. Because all of us hope to hear answers from God, we remain interested, and continue to hold conferences discussing Mormonism. However much our predecessors have tampered with and discarded from the original, the power in the ideals of that original still haunt all who have been exposed to them.

Even if the present-day interest for some is limited to a postmortem of a stillborn cult, critics must acknowledge the power of the original ideas of Joseph Smith.[193] Critics continue to complain because they remain interested, even if disaffected. They linger over the corpse as if they fear another resurrection.

Critics are justified to fear a Mormon revival. If God really did talk to Joseph, Mormonism may again assume the role of God's soapbox to address mankind. If all truth belongs to Mormonism, everyone looking for truth will want to become a part.

At one time Mormonism claimed that the true and only God of heaven, who sent His Son Jesus Christ to save mankind, still cared enough to talk to us. By participating *WE* become as important as the people who produced the Bible. The rest of Judaism and Christianity may have dead prophets and a silent God, but in Mormonism, God's voice spoke anew.

The presence of God's active voice is at the foundation of original Mormonism. If Mormons are able to hear God's voice regularly, it renders all other religions inferior. By implication, it also renders every other Judeo-Christian religion "an abomination" because it is obviously wrong to reject the voice of God calling you to come unto Him by becoming a Mormon.

Because God spoke, everything changed continually. It was an expanding changeling, never taking a final form. I am only going to refer to a handful of examples to illustrate the shifting contours of Mormonism during Joseph Smith's lifetime. Many others could be added.

Mormonism forces us to confront the choice: Mormonism, or the false Judeo-Christian religions that are "other than Mormonism." The breadth of this religious conflict leaves a choice between only two churches. The *Book of Mormon* explains, "Behold, there are save two churches only; the one is the church of the Lamb of God, and the other is the church of the devil; wherefore whoso belongeth not to the church of the Lamb of God belongeth to that great church[.]"[194] Whatever else the original of Mormonism involved, this claim made it important for every religious thinker to investigate.

This gets all the more interesting within the different factions of Mormonism itself. If "there are save two churches only," and only one is the church of the Lamb of God, splintered Mormonism cannot be the "one true church." It is now anything but monolithic. Which version is "true" (because it is impossible for squabbling and disagreeing versions to *all* be the "only true church")?[195] Mormonism has included, or does include:[196]

The Church of Christ,
the Pure Church of Christ,
the Church of Jesus Christ,
the Church of Jesus Christ of Latter-day Saints,
the Reorganized Church of Jesus Christ of Latter Day Saints—
later re-renamed the Community of Christ,
the Church of Jesus Christ, the Bride, the Lamb's Wife,
the Council of Friends,
the Latter Day Church of Christ,
the Apostolic United Brethren,
the Fundamentalist Church of Jesus Christ of Latter-day Saints,

---

[194] 1 Ne. 14:10.

[195] This is particularly so when the various factions have gone to the trouble of excommunicating one another.

[196] This is only a partial list.

the Church of the First Born of the Fulness of Times,

the Church of the Firstborn,

the Church of Jesus Christ in Solemn Assembly,

The Church of the Firstborn of the Lamb of God, the Righteous Branch of the Church of Jesus Christ of Latter-day Saints,

the School of the Prophets,

the Church of Jesus Christ of Latter-day Saints and the Kingdom of God,

the True and Living Church of Jesus Christ of Saints of the Last Days,

Church of Jesus Christ Original Doctrine Inc.,

the Church of Zion,

the United Order Family of Christ,

and many others.

It is an interesting list of names. If there is only one true Mormon church it ought to be "true and living" and "righteous" and "united"—so those words in the names of some of the various splinters are both apt and attention-getting.

Mormonism rose only briefly above the religious squabbling of its time. Following Joseph and Hyrum's murders, Mormonism has subsequently degenerated and splintered. It now can be described in the same terms Joseph Smith used to explain the Methodists, Baptists and Presbyterians of 1820:

> The whole of Mormonism is affected by an unusual excitement, and multitudes unite themselves to the different Mormon parties, which creates no small stir and division amongst the people, some crying, "Lo, here!" and others, "Lo, there!" Some are contending for the LDS faith, some for the RLDS, and some for the FLDS. But, notwithstanding the great love the converts to these different faiths express at the time of their conversion, and the great zeal manifest by the respective advocates, who are active in getting up and promoting this extraordinary scene of religious feeling, in order to have everybody converted, as they are pleased to call it, let them join what sect they pleased; yet when the converts begin to file off, some to one party and some to another, it is seen that the seemingly good feelings of both the priests and the converts are more pretended than real; for a

scene of great confusion and bad feeling ensues—
prophets, seers and revelators contending against
presidents, prophets, kings and revelators, and
pseudo-saint against pseudo-saint; so that all their
good feelings one for another, if they ever had any,
are entirely lost in a strife of words and a contest
about opinions.[197]

The theme of the 2016 Sunstone Conference was the result of
the divisions now found in Mormonism. Speakers at that Conference
addressed the: "Many Mormonisms and the Mormon Movement."
The divergences all reckon from a common starting point, and it is
that point of beginning I address. I am concerned with whether there
was an *original* Mormonism. To accept "Many Mormonisms" as a
welcome outcome is contrary to the first premise of "one true
church,"[198] all others being the devil's whores.[199] If Mormonism has
any eternal value it will be found by identifying the original—the one
God called "true and living" and was the "only one with which [He
was] well pleased."[200] What was that?

If there is any hope of successfully separating the many
Mormonisms into categories of more or less like what began with
Joseph Smith, the quest must begin by asking: how do we define the
original? The measure of "authenticity" can only be determined by a
comparison with an original, which requires us to clarify what is
meant by the term "the original."

William James once explained about those with revelatory
encounters with God,

A genuine first-hand religious experience like this is
bound to be a heterodoxy to its witnesses, the
prophet appearing as a mere lonely madman. If his
doctrine prove contagious enough to spread to any
others, it becomes a definite and labeled heresy. But
if it then still prove contagious enough to triumph

---

[197] This is adapted from JS-H 1:5-6. The LDS Church calls all other versions
of Mormonism "apostate." It even labels its own faithful members who are
insufficiently subordinate in opinion and speech to correlated history, and
praise of church leaders, as "apostate" because any heterodoxy is considered
subversive to their vulnerable historical fiction.
[198] See D&C 1:30.
[199] 1 Ne. 14:10.
[200] D&C 1:30.

over persecution, it becomes itself an orthodoxy; and when a religion has become an orthodoxy, its day of inwardness is over: the spring is dry; the faithful live at second hand exclusively and stone the prophets in their turn. The new church, in spite of whatever human goodness it may foster, can be henceforth counted on as a staunch ally in every attempt to stifle the spontaneous religious spirit, and to stop all later bubblings of the fountain from which in purer days it drew its own supply of inspiration. Unless, indeed, by adopting new movements of the spirit it can make capital out of them and use them for its selfish corporate designs![201]

We cannot look at the landscape today, separated from the martyrdom by 174 years and see anything but proprietary Mormon orthodoxies attempting to stifle the spontaneous and unruly springs of inspiration, revelation and 'conversing with the Lord through the veil.' There is in every splinter an hierarchy whose right alone it is to hear and announce God's voice. If any should come outside the hierarchies claiming revelation, dutiful followers believe they should test them, by asking they cut off an arm or some other member of the body, and then restore it again, so that we may know they come with power.[202] It does not matter the institutions fail to provide such miraculous signs. If the sheep donate enough, the power of constructing monuments with brick and mortar using the widow's mite is enough of a sign to show God supports the leadership. After all, if they build a great temple (or a tower to heaven[203]), isn't that sign enough?

So what was original Mormonism? That question is not as simple as it may seem. How would you describe it with certitude? During Joseph Smith's lifetime, Mormonism had the ill-defined visage

---

[201] *The Varieties of Religious Experience*, Being the Gifford Lectures on Natural Religion Delivered at Edinburgh in 1901-1902, Lectures XIV and XV: <u>The Value of Saintlessness</u>.

[202] Those familiar with the temple endowment before 1990 will recognize this language taken from the test the false minister obtained from Satan to be used to determine if Peter, James and John were true apostles. Those who only know of the post-1990 endowment may not understand the allusion without this explanation.

[203] Gen. 11:3-4.

of a kaleidoscope. As soon as one indispensible characteristic is identified for the original, we find discontinuity. The voice Joseph heard never stopped tampering, adjusting, modifying, adding and improving—unless of course you disliked what happened. For those he alienated, they concluded he fell from grace, and therefore did not improve but damaged the original before he died, leaving something others would need to reorganize and reclaim.[204]

While Joseph was alive, there was no approved creed or necessary body of beliefs. Joseph was opposed to constricting the beliefs of the saints. On April 8, 1843, while preaching about interpreting visions, Joseph tried to make it clear that Mormonism allowed differing views to be held by the saints. He referred to an audience member, Pelatiah Brown, who had been summoned before the High Council for preaching false doctrine. Joseph explained his view:

> I did not like the old man being called up for erring
> in doctrine. It looks too much like the Methodist,
> and not like the Latter Day Saints. Methodists have
> creeds which a man must believe or be asked out of
> their church. I want the liberty of thinking and
> believing as I please. It feels so good not to be
> trammeled. It does not prove that a man is not a
> good man because he errs in doctrine.[205]

Joseph Smith's tolerant broadmindedness does not mean Joseph Smith's silence about ideas circulating among the early Mormons was

---

[204] See, e.g., David Whitmer, *An Address to All Believers in Christ*.

[205] *DHC* 5:340; see also *JS Papers, Journals, Vol. 2*, p. 345: "should not have called up this subject if it had not been for this old white head before. Father [Pelatiah] Brown.—I did not like the old man being called up.(before the High council.)—for erring in doctrine.—why I feel so good to have the privilege of thinki[n]g & believing as I please." Also, *Words of Joseph Smith*, p. 183-184:"Er (Pelatiah) Brown has been the cause of this subject being now presented before you. He, is one of the wisest old heads we have among us, has been called up before the High Council on account of the beast. The old man has preached concerning the beast which was full of eyes before and behind and for this he was hauled up for trial. I never thought it was right to call up a man and try him because he erred in doctrine, it looks too much like Methodism and not like latter day Saintism. Methodists have creeds which a man must believe or be kicked out of their church. I want the liberty of believing as I please, it feels so good not to be tramelled. It dont prove that a man is not a good man, because he errs in doctrine."

64

an endorsement of those ideas. Mormons at the time were all first generation converts. They brought with them many ideas from their prior religious traditions. Joseph made little attempt to compel uniformity, choosing instead to "preach, teach, expound, and exhort"[206] a developing religion with increasingly nuanced broad features.

Prior to his conversion, Parley P. Pratt was a Campbellite preacher. He had been preaching a New Testament religion based on four principles: Faith, repentance, baptism and receiving the Holy Ghost.[207] These ideas were Campbellite before Mormonism began advocating them, and were seamlessly adopted by Mormons from the Campbellite movement.[208] After converting, Pratt filled in many of the Mormon lacunas. He was the most prolific pamphleteer in the early Mormon movement, and wrote what became to be regarded as foundational books explaining doctrine.[209] It is difficult to track the extent to which today's Mormon orthodoxy was created by Pratt, but it is clear he was influential both in his own right and in converting Sidney Rigdon. Rigdon would become a member of the first presidency of the LDS Church once that body was added. Ridgon would raise many questions that led to yet another Joseph Smith revelation. Rigdon was looking to restore a New Testament church years before he met Joseph Smith.[210] David Whitmer believed Rigdon exerted a powerfully negative influence on Joseph.[211] Because Joseph

---

[206] Part of the duties of any Mormon priest. (D&C 20:46.)

[207] See Gregory Armstrong, Matthew Grow and Dennis Siler, *Parley P. Pratt and the Making of Mormonism*, (Norman, Oklahoma: Arthur H. Clark Company, 2011), p. 41.

[208] Pratt was swept up into a religious movement led by Sidney Rigdon, who proclaimed a restorationist New Testament Christianity of faith, repentance, baptism, and the promise of the Gift of the Holy Ghost. Rigdon exhorted his followers to reject all creeds and take the Bible as the sole norm of faith. (*Id.*)

[209] *Voice of Warning*, written in 1837 and *Key to the Science of Theology*, written in 1855.

[210] "Rigdon's teachings were restorationist in a legalstic sense, seeking to re-create early Christianity as described in the New Testament." (See, *Parley P. Pratt and the Making of Mormonism*, supra, p. 23.) See also Richard Van Wagoner, *Sidney Rigdon: A Portrait of Religious Excess*, (Salt Lake: Signature Books, 2006).

[211] In David Whitmer's retrospective *Address to All Believers in Christ*, Chapter 4, he explained, "Sydney Rigdon was the cause of almost all the errors which were introduced while he was in the church. I believe Rigdon to have been

believed Mormons should be free to believe anything they wanted, unconstrained by creed, the contours of Mormonism during Joseph's life were left poorly defined. The contributions from Pratt, Rigdon and others complicate, rather than contribute, to clarifying the original.

Mormonism expanded continually during Joseph's life. The portions that existed in 1820, at the time of the First Vision, did not include the *Book of Mormon*,[212] which would be added in 1830. At the time Moroni (or Nephi) visited Joseph in 1823, it only included the promise that an untitled book "written upon gold plates giving an account of the former inhabitants of this continent" would be revealed.[213] Today, Mormons identify the angel who visited Joseph and informed him of the plates by the name "Moroni." But in the account Joseph Smith published in the *Times and Seasons* on April 15, 1842, his name was "Nephi."[214] By 1830, the *Book of Mormon* was in print and a church was organized with elders, priests and teachers. "Apostles" were added to Mormonism in 1831. The quorum of 12 apostles would not be organized until 1835.[215]

Mormonism's mercurial form during Joseph's lifetime can be seen through an examination of any feature, teaching, practice or

---

the instigator of the secret organization known as the 'Danites' which was formed in Far West Missouri in June, 1838. In Kirtland, Ohio, in 1831, Rigdon would expound the Old Testament scriptures of the Bible and Book of Mormon (in his way) to Joseph, concerning the priesthood, high priests, etc., and would persuade Brother Joseph to inquire of the Lord about this doctrine and that doctrine, and of course a revelation would always come just as they desired it. Rigdon finally persuaded Brother Joseph to believe that the high priests which had such great power in ancient times, should be in the Church of Christ to-day. He had Brother Joseph inquire of the Lord about it, and they received an answer according to their erring desires."

[212] JS-H 1:1-20.

[213] JS-H 1:34-35.

[214] See *Times and Seasons*, Vol. III, No. 12, <u>History of Joseph Smith, continued</u>. This is the same name as appears in the Joseph Smith History version of 1839 (which was a copy made by James Mulholland of the prior 1838 history). See *JS Papers, Histories Vol. 1*, p. 222. The 1839 copy was reviewed by Joseph Smith as it was read aloud while being copied. See *id.*, p. 201. The change from "Nephi" to "Moroni" happened after Joseph Smith's death and was done by "an unknown hand." *Id.*, p. 223, footnote 56.

[215] Individuals who in 1831 were called apostles, included Joseph Smith, Oliver Cowdery, David Whitmer, and later Orson Pratt.

organizational form. Everything changed continually. Perhaps the most stable practice of original Mormonism was baptism; so let's consider that.

It began before 1830. While the mode of baptism (by immersion) remained constant, the language and purposes changed. The original baptismal prayer set out in the Church Articles and Covenants[216] used the identical prayer found in the *Book of Mormon*.[217] The words of the prayer, after calling the initiate by their name, included "having <u>authority given me</u> of Jesus Christ, I baptize you"[218] and so on. Those words were changed in the 1835 *Doctrine and Covenants* to "having been <u>commissioned</u> of Jesus Christ, I baptize you,"[219] and so on. Once altered, the words were never changed back. So the *Book of Mormon* commands one baptismal prayer (given by Jesus Christ), and the *Doctrine and Covenants* (since 1835) commends a different prayer.

Proxy baptism of the living for the dead was added in 1840. Originally proxies of either sex could be baptized for both men and women. That later changed, and vicarious proxy work could only be done on behalf of the same sex only.

The purpose of baptism grew from remitting sins and joining the church, to include rebaptism as a means for rededication and purification,[220] and baptism for healing of the sick as well. Emma

---

[216] See *JS Papers, Revelations and Translations, Manuscript Revelations Book*, p. 75.

[217] 3 Ne. 11:25.

[218] *JS Papers, Revelations and Translations, supra*, p. 85.

[219] *JS Papers, Revelations and Translations Vol. 2*, p. 391. See also the side-by-side change in wording on the same volume on p. 208.

[220] Edwin Wilde provided some excerpts taken from his review of 178 early Mormon journals mentioning the widespread practice of rebaptism. Here are some of those excerpts: From the journal of Milo Andrus, (1814-1893): "In the spring of 1854, I was sent to Saint Louis to preside over the stake there. Stayed there one year, rebaptized and confirmed about 800 saints." From the journal of Elizabeth Brotherton: "March 19 1851 Mr. Pratt was appointed on a mission to the Pacific Coast to organize and set in order the Saints that had gone there not knowing where the church would locate. They went in the ship Brooklyn. I went with him to San Francisco, we traveled in company with A. Lyman, and C.C. Rich when they were going to San Bernerdino with a company of Saints. After a tiresome journey we arrived in San Francisco. Mr. Pratt remained there and rebaptized quite a number in about two months time." From William Clayton's diary: "May 9, 1841 Joseph preached on his side on baptism for the dead (see Record.)

Smith was rebaptized in October 1842 for her health.[221] In April

Afterwards a number was baptized both for remission of sins and for the dead. I was baptized first for myself and then for my Grandfather Thomas and Grandmother Ellen Clayton, Grandmother Mary Chritebly and Aunt Elizabeth Beurdwood." (Clayton was previously baptized October 21, 1837.) From the journal of Warren Foote: "24th. [March 1842] This is the day that I have appointed to go down into the waters of baptism and thereby fulfill the covenant I made to the Lord when I was near death's door. The meeting was at Elder Jacob Myers house about one mile from Father's. I walked down there and in company with Amos Kimmins, Franklin Allen, and his wife, Samuel Myers, and Lovina Myers, was baptized by Daniel A. Miller, President of this branch, between five and six o'clock P.M. The foregoing named persons, had been baptized before, and now felt to renew their covenants. As it was concluded to have an evening meeting I thought that I would stay to it. The wind blew up from the north very cool and in going home, I took cold." Other entries in Warren Foote's journal: "8th. [May 1842] Sunday. A very large congregation assembled to meeting. Sidney Rigdon preached. In the afternoon there were many baptized in the font in the basement of the Temple and forty three in the Mississippi River. They were mostly rebaptisms." "[MAY, 1844] 26th. Attended meeting at Bro. J. Clark's. After meeting I rebaptized Elihu Allen, Joseph Clark, and John B. Carpenter. We ordained E. Allen [a] priest, and Joseph Clark [a] teacher. It is so wet that we cannot plant corn." "[JUNE, 1844] 9th. Sunday. My wife with five others were rebaptized by Elder J. B. Carpenter." From the autobiography of Joseph Holbrook: "On Saturday, January 5, 1833…I told Brother Lyons and Rich I would like to be baptized if they thought I was worthy as I had brought my clothes for that purpose. So after breakfast I was baptized with my Aunt Phebe Angel by Leonard Rich…My wife was taken very sick on the 7th of July [1842] and grew worse until she died, being taken sick nine days (July 16, 1842), aged 37 years, 11 months and two days…After my wife's death, I was rebaptized in the Mississippi River by Brigham Young." From the autobiography of Joseph Hovey: "I, Joseph, for the first time bowed myself before God in secret and implored his mercy and asked him if what I had read out [of] the Book of Mormon was true and if the man, Joseph Smith, was the one who translated these marvelous records. I, Joseph, asked God for a testimony by the Holy Spirit and truly I got what I asked for and more abundantly. Therefore, my wife, Martha, and I did truly rejoice in the truth we had found in those records. We also searched the Bible daily and found that it did corroborate with the Book of Mormon. We were, therefore, born again and could see the kingdom. Hence, July 4, 1839, we were baptized with water and received the Holy Ghost by the laying on of hands. One brother, Mr. Draper, baptized us…there was a committee appointed by the God of Israel to superintend those houses in the fall of 1840. The fund to commence the building of the temple were

1842, additional clarifications limited baptism and rebaptism for the

raised through tithing, that is every man put in a tenth of his property and thereafter his earnings every tenth day. ...I, Joseph, did prosper well in good health but my wife, Martha, was not so well as myself. I, Joseph, did go to work in the stone quarry and I labored exceedingly for the Nauvoo House. I got out several hundred feet of stone during the season. I also worked on the Nauvoo temple cutting stone. In the meanwhile, my wife, Martha, was sick, even abortion took place and she was very low. But she was healed by going to the baptismal font and was immersed for her health and baptized for her dead." This is from the journal/autobiography of William Huntington Sr.: "In 1833, I found the Book of Mormon. I read the book, believed in the book that it was what it was represented to be. My mind thus being prepared to receive the gospel accordingly, in the month of April 1835, myself and my wife both united with the Church of Jesus Christ of Latter-day Saints. ...April 11th, 1841 Joseph [Smith] and Sidney [Rigdon] baptized each other for the remission of their sins as this order was then instituted in the Church. Accordingly, on the 27th of April [1841], I was baptized for the remission of my sins. Also, on the same day, was baptized for my brother Hyrum Huntington." This is from the autobiography of Benjamin F. Johnson: "In the spring of 1835 before I was baptized, my mother and all her children met at the house of my sister, Delcena Sherman, to receive from Patriarch Joseph Smith, Sr., our patriarchal blessings. He blessed all according to age until be came to Joseph E. and myself, when he placed his hands first upon my head. My mother told him I was the youngest, but he said that mattered not–to me was the first blessing; and in blessing me, among other great and glorious things, he told me the Lord would call me to do the work of brother Seth, who had been called away by death. In this promise there was to me more joy than ever before I had known; my dear brother was not to be robbed of his blessings, and if I could only live faithfully his work would be done, and I should do it for him. I felt this was the greatest boon the Lord could bestow upon me. ...Soon after this, I overstepped my father's objections and was baptized by Elder Lyman Johnson... On the 13th of October [1838] we crossed the Mississippi at Louisiana, and began to hear of great troubles among the Mormons at Far West, and we were warned of the great danger of proceeding, but our camp was only stirred to greater desire to go on. Here I remembered my former purpose to renew my covenant by baptism, and as one of my associates, D. D. McArthur, was to be baptized, I went with him and was baptized by Henry Hariman. [Harriman]" From the autobiography of Joel H. Johnson: "At the October [1856] Conference the heads of the Church preached the necessity of a reformation among the saints by confessing their own sins against God and their brethren and forsaking the same and by forgiving the sins of others and making restitution for all wrongs as much as possible. This glorious work of reformation and restitution soon commenced in Great Salt Lake City and spread with rapidity

living to be performed in living waters like a lake, stream or river.[222] Baptism for the dead or for healing the sick, were only to be performed in the temple font.[223]

---

to all the branches of the Church; and all who confessed and restored were rebaptized for the last time for the remission of their sins." "Thursday, September 18th [1856], I started with my wife Susan and little child accompanied by my son Nephi, with an ox team to go and visit our friends at Summit Creek in Utah County, and also in Salt Lake City, and attend the October conference, and to purchase and drive home a few sheep. We arrived at Summit Creek and Friday the 26th, and found our friends as well. We had a good visit with them and started on Tuesday the 30th for Salt Lake City, and arrived on Friday the 3rd of October, attending conference and done our business and started homeward on Friday the 10th. On our way we called at Lake City in Utah County and purchased 26 sheep, one of which died at Chicken Creek. We arrived safely home with the rest on the 25th and found all well, and was rebaptized on Wednesday, 29th [October 1856], at Fort Johnson by Isaac C. Height, President of the Stake of Cedar City." This is from a letter from Parley Pratt to Brigham Young, August 28, 1851; while he was in San Francisco: "Since I have arrived here I have been diligent in the duties of my calling every hour, and have called upon God for His Spirit to help me with all the energy I possessed, and without ceasing. The result is, the Spirit of the Lord God has been upon me continually, in such light, and joy, and testimony as I have seldom experienced. Brothers A. Lyman and C. C. Rich have been here with me some of the time; we have called together the old members and others, and preached repentance and reformation of life. We have re-baptized many of them, and have re-organized the Church." A statement by Orson Pratt found in the *JD* 18:156-61: "I will here state that Martin Harris, when he came to this [Utah] Territory a few years ago, was rebaptized, the same as every member of the Church from distant parts is on arriving here. That seems to be a kind of standing ordinance for all Latter-day Saints who emigrate here, from the First Presidency down; all are rebaptized and set out anew by renewing their covenants." There are many more.

221 "Wednesday 5th Sister E. [Emma Smith] is worse, many fears are entertained that she will not recover. She was baptized twice in the river which evidently did her much good." *JS Papers, Journals Vol. 2: December 1841-April 1843*, p. 161.

222 *Times and Seasons*, Vol. III, No. 12, April 15, 1842, Conference Minutes from a special conference held in Nauvoo April 6, 1842. Joseph said, "those coming into the church and those rebaptized may be done in the river."

223 *Id.*, Joseph said, "Baptisms for the dead, and for the healing of the body must be in the font."

So we see the practice of baptism expanded while Joseph was alive, even though it was perhaps the most stable feature of the original.

There is no single organized entity that began in 1830 that has remained intact till now.[224] Every one of the organized corporate forms of Mormonism has morphed, been superseded, or rolled into new legal entities and changed from whatever existed in New York on April 6, 1830.[225]

Despite common belief to the contrary, there was never a single corporate form of an original. In January 1841, an Illinois corporation was formed[226] and Joseph Smith elected the Trustee in Trust for the entity. This was likely the first legal organization of the church, as no formal documentation from New York has been discovered. But the Illinois law limited the corporation to owning no more than 5 acres. Upon Joseph's death, the Trustee was lost and disputes over property followed. Property held in Joseph's name may have belonged to the church—or not, if you were Emma Smith. Hopefully no one believed

---

[224] For a description of the changing internal organization see David J. Whittaker, *An Introduction to Mormon Administrative History*, Dialogue, Volume 15, No. 4, Winter 1982, p. 16.

[225] David Whitmer explained the Church of Christ existed *before* April 6, 1830 and had three branches: "Now, when April 6, 1830, had come, we had then established three branches of the 'Church of Christ,' in which three branches were about seventy members: One branch was at Fayette, N.Y.; one at Manchester, N.Y., and one at Colesville, Pa. It is all a mistake about the church being organized on April 6, 1830, as I will show. We were as fully organized -- spiritually -- before April 6th as we were on that day. The reason why we met on that day was this; the world had been telling us that we were not a regularly organized church, and we had no right to officiate in the ordinance of marriage, hold church property, etc., and that we should organize according to the laws of the land. On this account we met at my father's house in Fayette, N.Y., on April 6, 1830, to attend to this matter of organizing according to the laws of the land; you can see this from Sec. 17 Doctrine and Covenants: the church was organized on April 6th 'agreeable to the laws of our country.'" (*Address to All Believers in Christ*, Richmond, Missouri, 1887.) But since most people attending this symposium reckon the organization from April 6, 1830 I accept that date for purposes of this presentation.

[226] This may have been the first formal corporate form, the substance of the earlier New York organization is unknown and paperwork for that formation does not exist. The "United Firm" was apparently a partnership.

that salvation was tied in any way to which corporate entity owned what property upon the death of Joseph Smith.[227]

Each one of the proprietary, corporate forms of Mormonism are very pushy about insisting they are "the only true and living church upon the face of the whole earth."[228] But even if there were such a thing as continuity of a corporate entity from Joseph Smith until today, would that really be the original without doing, teaching, conducting and delivering what originally was done, taught, conducted and delivered? Can institutional identity decide religious authority apart from conduct? The LDS version of scripture rejects that idea.[229]

There was never a single name used to identify an original Mormon church. The organization changed names several times from the 1830s to 1841. In addition to different names, a series of entities, many of which were not legally separate from the individuals involved,[230] were formed to hold property belonging to the "Church of Christ."[231] The "United Firm" merged three business entities: N.K. Whitney & Co., a preexisting business formed by Newel Whitney and

---

[227] In the case of *The Reorganized Church of Jesus Christ of Latter Day Saints v. Williams, et. al.* ("et. al." including John Taylor, among others) Court of Common Pleas, Lake County, Painsville, Ohio (February 1880), the Reorganized LDS Church cleared title to the Kirtland Temple (which was dismissed without deciding any real issue of the case) and the RLDS have pointed to the case as legitimizing their claim to be THE original.

[228] D&C 1:30. The LDS version insists the term "Mormon" belongs to them and ought not be used to refer to any other group or organization. (See www.mormonnewsroom.org/style-guide.)

[229] If D&C 121:36-37, 40-42 is taken at face value, then priesthood can be easily forfeited. The revelation describing "the power and authority of the higher or Melchizedek priesthood is to hold the keys of all the spiritual blessings of the church... to have the heavens opened unto them—to commune with the general assembly and church of the first born, and to enjoy communion and presence of God the Father, and Jesus the Mediator of the new covenant." (*JS Papers, Revelations and Translations, Vol. 2*, p. 395; now also found in D&C 107:18-19.) This in all likelihood means that without the communion and presence of the Father and Son there is no higher priesthood authority or power. Mormons do not consider that meaning.

[230] The "United Firm" was apparently the first legal entity formed. It was likely a partnership. Later a series of Agricultural Companies were formed to own property in Far West.

[231] This name came from Christ's instruction given in 3 Ne. 27:7-8.

Sidney Gilbert in Kirtland, Ohio; Gilbert, Whitney & Co., an entity formed by Gilbert in Missouri in 1832; and The Literary Firm, supervised by W.W. Phelps, organized for the church's printing operations. Members of the United Firm were Joseph Smith, Sidney Rigdon, Oliver Cowdery, John Whitmer, William W. Phelps, Martin Harris, Edward Partridge, Newel K. Whitney, Sidney Gilbert, Frederick G. Williams and John Johnson. Profits from the three ventures were to be shared between businesses and to provide income for the member of the firm.[232]

The first name didn't last[233] and was occasionally replaced by the "Church of Jesus Christ." The third iteration was the "Church of the Latter Day Saints,"[234] and still later the "Church of Jesus Christ of Latter Day Saints." In a Marriage Certificate prepared by Joseph Smith on January 18, 1836 he identified the organization as "the church of christ of Latter-Day Saints."[235] On April 26, 1838,[236] a revelation settled the question of name as "the Church of Jesus Christ of Latter Day Saints," but the revealed name was not used until years later.

Today, in the published revelation in the *Doctrine and Covenants*,[237] the original revealed name has been altered, substituting a new "revealed name." The original name approved by God was "the Church of Jesus Christ of Latter Day Saints"[238] –no capitalizing "the" and no hyphen between "Latter" and "Day" (as the RLDS Church once spelled "Latter Day" in their name). In the LDS *Style Guide*, (something of such importance that a member of the quorum of the twelve introduced it) the name is now: "The Church of Jesus Christ

---

[232] For more on the venture see *JS Papers, Documents, Vol. 4: April 1834-September 1835*, pp. 19-38.

[233] The *Evening and Morning Star*, published between 1832-1834 uses "Church of Christ" 115 times and "Church of Jesus Christ" only once. In contrast, the *Times and Seasons* from 1839-1846 used "Church of Christ" 118 times and "Church of Jesus Christ 13 times.

[234] The name was changed in 1834. Minutes of the Conference of Elders when the change was adopted can be found at *JS Papers, Documents Vol. 4, April 1834-September 1835*, p. 44. The motion to change the name was made by Sidney Rigdon. The *Times and Seasons* used the "Church of the Latter Day Saints" 47 times.

[235] *JS Papers, Journals, Vol. 1: 2835-1836*, p. 164.

[236] D&C 115:4—the capitals and missing hyphen as in the original.

[237] The one published by The Church of Jesus Christ of Latter-day Saints.

[238] See *JS Papers*, Revelation 26 April 1838 (current D&C 115).

of Latter-day Saints."[239] If the name of the church matters to the degree indicated by a published revelation and the church's *Style Guide*, then the name God revealed has been abandoned. No organization exists today that uses the revealed, required name. The format for the LDS corporate church name only acquired a settled form with the *Style Guide*, adopted in 1972.[240]

The criteria for an "original" Mormonism must reckon from some form of continuity, but continuity of exactly what? Is it some form of practice? Practices changed markedly during Joseph's lifetime and never acquired a settled form. For example, it took six years from founding the church before washings and anointings were introduced on January 21, 1836 in Kirtland. Once introduced, they were changed.

Originally they were done with whisky[241] scented with cinnamon,[242] followed by perfumed olive oil.[243] Feet and face washing were added

---

[239] See www.mormonnewsroom.org/style-guide as well as the *Church News*, February 17, 2001, "Church Should be Called by its Revealed Name." The church also copyrighted in 2013 the fourth edition of a 91 page revised version of its *Style Guide for Publications of The Church of Jesus Christ of Latter-day Saints* which clarifies how the church's name ought to be spelled, hyphenated and capitalized.

[240] Lest you think the exact name is a trivial matter, I received a letter from a woman informing me that she knew I was a deceiver when she saw how I spelled the name of the church in *(Comforter: Conversing With the Lord Through the Veil* (Mill Creek Press: Salt Lake City, 2006). I had failed to capitalize "T" in "**T**he Church of Jesus Christ of Latter-day Saints," and therefore was in open rebellion against the church. For the want of a capital "T" I was branded apostate. The *Style Guide*, as explained to the press by Dallin H. Oaks, required such slavish conformity in the mind of that woman that any deviation was rebellion against God and His exacting expectations.

[241] This use of "strong drinks" was foreshadowed three years earlier in the 1833 revelation D&C 89:7.

[242] "[M]et in the evening with [B]ro. Joseph Smith, Jr. at his house, in company with [B]ro. John Corrill, and after pure water was prepared, called upon the Lord and proceeded to wash each other's bodies, and bathe the same with whiskey, perfumed with cinnamon. This we did that we might be clean before the Lord for the Sabbath, confessing our sins and covenanting to be faith to God. While performing this washing unto the Lord with solemnity, our minds were filled with many reflections upon the propriety of the same, and how the priests anciently used to wash always before ministering before the Lord." (*Oliver Cowdery Sketch Book*, 16 January 1836, pp. 4-5, archives, Historical Department, Church of Jesus Christ of Latter-day Saints, Salt Lake City, Utah). Also quoted in David Buerger, *The Mysteries*

after the Kirtland Temple dedication on March 27, 1836. The rites were revised in Nauvoo and tubs were added as a practical accommodation in the Nauvoo Temple. Joseph died before the construction of the Nauvoo Temple had been completed to the second floor, and therefore neither a building design for the upper floors, nor a ceremony for the endowment were completed by Joseph Smith before his death.[244]

Joseph declared, "Ordinances instituted in the heavens before the foundation of the world, in the priesthood, for the salvation of men, are not to be altered or changed. All must be saved on the same principles."[245] The first question this raises is whether Joseph contradicted himself by changing things. The only way to reconcile the many changes he instituted is to take note that he made only additive expansions, finishing and recovering the ordinances instituted in the heavens. He was transmitting what came from above to believers, and that happened incrementally. His changes never took

---

*of Godliness: A History of Mormon Temple Worship*, (Salt Lake: Signature Books, 2002), p. 11.

[243] This practice continued following Joseph's death. "The brethren rejoiced at the commencement again of the administration of these ordinances which had not been administered since they were in the Temple at Nauvoo. Pres[iden]t Young had procured and perfumed the oil which was consecrated at the circle on Sunday evening for the purpose." Devery Anderson, *The Development of LDS Temple Worship 1846-2000*, (Salt Lake: Signature Books, 2011), p. 25; quoting *Historian's Office Journal*, Dec. 31, 1866.

[244] Brigham Young completed the unfinished ceremony and attributed his authority to do so to Joseph Smith. According to L. John Nuttall's Diary, Brigham Young stated he received the endowment from Joseph before the temple was available and "after we got through Bro Joseph turned to me and said Bro Brigham this is not arranged right but we have done the best we could under the circumstances in which we are placed..." (Diary entry February 7, 1877, L. Tom Perry Special Collections, Harold B. Lee Library, Brigham Young University, Provo, Utah; cited with some additions in Anderson, Devery and Bergera, Gary, *Joseph Smith's Quorum of the Anointed, 1842-1845*, (Salt Lake: Signature Books, 2005), p. 7.)

[245] *TPJS*, p. 308. "Ordinances were instituted in heavn before the f[o]undation of the world of in the pri[e]sthood. for the salvation of man. not be alterd. not to be changed.—all must be saved upon the same principle." (*JS Papers, Journals, Vol. 3, May 1843-June 1844*, p. 32 (all as in original).

away from the ordinances, but frequently expanded on what was here before.

Joseph never did anything with "the ordinances instituted in the heavens" like the LDS Church has done. The elimination of the Christian minister from the endowment in 1990, along with the abandonment of the penalties from the ceremony at the same time, were purely deductive. Joseph never did that. Likewise, LDS washings and anointings were changed in 2011 to eliminate actual washing and actual anointing, replacing them with "simply symbolic" references. That was yet another deductive deviation from "the ordinances instituted in the heavens." It was another violation of Joseph's principal that they "are not to be altered or changed." The original Mormonism may have added, but it respected what was previously revealed. All later forms of corporate Mormonism have been deductive.

The RLDS (CofC) Church has made even greater deductions. They abandoned baptisms for the dead, washings, anointings, and the temple rites altogether. Subtraction from the ordinances is one clear way to confirm the original form of Mormonism no longer exists. If there is to be an original, it will require adding back what has been lost.

Fundamentalist versions of Mormonism have attempted to revive or preserve plural wivery, but the history that the practice was part of original Mormonism is anything but clear. Only a single document links Joseph Smith to the practice.[246] The single document Brian Hales has identified is the published version of D&C 132. However, that version of the document is an undated copy of something first written on July 12, 1843 by William Clayton. The one written by Clayton no longer exists.[247] But since the fundamentalists

---

[246]Brian Hales: "Establishing the Prophet's precise instructions is difficult due to a lack of contemporary accounts recording Joseph Smith's specific teachings on these lofty topics. Furthermore, a challenge arises regarding which sources should be considered authoritative for defining his theology, ideology, and cosmology. Of course, the most authoritative of sources would be the Prophet himself, but his writings and recorded instructions on plural marriage are limited to the revelation on celestial and plural marriage, Doctrine and Covenants 132." (*Joseph Smith's Polygamy: Volume 3, Theology*, chapter 6: Authoritative Sources for Joseph Smith's Theology, pp.69-84.)

[247] The original is gone, and the handwritten copy is in the hand of Joseph Kingsbury who was not a scribe for Joseph Smith at any time. It was not

accept the published version (it being the only one extant), they face the dilemma that it limits to "only one on the earth at a time"[248] who can hold authority to solemnize such relationships. Every one of the fundamentalist sects claim that they alone have that "one on the earth" possessing such authority. They obviously cannot all be right, but certainly could all be wrong.[249] This topic is treated separately in a later section of this paper.

The First Vision is a clear illustration of Joseph's practice of adding to the religion. Originally, the event was not part of the Mormon narrative. Once it was added, it changed over multiple tellings. The 1832 account focused on Joseph's personal salvation:

> [T]he Lord heard my cry in the wilderness and while in the attitude of calling upon the Lord, in the 16th year of my age a pillar of ~~fire~~ light above the brightness of the Sun at noon day come down fro above and rested upon me and I was filld with the Spirit of God and the Lord opened the heavens upon me and I Saw the Lord and he Spake unto me Saying Joseph my Son thy Sins are forgiven thee. Go they way walk in my Statutes and keep my commandments behold I am the Lord of glory I was crucified for the world that all those who believe on my name may have Eternal life…[250]

---

made public until 1852 and may well have been among the changed documentation referred to by Charles Wandell. Wandell noted in his diary: "I notice the interpolations because having been employed in the Historian's office at Navuoo by Doctor Richards, and employed, too, in 1845, in compiling this very autobiography, I know that after Joseph's death his memoir was 'doctored' to suit the new order of things, and this, too, by the direct order of Brigham Young to Doctor Richards and systematically by Richards." (See Richard S. Van Wagoner, *Sidney Rigdon: A Portrait of Religious Excess*, (Salt Lake: Signature Books, 1994), p. 322.) He was reacting to the publication of Joseph's history in the Deseret Evening News. The "new order of things" he referred to was the public practice of plural wives.

[248] D&C 132:7.

[249] I've written two papers on this topic available on my website, and also discuss the issue in *Beloved Enos* (Salt Lake: Mill Creek Press, 2009), and therefore do not repeat the discussion again.

[250] Milton Backman, Jr., *Joseph Smith's First Vision*, (Salt Lake: Bookcraft, 1980) 2nd Edition, Appendix A, p. 157.

The 1835 account is the first to mention a struggle with the devil:

> I made a fruitless attempt to pray My tongue seemed to be swoolen in my mouth, so that I could not utter, I heard a noise behind me like some one walking towards me. I strove again to pray, but come not; the noise of walking seemed to draw nearer, I sprang upon my feet and looked round, but saw no person or thing that was calculated to produce the noise of walking. I kneeled again, my mouth was opened and my tongue loosed; I called on the Lord in mighty prayer. A pillar of fire appeared above my head; which presently rested down upon me, and filled me with unspeakable joy. A personage appeared in the midst of this pillar of flame, which was spread all around and yet nothing consumed. Another personage soon appeared like unto the first: he said unto me thy sins are forgiven thee. He testified also unto me that Jesus Christ is the son of God. I saw many angels in this vision.[251]

The account evolved in the 1838 retelling to have cosmic implications for the salvation of all mankind. Both the Father and Son appeared, and the purpose was not to forgive Joseph's sins, but to confirm the entire Christian world "were all corrupt" and taught "the commandments of men" "having a form of godliness but they deny the power thereof." It is the 1838 version that is canonized in the *Pearl of Great Price*. Like everything else for so long as Joseph Smith was involved, the First Vision expanded, both in details and meaning, until it was no longer about Joseph the individual, but the salvation of all mankind.

The description of the Godhead, which was settled during Joseph's lifetime, became unsettled after his death. When *Lectures on Faith* was adopted as scripture by a conference in 1835,[252] the Godhead consisted of two personages: the Father and the Son. The Holy Ghost was not a person but "the mind" of the Father and Son.[253]

---

[251] *Id.*, Appendix B, p. 159.

[252] The details of adopting the volume as scripture by a vote of a solemn assembly, together with the various priesthood quorums sustaining the volume, is detailed in the section, *General Assembly*, pp. 255-257 of the 1835 *Doctrine and Covenants*.

It was described similarly in Moses 6:61, as a "record" or "truth of all things" and not an individually embodied spirit being.

A different definition gradually crept into LDS scripture, assuming the final form in 1921.[254] The 'Holy Ghost creep'[255] stemmed from a talk Joseph delivered on April 2, 1843. The note-takers who were present during that talk bequeathed an altered definition of the Holy Ghost. Their notes reflected what they believed they heard from Joseph. However, Brigham Young and Jedediah Grant approved a change from the notes in 1854, which then underwent a round of punctuation changes in 1858. A final version of the embodied Holy Ghost doctrine was approved by Heber J. Grant and a committee of six members of the twelve in 1921 (the same time they deleted the *Lectures on Faith* from the scriptures). The addition of the embodied Holy Ghost to LDS scripture created a doctrinal conflict with *Lecture Fifth*, and something had to give. So the *Lectures* were deleted.[256] Whatever else this process illustrates, it confirms there was confusion stemming from Joseph's comments in April 1843, and therefore Mormon beliefs remained unstable while Joseph was alive.

Mormonism's canon of scripture was still unsettled when Joseph died in 1844. Different Mormon sects rely on different canons as their sacred texts. Joseph retranslated the Bible, which is commonly referred to as the Joseph Smith Translation. He called this endeavor "the fullness of the scriptures" and it was only the Joseph Smith Translation that was used throughout *Lectures on Faith.* Joseph prophesied that the church would fail if the fullness of the scriptures were not completed.[257] Though finished, Joseph never published the

---

[253] See *Lecture Seventh* ¶3.

[254] See Ronald Bartholomew, *The Textual Development of D&C 130:22 and the Embodiment of the Holy Ghost*, BYU Studies Quarterly 52, no. 3 (2013).

[255] I coin this term as a quick way to describe the post-Joseph aggregation of changes that ultimately caused the conflict between the *D&C* Holy Ghost and the *Lectures on Faith* (and *PofGP*) Holy Ghost. The description in Moses 6:61 is comparable to *Lectures on Faith* in that the Holy Ghost is an impersonal record, not a being of spirit. The LDS changes made in 1921 failed to harmonize this verse in Moses with their change to the *D&C*.

[256] I discuss this in detail in *Preserving the Restoration* (Salt Lake: Mill Creek, 2015), where I urge believers to continue to regard *Lectures on Faith* as scripture.

[257] The minutes of a conference on October 25, 1831 meeting tell of Joseph

text. Upon his death, it became the property of Emma Smith. She bequeathed it to the RLDS (CofC) Church, and they subsequently published it. Excerpts are now in the LDS Bible in footnotes and an appendix.

This canonical disparity between Mormonisms is only possible because a completed authoritative canon was still expanding during Joseph's life. Ironically, the canonical exposition Joseph personally edited and vouched for, *Lectures on Faith*,[258] has been discarded by every Mormon sect.

---

Smith's need for assistance while he worked on "the fulness of the Scriptures." This reference to scriptures is defined by the LDS Church Historian as "JS's Bible revision." (*JS Papers, Documents Vol. 2: July 1831-January 1833*, p. 85, footnote 76.) The minutes include this statement by Joseph Smith: "God had often sealed up the heavens because of covetousness in the Church. Said the Lord would cut his work short in righteousness and except the church receive the fulness of the Scriptures that they would yet fall." (*Id.*, p. 85, as in original.) Although the scripture translation was completed by July 2, 1833, as Joseph mentioned in a letter to church leaders in Missouri: "[W]e this day finished the translating of the Scriptures for which we returned gratitude to our heavenly father[.]" (*JS Papers, Documents Vol. 3, February 1833-March 1834*, p. 166.) Despite this, Joseph never released them for publication to the church. The LDS Church Historian's Office notes, "the work was never fully published during JS's lifetime... neither the Bible revision nor the classification of scriptures project was ever published in JS's lifetime[.]" (*Id.*, p. 179.)

[258] "The first part of the book will be found to contain a series of Lectures as delivered before a Theological class in this place, and in consequence of their embracing the important doctrine of salvation, we have arranged them into the following work. ...We do not present this little volume with any other expectation than that we are to be called to answer to every principle advanced, in that day when the secrets of all hearts will be revealed, and the reward of a very man's labor be given him." (Preface, 1835 Doctrine and Covenants; appearing over the names of Joseph Smith, Oliver Cowdery, Sidney Rigdon and F. G. Williams.) In the preface to *Lectures on Faith* in the 1835 edition, (*JS Papers, Revelations and Translations, Vol. 2,* beginning on page 311) Joseph wrote: "We deem it to be unnecessary to entertain you with lengthy preface to the following volume, but merely to say that it contains in short the leading items of the religion which we have professed to believe. The first part of the book will be found to contain a series of lectures as delivered before a theological class in this place. And in consequence of their embracing the important doctrines of salvation, we have arranged them into the following work. We do not present this little volume with any other

Originally, like the *Book of Mormon*, the church had elders, priests and teachers. Then the term "apostle" began to be used. But the term "apostle" did not mean the same thing then that it does today. A quorum of twelve apostles did not exist in Mormonism until February 1835. Prior to that, many individuals were identified as "apostles." The term meant someone sent with a message from God.[259] The term was originally used to identify all the missionaries sent to preach the *Book of Mormon* and restoration. The revelations given through Joseph Smith specifically identified the following men as "apostles" in the following sections and dates:

-Oliver Cowdery and David Whitmer, D&C 18:9 (June 1829)

-Joseph Smith, D&C 20:2 and Oliver Cowdery, D&C 20:3 (April 1830)

-Joseph Smith, D&C 21:1 and Oliver Cowdery 21:10 (April 1830)

-Sidney Rigdon, Parley Pratt and Leman Copley, D&C 49:1, 11 (March 1831)—sending them forth "like unto mine apostle of old, whose name was Peter"

A series of revelations likewise referred to "apostles" and included admonitions, instructions, and commandments to different audiences composed of "apostles" before the organization of a quorum of twelve in 1835.[260] The Seventy were regarded as

---

expectation than that. We are to be called the answer to every principle advanced." He defended every principle advanced in Lectures on Faith. Before publishing it as scripture, it was presented to a council of the church to be sustained as scripture. "On 17 August 1835, a general assembly of the church met for the purpose of examining a book of Commandments and Covenants that had been compiled and written by the publications committee." [Joseph Smith headed the publications committee.] "This committee having finished the said book according to the instructions given them, it was deemed necessary to call the General Assembly of the Church to see if the book be approved or not by the authorities of the Church. That it may, if approved, become a law of the church, and a rule of faith and practice of the same." (*JS Papers, Revelations and Translations, Vol. 2,* p. 307.)

[259] The LDS Historian's Office acknowledges it meant, "A title indicating one sent forth to preach; later designated as a specific ecclesiastical office." (*JS Papers, Documents, Vol. 1, July 1828-June 1831,* p. 495—Glossary, "Apostle".) There has been no attempt to deal with the anachronism of applying the term "apostle" used in revelations before there was a twelve to mean exclusively those who belong to the twelve.

[260] November 1831 – D&C 1:14: "the day cometh that they who will not

hear the voice of the Lord, neither the voice of his servants, neither give heed to the words of the prophets and apostles, shall be cut off from among the people." This *did not, indeed could not,* refer to a non-existent quorum of the twelve. At that time, it referred to any of the "disciples" he sent out as missionaries in the early church as explained in the same revelation, D&C 1:4-9.

March 1830 – D&C 19:8: refers to giving information to Martin Harris because "it is meet unto you to know even as mine apostles." This meant that Martin Harris was entitled to have a mystery revealed to him.

The language in D&C 27:12 *is not part of the original revelation* given in August 1830. It was apparently added by Sidney Rigdon sometime between 1834 and 1835.

December 1830 – D&C 35:6 informs Joseph Smith and Sidney Rigdon that they could then give the gift of the Holy Ghost "by the laying on of the hands, even as the apostles of old." This is consistent with everywhere else in scripture that associates "laying on hands for the gift of the Holy Ghost" with the status of "apostle." See, e.g., D&C 20:38, 43; 3 Ne. 18:36-37; Moroni 2:2-3.

September 1831 – D&C 64:39: "they who are not apostles and prophets shall be known." Given to the elders of the church, many of who were calling themselves "apostles" as is mentioned two months later in the November 1831 revelation (D&C 1:14, discussed first above). Verses before this relate to establishing Zion (v. 34-38) making the exposure of false "apostles" a task required for those who will populate Zion. All the missionaries called themselves "apostles." The revelation meant that the unworthy who were sent as missionaries will be exposed to be unworthy.

September 1832 – D&C 84:63: "you are mine apostles" Given to the missionaries who were now returning, having been sent out the previous year. All the missionaries were identifying themselves as "apostles" and the Lord was acknowledging and confirming this was true.

June 1833 – D&C 95:4: "For the preparation wherewith I design to prepare mine apostles to prune my vineyard for the last time," Referring to the Kirtland Temple the Lord wanted built (and they had delayed starting). He said it was necessary to prepare all these "apostles" who were serving missions.

February 1834 – D&C 102—minutes of a meeting written by Oliver Cowdery which identifies the "traveling high council composed of the twelve apostles." This council would not come into existence for another year.

March 1835 – D&C 107:23: The twelve apostles are identified as "twelve traveling councilors" These particular "apostles" were a traveling council with authority equal to the many other "apostles" in the church. The apostles in the first presidency, and in the seventy, and in the other standing high councils are all equal in authority to these traveling high council apostles.

*Book of Mormon*, Oliver Cowdery, David Whitmer, and Martin Harris, were asked by Joseph Smith to choose the first twelve members of the newly announced quorum of the twelve. The Three Witnesses made their choices at a meeting on February 14, 1835. They also ordained the twelve chosen men to be apostles belonging to the new quorum. The ordinations took place between February and April 1835. Ordination was accompanied by a charge given by Oliver Cowdery that explained their ordination was not complete until they qualified. In part it included:

> It is necessary that you receive a testimony from heaven to yourselves; so that you can bear testimony to the truth of the Book of Mormon, and that you have seen the face of God. That is more than the testimony of an angel. When the proper time arrives, you shall be able to bear this testimony to the world. When you bear testimony that you have seen God, this testimony God will never suffer to fall, but will bear you out; although many will not give heed, yet others will. You will therefore see the necessity of getting this testimony from heaven. Never cease striving until you have seen God face to face. Strengthen your faith; cast off your doubts, your sins, and all your unbelief; and nothing can prevent you from coming to God. Your ordination is not full and complete till God has laid his hand upon you. We require as much to qualify us as did those who have gone before us; God is the same. If the Savior in former days laid his hands upon his disciples, why not in latter days? . . . The time is coming when you will be perfectly familiar with the things of God. . . . You have our best wishes, you have our most fervent prayers, that you may be able to bear this testimony, that you have seen the face of God. Therefore call upon him in faith in mighty prayer till you prevail, for it is your duty and your

---

[261] "on this day the council of the seventy meet to render an account of their travels and ministry, since they were ordained to that apostleship[.]" (*JS Papers, Journals Vol. 1, 1832-1839*, p. 139.)

privilege to bear such a testimony for yourselves. (*DHC*, 2:192-98.)

Oliver's charge was nothing new. Joseph Smith had already explained on January 23, 1833 to the "School of the Prophets" that to be an "apostle" required a visit from Christ and the Father.[262] Oliver was just repeating in 1835 what Joseph taught beginning in 1833.

Along with the administrative quorum of twelve apostles, in 1835 Joseph introduced a hierarchy of equal orders of three presidents, twelve apostles, 70 seventies and unlimited high councils.[263]

---

[262] *Minutes, Salt Lake City School of the Prophets*, October 3, 1883, (quoting from Zebedee Coltrin who was recounting events to the School): "At one of these meetings after the organization of the school, (the school being organized on the 23rd of January, 1833, when we were all together, Joseph having given instructions, and while engaged in silent prayer, kneeling, with our hands uplifted each one praying in silence, no one whispered above his breath, a personage walked through the room from east to west, and Joseph asked if we saw him. I saw him and suppose the others did and Joseph answered that is Jesus, the Son of God, our elder brother. Afterward Joseph told us to resume our former position in prayer, which we did. Another person came through; he was surrounded as with a flame of fire. He (Brother Coltrin) experienced a sensation that it might destroy the tabernacle as it was of consuming fire of great brightness. The Prophet Joseph said this was the Father of our Lord Jesus Christ. I saw Him.

"When asked about the kind of clothing the Father had on, Brother Coltrin said: I did not discover his clothing for he was surrounded as with a flame of fire, which was so brilliant that I could not discover anything else but his person. I saw his hands, his legs, his feet, his eyes, nose, mouth, head and body in the shape and form of a perfect man. He sat in a chair as a man would sit in a chair, but this appearance was so grand and overwhelming that it seemed I should melt down in his presence, and the sensation was so powerful that it thrilled through my whole system and I felt it in the marrow of my bones. The Prophet Joseph said: Brethren, now you are prepared to be the apostles of Jesus Christ, for you have seen both the Father and the Son and know that they exist and that they are two separate personages." (The part referring to the definition of an "apostle" is excerpted and quoted in *JS Papers, Documents, Vol. 3: February 1833-March 1834*, p. 43, ftnote 259.)

[263] The High Council in Nauvoo thought it had church-wide authority as evidenced by sending *An Epistle of the High Council of the Church of Jesus Christ of Latter Day Saints, in Nauvoo, to the saints scattered abroad, greeting*[.] It was published in the *Times and Seasons*, Vol. III, No. 15, June 1, 1842 with the direction to the church: "Now therefore let this epistle be read in all the branches of the church[.]"

All of these various councils were equal in authority possessing all the rights of presidency in the church.[264] In today's LDS vocabulary, each of these groups would "possess all the priesthood keys with the authority to exercise them."[265] Equality has been shattered, authority has been seized, scriptures have been ignored, and today's Mormonism in almost all the various iterations is dominated by a presiding, single authority figure supported by an oligarchy of paid, professional church authorities.

Joseph Smith took an inconsistent path identifying the center of power and influence in Mormonism. On the day the church was organized, a revelation identified Joseph as the church's "prophet, seer and revelator."[266] Five months later in September 1830, another revelation limited all revelations and commandments for the church to those coming through Joseph Smith.[267] David Whitmer thought Joseph Smith was led into error by pride when he assumed the role of "prophet, seer and revelator."[268]

---

[264] D&C 107:21-36.

[265] There was no single person, group or body holding "keys" which were exclusive property of that single person, group or body.

[266] D&C 21:1. In 1841 by revelation Hyrum joined Joseph in the role. (See D&C 124:94.) It was not until 1843, however, that Joseph put Hyrum into that role in a meeting at the stand in Nauvoo: "proposing Hyrum (Smith) as a prophet." (*JS Papers, Journals, Vol. 3: May 1843-June 1844*, p. 61.) (See also *Id.*, ftnote 270: "in the afternoon discourse he told the Saints to consider Hyrum Smith a prophet. According to William Clayton JS said that 'Hyrum held the office of prophet to the church by birth-right & he was going to have a reformation and the saints must regard Hyrum for he has authority.'")

[267] D&C 28:2: "But, behold, verily, verily, I say unto thee, no one shall be appointed to receive commandments and revelations in this church excepting my servant Joseph Smith, Jun., for he receiveth them even as Moses."

[268] See, *An Address to All Believers in Christ, Chapter IV, How the Church was Established in the Beginning, and How They Drifted into Error*, "Just before April 6, 1830, some of the brethren began to think that the church should have a leader, just like the children of Israel wanting a king. Brother Joseph finally inquired of the Lord about it. He must have had a desire himself to be their leader, which desire in any form is not of God, for Christ said 'If any man desire to be first, the same shall be last of all, and servant of all.' 'He that would be great, let him be your servant.' 'For he that is least among you all, the same shall be great.' A true and humble follower of Christ will never have any desire to lead or be first, or to seek the praise of men or brethren. Desiring any prominence whatever is not humility, but it is pride; it is

Despite the revelations making Joseph the primary revelator of commandments for the church, he never presumed to be the exclusive revelator. To the contrary, others were expected to receive them,[269] and he was pleased when others received visions, believed them to be authentic, and recorded them.[270] The year after revelation conferred status on Joseph as primary revelator, another revelation empowered everyone holding priesthood with the authority to reveal the mind of God: "they shall speak as they are moved upon by the Holy Ghost & whatsoever they shall speak when moved upon by the Holy Ghost shall be Scripture shall be the will of the Lord shall be the mind of the Lord shall be the voice of the Lord & shall be the power of God unto Salvation[.]"[271]

From October 31, 1838 to April 22, 1839, Joseph was on an unwelcome hiatus from leading the church. He spent most of those 173 days in the jail of Liberty, Missouri. On March 25, 1839 Joseph wrote in response to a letter Emma had sent him earlier in the month. He starts out with a salutation that rivals the Apostle Paul in terse prose:[272] "Your humble servant, Joseph Smith, Jun., prisoner for the

---

seeking praise of mortals instead of the praise of God. Joseph received a revelation that he should be the leader; that he should be ordained by Oliver Cowdery as 'Prophet Seer and Revelator' to the church, and that the church should receive his words as if from God's own mouth. Satan surely rejoiced on that day…"

[269] A revelation later at the end of the next year (not in the D&C) said "the duty of the Bishop shall be made known by the commandments which have been given and by the voice of the conference." (*JS Papers, Documents Vol. 3: July 1831-January 1833*, p. 150.) Another revelation (also not in the D&C) likewise expected the conference to obtain revelation: "it shall be made known unto them by the voice of the conference their severall missions." (*Id.*, p. 156.)

[270] For example: Joseph taught others should expect to have God appear to them: "[A]ll who are prepared and are sufficiently pure to abide the presence of the Lord, will see him in the solemn assembly." (*JS Papers, Histories Vol. 1: 1832-1844*, p. 123.) Later in the solemn assembly he recorded, "My Scribe also received his anointing (with us) and saw in a vision the armies of heaven protecting the Saints in their return to Zion—" (*JS Papers, Journal Vol. 1: 1832-1839*, p. 170.) "we ~~commenced~~ spent the time in rehearsing to each other the glorious scenes that transpired on the preceding evening, while attending to the ordinance of holy anointing." (*Id.*, p. 171.)

[271] *JS Papers, Documents Vol. 2: July 1831-January 1833*, p. 101; see also D&C 68:3-4.

Lord Jesus Christ's sake, and for the Saints, taken and held by the power of mobocracy, under the exterminating reign of his excellency, the governor, Lilburn W. Boggs…"[273]

During the half-year in prison, Joseph rethought the propriety of holding primary priestly power. Two events leading to his imprisonment were likely contributors to him rethinking all authority. The first was Rigdon's July 4th Salt Sermon that threatened "extermination" of Missourians. This thought apparently inspired Governor Boggs and was adopted by him in Missouri Executive Order 44, known as the "Extermination Order." But Mormons, not Missourians, were the targets for extermination.

The second was Sampson Avard's role in leading Mormon vigilantes against non-Mormons, burning homes, destroying crops and pillaging property. Joseph's preference was to take the high moral ground, and it was hard to go there when his followers engaged in morally reprehensible misconduct.

The day after his arrest, Joseph was sentenced to die. It was a perfunctory military tribunal conducted by General Lucas. Lucas issued this order: "To Brigadier-General Doniphan: Sir: You will take Joseph Smith and the other prisoners into the public square of Far West and shoot them at 9:00 tomorrow morning. Samuel D. Lucas, Major-General Commanding." Doniphan responded: "It is cold-blooded murder. I will not obey your order. My brigade shall march for Liberty tomorrow morning, at 8 o'clock; and if you execute these men, I will hold you responsible before an earthly tribunal, so help me God. A. W. Doniphan, Brigadier-General."[274] Nothing ever happened to General Doniphan for disobeying a direct order. Instead his response provoked a debate over the propriety of the state militia executing a civilian. On so thin a thread hung the lives of Joseph and seven others.

A civilian court was to decide the matter. The prisoners were transported to Richmond, where the chief witness against Joseph was the same Sampson Avard responsible for Danite depredations.

In the letter from Liberty Joseph advised the saints:

> …Nevertheless we would suggest the propriety

---

[272] See, *e.g.*, 1 Cor. 1:1-2; 2 Cor. 1:1-10; Philemon 1:1-3.

[273] For a complete transcript of the letter see *TPJS*, pp. 129-148.

[274] *History of Caldwell and Livingston Counties Missouri*, (St. Louis: National Historical Co., 1886), p. 137.

of being aware of an aspiring spirit, which spirit has
often times urged men forward to make foul
speeches, and influence the Church to reject milder
counsels, and has eventually been the means of
bringing much death and sorrow upon the Church.

The comments seem focused on the Mormon contribution to
the conflict, not on shirking blame and avoiding accountability. The
identities of those who made "foul speeches" are left to conjecture,
but the letter was for a Mormon audience, and therefore were likely
Mormons. Rigdon? Avard?

We would say, beware of pride also; for well and
truly hath the wise man said, that pride goeth before
destruction, and a haughty spirit before a fall. And
again, outward appearance is not always a criterion
by which to judge our fellow man; but the lips betray
the haughty and overbearing imaginations of the
heart; by his words and his deeds let him be judged.
Flattery also is a deadly poison. A frank and open
rebuke provoketh a good man to emulation; and in
the hour of trouble he will be your best friend; but
on the other hand, it will draw out all the corruptions
of corrupt hearts, and lying and the poison of asps is
under their tongues; and they do cause the pure in
heart to be cast into prison, because they want them
out of their way.

Joseph's reaction seems unexpected and out of context. A
religious leader imprisoned, under sentence of death, writing to
caution about pride and flattery. Pride and flattery have become tools
for advancing modern Mormonism.[275]

---

[275] See, e.g., Russell Ballard, *The Greatest Generation of Young Adults* (April 2015
General Conference); Julie Beck, *You Have a Noble Birthright* (April 2006
General Conference); Thomas Monson, *Be Thou an Example* (April 2005
General Conference); Neil Anderson, *You Know Enough* (October 2008
General Conference); President Gordon B. Hinckley, *Church News* interview,
June 7, 1995; Vaughn J. Featherstone, Champion of Youth (October 1987
General Conference); *Letter to the Youth of the Church*, (Church News, 9 May
1981); Neal A. Maxwell, *Notwithstanding My Weakness* (October 1976 General
Conference).

Joseph's counsel about using time wisely, particularly when Mormons meet for conferences, councils or conversations is a remarkable standard that has gone neglected. His letter from jail encouraged believers to be careful about letting fiction and vanity assume prominence:

> A fanciful and flowery and heated imagination beware of; because the things of God are of deep import; and time, and experience, and careful and ponderous and solemn thoughts can only find them out. Thy mind, O man! if thou wilt lead a soul unto salvation, must stretch as high as the utmost heavens, and search into and contemplate the darkest abyss, and the broad expanse of eternity-- thou must commune with God. How much more dignified and noble are the thoughts of God, than the vain imaginations of the human heart! None but fools will trifle with the souls of men.

> How vain and trifling have been our spirits, our conferences, our councils, our meetings, our private as well as public conversations--too low, too mean, too vulgar, too condescending for the dignified characters of the called and chosen of God, according to the purposes of His will, from before the foundation of the world!

Another passage echoes from Liberty and should trouble Mormonism a great deal more than it does. It is given little thought, but the imprisoned prophet-founder pondered about pride and petitioned his followers to avoid its practice:

> ... And if there are any among you who aspire after their own aggrandizement, and seek their own opulence, while their brethren are groaning in poverty, and are under sore trials and temptations, they cannot be benefited by the intercession of the Holy Spirit, which maketh intercession for us day and night with groanings that cannot be uttered.

> We ought at all times to be very careful that such high-mindedness shall never have place in our hearts; but condescend to men of low estate, and

with all long-suffering bear the infirmities of the weak.

These were ideals for original Mormonism that would challenge us still today (if we considered them still binding). Stratification of haves and have-nots is just part of our landscape.

The most remarkable part of the letter, however, addresses priestly domination. While in prison, suffering and oppressed by the state and political authorities, Joseph's concern turned to priestly abuse. Donatus Magnus[276] would agree with these words. Catholicism rejected the Donatist Heresy and concluded unfaithfulness was no impediment to priestly authority.[277] Joseph's letter vindicates the North African priest:

> ... Behold, there are many called, but few are chosen. And why are they not chosen? Because their hearts are set so much upon the things of this world, and aspire to the honors of men, that they do not learn this one lesson--that the rights of the Priesthood are inseparably connected with the powers of heaven, and that the powers of heaven cannot be controlled nor handed only upon the principles of righteousness. That they may be conferred upon us, it is true; but when we undertake to cover our sins, or to gratify our pride, our vain ambition, or to exorcise control, or dominion, or compulsion, upon the souls of the children of men, in any degree of unrighteousness, behold, the heavens withdraw themselves; the Spirit of the Lord is grieved; and when it is withdrawn, Amen to the Priesthood, or the authority of that men. Behold! ere he is aware, he is left unto himself, to kick against

---

[276] Donatus was the North African Bishop of Carthage in 313 ad. Roman Emperor Diocletian persecuted Christians, causing many to turn traitors to the cause. Donatus believed they forfeited their ecclesiastical authority when they betrayed the faith, requiring them to be re-baptized and re-ordained before holding authority. Likewise any ordinances performed by them during the period of apostasy were invalid. This view was rejected as heresy by the Catholic Church.

[277] See *Encyclopedia of Catholicism*, <u>Donatists</u> (<u>www.newadvent.com/cathen/</u> 05121.a.htm)

the pricks; to persecute the Saints, and to fight against God.

We have learned by sad experience that it is the nature and disposition of almost all men, as soon as they get a little authority, as they suppose, they will immediately begin to exercise unrighteous dominion. Hence many are called, but few are chosen.

No power or influence can or ought to be maintained by virtue of the Priesthood, only by persuasion, by long-suffering, by gentleness, and meekness, and by love unfeigned; by kindness, and pure knowledge, which shall greatly enlarge the soul without hypocrisy, and without guile, reproving betimes with sharpness, when moved upon by the Holy Ghost, and then showing forth afterwards an increase of love toward him whom thou hast reproved, lest he esteem thee to be his enemy; that he may know that thy faithfulness is stronger than the cords of death; let thy bowels also be full of charity towards all men, and to the household of faith, and virtue garnish thy thoughts unceasingly, then shall thy confidence wax strong in the presence of God, and the doctrine of the Priesthood shall distill upon thy soul as the dews from heaven. The Holy Ghost shall be thy constant companion, and thy sceptre an unchanging sceptre of righteousness and truth, and thy dominion shall be an everlasting dominion, and without compulsory means it shall flow unto thee forever and ever.

Early in the restoration, power and influence was consolidated into Joseph's hands alone. It began to erode by the following year. But in the meditative confines of Liberty Jail, Joseph saw the wisdom of removing all power and influence by virtue of priesthood alone.

Two months following the Liberty Jail confinement Joseph's advice to church leaders reflected his misgivings about power and authority in priesthood leaders. In an address to the twelve apostles and seventies, Joseph told them they needed to guard against self-sufficiency, self-righteousness and self-importance.[278] He was alarmed

---

[278] "I then addresst them, and gave much instruction calculated to if guard

by the idea leaders would think themselves better than church members, and would rise up in judgment, calling themselves more righteous than those they led. His warning to leaders included the following:

> I will give you one of the *Keys* of the mysteries of the Kingdom. It is an eternal principle, that has existed with God from all eternity: That man who rises up to condemn others, finding fault with the Church [meaning church members], saying that they are out of the way, while he himself is righteous, then know assuredly, that that man is in the high road to apostasy, and if he does not repent, will apostasize, as god lives.[279]

This caution has been turned on its head by the many Mormonisms of today. Hierarchies uniformly regard themselves as "righteous" even claiming they cannot lead their churches astray.[280] They presume to condemn and find fault with the church's members, saying the members are out of the way while the leaders are righteous. In short, the fears that began to mount in Joseph's heart while in Liberty Jail, which he voiced again in this sermon, have all come to pass.

In 1842 Joseph Smith lamented the Saints were depending too much on the prophet, darkened in their minds and neglecting the duties devolving on themselves. This position practically renounces a dominant role for a central leader.

If Apostle Samuel Richards can be trusted, the editorial in the Millennial Star on November 13, 1852 contained the words of Joseph Smith, and not himself. The editorial was titled "Priesthood" and in a voice attributed to Joseph declared:

> We have heard men who hold the priesthood remark that they would do anything they were told to do by those who preside over them even if they knew it was wrong; but such obedience is worse than folly to us; it is slavery in the extreme; and the man who

---

them against selfsuffiency, selfrighteousness & selfimportance[.]" *JS Papers, Journals Vol. 1: 1832-1839*, p. 344.
[279] See *DHC* 3:385.
[280] See, e.g., Gordon B. Hinckley, Ensign, First Presidency Message, January 2001, *A Prophet's Message and Counsel for Youth*, "I make you a promise that the authorities of this Church will never lead you astray."

would thus willingly degrade himself, should not claim a rank among intelligent beings, until he turns from his folly. A man of God would despise the idea. Others, in the extreme exercise of their almighty authority have taught that such obedience was necessary, and that no matter what the saints were told to do by their presidents, they should do it without any questions. When Elders of Israel will so far indulge in these extreme notions of obedience as to teach them to the people, it is generally because they have it in their hearts to do wrong themselves.[281]

Whatever early authority may have been centered on Joseph, by the early 1840s Mormon priestly domination was greatly diminished, if not altogether gone. It is impossible to reconcile the most virulent form of priestly power found in Correlated LDS Mormonism with the Liberty Jail edict that "no power or influence can, or ought, to be maintained by virtue of the priesthood." Joseph Smith's meditations on learning from sad experience that men abuse even "supposed" power[282] has been forgotten by modern Mormonisms. Unclear thinking critics aspire to join in the abuse, wanting ordination for women in the hope that females would be able to improve on the sad state of affairs. It is more likely that expanding participation would only expand the number of those who abuse authority while occupying the chief seats.[283] Fortunately, anyone can be a servant, kneeling to wash others' feet as the Master showed in His example,[284]

---

[281] See *Millennial Star*, Vol. 14, No. 2, Nov. 13, 1852. Even if the quote does not originate with Joseph, its publication in 1852 is in a consistent line with Joseph's changing thinking about limiting priesthood power.

[282] Fortunately the claims of priestly power by LDS Mormonism are now entirely hollow. When Joseph lamented men abused "a little authority, as they suppose" he was describing pretend priests. Immediately preceding that description he wrote of heaven's exclusive control over actual priestly status: "That the rights of the priesthood *are inseparably connected with the powers of heaven*, and that the powers of heaven *cannot be controlled nor handled only upon the principles of righteousness*. That they may be conferred upon us, it is true; but *when we undertake to cover our sins, or to gratify our pride, our vain ambition, or to exercise control or dominion or compulsion upon the souls of the children of men, in any degree of unrighteousness, behold, the heavens withdraw themselves; the Spirit of the Lord is grieved; and when it is withdrawn, Amen to the priesthood or the authority of that man.*" (D&C 121:36-37.)

[283] See Luke 20:46. A position Christ warned against.

whether they are ordained or not. Anyone can teach pure knowledge using persuasion and meekness. THAT is godly, and will save souls, whether the teacher is ordained or not.

In 1836, sacred rites were introduced in the Kirtland Temple. In 1843 different rites were contemplated, even partially celebrated. The new and improved temple rites were to be completed and housed in a new temple then under construction. A partial "endowment" was added to the already existing washings and anointings. The expanded rites also contemplated sealing marriages and adoption, or man-to-man sealings, all of which remained ill defined at the time of Joseph's death.

Joseph's original instruction about sealing dealt with connecting the living faithful to the "fathers" Abraham, Isaac and Jacob.[285] The connection was to be accomplished through adoption sealing, not genealogy. Joseph was connected to the "fathers" through his priesthood.[286] He and his brother Hyrum were to become 'fathers' of all who would live after them. Families were originally organized under Joseph as the father of the righteous in this dispensation.[287] Accordingly, men were sealed to Joseph Smith as their father, and they as his sons. This was referred to as 'adoption' because the family organization was not biological, but priestly, according to the law of God. As soon as Joseph died, the doctrine began to erode, ultimately replaced by the substitute practice of sealing genealogical lines

---

[284] John 13:4-5.

[285] "The spirit power & calling of Elijah is that ye have power to hold the keys of the revelations ordinances, oricles powers & endowments of the fulness of the Melchezedek Priesthood & of the Kingdom of God on the Earth & to receive, obtain and perform all the ordinances belonging to the Kingdom of God even unto the sealing of the hearts of the fathers unto the children & the hearts of the **children unto the fathers even those who are in heaven.**" (*The Words of Joseph Smith,* (Provo: BYU Religious Studies Center, 1980), p. 329, emphasis added). Abraham, Isaac and Jacob are in the heavens, sitting upon thrones. (D&C 132:37.) Connecting to the un-resurrected dead, as presently practiced by LDS Mormons, does nothing to reconnect to heaven.

[286] See, *e.g,* Abr. 2:10-11.

[287] Brigham Young made a clumsy allusion to this when he taught, "Joseph Smith holds the keys of this last dispensation, and is now engaged behind the vail in the great work of the last days...no man or woman in this dispensation will ever enter into the celestial kingdom of God without the consent of Joseph Smith...." October 9, 1859, (*JD* 7:289.)

together. In between the original adoptive sealing to Joseph Smith and the current practice of tracking genealogical/biological lines, there was an intermediate step when families were tracked back as far as research permitted, then the line was sealed to Joseph Smith. That practice is now forgotten, and certainly no longer practiced by any denomination within Mormonism.[288]

When Joseph died, any understanding of the practice of "adoption" was quickly lost. One writer explained:

> The period after Taylor's death in July 1887 appears to have been one of continued confusion regarding the law of adoption. Two months later in September 1887, John M. Whitaker, John Taylor's son-in-law wrote: "I went back to the office where I found [Apostle] Brother Lorenzo Snow and [First Council of the Seventy member] Jacob Gates. They conversed a long time. He finally entered into a deep subject on 'The Law of Adoption.' Brother Gates said he didn't believe in it as did also bother Snow. He reference back to the time that Brigham Young was in Kirtland[;] he had a person asked him about it and he said 'I don't know nothing about it.' President Taylor on one different occasion had a letter written to him for the following reason: it was [two undecipherable words] of Prophet J Smith or rather sister Eliza R. Snow Smith (Brother Gates didn't know which[;] a bout [sic] 70 persons were adopted into President J Smith's [family;] Sister Snow Smith said 'she didn't understand the law' but had no objections to them being sealed to her husband. And this led Brother Gates to write to President Taylor asking him if he knew anything about it. He never answered the letter. But on another occasion Brother Gates saw him and asked him plainly. President Taylor said he knew nothing about it. And also just lately when asked by Brother Snow, President Wilford Woodruff knew nothing about it. [']It hadn't been revealed to him.' I know this at this time to say [or show] a prevailing feeling

---

[288] *Passing the Heavenly Gift*, (Salt Lake: Mill Creek Press, 2011), pp. 481-482.

among the Twelve that they don't understand it. George [undecipherable] Cannon also said he didn't understand it.[289]

Mormonism never acquired a settled form of temple rites, the adoption process being poorly understood even while Joseph was alive.[290] For a short time temple sealings of ancestors went as far as information permitted, then the last known ancestor was sealed to Joseph Smith. But as Jonathan Stapley explained, "the idea of linking to Joseph Smith was eventually dismissed or forgotten."[291] The confusion over the subject once again confirms both the ever-changing nature of Mormonism and its failure to become complete during Joseph's life.

David Whitmer was disaffected because everything continually changed. His *Address to All Believers in Christ* began by addressing the issue of Mormonism-in-motion:

> They have departed in a great measure from the faith of the Church of Christ as it was first established, by heeding revelations given through Joseph Smith, who, after being called of God to translate his sacred word--the Book of Mormon --drifted into many errors and gave many revelations to introduce doctrines, ordinances and offices in the church, which are in conflict with Christ's teachings. They also changed the name of the church.

He thought the *Bible* and *Book of Mormon* were the only faithful canon, and all else was vanity and foolishness. He departed before the now-lost practice of adoption was introduced. Likewise, although he heard of the temple endowment, he never experienced it.

---

[289] Jonathan Stapley, *Adoptive Sealing Ritual in Mormonism*, The Journal of Mormon History, Vol. 37, No. 3, Summer 2011, pp. 53-117; citing to *John M. Whitaker, Diary, Book No. 4, September 16, 1887 to September 20, 1888*, November 16, 1887, MS 0002, Marriott Special Collection; transcription from Pitman shorthand by LaJean Purcell Carruth.

[290] His first public allusion to it was on October 15, 1843: "to see the kingdom of Good [God]. & subscribe the articles of adoption to enter therein." (*JS Papers, Journals Vol. 3: May 1843-June 1844*, p. 114.) Although his letter from Liberty Jail included language that foreshadowed adoptions: "There are many teachers, but, perhaps, not many fathers."

[291] Stapley, *Adoptive Sealing Ritual in Mormonism*, The Journal of Mormon History, supra, p. 53, 113-114.

In developing man's role in the cosmos, things began rather Protestant-like. Joseph eventually taught plainly that men could become gods.[292] Further, he asserted that God was once a man and had progressed to godhood.[293] LDS President Gordon B. Hinckley commenting on this topic stated, "I don't know that we teach it. I don't know that we emphasize it. I haven't heard it discussed for a long time in public discourse. I don't know. I don't know all the circumstances under which that statement was made. I understand the philosophical background behind it. But I don't know a lot about it and I don't know that others know a lot about it."[294] President Hinckley was right, of course. The idea crept into Mormonism late in Joseph's life, and never had an opportunity to be fully developed. So Mormons do not know a lot about it.

Joseph Smith's 'Magnum Opus,' the *King Follett Discourse*,[295] seems more like an introduction to something new than an older fully developed theology. Though the idea that man could progress to be like God had been disclosed earlier,[296] the idea that God was once like man and also learned His salvation was clearly something new, first revealed in this talk.[297] Joseph's April 1844 sermon finally closed an

---

[292] D&C 132:17-20.

[293] First, God himself, who sits enthroned in yonder heaven, is a man like one of you. That is the great secret. If the veil were rent today and you were to see the great God who holds this world in its orbit and upholds all things by his power, you would see him in the image and very form of a man; for Adam was created in the very fashion and image of God. ...I am going to tell you how God came to be God. We have imagined that God was God from all eternity. ...God himself, the Father of us all, dwelt on an earth the same as Jesus Christ himself did, ...Jesus, what are you going to do? To lay down my life as my Father did, and take it up again. ...Here, then, is eternal life--to know the only wise and true God. And you have got to learn how to be Gods yourselves--to be kings and priests to God, the same as all Gods have done--by going from a small degree to another, from grace to grace, from exaltation to exaltation, until you are able to sit in glory as do those who sit enthroned in everlasting power." (King Follette Discourse, *Times and Seasons*, 15 August 1844.)

[294] Biema, David Van. *Kingdom Come*, Time, August 4, 1997, page 56.

[295] The talk was first published posthumously in the *Times and Seasons*, August 15, 1844, although it was delivered April 7th of that year.

[296] Though the idea is Biblical (see, e.g., Rom. 8:16-17; Rev. 3:21; 1 John 3:2) it was considered novel when Joseph first revealed the idea in 1832 (D&C 76:55-60).

idea opened nine years earlier in the 1835 *Lectures on Faith*. In those lectures Joseph posed, and answered, the question:

> Where shall we find a saved being? For if we can find a saved being, we may ascertain without much difficulty what all others must be in order to be saved. We think that it will not be a matter of dispute, that two saved beings who are unlike each other cannot both be saved; for whatever constitutes the salvation of one will constitute of every creature that will be saved; and if we find one saved being in all existence, we may see what all others must be, or else not be saved. We ask then where is the prototype, or where is the saved being? We conclude as to the answer of this question, there will be no dispute among those who believe the Bible, that it is Christ: all will agree in this, that he is the prototype or standard of salvation; or, in other words, that he is a saved being. And if we should continue our interrogation and ask how it is that he is saved? The answer is because he is a just and holy being; and if he were anything different from what he is, he would not be saved; for his salvation depends on his being precisely what he is and nothing else; for if it were possible for him to change, in the least degree, so sure he would fail of salvation and lose all of his dominion, power, authority, and glory, which constitutes salvation; for salvation consists in the glory, authority, majesty, power, and dominion which Jehovah possesses and in nothing else; and no being can possess it but himself and one like him.[298]

---

[297] "God himself was once as we are now, and is an exalted man, and sits enthroned in yonder heavens! That is the great secret. If the veil were rent today, and the great God who holds this world in its orbit, and who upholds all worlds and all things by his power, was to make himself visible, --I say, if you were to see him today, you would see him like a man in form –like yourselves in all the person, image, and very form as a man: for Adam was created in the very fashion, image and likeness of God[.]" (*TPJS* p. 345.) Even the hint found in Ether 3:6-16 failed to clearly assert God was once like man.

[298] *Lecture Seventh*, ¶9

This 1835 teaching was just a prelude, left un-clarified and unexplained. The implications of this teaching escaped believers. Mormons were surprised to learn Christ did what His Father did[299] when He offered Himself as a sacrifice for sin. Like God the Father, Christ "laid down His life and took it up again" or, in other words, attained to the resurrection from the dead.[300] These ideas were consistent with earlier revelations, translations and writings, but *King Follett* signaled a whole new level of harmonizing ideas and adding upon the restoration.

Because Joseph was killed less than three months later, the talk was left as the introduction of something much grander to follow. But like the Nauvoo Temple and the temple rites, this fresh teaching was left undeveloped; a reminder of how great a loss one encounters when God takes an authentic prophet out of the community.

Mormonism failed to reach a finish line while Joseph was alive. God seems quite willing to give people what they want, even if it displeases Him.[301] The early eager Campbellite converts steered

---

[299] "What did Jesus say? (Mark it, Elder Rigdon!) The Scriptures inform us that Jesus said, As the Father hath power in Himself, even so hath the Son power—to do what? Why, what the Father did. The answer is obvious—in a manner to lay down His body and take it up again. Jesus, what are you going to do? To lay down my life as my Father did, and take it up again. Do we believe it? If you do not believe it, you do not believe the Bible." (*TPJS* p. 346, discussing John 5:19.)

[300] Attaining to the resurrection happens when the individual is able to come forth from the grave because death has no right or claim upon them. Christ delivers a form of resurrection to this creation, but the creation is dependent upon Him to rise again. In the theology introduced in this discourse, Joseph suggested the conquest of death happened only after proceeding from exaltation to exaltation until the individual arrived at the same station as Christ and His Father attained. "[Y]ou have got to learn how to be Gods yourselves, and to be kings and priests to God, the same as all Gods have done before you, namely, by going from one small degree to another, and from a small capacity to a great one: from grace to grace, from exaltation to exaltation, until you attain to the resurrection of the dead, and are able to dwell in everlasting burnings, and to sit in glory, as do those who sit enthroned in everlasting power." (*TPJS* pp. 346-347.)

[301] See, e.g., 1 Sam. 8:6-9; Eze. 14:7-10; "President Joseph Smith read the 14th chapter of Ezekiel–said the Lord had declared by the Prophet, that the people should each one stand for himself, and depend on no man or men in that state of corruption of the Jewish church–that righteous persons could

Joseph's inquiries, and over the following decade the restoration focused on organizing a restored, New Testament, Primitive Christian Church with all the original offices, teachings and practices. In the background of this preoccupation with New Testament Christianity, however, God pointed Joseph, and in turn us, toward something more ancient. God was attempting to return to the earth the original faith taught to Adam in the beginning. The first four Mormon missionaries were sent to proselytize American Indians or Lamanites in September 1830. Oliver Cowdery, Parley Pratt, Ziba Peterson and Peter Whitmer, Jr. were sent after one target but hit another. Pratt altered the mission trajectory as they passed through the Ohio area where he formerly served as a Campbellite advocate. This detour brought approximately 200 Campbellite converts into the Mormon ranks. The center of activity for Mormonism shifted from New York to Ohio. The focus of the "restoration" changed from a trek back to Eden, to a search for an authentic New Testament, Primitive Christian church with all the accouterments of the original. The Campbellites wanted, above all else, to have the authentic, original Primitive Church back again. They desired to confidently claim they were in sole possession of the restored original.

The religion of Adam was the objective of Mormonism. Joseph Smith was unable to fully restore that first religion of man. Joseph predicted the religion would include a future gathering in the "everlasting hills," (in all likelihood meaning the Rocky Mountains) where returning tribes would be "crowned" with glory in a New Jerusalem to be God's last days Zion.[302] The returning tribes did not gather in Kirtland, Jackson County, Far West, or Nauvoo. Joseph was dead before the trip westward to Salt Lake. Even the most ardent defender of the LDS version of Mormonism must concede there were things expected, even promised and prophesied to happen, that were left unrealized when Joseph died.

The LDS and RLDS organizations disagreed on many subjects, but four in particular separated them. These four were polygamy, succession in the presidency, plurality of Gods, and secret temple rites including baptism for the dead. Depending on which part of the

---

only deliver their own souls–applied it to the present state of the Church of Jesus Christ of Latter-day Saints–said if the people departed from the Lord, they must fall–that they were depending on the Prophet, hence were darkened in their minds…" (*TPJS*, p. 237.)
[302] D&C 133:23-35.

history was considered most important the outcome favored one over the other. One writer explained the disagreements this way, "I realized that as long as the focus was on Kirtland, the prairie Mormons [RLDS] held the advantage, but whenever the debate turned to Nauvoo, the mountain Mormons [LDS] would win."[303] The morphing faith under Joseph Smith was responsible for allowing this outcome. Anywhere along the timeline of his life as church leader, if there was a line drawn, what followed was different from before. It was dynamic, increasing, and consistent in building on what already existed, always in motion. It was an additive faith, never deductive. Nothing was abandoned, but expansions sometimes so transformed the earlier ideas, rites or practices that the new developments seemed to revolutionize the religion.

Because of the instability of Mormonism during Joseph Smith's life, it is reasonable to conclude that if there was an original, it cannot be defined by searching the teachings, practices, features, rites, or organization of the period from 1820 to 1844. One must look elsewhere to define an "original."

Apart from the changing organization, practices and teachings, there was the prophesied destiny of the faith. Many things are known to be undone because Joseph identified them as the targeted destiny for Mormonism. Perhaps the best and the only, way to identify an "original" Mormonism is to look at the aspirations for a religion that embraces all truth. If the goal of the original is considered, one can get much closer to defining it than by reassembling bits from its beginning. It is Mormonism's destiny that best tells us what Mormonism was, is, and is to come.[304] Anything else fails to meet the scriptural definition of truth.

---

[303] William Russell, *The LDS Church and Community of Christ: Clearer Differences and Closer Friends*, Mormon Dialogue, Vol. 36, No. 4, p. 177, 182. In that article he proposes that when Joseph Smith wrote the Wentworth Letter in 1842 he chose to omit the most exotic features of the Nauvoo developments, including temple rites. The Reorganized LDS movement followed most closely the features of Mormonism explained in the Wentworth Letter, and likewise rejected the Nauvoo additions. As he explained it, "we agreed with the Palmyra and Kirtland doctrines but rejected the later Nauvoo doctrines. We accepted the early part of the Mormon tradition but rejected the later, more extreme Mormon doctrines." (*Id.*, p. 184-185.)

[304] This is the definition of truth: "And truth is a knowledge of things as they

Christ compared the time when He would return in glory to the time of Noah.[305] Joseph added information about the time of Noah in the Joseph Smith Translation of Genesis, the relevant portion now being included in the *Pearl of Great Price*. Preliminary to the destruction of the wicked in Noah's day, mankind became wicked, murderous, and the world was filled with violence.[306] But if the wicked ripened in their behavior, so did the righteous. Not only were Noah and his family spared, but also Enoch's city,[307] and later many others were caught up to heaven.[308] To the same effect, Christ foretold that the time of His coming would be when the wheat and tares were both ripe.[309] Taken together, Mormonism exists with the expectation that there will come a time when violence overtakes the world, and like Enoch's people, a single place of peace will be established like in the days of Noah, as a refuge from that storm.

Ripened wheat occupying the future Zion are described in Mormonism with details of where, how and who will be involved. It is, however, important to clarify that there remains an unfinished role for Elijah before any expectation of Zion.

Joseph wrote a letter September 6, 1842 listing the heavenly visitors who helped create Mormonism. The list begins with an unidentified "voice mercy from heaven" followed by a "voice of truth out of the earth." Presumably these were Christ in the First Vision and Nephi or Moroni revealing the *Book of Mormon*. Then "Moroni," the "voice of the Lord" to the three witnesses, "Michael," the voice of God (conferring priesthood), Michael again, Gabriel, Raphael, and "divers angels from Michael or Adam down to the present time."[310] The letter was written six years after the Kirtland Temple dedication. There was no mention of Elijah in his letter. Oliver Cowdery failed to ever mention any visit from Elijah.[311] Joseph always referred to Elijah's return as a future event.[312] The original form of Mormonism

---

are, and as they were, and as they are to come." (D&C 93:24.)

[305] See Matt. 24:37-38; Luke 17:26-27.

[306] Moses 8:28-30.

[307] Moses 7:19-21.

[308] Moses 7:27.

[309] Matt. 13:25-30.

[310] See D&C 128:19-21.

[311] For a summary of Oliver's various statements see Richard Anderson, *The Credibility of the Book of Mormon Translators*, BYU Studies, Vol. 8, (1968), p. 277.

expected Elijah to return at some point after the 1840s.[313] Elijah's return will be one marker signaling the return of the original.

At the time of Abraham, generations of apostates separated father Abraham from the religion of Adam. But Abraham "sought for the blessings of the fathers" and wanted "to be one who possessed great knowledge." The result was Abraham "holding the right belonging to the fathers."[314] It was not easy to acquire, but as long as Shem was alive, it was still possible for Abraham to obtain it as "it came down from the fathers, from the beginning of time, yea, even from the beginning, or before the foundation of the earth, down to the present time, even the right of the firstborn, or the first man, who is Adam, or first father, through the fathers unto me."[315]

Joseph lived generations after the right descending from the fathers, or the first man, Adam, had been lost. Therefore, it was necessary for revelation, visitations and restoration; or in the language of Joseph Smith, "divers angels from Michael or Adam down to the present time, all declaring their dispensations, their rights, their keys, their honors, their majesty and glory, and the power of their priesthood; giving line upon line, precept upon precept; here a little, and there a little; giving us consolation by holding forth that which is to come, confirming our hope!"[316] But the original was "lost unto [Mormonism], or which [God] hath taken away, even the fullness of the priesthood" by January 1841.[317] God offered to "restore again" the fullness, on condition that the Mormons wanted it enough to provide a demonstration of faith.[318] They failed, and as a sign of their

---

[312] I have explained this in *Passing the Heavenly Gift* and elaborated on the reason for a needed future return in *The Mission of Elijah Reconsidered*, available on my website and in the book *Essays: Three Degrees* (Salt Lake: Mill Creek Press, 2013).

[313] On 13 August 1843 Joseph's journal recorded, "he shall send Elijah the prophet... and he shall reveal the covenants of the fathrs (in relation) to the children,--(originally written ) and the childrn and the covenant[n]ts of th[e] childr[en] in relati[o]n to the fathrs—" (*JS Papers, Journals Vol. 3, May 1843-June 1844*, p. 77, all as in original.)

[314] Abr. 1:2.

[315] Abr. 1:3.

[316] D&C 128:21.

[317] D&C 124:28.

[318] D&C 124:27-32. That same revelation made Hyrum Smith a "prophet, and a seer, and a revelator unto my church, as well as my servant Joseph[.]" (*Id.*, v. 94.) His position was above the twelve, because in December 1841 he

failure they received "instead of blessings…bring cursings, wrath, indignation, and judgments upon" them.[319] They did not enjoy God's protection, which would have included having a "holy spot" where, despite mobs and opposition, "they shall not be moved out."

If the original Mormonism needed to recover the fullness that was lost, then to revive an original, it will require a recovery of what was lost. If recovered, believers will be able to receive a holy spot, accepted and defended by God. In that place the in religion of Adam will be taught. The promised original religion includes the revelation of everything, "nothing shall be withheld." "All thrones and dominions, principalities and powers, shall be revealed and set forth[.]" Mormonism will recover information about "the sun, moon, [and] stars—All the times of their revolutions, all the appointed days, months, and years, and all the days of their days, months, and years,

---

presided over a conference in Ramus, Illinois at which four of the twelve were present, including Brigham Young. (See *JS Papers, Journals, Vol. 2, December 1841-April 1843*, p. 10.) In that role a few months later Hyrum published a revelation to the church: "[T]hey have neglected the House of the Lord, the Baptismal Font, in this place, wherein their dead may be redeemed, and the key of the knowledge that unfolds the dispensation of the fullness of times may be turned, and the mysteries of God be unfolded, upon which their salvation and the salvation of the world, and the redemption of their dead depends, for 'Thus saith the Lord, there shall not be a General Assembly for a general conference assembled together until the House of the Lord shall be finished, and the Baptismal Font, and if we are not diligent the church shall be rejected, and their dead also, Saith the Lord[.]'" Hyrum Smith, Patriarch for the whole church, *Times and Seasons*, Vol. 3, No. 1, November 15, 1841. In the same volume *An Epistle of the Twelve* stated, "[T]he first great object before us, and the saints generally, is to help forward the completion of the Temple and the Nauvoo House; buildings which are now in progress according to the revelations, and which must be completed to secure the salvation of the church in the last days, for God requires of his saints to build him a house wherein his servants may be instructed, and eudued with power from on high[.]" It was published over the names of Brigham Young, Heber C. Kimball, Orson Pratt, William Smith, Lyman Wight, Wilford Woodruff, John Taylor, Geo. A. Smith and Willard Richards. In the December 15, 1841 edition (Vol. 3, No. 4) another Epistle of the Twelve stated concerning the Nauvoo Temple, "[I]f this building is not completed, speedily, 'we shall be rejected as a church with our dead,' for the Lord out God hath spoken it[.]" It wasn't completed and the details are discussed in *Passing the Heavenly Gift*.
[319] D&C 124:44-48.

and all their glories, laws, and set times, shall be revealed in the days of the dispensation of the fullness of time—According to that which was ordained in the midst of the Council of the Eternal God of all other gods before this world was, that should be reserved unto the finishing and the end thereof, when every man shall enter into his eternal presence and into his immortal rest."[320]

These subjects seem disconnected with today's Mormonism, but the religion of Abraham (and therefore the religion of Adam) included "a knowledge of the beginning of the creation, and also of the planets, and of the stars, as they were made known unto the fathers."[321] The original Mormonism must grow in ancient knowledge until understanding reaches into the heavens. Not just spiritual understanding, but also physical understanding of the layout of the universe. The placement of the lights in the firmament was for "signs" to man,[322] and therefore were deliberately placed and contain information originally understood by Adam.

Almost from the beginning moments of Mormonism, the ambition to build a "New Jerusalem" on this continent was announced. Christ foretold The New Jerusalem in the *Book of Mormon*.[323] It was a later revelation to Joseph Smith that cemented the idea as part of the destiny for Mormonism. In January 1831, Mormons were promised they would be shown a location for that holy city.[324] That revelation explained how, after God reveals the location,[325] to collect funds for the purchase and construction of the city. To succeed, the New Jerusalem would require new covenants, which God also promised to reveal in due course.[326]

In March 1831, another revelation described the New Jerusalem as "Zion" which would be a place of glory and protection. It would

---

[320] D&C 121:28-32.

[321] Abr. 1:31.

[322] Gen. 1:14, also Abr. 1:31.

[323] See, 3 Ne. 20:22 (where not only is the New Jerusalem foretold, but Christ promises He will "be in the midst" of them) and 3 Ne. 21:23-25 (where gentiles are included with the promised city, and again He promises to "be in the midst" of them).

[324] D&C 42:9, 62

[325] *Id.*, v. 35, see also D&C 84:2-4 for the first approved location and D&C 124:42-45 for a later approved replacement location. Its final location will be "upon the mountains" (D&C 49:25).

[326] *Id.*, v. 67.

be a land of peace, a city of refuge where the glory of the Lord would be visible. "[T]he terror of the Lord also shall be there,[327] insomuch that the wicked will not come unto it, and it shall be called Zion." This revelation also contrasted the violence among the tares and peace among the wheat: "And it shall come to pass among the wicked, that every man that will not take his sword against his neighbor must needs flee unto Zion for safety. And there shall be gathered unto it out of every nation under heaven; and it shall be the only people that shall not be at war one with another. And it shall be said among the wicked: Let us not go up to battle against Zion, for the inhabitants of Zion are terrible; wherefore we cannot stand. And it shall come to pass that the righteous shall be gathered out from among all nations, and shall come to Zion, singing with songs of everlasting joy."[328]

The gathering to the New Jerusalem develops in time to the status of being "Zion" where God will visit. The growth is through refinement of the residents of the New Jerusalem.[329] In 1833, the Lord revealed that once developed into His Zion, nothing on earth or in hell can move it from the place God plants it. He will defend it, and although scourges will be dispensed to the ungodly, "the Lord's scourge shall pass over by night and by day, and the report thereof shall vex all people[.] …Nevertheless Zion shall escape if she observe to do all things whatsoever [God has] commanded her."[330] Zion's appearance on earth is a signal that all other governments will end.[331]

In 1834, the Lord explained that He, and not the residents of His Zion, would fight the coming battles. "For behold, I do not require at their hands to fight the battles of Zion; for as I said in a former commandment,[332] even so will I fulfill—I will fight your battles."[333]

---

[327] See also, D&C 133:56 where the Lord's return to live in Zion is to be accompanied by the resurrection of the dead.

[328] D&C 45:66-71.

[329] D&C 35:24.

[330] See, D&C 97:19-27.

[331] Joseph taught, "we believe god will not destroy the kingdoms of the earth till, he has set (up) his own kingdom." (*JS Papers, Journals Vol. 3, December 1842-June 1844*, p. 342.)

[332] Meaning D&C 98:37.

[333] D&C 105:14.

Because of prophecies made to the patriarchal fathers, the right to found this future city of peace descends from a specific ancient line. There will be an heir descended from both Jesse and Joseph[334] who will accomplish it.[335] Occupants of the community will likewise have lineal qualification. The last-day's Zion is an accomplishment promised earlier to the patriarchal fathers and it is through their descendants God intends to vindicate the promises.[336] The result of this alignment will be a priestly city of Zion that will "return to that power which she had lost."[337]

Many other details that are passed over are in the revelations to Joseph Smith.[338] But one promise requires particular mention. The city founded by Enoch, which was the original City of Zion, will return.[339] When it does, an earthly counterpart also named "Zion" is the place to which Enoch and his people will return. "Then shalt thou [Enoch], and all thy city meet them there, and we will receive them into our bosom, and they shall see us; and we will fall upon their necks, and they shall fall upon our necks, and we will kiss each other; And there shall be mine abode, and it shall be Zion, which shall come forth out of all the creations which I have made[.]"[340]

The original iteration of Mormonism was apocalyptic. But it was oddly practical about the apocalypse, assuming there were things that could be done to prepare. Not in haste, which was condemned,[341] but it was a physical and spiritual enterprise to be accomplished by the hard effort of those interested in welcoming the Lord's return.

The matter of plural wives, spiritual wives, polygamy or polygyny is certainly part of Joseph's life. However, the history and reliable documentation concerning this issue is anything but certain. There is debate even over when it first appeared. The date that makes the

---

[334] This lineage disqualified Joseph Smith, who was descended from Joseph, but not from Jesse. He was a "pure Ephraimite" according to the LDS Church. See Daniel H. Ludlow, *Of the House of Israel*, Ensign, January 1991, citing with approval Brigham Young's assertion in *JD* 2:268-269 as part of the article.
[335] D&C 113:5-6.
[336] D&C 113:7-8.
[337] *Id.*
[338] See, *e.g.*, D&C 133:12-35.
[339] See, Jude 1:14-15.
[340] Moses 7:63.
[341] See, e.g., D&C 63:24; 101:68; 133:15.

most sense is 1829. When Joseph and Oliver were translating the *Book of Mormon*, it provoked them into praying about baptism. Similarly when the issue of plural wives surfaced in the translation of Jacob 2, it also provoked an inquiry. Brigham Young made this statement:

> Said that while Joseph and Oliver were translating *The Book of Mormon*, they had a revelation that the order of patriarchal marriage and the sealing was right. Oliver said to Joseph, "Brother Joseph, why don't we go into the order of polygamy and practice it as the ancients did? We know it is true, then why delay?" Joseph's reply was, "I know we know it is true and from God, but the time is not yet come." This did not seem to suit Oliver who expressed the determination to go into the order of plural marriage anyhow, although he was ignorant of the order and the pattern and the results. Joseph said, "Oliver if you go into this thing, it is not with my faith or consent." Disregarding the counsel of Joseph, Oliver Cowdrey took to wife Miss Annie Lyman, cousin of George A. Smith.[342]

Brigham Young is quoting a private conversation between Oliver and Joseph that took place 32 years earlier, which he apparently recalled off the top of his head. He was not there when the conversation occurred. He could not know what was actually said yet he retells it as if quoting the actual words spoken between Joseph and Oliver. He likewise does not tell us the source of his information. Did it come from Joseph, or Oliver, Annie Lyman, George A. Smith, or someone who heard about it from one of them? There is no attempt to authenticate the account. The story may not be altogether accurate, at least as far as quoting what was said at the time, but the fact he positively claims the revelation happened in the 1829 time frame is plausible.

The chronology of Section 132 is NOT known, other than it was put into a lost writing for the first time on July 12, 1843. Then, once written, the original was destroyed and only a copy in the handwriting of Joseph Kingsbury (who was not present when the revelation was received) survives as a copy of whatever was first revealed.[343] The first

---

[342] See *The Complete Discourses of Brigham Young*, vol. 5, entry of July 26 of 1872, a talk given in Salt Lake City 14th Ward.

portion of Section 132 was likely composed in 1829 and was inspired by the material in Jacob Chapter 2 in the *Book of Mormon*, and not the later translation of the Old Testament as LDS traditions hold.[344] There are also potentially at least five separate portions consolidated into one document.

If the chronology begins in 1829, the possibility of plural wives was "on" then (at least as far as Oliver Cowdery was concerned), but Joseph hesitated to practice it, so it was also "off" then as to him. In

---

[343] If contemporary statements by Joseph and Hyrum can be trusted, the original revelation did not relate to present day marital relationships. In the City Council minutes of June 8 and 10, 1844 Joseph and Hyrum give an explanation of original revelation and its limitation:

"[Hyrum] referred to the revelation [he] read to the [Nauvoo Stake] High council — that it was in answer to a question concerning things which transpired in former days & had no reference to the present time — that W[illia]m Law[,] when sick[,] [confessed and] said ^he had been guilty of adultery &^ he was not fit to live or die, had sinned against his own soul...." (John S. Dinger, *Nauvoo City and High Council Minutes*, (Salt Lake: Signature Books, 2011) p. 241.) "[The mayor said]...They make [it] a criminality of for a man to have a wife on the earth while he has one in heaven — according to the keys of the holy priesthood, and [the mayor] read the statement of W[illia]m Law in the Expositor, where the truth of God was transformed into a lie. [He] read [the] statements of Austin Cowles — & said he had never had any private conversation with Austin Cowles on these subjects, that he preached on the stand from the bible showing the order in ancient days[,] having nothing to do with the present time..." (*Nauvoo City and High Council Minutes*, p. 254.) "C[ouncillor] H[yrum] Smith — spoke to show the falsehood of Austin Cowles in relation to the revelation referred to — that it referred to former days [and] not the present time as stated by Cowles. [The] Mayor said he had never preached the revelation in private as he had in public — had not taught it to the highest anointed in the Church ^in private^ which many confirmed.

"[The mayor said][,] on enquiring [of God regarding] the passage in [the Bible that in] the resurrection they neither marry &c[:] I received for [an] answer, Men in this life must be married in view of Eternity, [and that] was the [full] amount of the [content of the] revelation, otherwise [in the resurrection] they must remain as angels only in heaven, and [the mayor] spoke at considerable length in explanation of the[se] principles[.]" (*Nauvoo City and High Council Minutes*, pp. 255-256.) If you believe these statements, the original version of Section 132 could not read as the Joseph Kingsbury copy reads.

[344] Dating explained in *Passing the Heavenly Gift*.

the 1835 D&C, polygamy was definitely "off" with this official statement of position: "Inasmuch as this Church of Christ has been reproached with the crime of fornication and polygamy, we declare that we believe that one man should have one wife, and one woman but one husband, except in the case of death, when either is at liberty to marry again."[345]

It was alleged to be "on" again in 1838 when Cowdery accused Joseph, but apparently that was a false alarm. The earliest authoritative suggestion that Joseph had any involvement with plural wives was in in April 1838 at the disciplinary council proceeding before the Far West High Council. The case involved seven charges against Oliver Cowdrey. The council excommunicated Oliver Cowdrey from the church.[346] The second charge against Cowdery was, "for seeking to destroying the character of President Joseph Smith jr by falsly insinuating that he was guilty of adultery &c."[347] In the transcript of the hearing George W. Harris, one of the witnesses, testified Oliver Cowdrey,

> he seemed to insinuate that Joseph Smith jr was guilty of adultery, but when the question was put, if he (Joseph) had ever acknowledged to him that he was guilty of such a thing; when he answered No.[348]

Next another witness, David Patten, testified:

> he went to Oliver Cowdrey to enquire of him if a certain story was true respecting J. Smith's committing adultery with a certain girl,[349] when he

---

[345] D&C 101:4 (which remained in the scriptures until 1876, when it was removed and Section 132 added).

[346] The entire proceeding can be found in *Far West Record: Minutes of The Church of Jesus Christ of Latter-day Saints, 1830-1844*, Edited by Donald Q. Cannon, Lyndon W. Cook, (Salt Lake: Deseret Book, 1983), pp. 162-171.

[347] *Id.*, p. 163 all quotes as in original. Joseph Smith never used the term "Celestial Marriage" to describe plural wives, but he did use the term "adultery" to describe it.

[348] *Id.*, p. 167, meaning that Joseph never acknowledged it was true.

[349] The record is footnoted by Cannon and Cook to add, "The girl referred to here is Fanny Alger, Joseph Smith's first plural wife." *Id.* at p. 171, footnote 18. They cite as support a letter from Oliver Cowdery to Warren Cowdery January 21, 1838 in the Huntington Library, a copy of which is on microfilm at Church Archives, and another letter from Benjamin F. Johnson to Elder George S. Gibbs in 1911. A typewritten copy of the Johnson letter is at Brigham Young University.

turned on his heel and insinuated as though he was guilty; he then went on and gave a history of some circumstances respecting the adultery scrape stating that no doubt it was true.[350]

Thomas Marsh testified:

> while in Kirtland last summer, David W. Patten asked Oliver Cowdrey if he Joseph Smith jr had confessed to his wife that he was guilty of adultery with a certain girl, when Oliver cocked up his eye very knowingly and hesitated to answer the question, saying he did not know as he was bound to answer the question yet conveyed the idea that it was true.[351]

Joseph Smith testified in the hearing. His testimony is only summarized and the summary was ambiguous. However it is clear from the outcome of the hearing that Joseph necessarily denied he was involved in the practice, otherwise the decision of the council makes no sense. Here is the summary of his testimony:

> Joseph Smith jr testifies that Oliver Cowdrey had been his bosom friend, therefore he intrusted him with many things. He then gave a history respecting the girl business.[352]

The court's decision vindicated Joseph and condemned Cowdery. One of the reasons for condemning Cowdery was the false accusation of "adultery" against Joseph:

> After some remarks by the Councellors, it was decided by the Bishop and his Council that the 1st, 2nd, & 3rd charges were sustained...[353]

The second charge dealt with the false accusation against Joseph Smith that he committed adultery. The complaint that Oliver Cowdrey was falsely attributing to Joseph Smith the untrue claim he (Joseph) committed adultery justified the decision that Oliver Cowdery "was, therefore, considered no longer a member of the

---

[350] *Far West Record: Minutes of The Church of Jesus Christ of Latter-day Saints, 1830-1844*, p. 167—meaning that the accusation against Oliver Cowdery was true, i.e. he had insinuated this about Joseph Smith and adultery.

[351] *Id.* meaning it was true Oliver Cowdery did convey the false idea Joseph Smith committed adultery.

[352] *Id.*, p. 168.

[353] Id., p. 169

Church of Jesus Christ of Latter Day Saints."[354] So in 1838, plural wives was apparently "off."

Once John C. Bennett secretly taught there was such a thing as a "spiritual wife" to women in Nauvoo, something akin to plural wives was "on" again. Except it wasn't marriage, just some sort of spiritual relationship involving carnal relations. And once Joseph learned of Bennett's conduct Joseph tried to make plural wives "off" again. One of the great obstacles to getting the truth is Bennett. Because of who he was and what he did, his sexual improprieties were attributed to Joseph Smith. In the *Times and Seasons* edition for June 15, 1842, there was a little notice on the last page of the edition. The little notice said:

> NOTICE.
> The subscribers, Members of the First Presidency of the Church of Jesus Christ of Latter Day Saints, withdrew the hand of fellowship from General John C. Bennett, as a christian, he having been labored with from time to time, to persuade him to amend his conduct, apparently to no good effect.
> JOSEPH SMITH
> HYRUM SMITH
> WM. LAW
> The following members of the Quorum of Twelve concur in the above sentiments.
> BRIGHAM YOUNG
> HEBER C. KIMBALL
> LYMAN WIGHT
> WILLIAM SMITH
> JOHN E. PAGE
> JOHN TAYLOR
> WILFORD WOODRUFF
> GEORGE A. SMITH
> WILLARD RICHARDS
> We concur in the above sentiment.
> N.K. WHITNEYV. KNIGHT
> GEORGE MILLER
> Bishops of the above mentioned Church.
> Nauvoo, May 11th, 1842.

---

[354] *Id.*, p. 169.

That was the original notice. But John C Bennett 'did not go quietly into that good night.' As soon as the notice was published he went out of his way to change the account of his history to change himself into the good guy (just diddling about undercover—no pun intended—to access the naked truth about Mormonism). This in turn made Joseph Smith the lecherous leader of a libidinous theology that made a sacrament of reckless sex. He attributed to Joseph Smith and the Mormons things he had done. The July 1st edition of the *Times and Seasons* devoted almost the entire edition to debunking Bennett. The lead article begins with this statement:

> It becomes my[355] duty to lay before for the Church of Jesus Christ of Latter Day Saints, and the public generally, some important facts relative to the conduct and character of Dr. John C. Bennett, who has lately been expelled from the aforesaid Church; that the honorable part of the community may be aware of his proceedings, and be ready to treat and regard him as he ought to be regarded, viz: as an imposter and base adulterer.

The original notice in June said nothing about adultery. Because of Bennett's campaign they had to discuss the ugly facts. The article continues,

> ...a communication had been received at Nauvoo, from a person of respectable character, and residing in the vicinity where Bennett had lived. This letter cautioned us against him, setting forth that he was a very mean man, and had a wife, and two or three children in McConnelsville, Morgan county, Ohio; but knowing that it is no uncommon thing for good men to be evil spoken against, the above letter was kept quiet, but held in reserve.

Church leaders did not at first trust the information in the letter. But Bennett proved the content true by his misconduct in Nauvoo. Joseph was always willing to believe the best about people and to accept repentance at face value. The lead article explained how they dealt with him, "finally threatening him to expose him if he did not desist. This, to outward appearance, had the desired effect, and the

---

[355] Joseph Smith was the editor and publisher.

acquaintance between them was broken off." Meaning he admitted, and apparently stopped, his sexual exploits.

Sadly, the article reports, "he only broke off his publicly wicked actions, to sink deeper into iniquity and hypocrisy." Secretly, "he went to some of the females in the city, who knew nothing of him but as an honorable man, & began to teach them that promiscuous intercourse between the sexes, was a doctrine believed in by the Latter-Day Saints, and that there was no harm in it[.]"

The account continued, explaining, Bennett would "persuade them that [Joseph Smith] and others of the authorities of the church not only sanctioned, but practiced the same wicked acts; and when asked why I publicly preached so much against it, said that it was because of the prejudice of the public, and that it would cause trouble in my own house."

Bennett's explanation was a lie that lives on today. Bennett accused Joseph of hiding it because of expected criticism, and fear Emma would discover the practice. However, Joseph excommunicated Bennett, exposed numerous others, and clearly did not fear public exposure of wrongdoing. He welcomed public exposure of the sexual misdeeds in Nauvoo. The trials were public. News reporters from outside Nauvoo attended some of the proceedings and reported on their content, just as the newspaper Joseph edited and published covered the Bennett affair. Bennett clearly lied. Bennett "persuaded [his victims] that there would be no harm if they should not make it known." He seduced these females "by his lying." Joseph's *Times and Seasons* article explained that, "Not being contented with having disgraced one female, he made an attempt upon others, and by the same plausible tale, overcame them also[.]"

> "[I]t was a fact that Bennett had a wife and children living, and that she had left him because of his ill-treatment towards her. This letter was read to Bennett, which he did not attempt to deny; but candidly acknowledged the fact."

Action against Bennett was delayed because "Dr. Bennett made an attempt at suicide, by taking poison." This was wrongly interpreted to be a sign of remorse and shame, and gave some hope he would reform. However, "without any government over his passions, he was soon busily engaged in the same wicked career, and continued until a knowledge of the same reached my ears." In response to this news,

Joseph Smith "publicly proclaimed against it, and had those females notified to appear before the proper officers that the whole subject might be investigated and thoroughly exposed."

This edition of the *Times and Seasons* also reprinted an affidavit signed by John Bennett. It says:

> John C. Bennett, who being duly sworn according to law, deposeth and saith: that he never was taught anything in the least contrary to the strictest principles of the Gospel, or of virtue, or of the laws of God, or man, under any circumstances, or upon any occasion either directly or indirectly, in word or deed, by Joseph Smith; and that he never knew the said Smith to countenance any improper conduct whatever, even in public or private; and that he never did teach me in private that an illegal and illicit intercourse with females was, under any circumstances, justifiable; and that I never knew him so to teach others.
>
> JOHN C. BENNETT.

Next the Aldermen and members of the City Council, in this same edition of the *Times and Seasons* also signed an affidavit recounting Dr. Bennett's testimony before them:

> I publicly avow that anyone who has said that I have stated that General Joseph Smith has given me authority to hold illicit intercourse with women is a liar in the face of God, those who have said it are damn liars; they are infernal liars. He never, either in public or private, gave me any such authority or license, and any person who says it is a scoundrel and a liar.

Joseph asked Bennett in front of the Council, "Will you please state definitely whether you know anything against my character, either in public or in private?" General Bennett answered, "I do not. In all my intercourse with Gen. Smith, in private and in public, he has been strictly virtuous." The edition then reprints affidavits signed by George Miller, one of which mentions Bennett "was an expelled Mason."

The subject gets taken up again in the August 1st edition of the *Times and Seasons*. Yet more affidavits, more public statements, and more acknowledgments are given. This time William Law provided an affidavit defending the character of Joseph and condemning what John Bennett attributed to him. Law's affidavit recounts,

> I told him we could not bear with his conduct any longer—that there were many witnesses against him, and that they stated that he gave Joseph Smith as authority for his illicit intercourse with females. J.C. Bennett declared to me before God that Joseph Smith never taught him such doctrines, and that he never told any one that he (Joseph Smith) had taught any such things, and that any one who said so told base lies[.]
>
> ...
>
> These statements he made to me of his own free will, in a private conversation which we had on the subject; there was no compulsion or threats used on my part[.]
>
> ...
>
> On one occasion I heard him state before the city Council that Joseph Smith had never taught him any unrighteous principles, of any kind, and that if any one says that he ever said that Joseph taught such things they are base liars, or words to that effect.

In the Nauvoo City and High Council minutes there followed a number of trials as Joseph sought out the participants to expose their sexual misconduct and bring it to an end. He did not tolerate it, and did not hide it when he learned of it.

On May 11, 1842 Bennett resigned his mayoral post because he had been accused of "adultery, fornication, buggery and miscegenation."[356] Buggery is the euphemism used in that time period for homosexual relations. Miscegenation was the legal offense of a white person having intercourse with a black person, because that was improper mixing of the races. He was apparently indiscriminate about sex.

---

[356] *The Wasp*, July 27, 1842—a newspaper printed in Nauvoo but not an official church publication.

The minutes of the Nauvoo City Council for July 20, 1842, report the earlier testimony of Mayor John C. Bennett when he resigned office:

> John C. Bennett was not under duress at the time he testified before the city council, May 19, 1842, concerning Joseph Smith's innocence and virtue and pure teaching. ...there was no excitement at the time, nor was he in anywise threatened, menaced or intimidated. His appearance at the city council was voluntary; ...Joseph Smith asked him if he knew anything bad concerning his public or private character. He then delivered those statements contained in the testimony voluntarily, and on his own free will, and went of his own accord, as free as any member of the Council.
>
> WILSON LAW, GEO A. SMITH, JOHN TAYLOR, GEO W. HARRIS, WILFORD WOODRUFF, NEWEL K. WHITNEY, VINSON KNIGHT, BRIGHAM YOUNG, HEBER C. KIMBALL, CHARLES C. RICH, JOHN P. GREEN, ORSON SPENCER, WILLIAM MARKS.

Joseph Smith's 1838 history was originally written to admit:

> "I was left to all kinds of temptations, and mingling (with) all kinds of society I frequently (fell) into many foolish errors and displayed the weakness of youth and the corruption of human nature which I am sorry to say led me into divers temptations to the gratification of many appetites offensive in the sight of God." (*JS Papers, Histories Vol. 1*: 1832-1844, p. 220.)

The history of Joseph Smith was first published in the *Times and Seasons*. This part of his history was printed in an installment on April 1, 1842. (*Times and Seasons, Vol 3*, p. 749.) The explanation that Joseph was not guilty of "any great or malignant sins" had not yet been added in April 1842. The month after the publication of this installment of Joseph's history, on May 11, 1842, John C. Bennett was excommunicated from the church for adultery. Bennett did not go quietly, and therefore public notice of his excommunication was announced in print on June 15, 1842. Bennett got louder and more accusatory and on July 1, 1842 a full account of John C. Bennett's misconduct was explained in the *Times and Seasons*.

Because Bennett began his public accusations against Joseph Smith in 1842, on December 2, 1842 a note was added to Joseph's history. The LDS Historian's Office explains the note clarified his sins "were of a minor nature." (See, *JS Papers, History, Vol. 1*, p. 221, footnote 55.) The changed language is now what we read in the *Pearl of Great Price*:[357]

> "In making this confession, no one need suppose me guilty of any great or malignant sins. A disposition to commit such was never in my nature. But I was guilty of levity, and sometimes associated with jovial company, etc., not consistent with that character which ought to be maintained by one who was called of God as I had been." (JS-H 1:28.)

The addition of this clarification was in direct response to John C. Bennett's adultery, the discovery by Joseph Smith of a "spiritual wife" system being practiced in Nauvoo, and the accusation that he was aware of, believed in, and practiced adulterous relationships. As Joseph Smith stated publicly months later in a meeting in Nauvoo:

> What a thing it is for a man to be accused of committing adultery, and having seven wives, when I can only find one. I am the same man, and as innocent as I was fourteen years ago; and I can prove them all perjurers.[358]

When the context is considered, the timing of the edit change to Joseph's History denying he committed "any great or malignant sins," is in response to scandal brought to Joseph's attention through the John C. Bennett affair. Joseph was denying he was involved in the

---

[357] The addition/substitution is in Willard Richards' handwriting, and reads as follows:

"In making this confession, no one need suppose me guilty of any great or malignant sins: a disposition to commit such was never in my nature; but I was guilty of Levity, & sometimes associated with jovial company &c, not Consistent with that character which ought to be maintained by one who was called of God as I had been; but this will not seem very strange to any one who recollects my youth & is acquainted with my native cheerly Temperament." (*Manuscript History*, Note added December 2, 1842.)

[358] *DHC* 6:411, May 26, 1844.

"spiritual wife" system of adulterous relationships practiced in Nauvoo that was being attributed to him.[359]

To the extent Joseph exposed his thoughts about sex, they were dominated by sexual purity and self-control.[360] His public and private statements point to a man who prized chastity, fidelity and condemned promiscuity. His letters are consistent with his public statements. In an address to those present for a high council trial

---

[359] This subject requires conspiracy and lies. There is a choice between Joseph Smith being a liar, engaged with others in a Nauvoo conspiracy to hide abominable relationships, on the one hand; or Joseph being truthful and therefore, upon his death others engaged in a conspiracy to attribute their adulterous and abominable relationships to him and concocted revisionist accounts to justify themselves. Either theory makes early Mormons liars and conspirators. The question turns on whether you think Joseph was truthful. Until persuaded beyond reasonable doubt, I hesitate to call Joseph a liar and deceiver, although the majority of Mormons, including the LDS Church, regard him so. I know what is required to have God answer. The "key" to be able to ask and have God answer (which is what the "keys of the kingdom" means—see D&C 124:95; compare D&C 42:68-69, 84:19, 90:1-4, 115:18-19, 128:14, because without revelation to obtain God's answer, Mormonism is just as adrift in uncertainty as apostate Christianity. They are like Laman and Lemuel, who could not understand a revelation given their father. In response to Nephi's inquiry as to why they did not ask God, they responded: "the Lord maketh no such thing known unto us." 1 Ne. 15:9. It takes revelation to understand revelation.). That "key" is to sacrifice your life by obedience to God. Live humbly and meekly before God, obeying every word that proceeds from Him. This despite the rage of false religionists who will always condemn the things of God by pretending they, without revelation, can know what God meant, intended or is doing. They are pretenders, without authority. They fight against God. A man who has the "keys" must sacrifice all to know God. Joseph held the keys, and that compels me to assume Joseph's innocence until there is something far more compelling than the present record to stand as proof to the contrary.

[360] Joseph's August 18, 1842 letter to the parents of Sarah Ann Whitney has been represented as a love letter to her, instead of to her parents. He was in hiding, Emma Smith had encouraged him to change hiding places to avoid capture by Missouri hunters who wanted to capture and return him to Missouri. Emma also warned Joseph she was being followed. Joseph's letter telling the Whitneys they ought to "find out when Emma comes then you cannot be safe, but when she is not here, there is the most perfect safty" directly related to Emma's warning about Missouri spies following her.

before the Nauvoo High Council on November 25, 1843, Joseph Smith declared:

> [G]ave an address tending to do away with every evil, and exhorting them to practice virtue and holiness before the Lord; told them that the Church had not received any permission from me to commit fornication, adultery, or any corrupt action; but my every word and action has been to the contrary. If a man commit adultery, he cannot receive the celestial kingdom of God. Even if he is saved in any kingdom, it cannot be the celestial kingdom.[361]

In the minutes of the High Council for November 21, 1843 it was Joseph Smith who brought the charges. He accused Elder Harrison Sagars of two offenses:

> 1st. For trying to seduce a young girl, living in his house[,] by the name of Phebe Madison. 2nd. For using my name in a blasphemous manner, by saying that I tolerated such things in which he is guilty of lying &c &c. Joseph Smith.[362]

Joseph responded to the claim he authorized seduction of females by accusing those making the claim of "blasphemy." At the trial he denounced he ever gave permission for fornication, adultery or any corrupt action. A false accusation against a prophet, when there is insufficient proof to remove all doubt of the accusation, is a grave offense. It offends the injured party, but also the one who sent Him as His messenger.

Beginning in 1842, plural wivery was definitely "off." Except on July 12, 1843, according to William Clayton, Joseph dictated a revelation that made it somewhat "on" again. We do not have the original of that document. We have a copy in the handwriting of Joseph Kingsbury. We also have Emma Smith's testimony that Joseph didn't participate in plural marriages. So it was "off" then. Then in 1852 it was "on" again and, like Bennett, it was all Joseph's idea. At that point, the journals were altered, affidavits were ginned-up, and sermons were delivered asserting it was all Joseph's idea.

---

[361] *DHC* 6:81.

[362] *The Nauvoo City and High Council Minutes*, John S. Dinger, editor, (Salt Lake: Signature Books, 2011), pp. 479-480.

We are forced to choose between circumstantial proof, often from witnesses telling their tale decades after the events, compounded by the conjecture of the witness or the audience who heard the witness, to support the proposition that Joseph Smith was a vile hypocrite. Or, alternatively, we can take him at his word and accept what he said about himself, and believe and trust he did not advocate or practice sexual sin.

In the aftermath of John Bennett's misconduct, Joseph tracked down what happened in Nauvoo. On May 21, 1842, the high council met and "[A] charge [was] [preferred] against Chauncey L. Higbee by George Miller for unchaste and un-virtuous conduct with the widow [Sarah] Miller, and others."[363] In the trial, "Three witness[es] testified that he had seduced [several women] and at different times [had] been guilty of unchaste and unvirtuous conduct with them and taught the doctrine that it was right to have free intercourse with women if it was kept secret &c and also taught that Joseph Smith authorised him to practice these things &c"[364]

On May 25, the charge was preferred "against Ms. Catherine Warren by George Miller for unchaste and unvirtuous conduct with John C. Bennett and others. The defendant confessed to the charge and gave the names of several other [men] who had been guilty having unlawful intercourse with her[,] stating they taught the doctrine that it was right to have free intercourse with women and that the heads of the Church also taught and practiced it[,] ...learning that the heads of the church did not believe of [the] practice [of] such things[,] she was willing to confess her sins and did repent before God for what she had done and desired earnestly that the Council would forgive her."[365] She furnished the identities of the several men involved, resulting in yet more church court proceedings to stop the spread of Bennett's mischief.

On September 3, 1842, "[A] charge was preferred against Gustavius Hills by Elisha Everett[,] one of the teachers of the Church[,] for illicit intercourse with a certain woman by the name of Mary Clift by which she was with child[,] and for teaching the said Mary Clift that that the heads of the Church practiced such conduct

---

[363] *Nauvoo City and High Council Minutes*, p. 414, all as in original.

[364] *Id.*, pp. 414-415, as in original.

[365] *Id.*, p. 417, as in original.

& that time would come when men would have more wives than one &c"[366]

The next day, September 4, 1842, "Esther Smith gave evidence that [the] defendant[367] told her that it was lawful for people to have illicit intercourse if they only held their peac[e] & that ~~the time would~~ it was agreeable to the practice of some of the leading men or heads of the Church."[368]

More court proceedings were held in an effort to round up those who were involved in this practice. John Bennett, in response to the treatment given him by the church, set out to tell another story where he was a hero and Joseph was the villain. He wrote, lectured and campaigned against Mormonism, first to salvage his reputation, but ultimately as his profession.

Joseph left a record of public and private actions taken in opposing the plural wife system. These included: "I preached in the grove and pronounced a curse upon all adulterers and fornicators, and unvirtuous persons and those who have made use of my name to carry on their iniquitous designs."[369] Then there is the obviously altered Joseph Smith journal for Thursday 5th October 1843, which confirms there was an effort to alter documents to conform to later events and practices:

> (ORIGINAL) Evening at home and walked up and down the street with my scribe. Gave inst[r]uction to try those who were preaching teaching or practicing the doctrin of plurality of wives. on this Law. Joseph forbids it. and the practice ther[e]of— No man shall have but one wife.

> (REVISED) Evening at home and walked up and down the street with my scribe. Gave inst[r]uction to try those who were preaching teaching or practicing the doctrin of plurality of wives. on this law for according to the law i hold the keys of this power in the last days, for there is never but one on earth at a time on whom the power? and the keys are conferred - and I have continually said

---

[366] *Id.*, p. 424, as in original.

[367] Gustavius Hills.

[368] *Id.*, p. 425, as in original.

[369] *WJS*, p. 114, citing *Manuscript History* and *Book of the Law of the Lord*— Joseph Smith (Sermon at the Grove; Apr 10, 1842)

Joseph forbids it. and the practice ther[e]of No man
shall have but one wife at a time unless the Lord
directs otherwise

So it was "off" on October 5, 1843 until someone revised the
content at a later date. Once revised at a later date it was "on" again,
and perhaps retroactively "on" since the original alterations were not
possible to detect until the *Joseph Smith Papers* project made the
original available for public view.[370]

There was a published denunciation of polygamy in February
1844 in the newspaper Joseph edited:

As we have lately been credibly informed, that
an Elder of the Church of Jesus Christ, of Latter-day
Saints, by the name of Hiram Brown, has been
preaching Polygamy, and other false and corrupt
doctrines, in the county of Lapeer, state of Michigan.
This is to notify him and the Church in general, that
he has been cut off from the church, for his iniquity;
and he is further notified to appear at the Special
Conference, on the 6th of April next, to make
answer to these charges.[371]

The Relief Society later put out a more detailed document titled
*A Voice of Innocence from Nauvoo* that offered an even stronger denial of
plural marriage. It was penned by W. W. Phelps at the request of
Joseph Smith. The document was presented to a general meeting of
the church at which Joseph presided in March 1844, only three
months before he was killed:

A vast assembly of Saints met at the Temple of
the Lord at nine o'clock a. m., by a special
appointment of President Joseph Smith, for the
purpose of advancing the progress of the Temple,
&c. The Patriarch, Hyrum Smith, was present; also
of the Twelve Apostles Brigham Young, Heber C.
Kimball, Parley P. Pratt, Orson Pratt, Willard
Richards, Wilford Woodruff, John Taylor, and
George A. Smith; also the temple committee and
about eight thousand Saints....[later in the meeting]

---

[370]http://www.josephsmithpapers.org/paperSummary/history-draft-1-
march-31-december-1843&p=144#!/paperSummary/history-draft-1-march-
31-december-1843&p=143

[371] Joseph Smith & Hyrum Smith, *Times and Seasons* Vol. 5 (February 1, 1844).

an article was also read by W. W. Phelps, entitled, *A Voice of innocence from Nauvoo*, and all the assembly said 'Amen' twice.[372]

Here is the content of that document:

### Virtue Will Triumph.

At four overflowing meetings of the Ladies of Nauvoo, members of the Female Relief Society, (each meeting being composed of different members that all might have the opportunity of expressing their feelings) held at Gen. Smith's large assembly room on Saturdays the 9th and 16th of March 1844. The following preamble and resolutions were read and unanimously adopted at each meeting.

THE VOICE OF INNOCENCE FROM NAUVOO

The corruption of wickedness which manifested itself in such horrible deformity on the trial of O. F. Bostwick last week for slandering President Hyrum Smith and the widows of the city of Nauvoo, has awakened all the kindly feelings of female benevolence, compassion and pity, for the softer sex to spread forth the mantle of charity to shield the characters of the virtuous mothers, wives, and daughters of Nauvoo from the blasting breath and poisonous touch of debauchers, vagabonds and [?]akers, who have jammed themselves into our city to offer strange fire at the shrine of infamy, disgrace, and degradation: as they and their kindred spirits have done in all the great cities throughout the world, corrupting their ways on the earth, and bringing women, poor defenceless women, in wretchedness and ruin.

As such ignoble blood now begins to stain the peacable habitants of the saints, and taint the free air of the only city in the world that pretends to work righteousness in union, as the sine qua non, for happiness, joy, and salvation: and as such ungodly wretches, burning or smarting with the sting of their

---

[372] *DHC* 6:236, p 241.

own shame, have doubtless, transported with them, some of the miserable dupes of their licentousness, for the purpose of defiling the fame of this godly city: mildewing the honesty of our mothers, blasting the chastity of widows and wives, and corrupting the virtue of our unsuspecting daughters, it becomes us, in defence of our rights, for the glory of our fathers, for the honor of our mothers, for the happiness of our husbands, and for the welfare of our dear children, to rebuke such an outrage on the chastity of society: to thwart such a death blow at the hallowed marriage covenant: and to ward off such poisoned daggers from the hearts of our innocent daughters, for the honor of Nauvoo: and write with indellible ink upon every such villain: virtue perditorus! Beware of the wretch! and, so put in every virtuous woman's hand a rod, to scourge such tormentors of domestic felicity, with vengeance through the world: curse the man that preys upon female virtue! curse the man that slanders a woman! Let the righteous indignation of insulted innocence and virtue, spurn him from society: Let the dignity of the mothers of Israel kick the blood thirsty pimp from the pale of social communion. Let the widows and wives who tread in the footsteps of their queenly mother Eve, drive such fag ends of creation, as was Cain, to the land of Nod, and let the timid daughters of Nauvoo dread such CANKER WORMS more than the pestillence that walketh in darkness, and shun them as the serpent on the land and the shark in the sea. My God! My God! is there not female virtue and valor enough in this city to let such men die of the rot: - that the sexton may carry their putrid bodies beyond the limits of the city for food, for vultures, eagles and wolves. Refuse them female courtesy; deny them the pleasure of family correspondence and family intercourse; curse the woman that speaks to such rotten flesh, if she knows who they are; curse the man that will harbor them; and curse the lawyer that will stoop from the dignity

125

of his profession to plead for them; The apologizer is as mean as the murderer!

Female virtue is a pearl of great price, and should glitter in the abodes of men, as in the mansions of bliss, for the glory and honor of him, whose image she bears and whose help meet she is, and every attempt of man to seduce that virtue, is, next to murder, a robbery that cannot be restored.

If woman swerves from the rules of righteousness 'Ruin ensues, reproach and shame; And one false step bedims her fame; In vain the loss she may deplore, In vain renew her life before' With tears she must in anguish be 'Till God says, 'set that captive free'"

Many of the distinguished females of Nauvoo, have waded to their present habituations through persecution, sorrow, and death, robbed and insulted and bereaved of husbands and children by the combined powers, of priests, and spiritual wickedness in high places, but none of these piercing calamities of man touch the heart of woman with such severe poignancy, as the envenomed slander of O.F. Bostwick, that he could take a half bushel of meal, obtain his vile purpose, and get what accommodation he wanted with almost any woman in the city.

Wo to the wretch that can thus follow the blood stained mobbers of Missouri, in their hellish career, and deal his slander about the streets of Nauvoo, as he may imagine with impunity. Wo to the man or lawyer that filthifies himself by advocating such rotten hearted raven's rights, or recommends him to any but the sympathies of Satan.

Has any man a mother in this city? honor says clear such rubbish from her door. Has any many a wife? benevolence whispers, trap such beasts of the field that they may not worry the flock, nor kill the lambs. Has any man a widowed mother? humanity seems to caution him - thy mother is in danger, protect her, from the stench of such carrion. Has any man, daughters? the voice of reason compels him to exclaim: There is a wolf in the path, beware! Has any man, sisters? the blood of his kindred says, evil be to him that evil thinks: and let the whole virtuous female population of the city, with one voice, declare that the seducer of female chastity, the slanderer of female character, or the defamer of the character of the heads of the church, or the canker worms of our husband's peace: the prostitute, their pimps, whether in the character of elite, lawyer, doctor, or cicisbeo, shall have no place in our houses, in our affections, or in our society.

Wherefore,
Resolved unanimous, That Joseph Smith, the Mayor of the city, be tendered our thanks for the able and manly manner in which he defended injured innocence in the late trial of O.F. Bostwick for slandering President Hyrum Smith, and almost all the women of the city.

Resolved unanimously, That we view with unequaled disapprobation and scorn the conduct of any man or woman, whether in word or deed, that reflects dishonor upon the poor persecuted mothers, widows, wives and daughters of the Saints of Nauvoo; they have borne aspersions, slander and hardships enough; forbearance has ceased to be a virtue and retaliation, like the dagger or the bowl, ought to close the lips of such cowardly assassins.

Resolved unanimously, That while we render credence to the doctrines of Paul, that neither the man is without the woman; neither is the woman without the man in the Lord, yet we raise our voices and hands against John C. Bennett's "spiritual wife system," as a grand scheme of profligates to seduce women; and they that harp upon it, wish to make it popular for the convenience of their own cupidity; wherefore, while the marriage bed, undefiled is honorable, let polygamy, bigamy, fornication, adultery, and prostitution, be frowned out of the hearts of honest men to drop into the gulf of fallen nature, 'where the worm dieth not and the fire is not quenched! and let all the saints say, Amen!

EMMA SMITH, Prest.

H. M. Ells, Sec. pro tem

And so in March 1844 plural wives were definitely "off" and decidedly so. None of the Relief Society women in Nauvoo were available any longer.

A month before he was killed Joseph reiterated his opposition to plural wives, equating multiple wives to adultery:

What a thing it is for a man to be accused of committing adultery, and having seven wives, when I can only find one. I am the same man, and as innocent as I was fourteen years ago; and I can prove them all perjurers.[373]

So it was decidedly "off" in the months leading up to his death.

Although Joseph was accused of attempting to seduce Sarah Pratt, Joseph's son interviewed her and published the interview in the RLDS newspaper. Her answer was published after her death in the *Saints Herald*, a newspaper printed by the Reorganized Church of Jesus Christ of Latter Day Saints. Below is the account they published:

Did he ever at such time, or in any other time or place, make improper overtures to you or to proposals of an improper nature? Begging your pardon for the apparent indelicacy of this question. To this Mrs. Pratt replied quietly but firmly, "No. Joseph, your father, never said an improper word to me in his life. He knew better."

Sister Pratt, it has been frequently told that he behaved improperly in your presence, and I have been told that I dare not come to you and ask you about your relations with him, for fear you would tell me things which would be unwelcome to me. "You needn't have no such fear," she repeated, "your father was never guilty of an action or proposal with improper nature in my house, toward me, or in my

---

[373] Joseph Smith *DHC* 6:411, May 26, 1844.

presence, at any time or place. There is no truth in the reports that have been circulated about him in this regard. He was always the Christian gentleman and a noble man."[374]

This adds to the interpretive problem caused by John Bennett. Since he admits he lied to get the confidence of the Mormons, did he also lie when he told the story of Joseph attempting to seduce Sarah Pratt? Likewise, because Bennett's account was first confirmed by Sarah Pratt, (after she was disaffected), does that repair Bennett's account? And for Sarah, did she tell the truth to Joseph Smith III? Did she tell the truth when she later said Bennett was telling the truth about Joseph attempting to seduce her to be one of his spiritual wives? Are these witnesses credible and believable? There are many histories that accept the fact that while Orson Pratt was on a mission to England Joseph Smith approached his wife to be his plural wife. Are they right?

During Joseph's lifetime plural wives was never openly advocated, taught or practiced. If we can trust the copy of Section 132 in the handwriting of Kingsbury as authentic, there are difficulties in harmonizing the document with Joseph's public and private statements from 1842 to 1844. The record is inconclusive, despite the dogmatism of our historians.

Joseph Smith completed his work (he thought) in 1834 when he organized a complementary presidency in Zion. The president was David Whitmer, with counselors William W. Phelps and John Whitmer.[375] Four days following a council electing the new presidency Joseph spoke at another meeting confirming, "if he should now be taken away that he had accomplished the great work which the Lord had laid before him[.]"[376]

He wrote in his journal the following year (1835) that the church's permanent foundation was assured because of the Missouri president, who would take over if he were taken.[377] Unfortunately, in

---

[374] *Saints' Herald*, January 15, 1935, 80.

[375] *JS Papers, Documents Vol. 4: April 1834-September 1835*, p. 90: a transcript of the meeting of "a general Council of High Priests" on July 3, 1834: "It was agreed that David Whitmer should be first President and to be assisted by William W. Phelps and John Whitmer."

[376] See *Id.*, p. 93.

[377] "I had established this church on a permanent foundation when I went to the Missourie and indeed I did so, for if I had been taken away it would have

1838 the successor Whitmer resigned as president in Zion, joined the dissenters and contributed to the agitation that resulted in the Mormon War that began that year. He later organized his own competing church, and when 82 years old published *An Address to All Believers in Christ* retelling the events of 50 years earlier as he recalled them.

Presumably an active dissenter who had not participating in the church for 6 years was disqualified as Joseph's successor upon Joseph's death in 1844.

Another successor was appointed in 1841. Hyrum Smith was given the same status as Joseph by revelation.[378] Although Hyrum was faithful, he died moments before Joseph and left the "successor" unidentified. This was all the more unfortunate because Joseph alone had the power to appoint a successor.[379]

Unfortunate for Mormonism, Brigham Young substituted another answer in a post-martyrdom knee-slapping moment of necessity (which is always the 'mother of invention').[380] But that is another story I have addressed elsewhere.[381]

If there was an original Mormonism, it had an inclusiveness to it that welcomed all truth. Diverse, even opposing views held in good faith, were welcome—even expected.[382] The original would have

---

been enough[.]" (*JS Papers, Journals Vol. 1: 1832-1839*, p. 97.)

[378] Hyrum was to "take upon him the office of Priesthood and Patriarch …whatsoever he shall bind on earth shall be bound in heaven; and whatsoever he shall loose on earth shall be loosed in heaven. And from this time forth I appoint unto him that he may be a prophet, and a seer, and a revelator unto my church, as well as my servant Joseph[.]" (D&C 124:91-94.)

[379] "And this ye shall know assuredly—that there is none other appointed unto you to receive commandments and revelations until he be taken, if he abide in me. But verily, verily, I say unto you, that none else shall be appointed unto this gift except it be through him; for if it be taken from him he shall not have power except to appoint another in his stead." (D&C 43:3-4.)

[380] "'The first thing I thought of' Brigham said in his journal, 'was whether Joseph had taken the keys of the kingdom with him from the earth; brother Orson Pratt sat on my left; we were both leaning back on our chairs. Bringing my hand down on my knee, I said the keys of the kingdom are right here with the Church.'" (*The Complete Discourses of Brigham Young*, Edited by Richard Van Wagoner, (Salt Lake City: Signature Books, 2009), Vol. 1, p. 38, entry of July 16, 1844.)

[381] See *Passing the Heavenly Gift*, pp. 69-95.

welcomed Paul Toscano and Boyd Packer (and it is doubtful Packer would have authority to forcibly exclude Toscano).[383] The original would have welcomed the insights of both Kate Kelly and Dallin Oaks, and allowed their opposing views to be resolved by persuasion and long suffering. The original would have allowed D. Michael Quinn to have continued, unfettered access to the Historical Department archives to mine and publish the sins and excesses of the past. Confessing sins is good for the individual,[384] but it is even better for an institution. An original would not have leaders seeking to hide their sins or gratify their pride, or whose vain ambitions attempt through control, dominion and compulsion[385] to reign with intimidation over a flock that is only kept from the truth because they are not allowed to find it.[386]

In the original, Mormonism's general conferences would look a lot more like a Sunstone Symposium than the uniform and predictable events each April and October. General Conference now serves to remind us of how greatly we are separated from God's authentic voice once echoing in Mormon meetings when Joseph spoke.

We have lost the original. But we do not need to abandon it forever. After all, repentance means to turn to face God again. He is quite willing to speak still.

If James 1:5 were true for Joseph Smith, it should be true for us. We can ask God with real intent, and obtain a like measure of wisdom from on high. Mormonism may have been a briefly lit candle whose flame expired on June 27, 1844. But it left behind a smoldering spark that only needs another generation to breathe enough of the breath of

---

[382] One of the gifts of the Spirit is the "diversity of operations" which belongs to the family of believers. See D&C 46:16. The word "diversity" appears only four times in scripture: as varying "gifts" (1 Cor. 12:4), varying "operations" (1 Cor. 12:6 and D&C 46:16) and diverse "tongues" (1 Cor. 12:28). All these references imply the body of Christ (Church) will be dissimilar—perhaps even spectacular differences among the members. How tragic uniformity has made Mormonism! Being "one" is something "of the heart" and not of the countenance, vocabulary, viewpoint or thought. It means only that we should love one another.

[383] See D&C 121:37, 41-42.

[384] Proverbs 28:3; D&C 58:43.

[385] D&C 121:37.

[386] D&C 123:12.

life to reignite the flame. The breath of the spirit gave life to man originally.[387] It can still restore life.

Mormonism is (or ought to be) a very big religion. Such a faith as that always attracts adherents. We won't get there unless our attitude returns to something like Joseph's in the original Mormonism. Here is what he wrote about how broadly tolerant we ought to be in our religious views in his letter from Liberty Jail:

> [W]e ought always to be aware of those prejudices which sometimes so strangely present themselves, and are so congenial to human nature, against our friends, neighbors, and brethren of the world, who choose to differ from us in opinion and in matters of faith. Our religion is between us and our God. Their religion is between them and their God.

Joseph died with a clear conscience.[388] Too few Mormons since him have done likewise. A clear conscience requires us to live by God's voice, not man's. To have a clear conscience requires us to know we are doing God's will.[389]

Somehow LDS Mormonism has tolerated marital misconduct, adultery, concealing criminal misconduct by "lying for the Lord" to evade Federal investigations, aggregating wealth while neglecting the poor, exercising control to abrogate follower's consciences under the false claim it is the right of church leaders to do so. It has abandoned priestly adoptions, denounced eternal progression, de-canonized *Lectures on Faith* (without a vote of the members), and hidden in shame their use of church finances. It recently has stretched LDS "sustaining" into an oath-like obligation binding on LDS members to further subjugate them to the hierarchy.[390] LDS Mormonism has determined truth can be sometimes "unhelpful" to it. These deviations have happened as modern LDS Mormonism yet

---

[387] Gen. 2:7.

[388] See D&C 135:4.

[389] *Lecture Third*, ¶5 explains faith is based on "an actual knowledge that the course of life which he is pursuing, is according to [God's] will."

[390] Russell Nelson, *Sustaining the Prophets*, October 2014 General Conference. The approach advocated by Nelson enforces authoritarian Mormonism contrary to D&C 121:34-38.

claims Joseph as its founder. Modern Mormonism isn't—in any of the present forms. It has become something far deviant from the original, and as this Sunstone Conference shows, its deviations are metastasizing.

Joseph dreamt while in Carthage Jail, the night before his murder, the following:

> I was back in Kirtland, Ohio, and thought I would take a walk out by myself, and view my old farm, which I found grown up with weeds and brambles, and altogether bearing evidence of neglect and want of culture. I went into the barn, which I found without floor or doors, with the weather-boarding off, and was altogether in keeping with the farm.
>
> While I viewed the desolation around me, and was contemplating how it might be recovered from the curse upon it, there came rushing into the barn a company of furious men, who commenced to pick a quarrel with me.
>
> The leader of the party ordered me to leave the barn and farm, stating it was none of mine, and that I must give up all hope of ever possessing it.
>
> I told him the farm was given me, and although I had not had any use of it for some time back, still I had not sold it, and according to the righteous principles it belonged to me.
>
> He then grew furious and began to rail upon me, and threaten me, and said it never did belong to me.
>
> I then told him that I did not think it worth contending about, that I had no desire to live upon it in its present state, and if thought he had a better right I would not quarrel with him about it but leave; but my assurance that I would not trouble him at present did not seem to satisfy him, and he seemed determined to quarrel with me, and threatened me with the destruction of my body.
>
> While he was thus engaged, pouring out his bitter words upon me, a rabble rushed in and nearly filled the barn, drew out their knives, and began to

quarrel among themselves for the premises, and for a moment forgot me, at which time I took the opportunity to walk out of the barn about up to my ankles in mud.

While I was a little distance from the barn, I heard them screeching and screaming in a very distressed manner, as it appeared they had engaged in a general fight with their knives. While they were thus engaged, the vision ended.[391]

We now can see the fulfillment of Joseph's final vision about his "farm." The original is now the property of angry men, and those who believe as Joseph are no longer welcome. The original can only be recovered in the same way it began: By God's direct involvement. If an "original" returns, it will add elements that recover, finish, and fulfill—not just add upon, but greatly expand, and yet remain entirely consistent with, the original.

In the current environment of "Many Mormonisms," the original will likely be unnoticed, or dismissed as merely another schismatic breakaway from the party of angry men now occupying "Joseph's farm." But if the original of Mormonism was founded on God's voice,[392] then God's voice is abundant enough to recreate what is yet to be fully created.[393] That is, of course, assuming there is ever again someone foolish enough to hear and heed His voice.[394]

---

[391] *TPJS*, pp. 393-394, edited to remove insertions about the church that do not belong in the account.

[392] God's work in the restoration followed (and will yet follow) the pattern from "the beginning" when "God created the heaven and the earth:" He spoke: "And God said, Let there be light: and there was light." (Gen. 1:1, 3.) All His great works involve Him speaking and thereby causing/creating: "My works are without end, and also my words, for they never cease." (Moses 1:4.)

[393] Borrowing from The Doobie Brothers, *What a Fool Believes*: "Trying hard to recreate what had yet to be created once in her life."

[394] As the Apostle Paul put it: "Are they ministers of Christ? (I speak as a fool) I am more[.]" (2 Cor. 11:23.) "We are fools for Christ's sake." (I Cor. 4:10.) "For ye see your calling, brethren, how that not many wise men after the flesh, not many mighty, not many noble are called[.]" (I Cor. 1:26.)

This paper is only a survey of the many ways in which Mormonism was in a constant state of development while Joseph lived. Other topics could be added and would show the same evidence of transition. Likewise a great deal more could be said about the prophesied destiny for the restoration. A "dispensation of fullness of times" will not reach a conclusion without the full return back to the original religion of Adam and the patriarchs.

**Chapter 4: Other Sheep Indeed**
By Denver C. Snuffer, Jr. © 2017

The theme of the 2017 Sunstone Symposium was "The Least of These: Embracing All." The Symposium was intended to examine the topic: "Exploring how Mormonism and the Restoration address the invitation of Matthew 25: 40, 'Inasmuch as ye have done it unto one of the least of these my brethren, ye have done it unto me'."

The theme inspired me to wax scriptural, and do a little preaching as part of my contribution:

Mormonism[395] announced in its founding book of scripture that it is an incomplete, markedly unfinished religion searching for more truth to achieve its destiny. The completion is to be accomplished primarily by two means: restoring lost scripture and continuing revelation. But even the concept of "continuing revelation" has been institutionally curtailed. The only institutionally authorized source for revelation is a single leader. When he is not gifted with that capacity, the concept of "continuing revelation" is given lip service without any substantive proof. For example, minimal organizational adjustments in missionary ages are extolled as "revelation"[396] rather than merely a policy change.

Of all faiths, Mormonism has the greatest canonical incentive to search for and embrace truth known to others. The "keystone" of Mormonism is the Book of Mormon.[397] That book alerts its readers

---

[395] When using the word "Mormonism" in this essay I intend to include every denomination or individual who accepts the Book of Mormon as part of their faith, and not any particular group or institution.

[396] In the Press Conference held during General Conference Elder Jeffrey Holland called the policy change "inspired" and "revelatory." He explained, "God is hastening His work." See Mormon News Room video at 7:02, 8:00 and 14:20, respectively. (Available on YouTube under the title, *Press Conference for New Missionary Service Age Requirements*.) Elder Dale Evans of the LDS Seventy categorized the change as revelation, explaining: "'The Lord has promised that revelation would come line upon line and precept upon precept,' Elder Evans said. 'The implication is that when one revelation is given, the next revelation is needed.'" See, *One year later: Looking back at the worldwide impact of a prophet's announcement* (Deseret News, October 3, 2013).

[397] Joseph Smith said: "I told the brethren that the Book of Mormon was the

that there are many others from vastly different places with vastly different scriptures who are nonetheless Christ's sheep. Book of Mormon readers are expected to search for, welcome and learn from them. In contrast, institutional Mormonism of all stripes confine trustworthy new religious ideas to their authorized leaders.

Early in the text we learn that our faith, like our scriptures, is unfinished, and to anticipate a flood of additional sacred texts to help remove our ignorance. The portion of the Book of Mormon translated by Joseph Smith is carefully censored, with its greater content withheld.[398]

2 Nephi 29:11-12 states: *For I command all men, both in the east and in the west, and in the north, and in the south, and in the islands of the sea, that they shall write the words which I speak unto them; ...* Obviously the Gods of Mormonism[399] view Their role as all-inclusive. The entire world and all mankind belong to Them.[400] Their global audience has been received and recorded sacred words directly from the Gods' "one" mouth.[401] We have no way to define the extent to which that has happened. Nor do we have any concept of the number of sacred records that exist somewhere among unknown others, nor any idea what truths they were given that we lack.

Mormonism cannot, or at least should not, consider itself the exclusive possessor of THE sacred canon or that there is only one canon containing the Gods' teachings. There are words from heaven spread throughout our world by the deliberate planting of the Gods.

Continuing, *for out of the books which shall be written I will judge the world, every man according to their works, according to that which is written.*

---

most correct of any book on earth, and the keystone of our religion, and a man would get nearer to God by abiding by its precepts, than by any other book." (*DHC*, 4:461).

[398] See, e.g., 1 Ne. 14:25, 27; Ether 4:5-6; 3 Ne. 19:32-34; 3 Ne. 26:7-9, 11, among other places.

[399] Given Joseph Smith's declaration concerning the "plurality of Gods" (*DHC* 6:473-479) and the material in Abraham Chapter 4, I am compelled to use the plural. Mormonism's pantheon resembles ancient Egypt's more than it does post-Deuteronomist Judaism. For an interesting comparison of Bible wisdom texts with Egyptian literature see Patrick Clark, Wisdom Literature and the question of priority—*Solomon's Proverbs or Amenemope's Instructions*, Journal of Creation, Vol. 26, No. 2, (2012) pp. 50-56.

[400] Israel was scattered globally to spread covenant status far and wide. (See 2 Ne. 20:20-22.)

[401] It is the unity of purpose and understanding that makes the Gods "one".

These "books" hold terrible importance for Mormons because we are going to be judged by the Gods based on a comparison between our "works" and "that which is written." With such a warning we Mormons ought to be humble about our claims to know more than other faiths. We should be modest in thinking we are especially graced by the Gods' words and should be anxious to scour the globe to discover the sacred texts of other cultures. In humility, we should invite them to share the truths they value most with us because we have shown that we will respect what they regard as sacred.

To clarify this further the record continues, *For behold, I shall speak unto the Jews and they shall write it; and I shall also speak unto the Nephites and they shall write it; and I shall also speak unto the other tribes of the house of Israel, which I have led away, and they shall write it; ...* So far this describes a welcome Judeo-Christian boundary because the ancient Israelites are the backbone of the Gods' dealings with mankind. The Lost Ten Tribes continued to compose scripture, and their records will in time be recovered.

This passage continues by including yet others who are disconnected from any disclosed connection to Israel: *and I shall also speak unto all nations of the earth and they shall write it.*

Who? When? What was said?

"All nations of the earth" is broad enough to raise the troubling possibility that the Gods have spoken to others in India, Japan and China - to the peoples of Persia, Africa, and Native peoples of the Americas, Hawaii, Polynesia, and Australia. The Jaredite prophet, identified as "the brother of Jared," had some of the greatest revelation in all history. He lived many centuries before Abraham, and therefore before there were Israelites. We know Egypt was founded "seeking earnestly to imitate that order established by the first fathers in the first generation, in the days of the first patriarchal reign, even in the reign of Adam[.]"[402]

If we take the Book of Mormon seriously, the ecumenicalism of the Gods may have no recognizable or comprehensible limits. The Gods of Mormonism are far more pantheistic than Trinitarian. What a cruel embarrassment that proves to be for any sect that proselytizes primarily among other Christian denominations. Imagining Gods who speak to everyone is troubling enough, but for the Gods to expect Mormons to give high regard, even canonical credibility to the

---

[402] Abr. 1:26.

records of these truly "others" begins to buckle the knees and mangle the mantras of today's Mormons.

An unfortunate Mormon truism is the mistaken idea that we have a better and more complete religion than *all* others. 'WE have the most recent revelation, because the Gods spoke last to us' (...uh, well, so far as we know). Therefore, we can be prone to think of "the least of these" as all others who have failed to embrace Mormonism. This paper explores the possibility that we have vastly overrated the scope of our religion, and underrated our ignorance. Perhaps we have *no* reason to ever consider those outside of Mormonism as "less than" Mormons, or "the least" worthy before our Gods.

This humbling revelation of the Gods' universal attention to all mankind is reinforced by Christ's words to the Nephites at Bountiful. He declared to them in 3 Ne. 16:1-4: *I have other sheep, which are not of this land, neither of the land of Jerusalem, neither in any parts of that land round about whither I have been to minister.* His declaration was every bit as disorienting to the Nephites as was His mention of "other sheep" to the Jews. Both the Bible and Book of Mormon make it clear that bodies of sheep who have the Great Shepherd standing before them are perplexed at the idea that He has yet others He loves as much as them. Are there no favorites? The sheep probably considered, at least passingly, "You MUST love us best because you're here visiting us, right?" But any thought that audience was special is dashed by the Lord's next sentence:

*For they of whom I speak are they who have not as yet heard my voice; neither have I at any time manifested myself unto them. But I have received a commandment of the Father that I shall go unto them, and that they shall hear my voice, and shall be numbered among my sheep, that there may be one fold and one shepherd; therefore I go to show myself unto them.* Christ was interested in unifying His sheep. He sought for "one" fold that followed only Him. There is no "Number One" fold among them. No upper class, or special distinct body towering above others.

Our gentile culture is stratified. We divide into haves and have-nots, upper class and lower class, winners and losers. Everything is ranked, from sports teams to television shows, mileage to price-per-ounce. We WANT to have comparisons made: to be more and have more. That is one of the most persistent character flaws of 'gentileness.'

Gentile Mormons were not at Bountiful when the Lord appeared and taught the Nephites. But we would like to have at least a derivative advantage by assuming the Nephites were more special than all the other sheep. We hunger for prominence, and our ambitions extend into all things, even the Gods' regard for us.[403] We reason that the Nephites were apparently visited first after the Jews. And the Jews killed Him,[404] so really the Nephites were the first *worthy* audience and therefore more special. And this matters because we gentiles are the ones to whom the Book of Mormon was given.[405] So we are sort of first and therefore more better, or Mormon.[406] And, *ipso facto*, all others are less to the Gods.

That line of reasoning comes to naught when we realize Christ's visit to the Nephites was over eleven months after His crucifixion.[407] He ministered for 40 days around Jerusalem after His resurrection,[408]

---

[403] Luke 22:25: "And he said unto them, The kings of the Gentiles exercise lordship over them; and they that exercise authority upon them are called benefactors."

[404] 2 Ne. 10:3.

[405] The Title Page of the Book of Mormon explains, "to come forth in due time by way of the Gentile[.]"

[406] Joseph Smith wrote a letter stating: "I may safely say that the word Mormon stands independent of the learning and wisdom of this generation.—Before I give a definition, however, to the word, let me say that the Bible in its widest sense, means *good*; for the Savior says according to the gospel of John, 'I am the *good* shepherd;' and it will not be beyond the common use of terms, to say that good is among the most important in use, and though known by various names in different languages, still its meaning is the same, and is ever in opposition to *bad*. We say from the Saxon, *good*; the Dane, *god*; the Goth, *goda*; the German, *gut*; the Dutch, *goed*; the Latin, *bonus*; the Greek, *kalos*; the Hebrew , *tob*; and the Egyptian, *mon*. Hence, with the addition of more, or the contraction, *mor*, we have the word MORMON; which means, literally, *more good*." (*Times and Seasons*, 4:194 (15 May 1843).)

[407] Christ's death was accompanied by a great storm in the Americas. The dating of that storm, and therefore His crucifixion, is given in 3 Ne. 8:5: "in the thirty and fourth year, in the first month, on the fourth day of the month, there arose a great storm[.]" His appearance to the Nephites took place at the end of that year, as dated in 3 Ne. 10:18-19: "And it came to pass that in the ending of the thirty and fourth year, behold, I will show unto you that the people of Nephi who were spared, and also those who had been called Lamanites, who had been spared, did have great favors shown unto them, and great blessings poured out upon their heads, insomuch that soon after the ascension of Christ into heaven he did truly manifest himself unto them—Showing his body unto them, and ministering unto them[.]"

but He had nearly eleven months to visit undisclosed other sheep before the people of the Book of Mormon. We have no basis for thinking we have the record of those the Lord visited first, after His resurrection. For all we know we have the record of those he visited tenth, maybe eleventh. If He took as long with each group as He took with the Nephites, He had time to visit with dozens of other unidentified flocks of His sheep.[409]

Following His resurrection, as Christ visited with the Jews and Nephites, none of them had enough curiosity about "other sheep" to inquire about them. The account continues, *And I command you that ye shall write these sayings after I am gone, that if it so be that my people at Jerusalem, they who have seen me and been with me in my ministry, do not ask the Father in my name, that they may receive a knowledge of you by the Holy Ghost, and also of the other tribes whom they know not of, that these sayings which ye shall write shall be kept and shall be manifested unto the Gentiles, ...* It is perhaps a good thing Christ commanded them to "write these sayings" so we have a record clarifying that "other sheep" are indeed people completely out of view from any scripture in our possession. They exist. They were visited by Christ. They were taught by Him. They recorded what He taught. And we know nothing about any of it, apart from Christ confirming that He did visit and minister to scattered bodies of other sheep post-resurrection. He wanted them to become "one" and understand "plain and precious things"[410] that have been lost from our present, limited version of scripture.

What if they are also all gods to whom the word of God has been given?[411] What if the Gods intend to spread knowledge of how to attain divinity among all people?[412] That would indeed be a task worthy of the Gods!

---

[408] Acts 1:3: "To whom also he shewed himself alive after his passion by many infallible proofs, being seen of them forty days, and speaking of the things pertaining to the kingdom of God[.]"

[409] Yet Christ said He would continue His post-resurrection ministry even after the Nephites by going to visit "lost tribes of Israel." 3 Ne. 17:4. Did He visit with some, but not all, before the Nephites? Did He visit with non-Israelite "sheep" during the first eleven months, and put off visits with the Ten Tribes until after the Nephites? His statement does not clarify, but instead emphasizes our ignorance of that part of Christ's work.

[410] See, e.g., 1 Ne. 13:28.

[411] John 10:34-36.

141

Consider that for a moment. Have we gentile Mormons been told of the Gods' other sheep for some important reason? If so, is it to alert us that we are no more special, nor in any greater possession of Gods' words, than many others who have been scattered around the world and are known to the Gods, but unidentified to us? Is it to make us more careful about how we regard strangers? Ought it to suggest there are other religious equals in the world? May it suggest there are perhaps religious superiors in the world? In other words, have we received news of other sheep to help keep Mormons humble?

If these words from Christ are not enough to make us cautious about dismissing others, in the Book of Alma there is another reminder of how the Gods deal equally with all mankind. Alma 29:8 states, *For behold, the Lord doth grant unto all nations, of their own nation and tongue, to teach his word, yea, in wisdom, all that he seeth fit that they should have;* ... The Lord is concerned about "all nations" and not merely Israelites in their scattered condition.[413] Each nation, in its own tongue, has been given a portion of His teaching. It is measured according to what He "seeth fit that they should have." I do not believe this means that 'while God gives everyone something, we have the most.' I think it instead means, 'everyone is remembered by God, and when you close down revelation, you get less—humble people get more.' This more probable meaning is suggested by Alma 12:10 which explains, *he that will harden his heart, the same receiveth the lesser portion of the word; and he that will not harden his heart, to him is given the greater portion of the word, until it is given unto him to know the mysteries of God, until he know them in full.* It is abundantly clear that Mormons do not know the mysteries of God in full. The farther back we look in human history the more appears to have been lost. Earlier stages, including the patriarchal era, knew God and therefore understood His path better. How else would Enoch and Melchizedek have achieved their heavenly breakthroughs? Like mankind, institutional Mormonism continually atrophies, knowing less and less, year by year.

---

[412] Moses 1:39.

[413] The word "nations" generally means the scattered tribes of Israel. However, given that the lost tribes forgot their identity, intermarried with other groups, and are now unidentifiable, the term should be applied more broadly to include all nations of the world. Israel's blood is likely to now be found among all nations. See Abr. 2:11 "all the families of the earth" are to be blessed by "the literal seed of thy [Abraham's] body."

However significantly this may impact the truth-claims and arrogance of Mormonism, we must at least allow for the possibility that there are "other sheep" who are much better informed than are any of us Mormons.

The Alma 12 material helps clarify the remaining statement in Alma 29:8: *therefore we see that the Lord doth counsel in wisdom, according to that which is just and true.* The Gods' wise counsel does not regulate dispensing truth on things external to us, but on what is internal to us. We determine whether we have hard hearts or open hearts.[414] One of the ways to determine if our hearts are open and not hard is the degree to which we regard those who are "other," not only with respect and charity, but also curiosity.

Mormon revelation helpfully defines knowledge of the Gods' mysteries as "riches."[415] That definition helps explain a prophecy about the coming return of other sheep. Newly awakened dormant prophets in the north countries will lead scattered flocks to the boundaries of the everlasting hills. They will bring with them "rich treasures unto the children of Ephraim" who will welcome them.[416] This will not merely be a reunion, but an exchange of treasured wisdom, or in other words revelation, between those who have preserved sacred knowledge. That reunion, however, will depend on a body of believing Ephraimites established in the everlasting hills that will welcome such riches. These prophetically described people must be humble enough to be taught, and willing to appreciate sacred information from outside.

---

[414] Anciently the "heart" was considered the seat of understanding rather than emotion. Therefore an "open heart" belonged to the seeker, the asker, the knocker on the door. (See, e.g., Matt. 7:7-11.)

[415] D&C 11:7: "Seek not for riches but for wisdom; and, behold, the mysteries of God shall be unfolded unto you, and then shall you be made rich. Behold, he that hath eternal life is rich."

[416] D&C 133:26-32: "And they who are in the north countries shall come in remembrance before the Lord; and their prophets shall hear his voice, and shall no longer stay themselves; and they shall smite the rocks, and the ice shall flow down at their presence. ..And they shall bring forth their rich treasures unto the children of Ephraim, my servants. And the boundaries of the everlasting hills shall tremble at their presence. And there shall they fall down and be crowned with glory, even in Zion, by the hands of the servants of the Lord, even the children of Ephraim."

Think of Mormonism more expansively and you may begin to share its founder's vision for the faith. Joseph Smith explained to the editor of the Chicago Democrat that Mormons "believe in being honest, true, chaste, benevolent, virtuous and in doing good to all men."[417] Joseph's list compares favorably with the five traditional Buddhist vows of non-harm to others, truthfulness, non-theft from others, sexual propriety and avoiding intoxicants. Buddha confronted the issues of life by segregating our challenges into "the truth of suffering." Life is filled with suffering from birth until death. Struggling vainly to relieve ourselves from suffering causes us yet more suffering.

To understand our suffering we need to recognize the true "cause of suffering." The cause is found in our desires, appetites and passions. We cause our suffering by what we seek.

This leads to the way to "cease suffering" by forsaking our desires. Or, in a rather Buddhist mantra found in the Mormon temple ceremony, our "desires, appetites and passions are to be kept within the bounds the Lord has prescribed." Buddha would welcome the Mormon temple mantra as part of the third great truth.

Buddha offers us a final solution found in the noble path: the right view, right thought, right speech, right behavior, right livelihood, right effort, right mindfulness and right concentration. Or, if you are a Mormon, the 13th Article of Faith covers similar ground using different language. Apparently all truth **can** be circumscribed into one great whole.

So are the Buddhists in possession of truths Mormons ought to consider acquiring? Do they have sacred texts they have guarded for generations that will be brought to the attention of Mormons only if we show enough respect and restraint so that their owners share their pearls with us? Does our swine-like arrogance and conceit[418] prevent them from casting their most valuable pearls our way?

Why aren't people from around the world eager to teach Mormons? What would it be like if Mormons sent out missionaries to inquire if others had any great truths to share with us? We cannot learn anything new when the only sound in the conversation is our own voice. Mormons are a very hard audience, hard of both head and

---

[417] Taken from Joseph Smith's letter to John Wentworth in which he quotes the Apostle Paul.

[418] See, e.g., 3 Ne. 14:6; Matt. 7:6 where Jesus advised by the Jews and Nephites against sharing sacred truths with the unworthy and unappreciative.

heart. Most Mormons "know the church is true" and so what else could possibly matter to them? It calls to mind Hugh Nibley's observations about BYU's students:

> Our search for knowledge should be ceaseless, which means that it is open-ended, never resting on laurels, degrees, or past achievements. "If we get puffed up by thinking that we have much knowledge, we are apt to get a contentious spirit," and what is the cure? "Correct knowledge is necessary to cast out that spirit." The cure for inadequate knowledge is "ever more light and knowledge." But who is going to listen patiently to correct knowledge if he thinks he has the answers already? "There are a great many wise men and women too in our midst who are too wise to be taught; therefore they must die in their ignorance." "I have tried for a number of years to get the minds of the Saints prepared to receive the things of God; but we frequently see some of them . . . [that] will fly to pieces like glass as soon as anything comes that is contrary to their traditions: they cannot stand the fire at all . . . . [If I] go into an investigation into anything, that is not contained in the Bible . . . I think there are so many over-wise men here, that they would cry 'treason' and put me to death." But, he asks, "why be so certain that you comprehend the things of God, when all things with you are so uncertain?" True knowledge never shuts the door on more knowledge, but zeal often does. One thinks of the dictum: "We are not seeking for truth at the BYU; we have the truth!" So did Adam and Abraham have the truth, far greater and more truth than what we have, and yet the particular genius of each was that he was constantly "seeking for greater light and knowledge."[419]

---

[419] See, *Zeal Without Knowledge*, originally published in Dialogue: Journal of Mormon Thought, Summer 1978, subsequently republished in *Nibley on the Timely and the Timeless* (Salt Lake: Deseret Book, 1978).

Think about the impression we have made upon the Native Americans with our traditional Christian rivalries and contentions. It was Christian behavior that provoked Nez Perce Chief Joseph to declare: *We do not want schools: They will teach us to have churches. We do not want churches: They will teach us to quarrel about God. We do not want to learn that. We may quarrel with men sometimes about things on this earth, but we never quarrel about God. We do not want to learn that.* Mormons have not distinguished themselves as being any more tolerant or interested in learning Native American wisdom than the contentious general rank of Christians out of which Mormonism emerged.

I have been greatly impressed with Hinduism. There is a significant overlap in beliefs shared by Mormons and Hindus. But it would be almost impossible to have the average Mormon-in-the-pew acknowledge such overlapping beliefs. Many Mormons won't investigate to discover truth if it isn't correlated and approved by the top leaders. Institutional Mormons trust leaders to tell them everything worthy of notice. Their leaders, however, demonstrate every six months just how utterly incomplete and superficial their command of the restoration gospel remains.

Hinduism teaches, *The knowing Self is not born; It does not die. It has not sprung from anything; nothing has sprung from It. Birthless, eternal, everlasting, and ancient, It is not killed when the body is killed.*[420] This compares interestingly with Joseph Smith's statement found in D&C 93:29: *Man was also in the beginning with God. Intelligence, or the light of truth was not created or made, neither indeed can be.*[421] There may be important potential Hindu contributions on the topic of the eternal nature of man's existence that could be of worth to Mormons—if we did not regard them as deluded pagans. Rather than invite a Hindu over to listen to our family home evening lesson, we may obtain greater benefit by asking them over to teach us a lesson.

Long before the Sermon on the Mount taught us to bless those who curse us, and do good for those who hate us,[422] The Dhammapada taught, *Let us live in joy, never hating those who hate us.*[423]

---

[420] S. Radhakrishnan, *The Principal Upanishads*, Katha 1.2.18, (New York: Harper, 1994) p. 73.

[421] See also, Abraham 3:18.

[422] Matt. 5:44.

[423] *The Dhammapada* is a collection of Buddha's sayings in verse form and is considered one of the earliest texts for the faith.

And when Christ said in that same Sermon on the Mount: *And why beholdest thou the* **mote** *that is in thy brother's eye, but considerest not the* **beam** *that is in thine own eye?*[424] Several centuries earlier the writings of Buddha put it this way: *Do not give your attention to what others do or fail to do; give it to what you do or fail to do.* What higher light illuminated Buddha when he spoke these words? Was it the same light that illuminated our Lord? Well, our Mormon scripture puts all light and truth into one, singular source for this world. That source is God the Son.[425]

Consider the very ecumenical nature of the following revelation given to Joseph Smith: *For you shall live by every word that proceedeth forth from the mouth of God. For the word of the Lord is truth, and whatsoever is truth is light, and whatsoever is light is Spirit, even the Spirit of Jesus Christ. And the Spirit giveth light to every man that cometh into the world; and the Spirit enlighteneth every man through the world, that hearkeneth to the voice of the Spirit.*[426] Notice this is without any restriction on who can receive the light of the Spirit. "Every man that cometh into the world" receives equally. There is no individual, in any corner of the world, who does not have equal access to obtain "truth" and "light" from that same source, who is Jesus Christ. If any soul in any age hearkens, or listens and follows the "voice of the Spirit," they are in communication with Jesus Christ. To them He bestows light.

Compare the following sample of Biblical Proverbs with corresponding quotes from Buddha:

Proverbs 23:7 – *For as a man thinketh in his heart, so is he.*

The Dhammapada – *We become what we think.*

Proverbs 15:1– *A soft answer turneth away wrath.*

The Dhammapada – *Speak quietly to everyone, and they too will be gentle in their speech.*

Proverbs 16:32 – *He that is slow to* **anger** *is better than the mighty; and he that ruleth his spirit than he that taketh a city.*

The Dhammapada – *One who conquers himself is greater than another who conquers a thousand times a thousand men on the battlefield.*

The Gods of Mormonism literally mean it when they proclaim, *he doeth nothing save it be plain unto the children of men; and he inviteth them all to come unto him and partake of his goodness; and he denieth none that come unto*

---

[424] Matt. 7:3.

[425] See D&C 84:45-46; 88:6-13; 93:2, 9-10.

[426] D&C 84:44-46.

*him, black and white, bond and free, male and female; and he remembereth the heathen; and all are alike unto God, both Jew and Gentile.*[427] All, even those swarthy heathens, are included within the ambit of the Mormon Gods' concern. They speak through the Spirit the same truths to all mankind and have done so since the beginning of creation. To Mormons the Gods declare: *I am no respecter of persons.*[428] To the Hindus the Gods declare: *none are less dear to me and none are more dear.*[429] Both the Mormon and Hindu Gods respect all mankind equally.

At one time the account in Genesis read: *This is my work, to my glory, to bring to pass the immortality and eternal life of man.*[430] The Gods of Mormonism take seriously their commitment to the eternal advancement of mankind. That means ALL mankind, including the heathen, and none are above others.

This raises the question of "chosenness" of the Gods' special people. Israel, after all, was at one point "chosen" by the Gods as Their special people. But that does not mean what we think it means. Being "chosen" means we are put on display as either the faithful servant, elevating others, or the unwise steward who is condemned, beaten with a rod,[431] and made the display of Divine ire.

Christ explained He was sent to serve, not to be served. Taoism makes the same observation about how "chosen" ones are to demonstrate their "chosenness" in words that parallel the Lord's.

The Lord:– *If any man desire to be first, the same shall be last of all, and servant of all.*[432]

Tao Te Ching: – *If the sage wants to be above the people, in his words, he must put himself below them; If he wishes to be before the people, in his person, he must stand behind them.*[433]

The Lord:– *For whosoever exalteth himself shall be abased; and he that humbleth himself shall be exalted.*[434]

---

[427] 2 Ne. 26:33.

[428] D&C 38:16.

[429] The Bhagvad Gita.

[430] This was the earliest version of the language.

[431] See, e.g., Heb. 12:5-11; Rev. 3:19.

[432] Mark 9:35

[433] The Tao Te Ching is a fundamental text to Taoism. Its authorship and date of origin are debated and uncertain but is known to date back at least two millennia.

[434] Luke 14:11

Tao Te Ching – *The unyielding and mighty shall be brought low; the soft, supple, and delicate will be set above.*

The Lord:– *Give, and it shall be given unto you; good measure, pressed down, and shaken together, and running over, shall men give into your bosom.*[435]

Tao Te Ching – *The sage does not hoard. The more he does for others, the more he has himself; The more he gives to others, the more his own bounty increases.*

Likewise the Mohawk wisdom: *A good chief gives, he does not take.*

Like Taoism, quotes from what Christ taught also have parallels in Hindu teachings:

The Lord – *[H]e that loseth his life for my sake shall find it.*[436]

The Bhagavad Gita – *Through selfless service, you will always be fruitful and find the fulfillment of your desires: this is the promise of the Creator.*

The Lord – *If ye love me, keep my commandments. Abide in me . . . . If ye keep my commandments, ye shall abide in my love.*[437]

The Bhagavad Gita – *[T]hose who worship me with love live in me, and I come to life in them.*

Interesting comparisons can be made between the Hindu belief in "karma" and the Mormon teaching of "pre-existence." Karma includes the belief that what was done (or not done) in both this and previous states of existence will determine a person's condition now and in the future existence. Whatever blessings or burdens you encounter are of your own creation by your deeds. Your suffering is merited and deserved. But by doing well, acting justly, and showing kindness you can deserve to inherit a better existence in the next state.

Mormonism includes the declaration that what we experience now and in the future is based on our heed and diligence to the Gods' pathway.[438] While the Hindu karma has a robust body of teaching, Mormonism's explanation of pre-earth events is spartan: The spirits

---

[435] Luke 6:38.

[436] Matthew 10:39.

[437] John 14:15; 15:4,10.

[438] "Whatever principle of intelligence we attain unto in this life, it will rise with us in the resurrection. And if a person gains more knowledge and intelligence in this life through his diligence and obedience than another, he will have so much the advantage in the world to come There is a law, irrevocably decreed in heaven before the foundations of this world, upon which all blessings are predicated—And when we obtain any blessing from God, it is by obedience to that law upon which it is predicated." D&C 130:18-21.

of all mankind lived as separate personalities before birth.[439] This world was planned before it was created and people were assigned roles to fulfill in this creation. Some souls were more noble and great than others.[440] Prophets were chosen to have a role to "rule" or to teach in this lifetime.[441] Christ was chosen to be the Savior of mankind in the expected event they fell from grace and required saving.[442] Lucifer rebelled and others followed him.[443] All souls were free to make choices before coming to this stage of creation.

We can infer from these few, settled Mormon ideas that all our choices made before this creation mattered and affect us here and now. Likewise, all choices we make now will follow us into the hereafter and affect things there.

Both the Hindu teaching of karma and the Mormon teaching of "judgment" make us, not God, responsible for the outcome of eternity. Joseph Smith said plainly, "A man is his own tormenter and his own condemner. ...The torment of disappointment in the mind of man is as exquisite as a lake burning with fire and brimstone."[444] In the most expressive description of God's judgment in Mormon scripture, God is doing nothing to cause the man's suffering. Man is feeling the "torment of disappointment" Joseph described.[445] Similarly, karma puts all responsibility for all consequences on the

---

[439] D&C 93:29-30.

[440] Abraham 3:21-22.

[441] *Id.*, v. 23.

[442] *Id.*, v. 27; Alma 12:25, 30; Moses 5:57.

[443] Abraham 3:28. Rev. 12:4; D&C 76:25-27.

[444] *TPJS*, p. 357 (2006 leather bound edition).

[445] "[W]hen the Lord shall come, yea, even that great day when the earth shall be rolled together as a scroll, and the elements shall melt with fervent heat, yea, in that great day when ye shall be brought to stand before the Lamb of God—then will ye say that there is no God? Then will ye longer deny the Christ, or can ye behold the Lamb of God? Do ye suppose that ye shall dwell with him under a consciousness of your guilt? Do ye suppose that ye could be happy to dwell with that holy Being, when your souls are racked with a consciousness of guilt that ye have ever abused his laws? Behold, I say unto you that ye would be more miserable to dwell with a holy and just God, under a consciousness of your filthiness before him, than ye would to dwell with the damned souls in hell. For behold, when ye shall be brought to see your nakedness before God, and also the glory of God, and the holiness of Jesus Christ, it will kindle a flame of unquenchable fire upon you." (Mormon 9:2-4.)

choices freely made by mankind. God is immune from responsibility for our self-inflicted fate. The Shawnee tribe also believed, *Each person is his own judge*. Egyptians conceived of a death interview, wherein the individual's heart was weighed to determine where they would go next.

How much might Mormons yet discover if we are open to learn! The truth is or should be our goal.

We fear what we do not understand. Mormons derive security from knowing we are better informed about the Gods than others. No one likes the idea of being surprised by failure because we were too ignorant to avoid a cataclysm. Particularly if our failure is because we thought we understood what was on the test, but in fact never studied what we were being tested on. (That is an old high school nightmare many of us share.)

John the Beloved explained the relationship between two opposing forces: *There is no fear in love; but perfect love casteth out fear: because fear hath torment. He that feareth is not made perfect in love.*[446] The opposite of faith and love is fear. Fear lies at the root of our hatred, our revulsion, and our unkindness to one another. We fear the "other" because we do not understand them. They are different and we fear they might even be toxic.

It is foolish to assume we can be righteous when we allow fear to inform how we react to others. Second Ne. 9:40 teaches, *I know the words of truth are hard against all uncleanness; but the righteous fear them not, for they love the truth and are not shaken*. Truth can be painful because it cuts away our vanity, pride and foolishness. A righteous individual confident in his honest search for truth should be capable of listening without fear to the beliefs of others and to respond respectfully.

No matter who we are, we are all in the same predicament and facing the same challenge. We will all give a full accounting of what we did with our lives here. Our thoughts, deeds and words that result from our search for heavenly truth will be the basis for that evaluation. As to that coming accounting, the Book of Mormon describes it this way: *And even unto the great and last day, when all people, and all kindreds, and all nations and tongues shall stand before God, to be judged of their works, whether they be good or whether they be evil—If they be good, to the resurrection of everlasting life; and if they be evil, to the resurrection of damnation; being on a parallel, the one on the one hand and the other on the other*

---

[446] 1 John 4:18-19.

151

*hand; according to the mercy, and the justice, and the holiness which is in Christ, who was before the world began.*[447]

This brings to mind yet another Mormon-Buddhist parallel. This one from the Book of Mormon:

Mosiah 4:30 – *[I]f ye do not watch yourselves, and your thoughts, and your words, and your deeds, …ye must perish.*

The Dhammapada – *Guard your thoughts, words, and deeds. These three disciplines will speed you along the path to pure wisdom.*

If how we treat even "the least of these, my brethren" is a measure of how we treat Christ, then how carefully ought we form our thoughts? How kindly should we express our words? How gentle and careful ought deeds be done to others?

Thought is driven by what we know of the Gods. And thought precedes our spoken words. Thought precedes our acts. Therefore the battleground is in our thoughts. On this front the Bible and Buddha agree:

Proverbs 23:7 – *For as [a man] thinketh in his heart, so is he.*

The Dhammapada – *[W]e become what we think.*

There are "other sheep" belonging to Christ about whom we know nothing. I wonder if they think their "church is true" also, or if they look condescendingly at others who do not have their 'Book of Mormapada' (or whatever it may be titled). What if the "fullness of the mysteries of God" have been scattered, like pieces of a jigsaw puzzle, worldwide among remnants of believers who have received truths in different times and places? What if the only thing preventing mankind from coming into the unity of faith Paul hoped would be achieved by Christians,[448] is our fear of others? Paul's hope for unity of the faith and knowledge of God until we are perfect and each exhibit the stature of Christ's fullness[449] clearly has not been accomplished in Christianity before, and neither in Mormonism. Indeed the accelerating rate of Mormon fracturing leaves any reasonable expectation for Mormon unity in the future as unlikely as reuniting Protestants and Catholics[450] and then reunifying these with

---

[447] 3 Ne. 26:4-5.

[448] Eph. 4:13

[449] *Id.*

[450] But the Lutherans and Catholics have reconciled one contentious issue, faith vs. works, in their recent *Joint Declaration on the Doctrine of Justification, by the Lutheran World Federation and the Catholic Church.* This first step may provide incentive to these two institutions to accomplish more.

the Eastern Orthodox Christian fragments. What if that goal is unachievable because it is too little, not too much, to hope for? What if the unity of faith and knowledge can only be accomplished when our fears of others are replaced by our curiosity about Christ's "other sheep?"

If there are others whom God loves as much or more than us, then we have some things to ponder:

If God gives liberally to all who ask,[451] what have they asked that we have not?

If God has been determined to *"grant unto all nations, of their own nation and tongue, to teach his word, yea, in wisdom, all that he seeth fit that they should have"*[452] did God see fit to give other sheep something more than has been given to us?

If, *he that will harden his heart, and same receiveth the lesser portion of the word; and he that will not harden his heart, to him is given the greater portion of the word, until it is given unto him to know the mysteries of God, until he know them in full,*[453] do these others have more open hearts than do we? If so, do they know greater of the Gods' mysteries than we do?

All of this leads to the cautionary moral: we ought to be careful about how we deal with others. We may be thinking of them as understanding less, when they may, in fact, understand more than us. In thinking of the Sunstone theme for this year, the irony of the selected scripture is that we are probably not open to learning from others precisely because we are not willing to learn from the Lord. We have arrived at this point because of the inherited, aggregated xenophobia of the generations who went before us. If we fail to awaken to our awful plight, we do not just perpetuate it, we add to it. Sacred books of different traditions warn us that when we begin with small errors they will eventually bind us into great errors:

In Mormonism: *[Y]ea, and [the devil] leadeth them by the neck with a flaxen cord, until he bindeth them with his strong cords forever.*[454]

In Buddhism: *Little by little a person becomes evil, as a water pot is filled by drops of water.*[455]

---

[451] James 1:5.
[452] Alma 29:8.
[453] Alma 12:10.
[454] 2 Nephi 26:22
[455] The Dhammapada.

But there is the converse, and that is a happy note indeed. If we allow the "light of Christ" to enter us little by little, it will eventually fill us as well:

In Mormonism: *That which is of God is light; and he that receiveth light, and continueth in God, receiveth more light; and that light groweth brighter and brighter until the perfect day.*[456]

In Buddhism: *One must develop small moments of insight and understanding each day. These small, daily bits of enlightenment accumulate over time, until they culminate in a sudden flash of great enlightenment.*[457]

We are here to learn. We should rejoice at any chance the Gods give to us to become better informed about Their mysteries. But it is easy to become trapped by what we know to be familiar and to allow our fears to keep us imprisoned. The beliefs keeping us bound are like the old story of how the trainers control the elephant. A large, adult elephant can be controlled by nothing more than a small rope tied to its front leg. No chains or cages are needed. It is obvious that adult elephants trained this way could at any time break away from their bonds, but they do not. When they are very young, and much smaller, the same small rope is used to tie them. At that early age it is enough to hold them. As they grow, they are conditioned to believe that they cannot break away. They believe the small rope is still enough to hold them, and so they never try to break free. The adult has the strength to be free at any moment, but their belief in their captivity keeps them under control.

One of Islam's great thinkers taught: *We ought not be embarrassed of appreciating the truth and of obtaining it wherever it comes from, even if it comes from races distant and nations different from us. Nothing should be dearer to the seeker of truth than the truth itself, and there is no deterioration of the truth, nor belittling either of one who speaks it or conveys it.*[458] This beautiful sentiment is the opposite of institutional Mormonism. Rather than truthful content, Mormonism has been led to believe the focus must be upon authorized sources. Mormon authorities, many of whom are devoid of understanding, vacuous in teaching, and unacquainted with God are trusted. And if truth dares speak up, the contrast it provides is condemned as a counterfeit.

---

[456] D&C 50:24.

[457] Venerable Master Hsing Yun.

[458] From Abu Yusuf Ya'qub ibn 'Isaq as-Sabbah al-Kindi ("al-Kindi") (801-873), known as the father of Islamic or Arab philosophy.

154

I envision a future for Mormonism where some few believers are willing to seek diligently to recover the truth. That search begins by mining the lost truths of Mormonism itself, of which there are a surprising number of unrecovered teachings. When the effort to recover a lost and compromised "restoration" has advanced far enough, the search for the "other sheep" can begin in earnest. Eventually if those believers are true to Christ's teachings, and open to welcoming all truths, wherever found, the truth will search out those Mormons. It will draw into it from every nation, kindred and people, and all nations will come up to the house of the God of Jacob. The truth, or "rich treasures" from around the world will come to those who will welcome it.

The seed for that new, more open body of believers is being planted. But until it has an opportunity to grow and take form, it is doubtful the larger body of Mormonism, much less the world will recognize it. But great things often have a small beginning. Like a stone broken out of a mountain that seems obscure and unimportant, until it triggers a greater landslide that eventually fills and alters the whole landscape.

There is a Cherokee prayer: *Oh Great Spirit, help me always to speak the truth quietly, to listen with an open mina when others speak, ana to remember the peace that may be founa in silence.*

We speak too much and too loudly and we listen too little. The restoration has filled Mormonism with factions holding unstable and shifting beliefs that are loudly declared in words of certainty. But fractious Mormonism has anything but a stable form. Today, every form of institutional Mormonism is hardly related to the faith practiced by Joseph Smith. These deformities and unhealthy mutations are explained as "continuing revelation." While they do reveal a great truth about the instability of Mormonism, instability is no evidence of revelation. We can hope that somewhere in the bizarre assortment of mutated Mormon offspring there can be found a healthy descendant. However recessive that gene may prove, that hope ought not to be abandoned.

I have been laboring for years to attempt to reinvigorate the original. Thankfully institutional Mormonism is so well informed by their conceit that they doubt such a thing can be accomplished. Today's Mormon intellectual cabals are bemused that the idea an original Mormonism has virtue. They assume wife sharing and bed hopping was a fundamental part of Joseph Smith's legacy, ignoring all he did to denounce and oppose such things. Polygamy is Mormonism's most revealing 'inkblot test'.[459]

The search for authentic, original Mormonism is the quest to find a belief system that confidently searches for truth, wherever found. It does not claim to possess all truth, only to be searching openly to find it. As the original Mormon, Joseph Smith explained:

> Mormonism is truth, in other words the doctrine of the Latter-day Saints, is truth. …The first and fundamental principle of our holy religion is, that we believe that we have a right to embrace all, and every item of truth, without limitation or without being circumscribed or prohibited by the creeds or superstitious notions of men, or by the dominations of one another, when that truth is clearly demonstrated to our minds, and we have the highest degree of evidence of the same.[460]

The response of an authentic believer in Mormonism to the discovery of some new truth should be excited gratitude. There is too much fear in the world, and Mormonism has taken that spirit with gusto. A new revelation is greeted with suspicion and dread because the source from which new revelation springs is invariably considered heterodox. Those in control of the most successful brands of the faith are content to count their money. If the road from Jerusalem to Nicea was calamitous, the downward trek from Nauvoo to Salt Lake is typified by the barren landscape itself: from a watered paradise beside the largest river in North America to a desolate salt flat. That descent into desolation has been as much theological as environmental.

Institutional forms of Mormonism want to claim that God has finished His work for our day and given His authority to a select group of professional clergy.[461] Their jealousy and envy keep them out of the kingdom, and those under their control are prevented from entering God's kingdom.[462] What an odd outcome this is for

---

[459] Like the Rorschach inkblot test, which uses vague images to expose what is inside the one being tested, the vague and contradictory history of plural marriage allows Mormons to envision Joseph as anything from virtuous and innocent to promiscuous and guilty.

[460] Letter from Joseph Smith to Isaac Galland, March 22, 1839, published in *Times and Seasons*, Feb. 1840, pp. 53-54.

[461] See 2 Ne. 28:5.

institutional Mormonism when the religion was founded on the relentless search for truth, anywhere it may be found.

What then ought we do? Can we still embrace an original once the original has been so deformed and disfigured? Can Mormonism, whose visage has been so marred by its adherents, yet bring Jacob again to God?[463] Can Mormonism provide a covenant of the people for a light of the gentiles?[464] Can it again be a marvelous work among the gentiles of great worth to both them and the House of Israel?[465] Are there any with the inclination or desire to deal prudently with the marred visage of Mormonism so that some believers will yet see and consider the depth and breadth of the religion hidden from them?[466] Will Mormonism ever arise from the dust[467] and become evidence that the work of the Father has begun to prepare mankind for the glorious return of His Son?[468] It cannot be done unless those who accept the challenge of Mormonism become as a little child. We must return to the innocent, child-like quest for the truth where "others" are not dreaded but welcomed with curiosity. We should attract, not repel others by the interest we have for discovering whatever truth they have to offer. Plato observed, *We can easily forgive a child who is afraid of the dark; the real tragedy is when men are afraid of the light.* How can Mormonism ever achieve its destiny if it fears both the dark and the light, insisting that it knows only **it** can be true? We should rouse ourselves to vindicate Joseph's view of what constitutes true Mormonism:

> ...the things of God are of deep import; and time, and experience, and careful and ponderous and solemn thoughts can only find them out. Thy mind, O man! if thou wilt lead a soul unto salvation, must stretch as high as the utmost heavens, and search into and contemplate the darkest abyss, and the broad expanse of eternity--thou must commune with God. How much more dignified and noble are the thoughts of God, than the vain imaginations of the

---

[462] Matt. 23:13.
[463] 1 Ne. 21:5-6.
[464] Isa. 22:6-7; 1 Ne. 21:8.
[465] 1 Ne. 22:8-11
[466] 3 Ne. 20:43-46.
[467] 2 Ne. 26:13.
[468] 3 Ne. 21:1-7.

human heart! None but fools will trifle with the souls of men. How vain and trifling have been our spirits, our conferences, our councils, our meetings, our private as well as public conversations--too low, too mean, too vulgar, too condescending for the dignified characters of the called and chosen of God.[469]

There are indeed other sheep who belong to God; they should be welcomed, not scorned. If we do our part, we can awaken and arise and seek for a covenant from God, and then receive in turn from them "rich treasures" of knowledge.

In their present form, Buddhism, Hinduism, Islam and Taoism have not preserved a Christ-centered tradition. Perhaps if we were to recover earlier writings from these faiths in an unadulterated form we would find Christological centers were once part of them all. The post-resurrection visit to the Nephites suggests that possibility.

Avicenna said, *The world is divided into men who have wit and no religion and men who have religion and no wit.*[470]

Mormonism is only a "starter" religion based on an incipient planting by the Gods. It remains wanting. We Mormons should be people of wit and religion, willing to consider and value all truth from whatever source it springs. The greatness of Mormonism has not been realized in any of its past, and those who have managed to profit from organizing institutions based on its mere beginning are threatened by the idea that there is yet much more to be added.

Mormonism has been a dismal underachiever. Its most wealthy sect is riddled with errors, controlled by an oligarchy of priestcraft, jealous of their power, wealth and influence. It has a criminal past, an unstable present, and an insecure future. That empire is diversifying its portfolio into land development, banking and business enterprises[471] to replace the now diminishing tithing cash-stream upon which the empire was built.

The second largest sect has so watered down its teachings and principles that it can hardly be distinguished from any of the weak

---

[469] *TPJS*, p. 137.

[470] Islamic philosopher Avicenna lived from 980-1037 a.d. and authored many books.

[471] See, e.g., *LDS Church makes large timberland purchase in Florida Panhandle,* Nov. 10, 2013, Deseret News; *Mormon Church to Expand Development in Philadelphia,* Feb. 18, 2014, NY Times.

and diminishing liberal Christian sects. It barely gives lip service to Joseph or the Book of Mormon.

The scatterling polygamist sects are hardly Mormon at all, practicing what the Book of Mormon identifies as an abomination that has broken the hearts of wives and lost the confidence of their children.[472] All forms of institutional Mormonism are easily compromised because they have adopted a structure engineered by Brigham Young. Joseph established at least four bodies equal in authority,[473] making it impossible for one to rule and reign with blood and horror over others. Brigham destroyed that balance and promptly began to reign with blood and horror. He even succeeded in persuading Mormons to openly practice an abominable form of plural marriage as a sacrament in his deformed version of the faith. With Brigham Young at the helm, the twelve traveling ministers assumed authority over organized stakes for the first time. It was only a matter of time before their ambition overtook their righteousness. Emboldened by isolation and under the leadership of Brigham Young, Mormons engaged in such excesses, abuses, whoredoms, murders and criminality that the heavens have stared aghast at the wretched spectacle Mormonism made of itself! Marred visage indeed![474]

The greatness of Mormonism has been hijacked. It is time for devoted believers to find the virtue, glory and aspirations of the original. The disillusioned critics do have a point. But their point is aimed in the wrong direction. Mormonism's institutional factions, critics, apostates, and activists all seem too distracted by what is now Mormonism to contemplate what Mormonism promises ultimately to become. It is that unrealized destiny that ought to fire our imaginations and thrill our hearts. Because of its self-declared lack, the original version of Mormonism, with its confidence and curiosity, remains the only faith with any potential to unite within it all truth; therefore, by extension, the unrealized potential to also unite all people.

---

[472] Jacob 2:28, 35.
[473] See D&C 107:22-37.
[474] 3 Ne. 20:44-45.

## Chapter 5: The Restoration's Shattered Promises and Great Hope[475]

© Denver C. Snuffer, Jr. 2018

The 2018 Symposium addressed the theme: *"Threads in the Mormon Tapestry."* This essay is based on a talk I delivered at that symposium. The month before then, June 2018, I participated in a conference at Boise, Idaho that invited various religious groups claiming Joseph Smith as their founder to meet and share ideas. That conference was the first Joseph Smith Restoration Conference, which is hoped to become an annual event. The theme of that conference was, *"What Unites Us is Greater Than What Divides Us."*

Both the June 2018 Boise conference and the July Sunstone Symposium, reflected an undisputable fact about the restoration through Joseph Smith: It is fractured into over an hundred parts. All claiming Joseph Smith as their founder, these factions disagree with one another so strongly they refuse to fellowship with one another. The Boise conference was an attempt to replace division with dialogue. The two largest bodies refused to accept an invitation to send representatives to speak at the conference, but several others were represented. Perhaps the history of the two largest bodies accounts for their reluctance to participate.

The largest Mormon group is the one headquartered in Salt Lake City and controlled by the Corporation of the President of the Church of Jesus Christ of Latter-day Saints. But there is only one person who actually belongs to that corporation sole. Yet he claims to lead some 16 million followers at present, of which about 4 million are nominally active enough to self-identify as Latter-day Saints. I refer to this group of Mormons as "Latter-day Saints" in keeping with

---

[475] All citations and quotes from scripture in this essay are taken from the newly published Old Covenants (containing the Old Testament), New Covenants (containing the New Testament and Book of Mormon), and Teachings and Commandments (containing various revelations, documents and letters from the time of Joseph Smith to today). They are referred to in this paper by identifying "OC", "NC" and "T&C" followed by the location within the respective text. The OC and NC are the most complete version of the JST Bible ever published. The T&C uses the original revelation texts with such limited changes and corrections as Joseph Smith personally added.

the directive from one of their presidents, Gordon B. Hinckley, who pronounced that members of that group cease to refer to themselves as "Mormons."[476]

The Salt Lake City-based church has been the most fecund restorationist mother. Following her abandonment of plural wives, she gave birth to numerous fundamentalist organizations. Her progeny include:

The Council of Friends: an early polygamist group founded by Lorin C. Wooley in 1920. It in turn gave birth to numerous other polygamist offspring.

The Apostolic United Brethren, splintered from the Council of Friends, but like them, claims it's founding reckons from 1886 with authority given by John Taylor. It has an estimated 9,000 members.

The Fundamentalist Church of Jesus Christ of Latter-day Saints, founded by Leroy S. Johnson in 1954 also claims its authority came from the 1886 John Taylor incident.[477] It is progeny from the Council of Friends. It has an estimated 6,000 members.

The Latter-day Church of Christ (Kingston Clan) incorporated as a church in 1978 by Ortell Kingston, and has roots that go back to 1926 with Charles Kingston. It has an estimated 1,200 members.

The Church of Jesus Christ (Original Doctrine), Inc., is a daughter of the Fundamentalist Church of Jesus Christ of Latter-day Saints and great-grand daughter of Brigham Young's Salt Lake organization. It split from its mother because Bishop Winston thought Warren Jeffs was too dictatorial, and led 700 people away from that group. This organization has about 1,000 members today and is also referred to as the Blackmore Group.

---

[476] First Presidency Letter, February 23, 2001. See also Boyd K. Packer's General Conference talk, *Guided by the Holy Spirit*, April 2011. That change in nomenclature seems particularly appropriate since so many of the doctrines, principles and teachings of the Joseph Smith era have been abandoned by that group. Most of the Latter-day Saints now seem unaware of much of what Joseph taught.

[477] In 1886 John Taylor received a revelation that "celestial marriage" would never end. The text was not discovered until after his death. Because he purportedly foresaw its future abandonment by the LDS church, in September 1886 it is claimed that he gave authority to five men to continue the practice. I addressed these claims in my website posts (www.denversnuffer.com) on July 23 through 27, 2012 in a five-part explanation titled *"Sorting Things Out"* parts 1-5.

There is no accurate count of all the daughters, grand daughters and great-grand daughters that have come from splits from the Salt Lake City mother-church. The overwhelming cause of these departures has been the abandonment of plural wives. When the corporation sole chose property over principle, some believed the principle more important than fidelity to their mother. The daughters want both principle and property, but as Warren Jeffs' Fundamentalist Church has learned by sad experience, Federal Courts can still appoint receivers over sexually deviant religious cults that trade women like possessions.

The second largest church is headquartered in Independence, Missouri and is now called the Community of Christ. It claims to have 250,000 members. There was a time when the landscape of the restoration had the Brighamites in Utah and Josephites in Missouri,[478] both claiming they were the authorized successor to Joseph Smith. Brighamites - because Brigham Young eventually claimed the right to succeed Joseph as leader. Josephites - because Joseph Smith III was the direct lineal descendant of the slain founder.

Like its larger sister, the Community of Christ also has produced unwanted daughters. One new daughter from the Community of Christ is The Restoration Church of Jesus Christ of Latter Day Saints. It is also headquartered in Independence, and split from the Community of Christ in 1991. They were disaffected by the decision to ordain women and adopt other innovations. Those who have departed the Community of Christ for the Restoration Church have other reasons for their changed alliance. During the Boise Conference, a Restoration Church leader lamented the Community of Christ's change in attitude toward the Book of Mormon as one of his main reasons for changing his membership to the Restoration Church.

In 2001, a year following the name change from RLDS to Community of Christ, church president W. Grant McMurray admitted doubts about the Book of Mormon, declaring: "The proper

---

[478] There were also saints in Texas led by Lyman Wight and in Wisconsin led by James Strang. But these were not as large when their leaders were living. Wight's movement died out after his demise. Strangites still survive, although their numbers today are very small. The "Cutlerites" were led by Alpheus Cutler. Cutler was an inner-circle follower of Joseph Smith, a high priest, endowed in Nauvoo and a member of the Council of Fifty. He initially remained with Brigham Young's group but broke from them in 1853.

use of the Book of Mormon as sacred scripture has been under wide discussion in the 1970s and beyond, in part because of long-standing questions about its historicity and in part because of perceived theological inadequacies, including matters of race and ethnicity."[479] Then during the 2007 Community of Christ World Conference, church president Stephen M. Veazey ruled it out of order to consider a resolution to "reaffirm the Book of Mormon as a divinely inspired record." In so doing he stated "while the Church affirms the Book of Mormon as scripture, and makes it available for study and use in various languages, we do not attempt to mandate the degree of belief or use. This position is in keeping with our longstanding tradition that belief in the Book of Mormon is not to be used as a test of fellowship or membership in the church."[480]

Both of the largest two Mormon divisions have experienced significant splintering. They may have good reason to fear dialogue between these divisions. As part of encouraging dialogue, this paper deals with two issues. Both have been used to attack and criticize Joseph Smith. If you are conversant with historical or theological Mormon material you may have seen or heard of these subjects, but some of the branches of Mormonism may not have provided any information related to these subjects. The first, and more important topic is Joseph's ascent theology, encouraging man to seek reunion and at-one-ment with God and Christ in the heavens. The second defends Joseph against the accusation that he advocated and practiced the heresy of polygamy.

The institutions claiming to be an authentic version of what Joseph Smith founded have failed to produce the results Joseph foretold. This failure is due, in large measure, because Joseph's teachings have been abandoned or contradicted. There is still a great deal left undone.

Joseph told us to expect great events among the gentiles, Native Americans and remnant of Jewish people before Christ's victorious return. He did not live to see this happen. Upon his death, he left a great deal for others to complete.

---

[479] McMurray, W. Grant, *"They 'Shall Blossom as the Rose': Native Americans and the Dream of Zion"*, an address delivered on February 17, 2001.

[480] Andrew M. Shields, *"Official Minutes of Business Session, Wednesday March 28, 2007"*, in 2007 World Conference Thursday Bulletin, March 29, 2007.

Assuming the work Joseph began is to be finished, it will not happen by heaven laboring independent of us. We have work to do. At the conference in Boise, speaker James McKay from the Restoration Church in Missouri observed, there was still no holy city and no gathering of Israel. He posed the question: "whose fault is that; God's or ours?" The answer, according to the Book of Mormon, is that we must do the work, while God, as Master of the Vineyard, labors alongside us.[481] But fault lies with us. God has been willing to do His part of the labor from Joseph Smith's day until now. God directs the work, and in this way "labors alongside" us. We must resist the temptation to insert our own agenda for God's. If we fail to grasp that the direction must come from heaven rather than as part of an agenda created by uninspired corporate planners, imaginative and even well intended individuals, then we risk working at odds with heaven. God's kingdom is a kingdom in every sense of the word, and the King is entitled to direct all its affairs.

Today, we see all of the quarreling restoration mothers, daughters and siblings accusing the others of apostasy and preaching falsely. If you are trying to find a "true" version of what Joseph Smith founded from the quarreling contenders of today, you face the same query Joseph posed at the beginning: "Who of all these parties are right? Or are they all wrong together? And if any one of them be right, which is it? And how shall I know it?"[482]

Sadly, it seems now as the Lord said to Isaiah: "the daughters of Zion are haughty and walk with stretched forth necks and wanton eyes."[483] These daughters lust after women, and property, power, authority, and make merchandise of the souls of men.[484]

I was a one-time member of the largest branch, but as some of you know, was excommunicated over the demand I retract things I had written about their history. The resulting independence has allowed me to pursue a more unfettered search into Mormon origins, miscarriages, and missteps. Latter-day Saint history has been so

---

[481] NC Jacob 3:27: "And it came to pass that the servants did go and labor with their mights, and the Lord of the vineyard labored also with them. And they did obey the commandments of the Lord of the vineyard in all things."

[482] T&C 1: Part 2:3.
[483] OC Isa. 1:11.
[484] NC Rev. 7:4.

radically revised by revelations in the recent records released that anyone reading is left reeling. LDS history written before 1980 is antiquated. And we never had the more complete panoply of Brigham Young's conjectures, rants, and vulgarities until 2009.[485]

The vast expansion of available and reliable historical materials for those interested has increased the schism rate for all the restorationist groups.[486] There is a lot more kicking and pricking afoot, but it is increasingly more difficult to distinguish between kicks and pricks. The tapestry expands as more threads arrive.

But Mormonism's tapestry is not limited to the committed or devout. It now includes hundreds of thousands, perhaps more, disaffected former-Mormons who remain unable to fully depart. Mormonism exerts a religious gravitational pull almost impossible to fully escape. It remains with all of us, whether you are active in one of the two mother churches or one of their progeny. Mormon denominational splintering continues unabated.

Sunstone attracts believers and disbelievers, the disaffected, the orthodox and the apostate. Why does Mormonism exert that pull?

The religion Joseph Smith ignited echoes with the wonder and appeal of God doing among us what He once did long ago with the people in the Bible. The restoration suggests that the long, awaited moment of Christ's return is at last approaching. Therefore we either hope this to be true or need it to be exposed as a fraud. Either way, our fears or hopes are emphatic.

---

[485] That is when editor Richard Van Wagoner's *The Complete Discourses of Brigham Young*, 5 volumes, was first published by Smith-Pettit Foundation. It expanded available first-person sermons into five large volumes including many previously unpublished sermons or public remarks of Brigham Young. The texts were taken from manuscript collections at LDS Church Archives: Brigham Young Addresses, Brigham Young Minutes, Brigham Young Diaries, Brigham Young Office and Secretary Journals, Thomas Bullock Minutes, Willard Richards Diary, John D. Lee Journals, and Heber C. Kimball Journals, as well as all prior published talks in *History of Brigham Young*, *Journal History of the Church*, *Deseret News*, *History of the Church*, *Journal of Discourses*, and *Millennial Star*.

[486] The Latter-day Saints have announced plans to write a new version of Mormon history. This seems ominous, given the many errors contained in the editorial insertions into the *Joseph Smith Papers*. The LDS Historian's Office even have the audacity to contradict historical records while they introduce them.

Accordingly, we all must decide what to make of Joseph Smith. All our fear, wonder and hope rests on resolving what to make of the life of Joseph:

This frames the dichotomy in the legacy of that man:
-With hope in his authenticity, we see him as God's messenger.
-With doubts about him, we see him as a charlatan.

Those polar opposites are inherent in his life, and were foretold at the beginning and reconfirmed toward the end.

The angel who appeared to Joseph in September 1823 said: "He called me by name, and said unto me that he was a messenger sent from the presence of God to me and that his name was Nephi,[487] that God had a work for me to do, and that my name should be

---

[487] All of the Joseph Smith written accounts that name the angel identify him as "Nephi" and not "Moroni." In the *Joseph Smith Papers, Histories*, Vol. 1, we learn Joseph read and corrected his history: "…it suggests that JS [Joseph Smith] read aloud from Draft 2 in the large manuscript volume, directing editorial changes as he read." (*Id.* at p. 201.) Here is how Draft 2 reads, describing the visit of the angel to him in his bedroom on the night of September 21, 1823: "When I first looked upon him I was afraid, but the fear soon left me. He called me by name and said unto me that he was a messenger sent from the presence of God to me and that his name was Nephi." (*Id.* p. 222.) Under Joseph's direction a Draft 3 was prepared by Howard Coray. This version reads as follows: "When I first looked upon (him) it I was afraid; but the far soon left me: calling me by name, (he) said, that he was a messenger, sent from the presence of God to me, and that his name was Nephi–" (*Id.* p. 223.)
There is a *JSP* footnote that explains someone, unidentified as to whom or when, changed the name from "Nephi" to "Moroni" because of what the editors refer to as a "clerical error." The same footnote explains that throughout Joseph Smith's lifetime, in any history he supervised, the name was always "Nephi". Here is an excerpt from footnote 56 on page 223 of *Joseph Smith Papers, Histories*, Vol. 1: "A later redaction in an unidentified hand changed 'Nephi' to 'Moroni' and noted that the original attribution was a 'clerical error.' Early sources often did not name the angelic visitor, but sources naming Moroni include Oliver Cowdery's historical letter published in the April 1835 *LDS Messenger and Advocate*, an expanded version of a circa August 1830 revelation, as published in the 1835 edition of the Doctrine and Covenants; and a JS editorial published in the *Elders' Journal* in July 1838. The present history is the earliest extant source to name Nephi as the messenger, and subsequent publications based on this history perpetuated the attribution during JS's lifetime." (*Id.* p. 223.)

had for good and evil among all nations, kindreds, and tongues, or that it should be both good and evil spoken of among all people."

My mother taught me to hold Joseph for evil. I've studied his life carefully, read what his critics and admirers have claimed for and about him. I've tried not to be hasty in reaching a conclusion. After four-and-a-half decades I have decided to hold Joseph for good. I'm all in. To me he is the real thing: a messenger sent from God to deliver a message that we reject at our peril and accept to our blessing. He had a great soul that searched, stretched, believed, hoped, fought fiercely, defied pain and persecution, and bore the hallmarks we should expect from a prophet messenger from God. He was a brilliant light: rough cut, homespun, and rustic. But he was also ablaze with insight, keen and penetrating, able to capture with a phrase a glimpse of the infinite.

At the beginning, Joseph Smith's restored religion included noble, thrilling and aspirational words, worthy enough for them to belong to God. If you divorce these words from an opinion of Joseph, and allow them to be independent ideas, they are worthy of meditation. Joseph Smith left religious writings and sermons that are the equal of the New Testament. They are the equivalent to the Vedas. They are as worthy as the Tibetan Book of the Dead.[488] They stand alongside the Tao Te Ching. But they trace their origin to Joseph Smith, and therein lies the rub.

I was raised among those who had Joseph's name for evil. Baptists regard Joseph as a deceiver, liar and imposter. They find the English vocabulary has an insufficient supply of caustic adjectives to heap enough scorn on him. To paraphrase Billy Beane's description of his Oakland A's:[489] 'There's bad men; and then there's devils. Then there's 50 feet of crap. And then there's Joseph Smith.'

When Mormon missionaries began pestering me in New Hampshire, I was amused at their sincerity and could not take seriously anything they offered. To me, they defended a false cult founded by a charlatan. I experienced an internal conflict between my mother's credo to be polite to others and her instruction that Joseph

---

[488] The lyrics to *Tomorrow Never Knows*, a Beatle song composed by John Lennon, was inspired by the *Tibetan Book of the Dead*. It was a revolutionary musical landmark when first released and remains an influential song 52 years after its appearance on the *Revolver* album.

[489] *Moneyball*: "There are rich teams and there are poor teams. Then there's 50 feet of crap. And then there's us."

Smith was a fraud. Without resolving that conflict, I listened politely while pondering profanity.

Having nothing better to do one weekend, I went with the Mormons to a campout in Sharon, Vermont, the birthplace of Joseph Smith. There I obtained a copy of the Doctrine & Covenants from the visitor's center. Steve Klaproth, himself a convert, showed me Section 76. Reading it was the first time I took seriously anything that came from Joseph. The words gripped me. They inspired my mind to deep reflection. They had value. It shattered the paradigm and left me unable to trust a dismissive view for Joseph. He required evaluation. Joseph's words inspired my investigation of the restoration.

In Joseph Smith's History there is a passage that still appeals to my heart and mind. He wrote, "During the space of time which intervened between the time I had the vision and the year eighteen hundred and twenty-three, (having been forbidden to join any of the religious sects of the day, and being of very tender years, and persecuted by those who ought to have been my friends and to have treated me kindly — and if they supposed me to be deluded, to have endeavored in a proper and affectionate manner to have reclaimed me)..."[490] THAT is still going on. Joseph is still being posthumously persecuted.

Persecution is what happens when an idea cannot be opposed on its merit. Persecution is the product of fear typically experienced by those lacking knowledge. There are two great competing forces in the whole of creation: Love and fear. I think God's love for us is exemplified in Him speaking to Joseph Smith. And I am grateful for how that has enriched my life.

Here are some of the great thoughts God inspired and Joseph Smith conveyed to us:

> It is given unto many to know the mysteries of God. Nevertheless, they are laid under a strict command that they shall not impart, only according to the portion of his word which he doth grant unto the children of men, according to the heed and diligence which they give unto him. And therefore, he that will harden his heart, the same receiveth the lesser portion of the word. And he that will not harden his heart, to him is given the greater portion of the word

---

[490] T&C 2:10.

until it is given unto him to know the mysteries of God until they know them in full. And they that will harden their hearts, to them is given the lesser portion of the word until they know nothing concerning his mysteries;[491]

This is one of the great and succinct declarations about coming to know God. Finding Them is deeply personal. We come to God by giving "heed and diligence" to what God asks of us. I cannot do that for you, nor can you do it for me. It is the sojourn of every individual.

The path requires movement. We remain in motion all the time. There is no stasis, no holding a position. We advance (that is, experience restoration) or we recede (that is, experience apostasy). There is no avoiding movement.

The mysteries of God are His hidden but simple truths. They can set a man's bones on fire.[492]

To pay heed to God requires that we not harden our hearts. When we have hard hearts we know less. Even what we once knew can be lost. Eventually, we know nothing of God's mysteries and we are left alone, without God in the world.[493]

Another similar inspired thought:

Woe be unto him that crieth, All is well. Yea, woe be unto him that hearkeneth unto the precepts of men and denieth the power of God and the gift of the Holy Ghost. Yea, woe be unto him that saith, We have received and we need no more. And in fine, woe unto all those who tremble and are angry because of the truth of God. For behold, he that is built upon the rock receiveth it with gladness, and he that is built upon a sandy foundation trembleth, lest he shall fall.

Woe be unto him that shall say, We have received the word of God, and we need no more of the word of God for we have enough. For behold, thus saith the Lord God, I will give unto the children of men line upon line, precept upon precept, here a little and there a little. And blessed are those who

---

[491] NC Alma 9:3.

[492] See, OC Jeremiah 8:7. Paul declared: "Our God is a consuming fire." (NC Heb. 1:57.)

[493] See, NC Alma 19:10.

hearken unto my precepts and lend an ear unto my counsel, for they shall learn wisdom. For unto him that receiveth I will give more, and from them that shall say, We have enough, from them shall be taken away even that which they have. (NC 2 Ne. 12:5-6)

All truth must come from God. The precepts of men are not only unreliable but they are corrupted by their source. God's truths do not end. This thought, like the one before, reminds us that we must seek the constant nourishment of our minds and souls to be in God's path. When God is silent, then you are cut off from truth. Those God can save are those who listen for His voice. No matter how unlikely the source from which God's voice comes, if it is God's word it is to be prized. Even when it comes from the Joseph Smith your mother warned you about.

The hallmark reaction from those disinterested in what God is saying is their angry rejection and refusal to acknowledge more. When you are content - you perish. When you hunger and thirst - you live.

Then another profound declaration along the same line:

And because that I have spoken one word, ye need not suppose that I cannot speak another, for my work is not yet finished, neither shall it be until the end of man, neither from that time henceforth and forever. Wherefore, because that ye have a bible ye need not suppose that it contains all my words, neither need ye suppose that I have not caused more to be written. (NC 2 Ne. 12:10)

At the 2017 Sunstone Symposium I delivered a talk titled *Other Sheep Indeed.* In it I invited others with sacred writings to come and bring them. That invitation was first offered by Joseph Smith in 1840. He anticipated a temple to be built in Nauvoo to which records would be brought from all over the world "bring every thing you can bring and build the house of God and we will have a tremendous City which shall reverberate afar... then comes all the ancient records dig them up... where the Saints g[ather] is Zion."[494] Not all of God's words are in the Bible. God has spoken to every nation (meaning religious body of people).[495] Truth is everywhere, among all people. If

---

[494] *JS Papers, Documents Vol. 7,* p. 336.

[495] "For behold, the Lord doth grant unto all nations of their own nation and tongue, to teach his word; yea, in his wisdom, all that he seeth fit that they should have; therefore we see that the Lord doth counsel in wisdom,

we love God and truth we will want to search for it. We will not be content to leave it unexplored, undiscovered. Blessed are those who hunger and thirst after more righteousness.[496] Blessed are those who are followers of righteousness, desiring to possess great knowledge, and to be greater followers of righteousness and to possess greater knowledge.[497] And blessed are those who do not suppose the scriptures contain all God's words and They (the Gods) have not provided more.

One of the world's greatest religious epistles was composed in Liberty Jail. It includes the following passage:

[T]he things of God are of deep import, and time, and experience, and careful and ponderous and solemn thoughts can only find them out. Your mind, O man, if you will lead a soul unto salvation, must stretch as high as the utmost Heavens, and search into and contemplate the lowest considerations of the darkest abyss, and expand upon the broad considerations of Eternal expanse. You must commune with God. How much more dignified and noble are the thoughts of God than the vain imagination of the human heart? None but fools will trifle with the souls of men.

How vain and trifling have been our spirits, our conferences, our councils, our meetings, our private as well as public conversations: too low, too mean, too vulgar, too condescending for the dignified characters of the called and chosen of God, according to the purposes of his will from before the foundation of the world[.][498]

These words enlarge the soul. Only a great religion challenges us to stretch as high as the utmost heavens! Search into and contemplate the darkest abyss! An expansive religion that urges us to become godlike in our interest, in our search for truth! We are clearly directed to turn our attention to the heavens and learn how they function, what they are, and who is to be found there. This is a vast religion. It is not confined to the earthly, and certainly not under the control of

---

according to that which is just and true." NC Alma 15:13.

[496] NC 3 Ne. 5:10.

[497] T&C 145:1:1.

[498] T&C 138:18-19.

any institution's administrative regimentation, or stifling controls. It cannot be what institutional Mormonism has become:

"O God, God!
How weary, stale, flat, and unprofitable
Seem to me all the uses of [modern Mormonism]!
Fie on 't, ah fie!
'Tis an unweeded garden
That grows to seed.
Things rank and gross in nature
Possess it merely.
That it should come to this."[499]

The restoration is far too great to have been reduced to the vain, trifling, low, mean, vulgar, and condescending versions presented in today's Mormon institutions. If we are going to hold a conference, it should aspire to stretch our minds upward! To make us reach beyond, and never remain content. This Sunstone Symposium deals with diverse, interesting thought, important issues and wonderful contrasts. God is being honored here. Churches should aspire to be as informative and thought-provoking.

This search into the highest heaven is the search to find holiness. Joseph Smith wanted us to ascend, like the ancients, into that realm of light and truth. How can any of us be content to listen to the institutional fare? It is incapable of sustaining spiritual life. Joseph's ideas and teachings are as far above those teachings of today as the heavens are above the earth. The restoration once sought to find what God declared as "His way" to Isaiah: "For my thoughts are not your thoughts, neither are your ways my ways, says the Lord. For as the heavens are higher than the earth, so are my ways higher than your ways, and my thoughts than your thoughts."[500] How the restoration has fallen! It is little wonder so many now hold Mormonism in contempt. It has become unnecessarily contemptible when it ought to be inspiring.[501]

---

[499] *Hamlet*, Act 1, Scene 2.

[500] OC Isa. 20:2.

[501] Joseph Smith's teachings and doctrines are not emphasized, and many are not even known in the scatterlings of Mormonism. Institutions have revised the concept of a prophet and seer to now consist of an administrative head controlling the body beneath him. This, too, while denigrating the founding Prophet who did access the heavens and ascended into the realm of light above.

The restoration's delight has turned to dismay; its ingenuity turned to ineptitude. Silk has become burlap. How have we allowed it to become so?

During confinement in Liberty Jail, Joseph reflected on the tragic and sudden disarray that priesthood leaders inflict on the restoration. Whereas Joseph first envisioned an authoritative administration for the incipient faith, in Liberty Jail he stripped priesthood of all its right to exercise control and dominion. These inspired words not only undo Joseph's initial investiture of priestly authority, it also rejects the long-established Roman Catholic decision to make priesthood non-forfeitable and independent of individual worthiness:[502]

> Behold, there are many called, but few are chosen, and why are they not chosen? Because their hearts are set so much upon the things of this world, and aspire to the honors of men, that they do not learn this one lesson — that the rights of the Priesthood are inseparably connected with the Powers of Heaven, and that the Powers of Heaven cannot be controlled nor handled, only upon the principles of righteousness. That they may be conferred upon us, it is true, but when we undertake to cover our sins or to gratify our pride, our vain ambition, or to exercise control, or dominion, or compulsion, upon the souls of the children of men, in any degree of unrighteousness, behold, the Heavens withdraw themselves, the Spirit of the Lord is grieved, and when it is withdrawn, Amen to the Priesthood or the authority of that man. Behold, ere he is aware, he is left unto himself to kick against the pricks, to persecute the Saints, and to fight against

---

[502] Catholics faced this issue because Donatus, a faithful priest, endured persecution when the Bishop of Alexandria fled. Donatus argued that fleeing the flock in a time of trouble was such a betrayal of the faith that the Bishop lost priesthood authority. Donatists believed that priesthood required righteousness of the ordained man. This controversy lasted several centuries before it was resolved. In 314, the first Council of Arles rejected the idea, and later Augustine of Hippo's active campaign in opposition to Donatus' position and permanently shifted momentum. By the 6th Century Donatism was rejected.

God. We have learned by sad experience that it is the nature and disposition of almost all men, as soon as they get a little authority, as they suppose, they will immediately begin to exercise unrighteous dominion. Hence many are called, but few are chosen.

No power or influence can or ought to be maintained by virtue of the Priesthood; only by persuasion, by long-suffering, by gentleness and meekness, and by love unfeigned, by kindness and pure knowledge, which shall greatly enlarge the soul, without hypocrisy and without guile, reproving betimes with sharpness when moved upon by the Holy Ghost and then showing forth afterwards an increase of love toward him whom you have reproved, lest he esteem you to be his enemy, that he may know that your faithfulness is stronger than the cords of death; your bowels also being full of charity towards all men, and to the Household of faith, and virtue garnish your thoughts unceasingly. Then shall your confidence wax strong in the presence of God, and the doctrines of the Priesthood shall distill upon your soul as the dews from heaven. The Holy Ghost shall be your constant companion, and your scepter an unchanging scepter of righteousness and truth, and your dominion shall be an everlasting dominion, and without compulsory means it shall flow unto you for ever and ever. (T&C 139:5-6)

Consider how these ideas affect religion. A calling to priesthood does not accomplish anything if the individual is not "chosen" by God. We can ordain men but heaven must ratify and elect that man.[503]

---

[503] The power of the priesthood cannot be controlled by men. It comes from heaven or it does not come at all. There has never been an institution entrusted with the power of heaven. "That the rights of the priesthood are inseparably connected with the powers of heaven, and that the powers of heaven cannot be controlled nor handled only upon the principles of righteousness." (T&C 139:5.) A gentile church can convey authority for men to rule over one another throughout the world. But the power of the priesthood comes only one way, and, as the revelation to Joseph Smith states, men do not have any right to either confer it, or prevent it from being conferred. Heaven alone determines if a man will be permitted to act as one

174

No one is permitted to function on God's behalf without God's personal imprimatur of approval.

Priesthood is connected to heaven. Without a connection to heaven, there is no priesthood. The "powers of heaven" are, of course, the angels themselves. Priests must have angelic accompaniment to claim priesthood. And angels cannot be manipulated by the ambition, self-will, or worldly ambition of men.

The called but unchosen use office and position to cover their sins or to gratify their pride and vain ambition. They are like the Jews who persecuted Christ, while sitting in the chief seats. Likewise, there is no priesthood in the possession of any man who exercises control, dominion, or compulsion upon the souls of the children of men in any degree of unrighteousness. Christ's gentle example of kneeling to serve presents a neon-bright example of how priesthood is to be used. He came to serve, not to be served.[504]

He taught, invited, bid others to repent, and clarified a better understanding of the scriptures for others. He did not demand support. He ministered light and truth for all who would listen. Any other kind of conduct antagonizes the heavens, which then withdraw themselves. The Spirit of the Lord is grieved, and when it is withdrawn, that is an end to the Priesthood or the authority of that man.

Imagine how different things are when you know that there is no power or authority in the priesthood itself. But the power to influence others comes only by persuasion, long-suffering, gentleness, meekness, love unfeigned, and by kindly presenting pure knowledge. Imagine that a teacher must greatly enlarge your soul to actually claim

---

of Heaven's chosen high priests. For example, Nephi's younger brother Jacob was ordained to the priesthood by Nephi. (See 2 Ne. 6: 2: "Behold, my beloved brethren, I, Jacob, having been called of God, and ordained after the manner of his holy order, and having been consecrated by my brother Nephi, unto whom ye look as a king or a protector, and on whom ye depend for safety, behold ye know that I have spoken unto you exceedingly many things.") He preached and taught after that ordination. However, when he replaced his older brother as prophet, he explained that he obtained that errand from the Lord. (See Jacob 1: 17: "Wherefore I, Jacob, gave unto them these words as I taught them in the temple, having first obtained mine errand from the Lord.") Many other examples are in scripture. Ordination invites. God alone confers His power.

[504] NC Luke 13:6.

priesthood. How different would it be for you? You would be drawn to attend a meeting for what great light it could provide to you. You would no longer endure those meetings, conferences and conversations that are low, mean, vulgar and condescending; leave if they do not edify or enlighten you soul. Religious classes and meetings that bore us are an obscenity. Discussions filled with a myriad of unenlightened personal opinion are the real pornography of today's Mormonism.

Joseph Smith revoked the right of priesthood to govern, and replaced it with the priesthood's obligation to teach and inspire. This ideal should still be central. We should all repent and forsake the false models of a controlling hierarchy. All the accretions of power, wealth, compulsion and dominion of the various Mormon sects should end this instant.

Another statement from Joseph makes it clear the restoration *was* intended to reintroduce the original religion of the Bible, not the diluted "Christianity" of his day. The original faith, in the first dispensations, had more understanding than what we find preserved in the Bible. Joseph was searching back into these beginnings. His heart was "turned to the fathers" of the first generations. He wanted a return of their original as part of the end. It was to be nothing less. Consider this declaration:

> [H]as the day of miracles ceased? Or have angels ceased to appear unto the children of men? Or has he withheld the power of the Holy Ghost from them? Or will he so long as time shall last, or the Earth shall stand, or there shall be one man upon the face thereof to be saved? Behold, I say unto you, Nay. For it is by faith that miracles are wrought. And it is by faith that angels appear and minister unto men. Wherefore, if these things have ceased, woe be unto the children of men, for it is because of unbelief, and all is vain. For no man can be saved, according to the words of Christ, save they shall have faith in his name. Wherefore, if these things have ceased, then has faith ceased also, and awful is the state of man, for they are as though there had been no redemption made.[505]

---

[505] NC Moroni 7:7.

If the heavens open to us, we have faith. If the heavens are brass, we are faithless. And without faith, it is as if Christ provided us no redemption. These words are as inspiring as they are sobering.[506]

At the conclusion of the vision of the three-heavens, Joseph wrote the following. It clarifies that we are supposed to access heaven, and see for ourselves the glory to be found there:

> But great and marvelous are the works of the Lord, and the mysteries of his Kingdom which he showed unto us, which surpasses all understanding, in glory, and in might, and in dominion, which he commanded us we should not write while we were yet in the Spirit, and are not lawful for men to utter, neither is man capable to make them known, for they are only to be seen and understood by the power of the Holy Spirit, which God bestows on those who love him and purify themselves before him, to whom he grants the privilege of seeing and knowing for themselves that through the power and manifestation of the Spirit, while in the flesh, they may be able to bear his presence in the world of glory.[507]

This privilege of seeing and knowing for ourselves is available to us "while in the flesh." The restoration aimed to reconnect us to heaven in a literal way. This is the same that transpired with Enoch and others in earlier dispensations.

The Book of Mormon is filled with ascension lessons and examples.[508] There is one verse that captures Joseph Smith's ascent theology. That verse compresses it into a single sentence. It explains

---

[506] Religious scholar Harold Bloom may understand Joseph Smith's intention better than modern Mormon sects. He wrote that Joseph Smith was "accomplishing a transumption of his Latter-day Saints to the ever-earliness of the great patriarchs and to Enoch in particular." Being "highly conscious of restoring ancient mysteries associated with Enoch" to repeat "the union of Patriarch and angel in Enoch ...for the ecstasy of union with the Divine principle, for the actual fusion of man with God." (Harold Bloom, *The American Religion*, pp. 100-102.)

[507] T&C 69:29.

[508] This is why the Book of Mormon is the primary text I used in *The Second Comforter: Conversing With the Lord Through the Veil*.

177

why the Book of Mormon contains the "fullness of the gospel." Here is the inspired declaration as a first-person promise from the Lord:

> Verily thus says the Lord: It shall come to pass that every soul who forsakes their sins, and comes unto me, and calls on my name, and obeys my Voice, and keeps all my commandments, shall see my face and know that I Am, and that I am the true light that lights every man who comes into the world[.][509]

"Every soul" includes you and me. Every one of us has equal access to the Lord. The conditions are the same for all. Forsake sins; come to Christ; call on His name; obey His voice; keep his commandments. This is far more challenging than obedience to a handful of 'thou shalt nots' because so much is required to be done, so much required to be known. A great deal of study and prayer is required to stand in the presence of the Lord. Once done, we shall see His face and know that He is the true light that enlightens every one. He is the God of the whole world.

Immediately after His resurrection, Christ did not minister to gentiles.[510] But after the Book of Mormon came forth, gentiles are also eligible for Christ's ministry in very deed:

> And it shall come to pass that if the gentiles shall hearken unto the Lamb of God in that day that he shall manifest himself unto them in word and also in power, in very deed, unto the taking away of their stumbling blocks, and harden not their hearts against the Lamb of God, they shall be numbered among the seed of thy father. Yea, they shall be numbered among the house of Israel and they shall be a blessed people upon the promised land forever[.][511]

His promise to us is predicated on "hearkening" to the Lamb. Gentiles failed to do so, and upon Joseph's death, a great dearth set upon the restoration. Until there is gentile repenting and returning, it

---

[509] T&C 93:1.

[510] "[T]hey understood not that the gentiles should be converted through their preaching. And they understood me not that I said, They shall hear my voice. And they understood me not that the gentiles should not at that time hear my voice, that I should not manifest myself unto them save it were by the Holy Ghost." (NC 3 Ne. 7:3.)

[511] NC 1 Ne. 3:25.

will continue to unwind. Since June 27, 1844 we have a restoration slow-moving car wreck. The pace of that decay is accelerating.

We must rage against the fading of that light.[512] "And seek the face of the Lord always, that in patience you may possess your souls, and you shall have Eternal life."[513]

Evidence of Christ is everywhere. Joseph used cosmological terms in the following passage describing the importance of light coming from Christ and His Father:

> [H]e is in the sun and the light of the sun, and the power thereof by which it was made. As also he is in the moon and is the light of the moon, and the power thereof by which it was made, as also the light of the stars and the power thereof by which they were made, and the earth also, and the power thereof, even the earth upon which you stand. And the light which now shines, which gives you light, is through him who enlightens your eyes, which is the same light that quickens your understandings, which light proceeds forth from the presence of God, to fill the immensity of space: the light which is in all things, which gives life to all things, which is the law by which all things are governed, even the power of God[.][514]

If you are alive, you are connected to Christ. If you detect the light of the sun, you detect a testimony of Christ. If you behold the moon moving in her cycles overhead, you behold a testimony of Christ.

There is another cosmic observation about our relationship to God and how we are gaining experience in this creation:

> All truth is independent in that sphere in which God has placed it to act for itself, as all intelligence also, otherwise there is no existence. Behold, here is the

---

[512] Dylan Thomas, *Do not go gentle into that good night.* The final two lines are: "Do not go gentle into that good night. Rage, rage against the dying of the light." Dylan so inspired Bob Zimmerman that he changed his name to Bob Dylan. American Poet, Elizabeth Bishop, wrote of his passing: "Thomas's poetry is so narrow—just a straight conduit between birth & death, I suppose—with not much space for living along the way."

[513] T&C 101:6.

[514] T&C 86:1.

agency of man, and here is the condemnation of man, because that which was from the beginning is plainly manifest unto them, and they receive not the light, and every man whose spirit receives not the light is under condemnation. For man is spirit, the elements are eternal, and spirit and element, inseparably connected, receive a fullness of joy; ...The glory of God is intelligence, or in other words, Light and Truth. Light and Truth forsake that evil one. ...And that wicked one comes and takes away light and truth through disobedience, from the children of men, and because of the tradition of their fathers.[515]

False traditions are as destructive for us as outright disobedience. The result is the same. The difference is when we know we disobey we feel guilt. But false traditions fool us into thinking we are obedient when we are merely misled. Thus Satan leads to destruction as mankind follows darkness rather than Christ's light.

Joseph Smith also provided us with Christ's personal explanation of what He endured to atone for our sins. It is a profound a statement as anything found in the Four Gospels.

[S]urely every man must repent or suffer, for I God am endless, wherefore, I revoke not the judgments which I shall pass, but woes shall go forth: weeping, wailing, and gnashing of teeth, yea, to those who are found on my left hand.

Nevertheless, it is not written that there shall be no end to this torment, but it is written endless torment. Again, it is written Eternal damnation, wherefore, it is more express than other scriptures that it might work upon the hearts of the children of men altogether for my name's glory. Wherefore, I will explain unto you this mystery, for it is mete unto you to know, even as mine apostles. I speak unto you that are chosen in this thing, even as one, that you may enter into my rest, for behold, the mystery of godliness, how great is it? For behold, I am Endless, and the punishment which is given from

---

[515] T&C 93:10-11.

my hand is Endless punishment, for Endless is my
name. Wherefore –

*Eternal punishment is God's punishment.*
*Endless punishment is God's punishment.*

Wherefore, I command you by my name, and
by my Almighty power that you repent, repent lest I
smite you by the rod of my mouth, and by my wrath
and by my anger, and your sufferings be sore, how
sore you know not, how exquisite you know not, yea,
how hard to bear you know not. For behold, I God
have suffered these things for all that they might not
suffer, if they would repent. But if they would not
repent, they must suffer even as I, which suffering
caused myself, even God, the greatest of all, to
tremble because of pain and to bleed at every pore,
to suffer, both body and spirit, and would that I
might not drink the bitter cup and shrink.
Nevertheless, glory be to the Father, and I partook
and finished my preparations unto the children of
men.[516]

This harrowing plea in the first-person account begs us to accept
Christ's sacrificial gift. But it warns us there is a price to be paid if we
reject what He offers. He only finished "his preparations" for us. If
we reject what He prepared, we are left to face the consequences
without His intervention. There is to be punishment for sins, but it is
avoidable punishment and need not be endured. All He asks is that
we accept the gift on His simple terms: Repent, be baptized and
follow Him.

Joseph wrote this harrowing request for us to accept Christ:
"[H]e loveth those who will have him to be their God."[517] We just
won't respond to that plaintive plea.

This plea reminds me of another Joseph Smith declaration. This
one comes from Nephi, son of Lehi, in the Book of Mormon:

I will go and do the things which the Lord hath
commanded, for I know that the Lord giveth no
commandments unto the children of men save he

---

[516] T&C 4:1-5.
[517] NC 1 Ne. 5:20.

shall prepare a way for them that they may accomplish the thing which he commandeth them.[518]

Nothing is asked of you that you cannot accomplish. You can have Christ to be your God, if you accept His invitation and keep His commandments. No commandment has been given that is beyond your capacity to perform. Repenting and being baptized is simple enough that any person of age can choose to comply. We are in control of our destiny.

There are hundreds of potential quotes that could be added to this paper. One final quote to end this part of the paper: "[W]hen ye are in the service of your fellow beings, ye are only in the service of your God."[519]

This was how Christ lived His life. He showed forth the glory of God the Father by serving and elevating others. We, too, can serve God by giving comfort to our fellow men and women. There is no end to the opportunities to help others. This life is abundant in opportunity to reflect God's grace, kindness and help by service to others. If you act that part, you are in God's service. Think Sub-for-Santa and consider joining Sub-for-God. It will add 364 days of opportunity.

The angel who visited Joseph in 1823 said his name would be had for good and evil among all people. A similar message was repeated 16 years later in March 1839 when the voice of the Lord spoke to Joseph in Liberty Jail. God said to Joseph, "The ends of the earth shall inquire after your name, and fools shall have you in derision, and Hell shall rage against you, while the pure in heart, and the wise, and the noble, and the virtuous shall seek counsel, and authority, and blessings constantly from under your hand. And your people shall never be turned against you by the testimony of traitors, and although their influence shall cast you into trouble, and into bars and walls, you shall be had in honor." Although these two are similar, there is a profound difference between the angel's statement in 1823 and the voice of God in 1839. The angel only said people would speak good and evil of Joseph. But God added a description of those who would speak evil, and those who would speak good of Joseph.

That voice of God said, "fools shall have [Joseph] in derision." Because I accept this statement as God's, I am led to conclude all

---

[518] NC 1 Ne. 1:10.
[519] NC Mosiah 1:8.

who have spoken derisively of Joseph have done so foolishly. We ought to stop our foolishness. We need to end the derision of Joseph.

God also condemned the "testimony of traitors" against Joseph. While alive, Joseph identified some of his contemporary traitors and named them: George Hinkle,[520] John Corrill, Reed Peck, David Whitmer, W.W. Phelps,[521] Sampson Avard,[522] William McLellin, John

---

[520] "Joseph Smith Jr is now unlawfully confined and restrained of his liberty in Liberty jail Clay County (Mo) that he has been restrained of his liberty near five months your petitioners clame that the whole transaction which has been the cause of his confinement (is) unlawfull from the first to the Last he was taken from his home by a fraude being practised upon him by a man by the name of George M Hinkle..." (*JSP, Documents Vol. 6*, p. 344; as in original.)

[521] "Look at Mr [George M.] Hinkle. A wolf in sheep's clothing. Look at his brother John Corrill Look at the beloved brother Reed Peck who aided him in leading us, as the savior was led, into the camp as a lamb prepared for the slaughter and a sheep dumb before his shearer so we opened not our mouth But these men like Balaam being greedy for a reward sold us into the hands of those who loved them, for the world loves his own. I would remember W[illiam] W. Phelps who comes up before us as one of Job's comforters. God suffered such kind of beings to afflict Job, but it never entered into their hearts that Job would get out of it all. This poor man who professes to be much of a prophet has no other dumb ass to ride but David Whitmer to forbid his madness when he goes up to curse Israel, and this ass not being of the same kind of Balaams therefore the angel notwithstanding appeared unto him yet he could not penetrate his understanding sufficiently so but what he brays out cursings instead of blessings." (*JSP, Documents Vol. 6*, p. 300-301; as in original.)

[522] We have learned also since we have been in prison that many false and pernicious things which were calculated to lead the saints far astray and to do great injury (have been taught by Dr. [Sampson] Avard) as coming from the Presidency and we have reason to fear (that) many (other) designing and corrupt characters like unto himself (have been teaching many things) which the presidency never knew of being taught in the church by any body untill after they were made prisoners, which if they had known of, they would have spurned them and their authors from them as they would the gates of hell. Thus we find that there has been frauds and secret abominations and evil works of darkness going on leading the minds of the weak and unwary into confusion and distraction, and palming it all the time upon upon the presidency while mean time the presidency were ignorant as well as innocent

Whitmer, Oliver Cowdery, Martin Harris, Thomas Marsh, and Orson Hyde.[523] These had been prominent leaders, trusted friends, and one-time believers in Mormonism. It was false testimony by those from within the flock that led to imprisonment of Joseph and other leaders.

The traitors of 1838 were joined by yet more traitors between 1842-44. In Missouri, Joseph was accused of treason and inciting violence. In 1842-44 Joseph's traitors accused him of adultery, polygamy and lying. John C. Bennett was a sexual predator who claimed amidst his secret seductions that Joseph Smith authorized him to engage in his promiscuity.

When his misconduct came to light, Bennett admitted Joseph authorized no such wickedness. He swore under oath, "that he never was taught any thing in the least contrary to the strictest principles of the Gospel, or of virtue, or of the laws of God, or man, under any circumstances, or upon any occasion either directly or indirectly, in word or deed, by Joseph Smith: and that he never knew the said Smith to countenance any improper conduct whatever, either in pubic or private; and that he never did teach me in private that an illegal illicit intercourse with the females was, under any circumstances, justifiable; and that I never knew him so to teach others."[524]

---

of these things, which were practicing in the church in their name[.]" (*JSP, Documents Vol. 6*, p. 306)

[523] Such characters as [William E.] McLellin, John Whitmer, O[liver] Cowdery, Martin Harris, who are too mean to mention and we had liked to have forgotten them. [Thomas B.] Marsh & [Orson] Hyde whose hearts are full of corruption, whose cloak of hypocrisy was not sufficient to shield them or to hold them up in the hour of trouble, who after having escaped the pollutions of the world through the knowledge of God and become again entangled and overcome the latter end is worse than the first. But it has happened unto them according to the words of the savior, the dog has returned to his vomit, and the sow that was washed to her wallowing in the mire. Again if we sin wilfully after we have received the knowledge of the truth, there remaineth no more sacrifice for sin, but a certain fearful looking (for) of judgement and firey indignation to come which shall devour these adversaries. For he who despiseth Moses' law died without mercy under two or three witnesses of how much more severe punishment suppose ye shall he be thought worthy who hath sold his brother and denied the new and everlasting covenant[.]" (*JSP Documents Vol. 6*, pp. 307-308.)

[524] Affidavit of John C. Bennett dated 17 May 1842 and published in the

William Law was also involved in secret adultery, and Joseph Smith refused to seal Law's marriage. A conspiracy of traitors in 1844 included William Law, Charles Ivins, Francis Higbee, Chauncey Higbee, Robert Foster and Charles Foster who published the Nauvoo Expositor accusing Joseph Smith of the very evil Joseph had been hunting down and eradicating through high council proceedings since the Bennett affair had become public.[525]

---

*Times & Seasons* on July 1, 1842 in Vol. III, No. 17, at p. 839.

[525] In the aftermath of John Bennett's misconduct, Joseph pursued an effort to track down what had happened in Nauvoo. By May 21, 1842, the high council met and, "[A] charge [was] [preferred] against Chauncey L. Higbee by George Miller for unchaste and un-virtuous conduct with the widow [Sarah] Miller, and others." (*Nauvoo City and High Council Minutes*, p. 414, all as in original.) In the trial, "Three witness[es] testified that he had seduced [several women] and at different times [had] been guilty of unchaste and unvirtuous conduct with them and taught the doctrine that it was right to have free intercourse with women if it was kept secret &c and also taught that Joseph Smith authorised him to practice these things &c" (*Id.*, pp. 414-415, as in original.)

On May 25 the charge was preferred "against Ms. Catherine Warren by George Miller for unchaste and unvirtuous conduct with John C. Bennett and others. The defendant confessed to the charge and gave the names of several other [men] who had been guilty having unlawful intercourse with her[,] stating they taught the doctrine that it was right to have free intercourse with women and that the heads of the Church also taught and practiced it[,] ...learning that the heads of the church did not believe of [the] practice [of] such things[,] she was willing to confess her sins and did repent before God for what she had done and desired earnestly that the Council would forgive her."(*Id.*, p. 417, as in original.) She furnished the identities of the several men involved, resulting in more church court proceedings to stop the spread of Bennett's mischief.

On September 3, 1842, "[A] charge was preferred against Gustavius Hills by Elisha Everett[,] one of the teachers of the Church[,] for illicit intercourse with a certain woman by the name of Mary Clift by which she was with child[,] and for teaching the said Mary Clift ~~that~~ that the heads of the Church practiced such conduct & that time would come when men would have more wives than one &c" (*Id.*, p. 424, as in original.)

The next day, September 4, 1842, "Esther Smith gave evidence that [the] defendant [Gustavius Hills] told her that it was lawful for people to have illicit intercourse if they only held their peac[e] & that ~~the time would~~ it was agreeable to the practice of some of the leading men or heads of the Church." (*Id.*, p. 425, as in original.)

185

Joseph was unequivocal in his opposition to adultery and plural wife taking. About the time Bennett's misconduct was beginning to come to light, Joseph organized the Female Relief Society to encourage moral and chaste conduct in Nauvoo.[526] In addition to the steps he took privately to discipline those involved directly, he made many public declarations against plural wives and in favor of chastity and moral purity. These included, among many others:

> Inasmuch as the public mind has been unjustly abused through the fallacy of Dr. Bennett's letters, we make an extract on the subject of marriage, showing the rule of the church on this important matter. The extract is from the Book of Doctrine and Covenants, and is the only rule allowed by the Church. 'Inasmuch as this church of Christ has been reproached with the crime of fornication, and polygamy; we declare that we believe, that one man should have one wife; and one woman, but one

---

Yet more courts were held as the effort to round up those who were involved in this practice. John Bennett, in response to the treatment given him by the church, set out to tell another story in which he was the hero and Joseph was the villain. He wrote, lectured and campaigned against Mormonism, first to salvage his reputation, but ultimately as his profession.

Joseph left a record of public and private actions taken in opposing the plural wife system. These included: "I preached in the grove and pronounced a curse upon all adulterers and fornicators, and unvirtuous persons and those who have made use of my name to carry on their iniquitous designs." (Joseph Smith (Sermon at the Grove; Apr 10, 1842)

[526] "Spoke of the organization of the Female Relief Society; said he was deeply interested, that is might be built up to the Most High in an acceptable manner; that its rules must be observed; that none should be received into it but those who were worthy; proposed a close examination of every candidate; that the society was growing too fast. It should grow up by degrees, should commence with a few individuals, thus have a select society of the virtuous, and those who would walk circumspectly; commended them for their zeal, but said sometimes their zeal was not according to knowledge. One principle object of the institution was to purge out iniquity; said they must be extremely careful in all their examinations, or the consequences would be serious. ...[T]he Saints should be a select people, separate from all the evils of the world– choice, virtuous and holy." (*TPJS*, p. 201-202, March 30, 1842.)

husband, except in case of death, when either is at liberty to marry again.'[527]

. . .

As we have lately been credibly informed, that an Elder of the Church of Jesus Christ, of Latter-day Saints, by the name of Hiram Brown, has been preaching Polygamy, and other false and corrupt doctrines, in the county of Lapeer, state of Michigan. This is to notify him and the Church in general, that he has been cut off from the church, for his iniquity; and he is further notified to appear at the Special Conference, on the 6th of April next, to make answer to these charges.[528]

. . .

What a thing it is for a man to be accused of committing adultery, and having seven wives, when I can only find one. I am the same man, and as innocent as I was fourteen years ago; and I can prove them all perjurers.[529]

He also encouraged the Relief Society to adopt a declaration titled *A Voice of Innocence*.[530] It was read publicly by W.W. Phelps on

---

[527] *Times & Seasons* Vol. 3, p. 909, Sept. 1, 1842.

[528] Joseph Smith & Hyrum Smith, *Times and Seasons* Vol. 5 (February 1, 1844).

[529] *DHC* 6:411, May 26, 1844.

[530] It states in part: "The corruption of wickedness which manifested itself in such horrible deformity on the trial of Orsemus F. Bostwick last week, for slandering President Hyrum Smith and the Widows of the City of Nauvoo, has awakened all the kindly feelings of female benevolence, compassion and pity, for the softer sex to spread forth the mantle of charity to shield the characters of the virtuous mothers, wives and daughters of Nauvoo, from the blasting breath and poisonous touch of debauchees, vagabonds, and rakes, who have jammed themselves into our city to offer strange fire at the shrines of infamy, disgrace and degradation; as they and their kindred spirits have done in all the great cities throughout the world: corrupting their way: on the earth, and bringing woman, poor defenseless woman, to wretchedness and ruin. ... and, as such ungodly wretches, burning or smarting with the sting of their own shame, have doubtless, transported with them; some of the miserable dupes of their licentiousness, for the purpose of defiling the fame of this goodly city: mildewing the honesty of our mothers: blasting the chastity of widows and wives, and corrupting the virtue of our unsuspecting daughters, it becomes US in defense of our rights, for the glory

of our mothers fathers; for the honor of our Mothers; for the happiness of our husbands; and for the well fare of our dear children, to rebuke such an outrage upon the sanctity of Society; to thwart such a death blow at the hallowed marriage covenant: and to ward off such poisoned daggers from the hearts of our innocent daughters, ... Curse the man that preys upon female virtue! Curse the man that slanders a woman: Let the righteous indignation of insulted innocence, and virtue spurn him from society; Let the dignity of the Mother's of Israel kick the blood thirsty pimp from the pale of social communion. Let the widows and wives who tread in the foot steps of their queenly mother Eve, drive such fag ends of creation, as was Cain, to the Land of Nod, and let the timid daughters of Nauvoo, dread such Canker worms more than the pestilence that walketh in darkness, and spurn shun them as the serpent on the land and the shark in the Sea. My God! My God! is there not female virtue and valor enough in this City to let such mean men die of the rot...

"Female virtue is a pearl of great price, and should glitter in the abodes of men; as in the Mansions of bliss for the glory and honor of him, whose image she bears and whose help meet she is, and every attempt of man to seduce that virtue, is, next to murder, a robbery that cannot be restored. If woman swerves from the rules of righteousness:

"...Wherefore,

"Resolved unanimously that Joseph Smith, the Mayor of the City, be tendered our thanks for the able and manly manner in which he defended injured innocence in the late trial of O.F. Bostwick for slandering president Hyrum Smith 'and almost all the women of the City.'

Resolved unanimously that we view with unqualified disapprobation and scorn the conduct of any man or woman, whether in word or deed, that reflects dishonor, upon the poor persecuted mothers, widows, wives and daughters of the Saints of Nauvoo: they have borne aspersions, slanders and hardships enough: forbearance has ceased to be a virtue, and retaliation, like the 'dagger or the bowl' ought to close the lips of such cowardly aspersions assassins

"Resolved unanimously that while we render credence to the doctrines of Paul, that neither the man is without the woman; neither is woman without the man in the Lord, yet we raise our voices and hands against John C. Bennett's 'Spiritual Wife System,' as a scheme of profligates to seduce women; and they that harp upon it, wish to make it popular for the convenience of their own cupidity: wherefore, while the marriage bed, undefiled is honorable, let polygamy, bigamy, fornication, adultery, and prostitution, be frowned out of the hearts of honest men to drop in the gulf of fallen nature, 'where the worm dieth not, and the fire is not quenched!' and let all the Saints say: Amen!"

Society, and published in the *Nauvoo Neighbor* on March 20, 1844.

Because of the testimony of traitors, Joseph Smith has been held in derision from 1842 to the present. He is accused of being a sexual predator, liar, and adulterer. Fools have repeated the accusations originally made by the adulterer John C. Bennett, though Bennett testified under oath that Joseph was not responsible and never behaved in any improper way toward women.

The derision of Joseph now comes from the LDS Church, which claims him as their founder. It comes from Brian Hales, who claims to be an accurate biographer.[531] It comes from anti-Mormons,

---

[531] Hales wrote a three volume series titled *Joseph Smith's Polygamy*. In it he accepts and advocates Joseph was a secretive polygamist. Adrian Larsen, in a private email exchange with Hales, described the effect of that work best: "But having looked at the evidence, rather than taking Joseph's side, you have sided with the Nauvoo Expositor in calling Joseph's statements lies, designed to conceal the truth that he was secretly practicing polygamy while publicly condemning it. You have taught he was, therefore, a liar, deceiver, adulterer, and the worst kind of hypocrite. You have provided the most volatile fuel to the anti-Mormon fire, and robbed the Lord's prophet of all credibility in other areas, including scripture. All arguments to the contrary fall on deaf ears, who point to you as an authority. You have contributed in major and direct ways to the apostasy and loss of many thousands of souls, based on your agenda-driven analysis of very equivocal evidence." (Email from Adrian Larsen to Brian Hales, May 15, 2018-copy in possession of author; used with permission fro the author.) Rock Waterman likewise is critical of the Hales' approach: "The story of The Angel With The Flaming Sword is a perfect example. (*Joseph Smith's Polygamy*, (Salt Lake: Greg Kofford Books, 2013), Vol 1: History, beginning on p. 194.) That story has a number of permutations, depending on the person 'remembering' Joseph telling it to him. But ultimately it evolves into a story about an angel with a flaming sword appearing to Joseph threatening to slay him unless he can get Emma to accept plural marriage. Brian's research on this matter is painstaking; he's documented every source, every version of the telling of it, until what we wind up with is a tale that gets embellished and more fantastic with every telling.

"If such an incident actually HAD occurred, it was the most fantastic event in Joseph's life since the First Vision (but it does starkly contradict everything we know about God allowing Joseph his free agency). Fantastic as it is, we hear absolutely nothing of this incredible tale from Joseph Smith himself; there are no records of him telling anyone any version of this story whatsoever when he was alive. The stories don't begin circulating until a decade after his death, and the story kept changing and getting more

and Christian ministers, and fundamentalists who have created a caricature they claim to be Joseph. There is little difference between these people and William Law, Charles Ivins, Francis Higbee, Chauncey Higbee, Robert Foster and Charles Foster who published the *Nauvoo Expositor.* There is an immense chorus of fools holding Joseph in derision, even among those who claim to be devout followers of the faith he restored.

I think the voice Joseph heard in Liberty Jail *was* God's. If I am right, then God's advice to the pure in heart, wise, noble and virtuous is to seek counsel, authority and blessing from Joseph. God's advice leads me to adopt a view of Joseph that is consistent with nobility and virtue. I do not believe you can regard Joseph as a sexual predator, liar and adulterer without holding him in derision. The chief and unavoidable result of thinking of Joseph so has been a legacy of excusing institutional lying, and promoting adulterous thoughts, and inappropriately entertaining the concept of women as mere breeding stock for the use of men.

It is not possible to harbor lustful, deceitful and adulterous thoughts in your heart and claim to be pure in heart. I do not believe you can conspire to commit bigamy and adultery and claim to be virtuous. I do not believe you can decide to trust the words of traitors and villains who contradict Joseph's account of his marital fidelity to Emma and claim to seek counsel from Joseph. In short, those who claim to accept the restoration, but believe Joseph was a sexual predator, do not qualify as noble, wise, virtuous or pure in thought.

---

fantastic every time it was repeated.

"What all this reminded me of was a party game they used to call 'Gossip' or 'Chinese Telephone,' where someone whispers something into the ear of the person next to him, the next person whispers what he thought he heard into the ear of the next person, and on down the line until what the last person repeats aloud is hilariously mangled. I told Brian his research was invaluable, but that in my view it tends to prove the opposite of what he thinks it does. I think this Angel story, like so many others that did not surface until long after Joseph's death, tends to cast serious doubt on Brian's thesis, rather than confirming it. I felt Brian had an obligation to deconstruct the rumors for his readers and help them see the absurdity of it all, but this he did not do. The prophet spent the last months of his life constantly denouncing the insidious 'spiritual wifery' that had begun to infest Nauvoo, yet we don't find those vigorous denunciations in any of our official histories. Instead we are bombarded with hearsay and silly rumors that don't hold up under critical examination." (Rock Waterman email to Denver Snuffer on July 24, 2018.)

All the restorationist groups that descend from the Brighamites are religious polygamists. Whether they think it right to practice that abomination at present, or only think it a true part of their religion,[532] they are polygamists. Their faith descends from a great whore, and her daughters are likewise whores. It is time for those involved to awaken to their awful situation and admit their mother is a whore.

Joseph said and wrote a great deal publicly to condemn plural marriage. He said nothing in public to defend or justify it. Clearly he did not want to be known as its advocate. He wanted to be understood as a staunch opponent of it.

It is important to realize the restoration was hijacked by polygamy and has never regained the momentum Joseph envisioned. That abomination has darkened men's hearts and broken women's hearts. It is used to justify looking upon women with lust in men's hearts, contrary to the Lord's command in the Sermon on the Mount.[533]

I hold Joseph in some considerable esteem. On the lightening-rod issue of plural wives, I've decided the historical record does not convict Joseph of polygamy, lying, deception, sexual improprieties, or exploitation of women. If I thought of Joseph Smith capable of such things I would join his traitors in deriding him. I prefer to think him virtuous and noble. I think it is only possible for any person whose heart is pure, and who prizes virtue, wisdom and nobility to respect Joseph Smith by regarding him as pure, wise, noble and virtuous. To me, adultery, promiscuity and deceit are none of those things.

I reject adultery by any name or description. It is morally wrong if you call it plural wives, polygamy, "celestial marriage" or any other misnomer. Adultery is prohibited in the Ten Commandments, and remains an important prohibition for any moral society.

Mormonism should never have been saddled with Brigham Young's program of making adultery a sacrament. But Mormonism should not have been saddled with many institutional accretions.

---

[532] Section 132 of the LDS Doctrine and Covenants makes plural wives a tenet of their religion.

[533] "Behold, it is written by them of old time that you shall not commit adultery. But I say unto you that whoever looks on a woman to lust after her, has committed adultery with her in his heart already. Behold, I give unto you a commandment that you suffer none of these things to enter into your heart; for it is better that you should deny yourselves of these things, wherein you will take up your cross, than that you should be cast into hell." (NC Matt. 3:21.)

Between June 27, 1844 and today, there have been too many incorrect subtractions, and far too many uninspired additions. Mormonism today requires both dramatic subtractions and necessary additions. No-one seems willing to do that with the precision required to "Strive to show yourself approved unto God, a workman that need not to be ashamed, rightly dividing the word of truth."[534]

Brigham Young was not the only one who betrayed Joseph and caused his memory to be held in derision. David Whitmer betrayed Joseph in 1838, testified against him, and helped cause his Missouri imprisonment. Many years later, Whitmer's testimony as a traitor and accuser was published in *An Address to All Believers in Christ*. Though he had been excommunicated in 1838 and never lived in Nauvoo, he accepted and echoed the *Nauvoo Expositor's* claims about polygamy.[535]

The band Bastille posed the question, "Where do we begin? The rubble or our sins?"[536] I think it begins with our sins. They first have to be set aside through Christ. But afterwards we have a Mormon landscape filled with rubble, out of joint, out of level, out of plumb, collapsed or collapsing. Mormonism's founding text tells us this is as it should be for the present. We were never supposed to see Zion before we witnessed gentile failure and apostasy.

Christ declared to the Nephites a warning to the gentiles:

> "And thus commandeth the Father that I should say unto you, At that day when the gentiles shall sin against my gospel and shall reject the fullness of my gospel and shall be lifted up in the pride of their hearts above all nations and above all the people of the whole earth, and shall be filled with all manner of lyings and of deceits and of mischiefs, and all manner of hypocrisy and murders and priestcrafts and whoredoms and of secret abominations, and if they shall do all those things and shall reject the fullness of my gospel, Behold, saith the Father, I will bring the fullness of my gospel from among them."[537]

---

[534] NC 2 Tim. 1:6.

[535] He had no reason to question the *Nauvoo Expositor* once Brigham Young's organization publicly advocated plural wivery from 1852.

[536] Daniel Smith, *Pompeii*.

[537] NC 3 Ne. 7:5.

This is not phrased as a possibility but as an inevitability. It was never a question of "if" the gentiles would reject the fullness. It has always been only a matter of "when" it would take place. The various institutions quarrel over whether it has happened. Some of them deny it can or will happen. The soothing mantra "we will never lead you astray" defies the message Christ was commanded by the Father to declare to us.

Joseph Smith has been held in derision for too long. Even those who claim to follow the commandments from God that came through him, deride his memory. This has gone on unchecked for far too long. The saints fell under condemnation in 1832 for taking lightly the Book of Mormon and former commandments given through Joseph Smith.[538] Then eight years later were warned it was foolish to hold Joseph in derision.[539] Reclaiming the restoration requires repentance. First, recovering and accepting the text of the Book of Mormon, and restoring the former commandments to what God originally spoke. That has been done by a small group of repentant believers. But second, we need to end the derision of Joseph and acknowledge he was pure of heart, noble and virtuous and to act accordingly. It is foolish to magnify his errors to justify our own. It is wicked to attribute uncommitted sins to him to give ourselves a license to sin. Generations have been cursed for this error.[540] We *have* been led astray. All of us in every branch of Mormonism err.

We stumble, and we have fallen down. We have discarded the expansive theology of Joseph Smith. The earliest dispensations had truth from heaven as their guide. Joseph began reassembling what was lost, but was slain before it was completed. We are the offspring of heaven, and are capable of reuniting with heaven while mortal. We

---

[538] T&C 82:20.

[539] T&C 139:7.

[540] "Cursed are all those that shall lift up the heel against my anointed, says the Lord, and cry, They have sinned, when they have not sinned before me, says the Lord, but have done that which was meet in my eyes, and which I commanded them. But those who cry transgression do it because they are the servants of sin, and are the children of disobedience themselves, and those who swear false against my servants, that they might bring them unto bondage and death, woe unto them because they have offended my little ones. They shall be severed from the ordinances of my house, their basket shall not be full, their Houses and their barns shall famish, and they themselves shall be despised by those that flattered them." (T&C 138:13.)

also have the opportunity, through eons of progression, to become as our Parents, the Gods.

Now it is time to awaken, arise, and shake off the dust.[541]

Some will awaken, arise, shake off the dust and push forward to recover the restoration. God will set His hand a second time to accomplish His covenants. We are promised there will be a last-days' Zion established on this, the American continent. We know that when it is here:

> "[E]very man that will not take his sword against his neighbor must needs flee unto Zion for safety, and there shall be gathered unto it out of every nation under Heaven, and it shall be the only people that shall not be at war one with another. And it shall be said among the wicked, Let us not go up to battle against Zion, for the inhabitants of Zion are terrible, wherefore we cannot stand. And it shall come to pass that the righteous shall be gathered out from among all nations, and shall come to Zion singing with songs of everlasting joy."[542]

The restoration has indeed squandered many opportunities by those who went before. Most of those who accept Joseph Smith as a founder of their religion are still squandering the opportunity to see the work continue. But God's purposes do not fail and we have the option to proceed now. Some generation, at some point, still has a glorious, promised completion to anticipate. As long as some, even a very few, are willing to walk in God's path, they will see the completion of this glorious, final work. "This is the purpose that is purposed upon the whole earth, and this is the hand that is stretched out upon all the nations. For the Lord of hosts has purposed, and who shall disannul? And his hand is stretched out, and who shall turn it back?"[543]

Why not now? Why not us? All that is required is to repent and return. The promise we have in exchange for our returning to the path is the stuff all the prophets and righteous from the days of Adam have eagerly anticipated.

---

[541] NC 2 Ne. 5:11.
[542] T&C 31:15.
[543] OC Isa. 6:7.

**Chapter 6: The Holy Order**
©Denver C. Snuffer, 2017

I was asked to discuss the topic of "priesthood." The biggest challenge in discussing the topic is that those most interested already have a context in their mind and so whatever is said about priesthood is distorted by their misunderstandings. It becomes almost impossible to make any meaningful forward movement in understanding a much bigger picture. To make progress, this discussion should be looked at as introducing something very different from how you now understand priesthood. Consider new ideas that may change the picture altogether.

I will be using quotes from Joseph Smith that frequently use the word "keys." That word is horribly misunderstood. I have made it a practice to not use the word because of all the foolish and vain ideas that have accumulated around it. Joseph used the term in a variety of ways. For example, to mean "authority,"[544] or opportunity,[545] and in others it refers to a correct idea.[546] The term in the context of priesthood is completely absent from the Book of Mormon; and that book is the keystone of our religion, containing the fullness of the gospel. The only time the word "keys" is referenced in the Book of Mormon, it refers to a physical set of keys to unlock a door to the treasury controlled by Laban.[547] Although Joseph used the term often and meant many things by it, the challenge is to understand priesthood without being distracted by a poorly defined, and often used term.

Mormon institutions now use the term most often to connote that there is exclusive right, license or control. The LDS *Handbook of Instructions* states the following, "Priesthood keys are the authority God has given to priesthood leaders to direct, control, and govern the use of His priesthood on earth."[548] This definition is the opposite of the way scripture directs priesthood be used:

> We have learned by sad experience that it is the
> nature and disposition of almost all men, as soon as
> they get a little authority, as they suppose, they will

---

[544] See, D&C 107:15.
[545] See, D&C 107:20.
[546] See, D&C 129:9. This is the most important meaning.
[547] See, 1 Ne. 4:20.
[548] *Handbook of Instructions* 2, 2.1.1.

immediately begin to exercise unrighteous dominion. Hence many are called, but few are chosen. No power or influence can or ought to be maintained by virtue of the priesthood, only by persuasion, by long-suffering, by gentleness and meekness, and by love unfeigned; By kindness, and pure knowledge, which shall greatly enlarge the soul without hypocrisy, and without guile[.]" (D&C 121:39-42.)

The LDS *Handbook* approach turns this scripture upside down and backwards: by virtue of priesthood keys they have the right to direct, control and exercise influence over others. Mormon institutions in general all use their preferred meaning of the term "keys" to denounce anything or anyone they view as a rival. That is nonsense, and I avoid using the term because of widespread abusive practice.

The greatest "key" to unlock truth is "pure knowledge, which shall greatly enlarge the soul." This is how the Brother of Jared was able to pierce the veil. "And because of the knowledge of this man he could not be kept from beholding within the veil[.]" (Ether 3:19.) It was the pursuit of "greater knowledge" that led Abraham to find God.

When God gives a man a dispensation from heaven, there is a labor to be done in His vineyard. The authority to complete the labor is implicit with the assignment given by God. When someone receives a dispensation and discharges the assignment with honor, he holds the keys, owns the rights, enjoys the honors, and possesses the dispensation of that assignment to all eternity.[549] A new dispensation is founded on knowledge from those who went before who "all [declare] their dispensation, their rights, their keys, their honors, their majesty and glory, and the power of their priesthood; giving line upon line, precept upon precept; here a little, and there a little"[550] to the new dispensation. An unchanging God bestows an unchanging gospel. Therefore, there is continuity and understanding shared along the path. These servants obtained rights and honors and are expected

---

[549] See, D&C 128: 21—the reason these ministers returned to visit Joseph was because they acquired the "keys" after successfully completing the assignment God gave them. Joseph needed this endowment to lay the foundation for a new dispensation.

[550] *Id.*

to come to the great future meeting when Adam-ondi-Ahman occurs[551] in the last days. At that meeting an accounting will be given in the presence of Christ to Father Adam, preliminary to Christ's return as the One whose right it is to preside over all things. If a dispensation was given and the recipient failed to complete the work God assigned, then he acquires no key, no honor, no right, no authority from the Lord and therefore has nothing to account for to Adam.

All who are invited to the future meeting when Adam-ondi-Ahman occurs again will give an account of their labor. This means it is necessary for servants to perform what God assigns to them in strict conformity to the assignment to honor and serve God. The notion that someone can obtain "keys" without receiving a dispensation from the Lord and successfully completing the work of God, is an idea that should be rejected.

To be clear, for the foregoing reasons, and because many Mormons misunderstand and misapply the word "keys" to mean authority to control and direct, I avoid using the term. Many people believe that one dispensation must resemble another. There are those are critical or ignorant of what God is doing now because it is different from what Joseph Smith did. There have been only two successful models since the fall of man. The scriptures disclose little about Enoch and Melchizedek's dispensations, but there is enough to know they did not establish an hierarchical institution with inequality between people. The work of God today will be done as He alone directs. It is apparent from what has already taken place, that God intends to complete many things that Joseph Smith only hinted at and never had the opportunity to accomplish.

As events progressed in Joseph Smith's life, he used some words with specific intended meanings based on events at a specific moment in time. For example, "fullness of the priesthood" was used by Joseph Smith at different times with different meanings. It always conveyed that the recipient had accepted all that had been given to a point in time. The willing readiness to accept all that had been offered at the time of the dedication of the Kirtland Temple meant the believer had

---

[551] The phrase means "Adam in the presence of Son Ahman." The first time this happened was near Spring Hill in Missouri. Since it was an event, and the location acquired significance because of what happened there, I use the term to describe a future event rather than a fixed location. Latter-day Saints think the future event will take place at the same location as the first event, but —like the location of the New Jerusalem—may happen elsewhere.

been ordained to the Aaronic and Melchizedek priesthoods, been baptized and, as the then-current practice involved, been rebaptized, and passed through an initiatory washing and anointing. The term used during the late-Nauvoo period of Joseph Smith's life involved all of the foregoing and, an endowment and sealing, second anointing, and finally an adoption process tying the individual into a family relationship that would endure after death. Because Joseph Smith used the phrase "fullness of the priesthood" dynamically and not statically, his various revelations making use of the term should not be read as having a single meaning. In a final sense, *fullness of priesthood* will be post-resurrection, and will come to those who have continually manifested a willingness to accept the dynamic and progressive fullness of the priesthood offered by God to man in the development and restoration of all things.

There is a reason the temple ceremony begins by telling the story of the creation and involves our first parents, Adam and Eve. Priesthood, at least the Holy Order, should not be divorced from the creation and from the first man and woman. We do not appreciate the significance of the beginning. Adam was given a fullness, and possessed the Holy Order after the Order of the Son of God. It was given to him in the beginning. (Abr. 1:3.) There was more to this than is involved in later priestly service.[552]

The Holy Order was much greater in scope than later priesthoods. Later priesthood functions should not be used to apprehend understanding of the original. Something as narrow and limited as a man (or angel) laying hands on another man did not and could not convey the original Holy Order.

After Eden, conveying the original Holy Order required either a temple or an ascent into heaven. It is one of the reasons why prophecy foretells of a last days temple. Information, instruction and revelation were essential to the Holy Order. The man and woman who entered into the Holy Order were taught truths about the

---

[552] Although I am going to discuss this topic in only a limited way, each time I convey more of what God is now doing it gives God's opponents more information they can use to deceive others. I hesitate to equip the pretenders, the well intentioned but deceived, and the foolish more ammunition to make a better pretense. Even those who hold good intentions, are often tempted to run into errors because they possess only a tiny fraction of the truth. We should all only disclose what God approves to be given, when He directs, and how He directs.

creation, heaven and man's relationship to the universe. When Abraham was seeking to obtain what was given to Father Adam, he studied records that came down from "the fathers." This included not just a chronology back to Adam, but also "to the beginning of the creation, for the records have come into my hands[.]" (Abr. 1:28.) This knowledge is conveyed to those who belong to the Holy Order. When the return of the original Holy Order is contemplated, consider that it will involve restoring great knowledge that is hidden from the world. The fathers knew it would be restored in the last days. Joseph Smith also prophesied of its return and explained the forefathers of mankind anxiously anticipated its return.[553]

Isaiah's prophecy concerning the last days' temple clearly identifies it as a house where man will be instructed in God's path. It will be a facility where the God of Jacob will teach His pathway of ascent back to the Throne of God. Mankind will learn the laws governing that pathway.[554]

---

[553] The following is in D&C 121:26-32: "God shall give unto you knowledge by his Holy Spirit, yea, by the unspeakable gift of the Holy Ghost, that has not been revealed since the world was until now; Which our forefathers have awaited with anxious expectation to be revealed in the last times, which their minds were pointed to by the angels, as held in reserve for the fulness of their glory; A time to come in the which nothing shall be withheld, whether there be one God or many gods, they shall be manifest. All thrones and dominions, principalities and powers, shall be revealed and set forth upon all who have endured valiantly for the gospel of Jesus Christ. And also, if there be bounds set to the heavens or to the seas, or to the dry land, or to the sun, moon, or stars—All the times of their revolutions, all the appointed days, months, and years, and all the days of their days, months, and years, and all their glories, laws, and set times, shall be revealed in the days of the dispensation of the fulness of times—According to that which was ordained in the midst of the Council of the Eternal God of all other gods before this world was, that should be reserved unto the finishing and the end thereof, when every man shall enter into his eternal presence and into his immortal rest."

[554] Isaiah 2:2-3: "And it shall come to pass in the last days, that the mountain of the Lord's house shall be established in the top of the mountains, and shall be exalted above the hills; and all nations shall flow unto it. And many people shall go and say, Come ye, and let us go up to the mountain of the Lord, to the house of the God of Jacob; and he will teach us of his ways, and we will walk in his paths: for out of Zion shall go forth the law[.]"

Therefore, when the Holy Order returns, those who are initiated will be given more than just the laying on of hands. It will include men and women, as husband and wife. They will be given understanding of things which the world cannot know because it is forbidden for the profane to obtain what God decrees for the righteous alone to maintain in holiness. The unholy are excluded from this knowledge.[555]

The Holy Order in its truest sense is much more comprehensive and far reaching than just laying on hands to convey permission to perform ordinances. This discussion will focus on the return of the original Holy Order belonging to the first fathers. Begin by assuming that you know almost nothing about the Holy Order, and that the Holy Order is not the priesthood as currently understood. It is distinct and broader than something commonly called "priesthood." Some of the quotes from Joseph use the word "priesthood" in the original. I will use the words "Holy Order" to help clarify this is a different subject and needs to be separate from the inherited traditions.

Joseph said, "The [Holy Order] was first given to Adam; he obtained the First Presidency." As an aside, when Joseph explained this in 1839 there was a church position called "the First Presidency." The church position was a proper noun. When the *Teachings of the Prophet Joseph Smith* was published, the publisher was the LDS church, and so when "First Presidency" was used it was treated as if it referred to the church position. However, the position Adam occupied was the first presiding father, or first presidency of the family of God; not a church position. The family of God is not the same thing as an institutional church. The institutional church will never comprise the family of God, although it was intended as a tool to bring about the recovery of the family of God. Unfortunately, the

---

[555] The Book of Mormon excludes sacred information from the ungodly (see, e.g., 1 Ne. 14:28; 3 Ne. 26:11-12, 16; 3 Ne. 27:23). Joseph Smith did not reveal everything entrusted to him (D&C 76:114-116; JS-H 1:20). Information can be sacred. It can be controlled by God so that when He determines to communicate it to man He will do so either by catching the individual up into the heavenly realm or by commanding that a temple be built to house His revelations. Either option will require that those who enter in must be approved by His decree, because the way is guarded by sentinels who protect what is Holy from those who are profane.

institution grew to hinder the restoration of the family of God. God must now use a different means to fulfill His promises.

[The Holy Order] was first given to Adam; he obtained the [first presiding position on the Earth], and held the keys of it from generation to generation. He obtained it in the Creation, before the world was formed, as in Genesis 1:26, 27, 28. He had dominion given him over every living creature. He is Michael the Archangel, spoken of in the Scriptures. Then to Noah, who is Gabriel; he stands next in authority to Adam in the [Holy Order]; he was called of God to this office, and was the Father of all living in this day, and to him was given the dominion. These men held keys first on earth, and then in heaven.

The [Holy Order] is an everlasting principle, and existed with God from eternity, and will to eternity, without beginning of days or end of years. The keys have to be brought from heaven, whenever the Gospel is sent. When they are revealed from Heaven, it is by Adam's authority.

...He (Adam) is the father of the human family, and presides over the spirits of all men, and all that have had the keys must stand before him in this grand council. This may take place before some of us leave this stage of action. The Son of Man stands before him, and there is given him glory and dominion. Adam delivers up his stewardship to Christ, that which was delivered to him as holding the keys the of the universe but retains his standing as the head of the human family.[556]

So, the Holy Order really commences before the world with Adam. In Luke 3:38, he, the first man, is called "the son of God." Adam obtained the Holy Order in the beginning and before the world. Included with it is the right to preside over all of the human family and the right to minister to Adam's posterity. Adam continues to hold that presiding position and will do so until the end of time.

---

[556] *TPJS*, p. 157.

In those remarks Joseph skipped from Adam down to Noah because Adam had dominion and rights over all of humanity as the father of all mankind. Noah occupied the same position. Both of these men were the genealogical fathers of all mankind born after them. In the case of Noah, the right descended to him through the Fathers: Adam, Seth, Enos, Cainan, Mahalaleel, Jared, Enoch, Methuselah, Lamech and then Noah.[557] All of these fathers held that same Holy Order, but they had siblings and other relations who were not their descendants. Therefore, although they were within the Holy Order, unlike Adam and unlike Noah, there were other people living who would descend outside of their genealogical line.

The Holy Order was passed down through these fathers. Joseph discussed the subject from the perspective of identifying those who were the genealogical fathers of all living. That is why he referred to Adam and Noah, omitting the others.

Joseph said,

> there are two priesthoods spoken of in the Scriptures, viz., the Melchizedek and the Aaronic or Levitical. Although there are two priesthoods, yet the Melchizedek Priesthood comprehends the Aaronic or Levitical Priesthood, and is the grand head, and holds the highest authority which pertains to [the Holy Order] and the keys of the Kingdom of God in all ages of the world, to the latest posterity on the earth; and is the channel through which all knowledge, doctrine, the plan of salvation, and every important matter is revealed from heaven.[558]

---

[557] It was the responsibility of the oldest living holder of the Order to ordain. So long as Adam was alive, it was Adam who ordained those in this line. Adam ordained Seth (D&C 107:42), Enos (v. 44), Cainan (v. 45), Mahalaleel (v. 46), Jared (v. 47), and Methuselah (v. 50). When Adam died it was Seth who ordained Lamech (v. 51). Noah was ordained by Methuselah (v. 52), the oldest living holder of the Order at that time.

[558] In a letter written September 1842 Joseph Smith referred to this same principle: "Now the great and grand secret of the whole matter, and the summum bonum of the whole subject that is lying before us, consists in obtaining the powers of the Holy Priesthood. For him to whom these keys are given there is no difficulty in obtaining a knowledge of facts in relation to the salvation of the children of men, both as well for the dead as for the living." (D&C 128:11.)

"Its institution was prior to 'the foundation of this earth, or the morning stars sang together, or the Sons of God shouted for joy' and is the highest and holiest [order] after the order of the Son of God.[559]

We think that the renaming of the Holy Order to the Melchizedek priesthood in order to avoid the too frequent repetition of the name of the Son of God,[560] was done out of respect for the Messiah, Jesus Christ, and that is true enough. However, the Holy Order after the Order of the Son of God includes the first man, Adam, who is also identified as a "son of God."[561] There are other "sons of God." The apostle John wrote in his first epistle to those he had taught. He gave them what he had received from Christ. He explained,

> Behold what manner of love the Father hath bestowed upon us that we should be called the sons of God. Therefore, the world knoweth us not because it knew Him not. Beloved now are we the sons of God. And it doth not yet appear what we shall be, but we know that, when He shall appear, we shall be like Him, for we shall see Him as He is. Every man that hath this hope in him, purifieth himself, even as He is pure.[562]

The Holy Order after the Order of the Son of God makes those who inherit it by definition the sons of God. Therefore, in a way, calling it the Holy Order after the Order of the Son of God is a way of identifying the recipient as someone who has become one of God's sons. Of course it is also appropriate to regard the primary Son of God to be Jesus Christ and Jesus Christ alone. He is the only one in this cycle of creation who has attained to the resurrection. It is through the power of His resurrection that we are going to come forth from the grave. We do not have the power in ourselves to rise from the dead. The wages of sin are death,[563] we have earned those wages, and we will die. The Savior did not earn those wages, but He nonetheless died, and His death was unjust. The law of justice was broken when He died and so whenever justice makes a claim on any of us, He can point to the fact that justice extracted from Him eternal

---

[559] *TPJS*, p. 166-167.
[560] See, D&C 107:2-4.
[561] Luke 3:38.
[562] 1 John 3:2-3.
[563] Rom. 6:23.

life. That was an infinite price for Him to have paid. He has compensated for all of mankind's shortcomings, failures, and Christ is the means by which we lay hold upon the promises. It is His intention to make of us all sons of God.

The Holy Order after the Order of the Son of God identifies the persons holding the Order as God's sons. Even though the couple may be mortals in the flesh, they are by definition "sons of God" if they belong to the Order.[564] This is one reason why the sacrament prayer for the bread that is eaten by both men and women includes "take upon them the name of thy Son."[565]

In *Preserving the Restoration*, pages 509-510, the following answers from the Lord are recounted:

> Because of the potential and actual abuse by some priesthood holding men, I asked the Lord to extend priesthood to women. I was told as to public rites, "priesthood is confined to men because of the Fall and the conditions ordained at that time."[566] Until things are reversed at the Millennium, it will remain for men alone to perform the public ordinances thus far given to us. This order is not going to change until the Millennium. I asked the Lord that if only men were to hold priesthood for our public ordinances, then could only women vote to sustain them. This pleased the Lord, for it was already in His heart. But He added: "There shall be a minimum of seven women[567] to sustain the man in

---

[564] It is the nature of this Holy Order that it is conferred upon the man and woman jointly. See 1 Cor. 11:11. It was never "good for man to be alone." See Gen. 2:18; Moses 3:18; Abr. 5:14. See also the Answer to Prayer for Covenant providing a new revelation on marriage, which states in part: "And again, I say to you, Abraham and Sarah sit upon a Throne, for he could not be there if not for Sarah's covenant with him. Isaac and Rebecca sit upon a Throne, and Isaac likewise could not be there if not for Rebecca's covenant with him. And Jacob and Rachel sit upon a Throne, and Jacob could not be there if not for Rachel's covenant with him. And all these have ascended above Dominions and Principalities and Powers, to abide in my Kingdom. Therefore the marriage covenant is needed for all those who would likewise seek to obtain from me the right to continue their seed into eternity, for only through marriage can Thrones and Kingdoms be established."
[565] Moroni 4:3.
[566] Moses 4:22; Gen. 3:16.

any vote, and if the man is married, his wife shall be one of them." If you have already been ordained then you have the right to continue to minister to your family as a matter of right. But outside your family it is different. Even though already ordained, a community needs to recognize and authorize anyone to minister for them.

For any who would like to qualify to minister outside his family, he must meet in a community and obtain a sustaining vote of a minimum of seven women.[568] When that is done, all seven who vote to sustain should sign a certificate.

This answer refers to "public rites" and not to those rites and performances the public are excluded from knowing. The Holy Order conveys blessings and information that is withheld from the world. But men and women jointly obtain the Holy Order.

Joseph continued, "...all other priesthoods are only parts, ramifications, powers and blessings belonging to the same, and are held, controlled, and directed by it. It is the channel through which the Almighty commenced revealing His glory at the beginning of the creation of this earth, and through which He has continued to reveal Himself to the children of men to the present time, and through which He will make known His purposes to the end of time." (*TPJS*, p. 167.) Among other things, the purpose of the Holy Order is to put in place a mechanism by which God can reveal from heaven what is necessary for the salvation of man on Earth. In every generation when God has provided salvation for mankind, it is the Holy Order used by God to fix what is broken, restore what has been lost, repair, heal, forgive, and reconnect those who are willing to give heed to the

---

[567] Several people suggested to me that this requirement of seven women sustaining is a last-days' fulfillment of Isa. 4:1-2 and 2 Ne. 14:1. If so, this would mean the prophecy of being "called by thy name" refers to the name of Christ. Seven women sustaining a man to priesthood precedes the ordinance of baptism itself. When baptized, we take upon us the name of Christ. It is the name of Christ through baptism that will "take away our reproach," or in other words provide the remission of sins, as mentioned in Isa. 4:2.

[568] This is information provided to me by the Lord on the morning of July 27, 2014 only after the talk given in St. George, Utah the day before.

message sent from Heaven to enable mankind to become sons of God.

Early events in man's history involve conflicts to control the Holy Order. There was a war in heaven[569] that continues on earth.[570] In the earliest generations Adam and Eve taught their children to worship God.[571] But "Satan came among them, saying I am also a son of God; and he commanded them, saying: Believe it not; and they believed it not, and they loved Satan more than God. And men began from that time forth to be carnal, sensual, and devilish." (Moses 5:13.)

There is an opposition in all things.[572] Having opposition gives mankind a choice. But mankind's choice is dependent on being pulled in different directions.[573] Man must be afforded the freedom to choose between these opposing sides. Without the freedom to choose there is no existence.[574] Satan wanted to destroy the agency of man.[575] This in turn would end mankind's ability to choose for themselves. In other words, it would destroy their existence. Mankind can only be held accountable for their choices if they are free to make a choice.[576] Satan wanted to eliminate the right to choose, and also eliminate any accountability for man's choices. The reason his plan attracted enough followers in heaven to cause a war was because he wanted to eliminate any law or commandment against sin. In the absence of a law against whatever a person chooses to do then there would be no condemnation and no judgment.[577]

Adam and Eve taught about repentance from sins.[578] Satan offered another path that did not require desires, appetites and passions to be controlled. The result was carnality, sensuality and licentiousness.[579] The descendants of Adam and Eve were overcome by what Satan offered. In the earliest generations, the war Satan began and lost in heaven continued on earth with overwhelming success.

---

[569] Rev. 12:7.
[570] Rev. 12:12.
[571] Moses 5:12.
[572] 2 Ne. 2:11.
[573] 2 Ne. 2:16.
[574] D&C 93:30.
[575] Moses 4:3.
[576] D&C 101:78.
[577] 2 Ne. 2:13.
[578] Moses 5:14-15.
[579] Moses 5:13.

After generations there was a son born to Adam and Eve who exhibited the inclination to follow God. Eve rejoiced over Cain and declared, "I have gotten a man from the Lord; wherefore he may not reject his words." (Moses 5:16.) Had Cain remained faithful he would have succeeded Adam as the one given the Holy Order, holding dominion over the earth. Through his line the promised Messiah[580] would have descended and Cain would be a patriarch over him.

Satan wanted to be chosen as the Savior so that he could implement his plan to save all mankind. Both he and his plan were rejected.[581] If he had been given the role of Savior he could have implemented his plan making it a condition for saving mankind. When he was not chosen, Satan wanted to become Adam, the first man, and stand as the patriarch over the entire family of man. This would have given him leverage to exert dominion over the creation and accomplish the same result. When he was rejected again, he rebelled and was cast out. As an exile from heaven, he targeted Adam and Eve to lead them to transgress God's commands.[582] When Cain became the probable heir of Adam, to receive the Holy Order and father the line through which the promised Messiah would come, Satan's attention turned to corrupting Cain.

A younger brother, Abel, also followed God. There had been universal rebellion (or apostasy) against God by the children of Adam and Eve until Cain. But then both Cain and Abel showed interest in following God. It is probable that Cain's example influenced Abel for the good. Since the Order would follow the oldest, righteous son, Cain would be the heir. Abel's righteous could not displace Cain, had Cain remained faithful.

Cain followed Satan and obeyed Satan's command to offer a sacrifice. Abel followed God and obeyed God's command to offer a sacrifice. The contrast between Cain and Abel provoked God to accept Abel's sacrifice and reject Cain's.[583] Cain was offended at God's rejection, but God offered to accept Cain if he would repent and return.[584]

---

[580] Adam and Eve were taught by an angel of a future Messiah, called the "Only Begotten" who would be offered a sacrifice for sin and redeem Adam and his posterity. Moses 5:6-9.

[581] Moses 4:1; Abr. 3:27-28.

[582] Moses 4:3-4, 18-19.

[583] Moses 5:18-21.

[584] Moses 5:22-23.

This was a conflict that involved who would inherit the Holy Order. Satan wanted to destroy the plan of God. If he could gain control over the right of dominion, and make the coming Messiah subject to a patriarch who would support Satan's ambition, he hoped to still prevail in the conflict over this creation. Cain could have repented and retained his right to inherit from Adam. God offered him that. Adam and Eve also urged Cain to repent. Abel pled with Cain to repent.[585] Cain rejected them all, took a wife and left the company of his parents and brother Abel.

There is no record of how many years passed, but the ambition to control and corrupt this creation was never out of the heart of Satan. Desperate ambitions lead to desperate acts, and the solution Satan inspired was for Cain to murder his brother.[586] This was an attempt to get control over the entire creation by overthrowing the government of God and confiscate the birthright and associated Holy Order that accompanied it. The "flocks of my brother" Cain wanted to control as his "gain" was the lineage through whom the Messiah would descend.[587]

This is an important part of the plot of the adversary because if he can control any position under Adam involving the Holy Order, this creation can be compromised. God has a house of order. When the world was created it belonged to God. By His word He gave dominion over His creation to Adam and Eve. It became theirs and Adam holds the right to preside over it, as Joseph Smith explained. That right must be returned to Jesus Christ before His return.[588] If anyone who has held a position in the Holy Order refuses to return dominion back to Christ, it can create a conflict that continues the same war that began in heaven. If Cain were to hold dominion over this creation, he could impose conditions Satan put into his heart before returning the right of dominion back to the Savior. By extension, if any disciple of Satan were ever to obtain the Holy Order with the right of dominion the conditions Satan demanded in the preexistence, which were designed to destroy the agency of man, could become the condition for redeeming this creation. Cain's

---

[585] Moses 5:26-27.

[586] Moses 5:28-31.

[587] Moses 5:31-33.

[588] "Adam delivers up his stewardship to Christ, that which was delivered to him as holding the keys the of the universe but retains his standing as the head of the human family." (*TPJS*, p. 157.) See also D&C 116:1; Dan. 7:9-10.

apostasy was a continuation of the war in heaven and a threat to the salvation of everyone who would live thereafter. Threatening salvation of mankind has been the aim of our adversary since the beginning. There is still a great conspiracy to destroy the souls of men and to capture this creation. The Holy Order is guarded by carefully qualifying those who receive it. It is under God's control and supervised by Adam and Eve.

Despite the enormity of Cain's sin, his punishment was not death. His parents wept over him, and he was driven from their society. The earth was told to not give her yield to Cain, making him a vagabond and a hunter, slaying animals for his sustenance.[589] He killed his brother because of ambition and then was required to continue killing to eat. But he was allowed to live.

To understand the Holy Order one must start with the beginning. Jumping ahead to the time of Moses and the Aaronic priests, or even the time of Joseph Smith, misses the mark. Priesthood in its most meaningful sense involves the Holy Order after the Order of the Son of God. The restoration at the end of creation must return to the beginning. Before the return of Christ, everything, including the original Holy Order with all its components, must be restored. That has not yet been revealed.

The Holy Order did not return with the ordinations in June 1831.[590] It was not accomplished when the three witnesses ordained the quorum of the twelve.[591] There is something far greater within the Holy Order. It includes the right of dominion over all creation, or the same right originally given to Adam that belonged to God. The right of dominion over this creation is why God is God. In essence, the Holy Order is to create of flesh and blood a living, mortal surrogate for the Father and Mother. Cain fell, Able was murdered, and the right passed to Seth. Seth stands next in the line followed in turn by Enos, Cainan, Mahalaleel, Jared, Enoch, Methuselah, Lamech and then Noah. All these lived before the flood. Noah alone remained on earth with his family. His son Shem inherited the Holy Order. Shem was a great high priest[592] after the Order of the Son of God. Shem obtained the right of dominion, and was referred to as a "king." He

---

[589] Moses 5:36-37.
[590] See the discussion on pp. 17-34 in *A Man Without Doubt*. 45 See, *DHC*, Vol 2, pp. 186-191.
[591] See, *DHC*, Vol 2, pp. 186-191
[592] D&C 107:2; 138:41.

also held the right to preach righteousness and was referred to as a "priest." Melchizedek is a new name given to him and means "king and priest." That new name was then also adopted as the name for the Holy Order itself.[593]

The line was then broken for generations. This was the first gap between Adam and his posterity who held the Holy Order. Until Abraham,[594] this break lasted nine generations. After this long gap, a man lived whose heart longed for what once was. He wanted to recover and restore what had been lost. He wrote, "[F]inding there was greater happiness and peace and rest for me, I sought for the blessings of the fathers..." (Abr. 1:2.) The "blessings of the fathers" he wanted to obtain was the original Holy Order. He wanted to be like the first fathers.

Abraham "sought for the blessings of the fathers and the right whereunto I should be ordained to administer the same, having been myself a follower of righteousness, desiring also to be one who possessed great knowledge and to be a greater follower of righteousness, and to possess a greater knowledge[.]" (Abr. 1:2.) Knowledge is a critical component of the Holy Order. Rather than worldly status or rank, the Holy Order involves "great knowledge" from God. The greater knowledge of the Holy Order is the reason a man cannot be saved in ignorance. "It is impossible for a man to be saved in ignorance." (D&C 131:6.) "A man is saved no faster than he gets knowledge, for if he does not get knowledge, he will be brought into captivity by some evil power in the other world, as evil spirits will have more knowledge, and consequently more power than many men who are on the earth. Hence it needs revelation to assist us, and give

---

[593] D&C 107:2-4.

[594] The generations were: Shem/Melchizedek-Arphaxad-Cainan-unnamed daughter-Eber-Peleg-Reu-Serug-Nahor-Terah-Abraham. Abraham described his forefathers in these words: "My fathers, having turned from their righteousness, and from the holy commandments which the Lord their God had given unto them, unto the worshiping of the gods of the heathen, utterly refused to hearken to my voice; For their hearts were set to do evil, and were wholly turned to the god of Elkenah, and the god of Libnah, and the god of Mahmackrah, and the god of Korash, and the god of Pharaoh, king of Egypt; Therefore they turned their hearts to the sacrifice of the heathen in offering up their children unto these dumb idols, and hearkened not unto my voice, but endeavored to take away my life by the hand of the priest of Elkenah. The priest of Elkenah was also the priest of Pharaoh."

us knowledge of the things of God." (*TPJS*, p. 217.) The "knowledge" Joseph Smith refers to is that same "knowledge" Abraham sought after.[595] Its purpose is to allow the one who possesses it to become a greater follower of righteousness. Godly knowledge must be implemented to save one's soul. There is no salvation without obedience to the principles of righteousness learned. It is the same for everyone as it was for Abraham: "[T]o posess a greater knowledge and to be a father of many nations, a prince of peace, and desiring to receive instructions, and to keep the commandments of God." This is what made him " a rightful heir." (Abr. 1:2.)

At this point in history, Adam was the father of all who were living. Noah would also have been the father of all. All the early members of the Holy Order fathered nations. Abraham knew that was part of what the Holy Order involved. It was not merely knowledge for knowledge's sake that motivated Abraham. He knew it would put him at the head of a righteous posterity. At that point in history, it also meant the promised Messiah would descend from his fatherhood. Abraham anticipated obtaining a posterity of "nations" that would look to him, as he looked to Noah and to Adam, as his fathers.

This role of fatherhood was (and is) an opportunity to nurture, assist, provide for, care for and bring along descendants. It gives the father and mother the challenge and opportunity to take a child who is innocent and teachable and help develop them into something Godlike, responsible and capable. Someone who can stand on her own two legs and defend the truth when called upon to do so: someone who can become a vessel of righteousness. What Abraham desired was to be a servant who would be a father of nations.

And so he "became a rightful heir, holding the right belonging to the fathers, it was conferred upon me from the fathers. It came down from the fathers from the beginning of time, even from the beginning, before the foundation of the earth, down to the present time, even the right of the firstborn or the first man who was Adam or the first father, through the fathers unto me." (Abr. 1:2-3.)

---

[595] "Knowledge saves a man; and in the world of spirits no man can be exalted but by knowledge. So long as a man will not give heed to the commandments, he must abide without salvation. If a man has knowledge, he can be saved; although, if he has been guilty of great sins, he will be punished for them." (*TPJS*, p. 357.)

Abraham identifies what he sought and obtained. It was the original Holy Order that began with Adam or the first father.

Abraham's right was non-genealogical because generations separated him from Shem. Like today, Abraham was living in a world of apostasy, isolated from God's Holy Order. Like Abraham, we should be looking to reconnect to Heaven.

He is the first example of a man in a world of apostasy reconnecting to Heaven. Despite the generations separating Abraham from Shem, he qualified to receive the rights belonging to the fathers because he sought for his appointment, he possessed knowledge, he lived consistent with the knowledge he had and wished to have greater knowledge, and he wanted to obey more commandments to gain further light and knowledge by the things he learned through obedience. When Abraham received the Holy Order by ordination from the oldest living holder,[596] Melchizedek, the Lord accepted Abraham and declared to him: "My name is Jehovah, and I know the end from the beginning; therefore my hand shall be over thee. And I will make of thee a great nation, and I will bless thee above measure, and make thy name great among all nations, and thou shalt be a blessing unto thy seed after thee, that in their hands they shall bear this ministry and Priesthood unto all nations; And I will bless them through thy name; for as many as receive this Gospel shall be called after thy name, and shall be accounted thy seed, and shall rise up and bless thee, as their father" (Abr. 2:8-10.) This future for the Holy Order is also non-genealogical in that there have been and will be distant generations separated from Abraham who will inherit the Holy Order. It was and will be the same process through which Abraham became a descendant of the first fathers. The reconnecting has and does happen after generations of apostasy. Whoever does, in whatever generation, is a descendant and can call Abraham their father.

The Lord declared to Abraham, "I will bless them that bless thee and curse them that curse thee and in thee (that is in thy Holy Order) and in thy seed (that is the Holy Order) for I will give unto thee a promise that this right shall continue in thee and in thy seed after thee (that is to say the literal seed, or the seed of the body) shall all the families of the earth be blessed, even with the blessings of the Gospel, which are the blessings of salvation, even of eternal life." (Abr. 2:11.)

---

[596] D&C 84:14.

Any person in any generation (after Abraham) who becomes part of the Holy Order will be grafted into the line of the fathers, and become a descendant of Father Abraham.

When the Lord said these things to Abraham, he reflected soberly on what had transpired and recorded, "After the Lord had withdrawn from speaking with me, and withdrawn His face from me, I said in my heart, Thy servant has sought thee earnestly, now I have found thee." (Abr. 2:12.)

In verse 10, the Lord refers to "this Gospel." That is not necessarily referring to what the gospel is today. In Abraham's case, he had both "great knowledge" as well as "greater knowledge." Those are important words and were important parts of "this Gospel" to which God made reference. It is very difficult to bring "this Gospel" back to the earth. When the process begins, men almost immediately rebel and close their minds. It stirs up the adversary to action. Religious people seem particularly influenced to fight against the return of the Holy Order. They always fight against the prophets and messengers because they are in Satan's employ without realizing it. The temple endowment (before 1990) included the role of the false minister. Despite its removal, that role belongs in the endowment. The point of the character was that he worked for Satan but believed he was following God.[597] When God referred to "this Gospel" it is a body of teachings and rights that are very hard to recover. Mankind is disinterested God's words and continually insists they already have enough and cannot tolerate God giving more.[598]

There was a great deal more to be recovered, restored and returned left undone at Joseph's death.[599] When "this Gospel,"

---

[597] Peter asked the false minister: "Do you know who that man is? He is Satan." The fooled preacher responded: "What? The devil?" Peter answered: "That is one of his names." Then the deceived preacher explained: "He is quite a different person from what he told me the devil is. He said the devil has claws like a bear's on his hands, horns on his head, and a cloven foot, and that when he speaks he has the roar of a lion." Peter then responded: "He has said this to deceive you, and I would advise you to get out of his employ."

[598] 2 Ne. 29:8-10.

[599] In January 1841 the potential for the "fullness of the priesthood" to be given the church had been lost and could only be restored in a temple. (D&C 124:27-28.) In the letter to John Wentworth first published in March 1842 Joseph Smith wrote, "we believe that [God] will yet reveal many great and

meaning the one Abraham received, is on the earth at any time, the possessor is a descendant of Abraham. They are part of the family of Abraham and he is their father. In this way he became the father of many nations.

Today the status of "father of many nations" still applies to the Holy Order, but the process is inverted. Instead of being the father through descendants of the body, the Holy Order contains the right to redeem the dead. But the dead do not remain as ancestors but become posterity. The living members of the Holy Order are the fathers and mothers of the dead whom they redeem. But that topic is best left for the future time when the temple exists. If this generation fails to obtain the right, and neglects the responsibility to prepare for the coming commandment to build a temple, then the information will be useless to those living today. Therefore, if there is ever a temple built at God's command, this topic will become important then. It is enough for now to note that the Holy Order still includes becoming a "father of many nations." But the method at the end is different than it was in the time of the first patriarchs, including Abraham.

I addressed the subject of reconnecting to the fathers, and redeeming the dead, in *The Mission of Elijah Reconsidered*, one of the essays in the book *Essays: Three Degrees*. Below is an excerpt from that essay:

> Joseph revisited the topic of Elijah's meaning again in a talk given on March 10, 1844. When he picks up the subject again to discuss Elijah, he says, "The spirit power & calling of Elijah is that ye have power to hold the keys of the revelations ordinances, oricles powers & endowments of the fulness of the Melchezedek Priesthood & of the Kingdom of God on the Earth & to receive, obtain and perform all the ordinances belonging to the Kingdom of God even unto the sealing of the hearts of the fathers unto the children & the hearts of the **children unto the fathers even those who are in heaven.**"[600]

---

important things pertaining to the Kingdom of God." The required temple for returning the Holy Order was not completed before Joseph and Hyrum were killed June 27, 1844

[600] *Id.* p. 329, emphasis added.

Notice the connection between these parties. It is not to connect you to your kindred dead. They are in the world of spirits. They are not "in heaven." Joseph is talking about a connection of your hearts to "the hearts of the fathers who are in heaven." That is the mission of Elijah. If you will receive it, this is the spirit of Elijah: That we redeem our dead, but then connect ourselves with our "fathers which are in heaven." Our dead are saved through us, but we are saved by connecting to our "fathers in heaven." Who are our "fathers in heaven" to whom we must be connected? If all we do is connect ourselves to our dead, then neither they nor we are connected to the "fathers in heaven." So it becomes quite important to understand why Joseph is talking in these strange terms. Who are these "fathers in heaven" to whom we must form a connection? We want the power of Elijah to seal those who dwell on earth to those which dwell "in heaven." Merely connecting the earthly to their kindred dead will not suffice. Joseph is explaining something more cosmic in this integration of generations. It is greater than mere genealogy.

Remember, those who are in the spirit world, our dead, are in need of redemption. They don't have these ordinances yet. We are supposed to take care of that for them. Our dead are the ones that need redemption from us, and cannot be the "fathers in heaven" Joseph is discussing. They cannot be "in heaven," because they need us to be redeemed. We need to be redeemed by our connecting to "the fathers who are in heaven."

This is important enough for Joseph to have focused on it in the remaining months of his life. As we have seen, Joseph expressed exasperation at the hard heads of the Saints, who would not listen to new information. Let us not repeat the error. We must do something more to avoid being "utterly wasted" at the Lord's return.[601] We must connect

216

ourselves to "the fathers in heaven." Joseph understood this doctrine. (Emphasis in original.)[602]

Abraham passed along the same Holy Order to Isaac, which then passed to Jacob, then to Joseph, and then to Ephraim. We lose track of the right for some generations until the time of Moses. Moses didn't belong to the birthright tribe. He lived approximately three centuries distant from Joseph and Ephraim. During those centuries, through intermarriage, Moses would have inherited blood of Judah, blood of Ephraim, blood of Benjamin, and other tribes of Israel, but his genealogy is reckoned from the Tribe of Levi.[603]

To understand how tribal affiliation was identified in ancient Israel, it is useful to refer to the tribal practice among some Indian tribes. The tribes have sub-clans that are comparable to separate villages. Intermarriage within the clan is prohibited. When a daughter gets to be marital age, she must marry outside her clan. Her husband from the other clan takes her to live with his clan once they marry. If the daughter was from the Water Clan and she marries a husband from the Bear Clan, she is then regarded as part of the Bear Clan. Their children also are members of the Bear Clan. The Water Clan identity of the wife is lost. Genealogically, she is Water Clan. But her family identification becomes Bear Clan.[604]

Moses' identification with the tribe of Levi is not based on DNA, but on the way ancient Israel assigned tribal affiliation. In any event, Moses offered Israel an opportunity to reconnect fully with God. Unfortunately that opportunity was forfeited and Israel lost their chance and received a lesser priesthood and lesser knowledge.[605]

---

[601] D&C 2: 3.

[602] For a more extended discussion of the subject, see that essay.

[603] Exo. 2:2.

[604] This example is adapted to a "patriarchal" society to illustrate the pattern of ancient Israel and their reckoning of tribal identities. In almost all modern Native American societies the reckoning is "matriarchal" and the husband would relocate to his wife's clan. In Hopi tradition, for example, home ownership is passed through the mother's line to the daughter.

[605] See, D&C 84:19-27. The "greater priesthood" referred to in the revelation includes the "mysteries of the kingdom, even the key of the knowledge of God" means the Holy Order held by Moses. The "ordinances" that allow the "power of godliness" to be shown to man in the flesh are also referring to an inheritance of greater knowledge that brings mankind into the presence of God the Father.

Moses represented an isolated restoration of a single person who could have brought all of Israel back into God's presence and could have established Zion. But Israel, after three centuries of slavery, was not willing to ascend the mountain. Today we are slaves of traditions that are just as limiting. Awake and arise. That is what I have been stirring people to do.

Following Moses, there were prophets who ascended and became ministering servants. Joseph had this to say about those prophets: "All the prophets had the [Holy Order] and were ordained by God himself." (*TPJS*, p. 181.) If they didn't have what was required, they would not be in possession of "the channel through which all knowledge, doctrine, the plan of salvation, and every important matter is revealed from Heaven." (*TPJS*, p. 167.) They would not have possessed "the channel through which the Almighty commenced revealing His glory at the beginning of the creation of this earth, and through which he has continued revealing himself to the children of men to the present time." (*Id.*) It was essential that they were qualified to minister in a way that guaranteed, for anyone would listen, salvation.

Remember that Father Adam presides over every dispensation of the gospel.[606] But Joseph wrote that it was "The voice of Peter, James, and John in the wilderness between Harmony, Susquehanna county, and Colesville, Broome county, on the Susquehanna river, declaring themselves as possessing the keys of the kingdom, and of the dispensation of the fulness of times!" (D&C 128:20.) There is no conflict. Although Father Adam is at the head as the first father and still holds dominion over this creation, Peter, James and John were assigned to assist in this dispensation as well. Adam holds keys in order to bring about every dispensation from the time of Adam down to the very end of time. But Adam did not live through every dispensation from the beginning to the very end of time. Adam is in possession of authority or "keys" over the Holy Order. He has a say who will be involved in each dispensation. He now exercises the right of dominion in the councils of Heaven as a resurrected man. But salvation for the living must involve those who are living to bear the burden to preach repentance and faith on Christ. Salvation is, was and always will be a mortal challenge and mortal obligation. It is not a test to prove those who are immortal. It is to prove the living.[607]

---

[606] *TPJS*, p. 157 discussed supra.

218

Whether we are saved depends on what we do during our mortal probation. Angels do not fix our errors or finish our tests for us. When immortals return, it will be to destroy the wicked and visit with those who are wheat. The best way to understand it is to refer to what we know about the immortals that are still on earth. We have two examples: the Three Nephites and John the Beloved.

Once the mortal lives of the three Nephite disciples who tarried on the earth ended, they, like John, ministered as angels to mortal prophets. They did not minister openly to the world. They acted as angels whose ministry is explained in Moroni:

> [N]either have angels ceased to minister unto the children of men. For behold, they are subject unto him, to minister according to the word of his command, showing themselves unto them of strong faith and a firm mind in every form of godliness. And the office of their ministry is to call men unto repentance, and to fulfil and to do the work of the covenants of the Father, which he hath made unto the children of men, to prepare the way among the children of men, by **declaring the word of Christ unto the chosen vessels of the Lord, that they may bear testimony of him. And by so doing, the Lord God prepareth the way that the residue of men may have faith in Christ**, that the Holy Ghost may have place in their hearts, according to the power thereof; and after this manner bringeth to pass the Father, the covenants which he hath made unto the children of men.[608]

Angels minister to "chosen vessels" or mortal messengers, as the Three Nephites did with Mormon and Moroni.[609] Then these vessels testify and bear testimony so that the way is prepared "that the residue of men may have faith in Christ." These three visited with Mormon, but the people to whom Mormon ministered didn't see them. They ministered to Moroni and those to whom Moroni ministered didn't see them. The chosen vessels[610] also become as

---

[607] See, Abr. 3:24-25. The proving is done to those who dwell on earth.

[608] Moroni 7:29-32, emphasis added.

[609] Mormon 8:11.

[610] Heaven's "chosen vessels" may seem most unlikely. In the cases of Alma the Younger and Saul of Tarsus they were wicked when they were chosen.

ministering angels. Many people have received ministering angels. Men, women and children have, can and do receive angelic ministers.[611] Angels minister to those with faith, who are supposed to then preach salvation to others. Likewise, John the Beloved became a ministering angel.[612] He has a ministry "for those who shall be heirs of salvation." Do not expect him to make appearances to the world, and do what flesh and blood are required to do. When the world has faith enough to receive angels, then angels will minister to them. But until then, they minister in private to those with faith to receive them. Appearing to the world would be unjust. It would be unfair if any single generation had all the heavy-lifting of salvation performed for them by immortals. If angels suddenly accomplish things that, from the days of Adam have been the duty of mortals, an apology would be owed to every other generation.

Appearances of angels, like the post-resurrection ministry of Christ, happen with the faithful. Christ appeared as a resurrected minister only to the faithful in Jerusalem. Likewise, He showed Himself to "the more righteous" who had been spared among the Nephites.[613]

The history of priesthood in this dispensation is made more difficult to understand because some important events are not recorded, and what is recorded has been altered. In *JSP Documents, Vol. 5*, p. 509 the LDS Church Historian's Office explains how some important documents were altered by Oliver Cowdery, apparently without Joseph Smith's knowledge. Here is how they explain the altered documents:

> Cowdery then took those loose pages and recorded the blessings in the patriarchal blessing book on 3 October 1835.
>
> Though it is possible that JS worked with Cowdery on the changes or instructed him to expand the blessings on his own, it seems more likely that Cowdery made the expansions without direction from JS. This would not have been the only occasion he did so: there is evidence

---

Yet both would later become ministering servants who preached righteousness to the residue of men.

[611] Alma 32:23. When they minister to you it is to enable you to testify and help others to likewise have faith in Christ.

[612] D&C 7:6.

[613] 3 Ne. 10:12.

that Cowdery altered at least one other blessing text—his own—when he recorded it in the volume.

...In summary, there is no direct evidence that JS was involved in expanding and editing the 1833 blessings in September or October of 1835, and there are reasons to think he was not[.]

This incident is one of the few instances where the LDS Historian's Office acknowledges a problem that is more widespread than the example of patriarchal blessing alterations. Alterations in the records began in the 1850s and under the control of the LDS Historian's Office. Richard Van Wagoner referred to this problem and quoted from one employed in the Historian's Office:

The official *History of the Church of Jesus Christ of Latter-day Saints*[614] was published in book form under the direction of the First Presidency in 1902. The introductory assurance that "no historical or doctrinal statement has been changed" is demonstrably wrong. Overshadowed by editorial censorship, hundreds of deletions, additions, and alterations, these seven volumes are not always reliable. ...The nineteenth-century propaganda mill was so adroit that few outside Brigham Young's inner circle were aware of the behind-the-scenes alterations so seamlessly stitched into church history. Charles Wesley Wandell, an assistant church historian, was aghast at these emendations. Commenting on the many changes made in the historical work as it was being serialized in the Deseret News, Wandell noted in his diary: "I notice the interpolations because having been employed in the Historian's office at Nauvoo by Doctor Richards, and employed, too, in 1845, in compiling this very autobiography, I know that after Joseph's death his memoir was 'doctored' to suit the new order of things,[615] and this, too, by the direct order of Brigham Young to Doctor Richards and systematically by Richards." The Quorum of the Twelve, under Brigham Young's leadership, began altering the historical

---

[614] Commonly referred to as the *Documentary History of the Church*, or "*DHC*."
[615] The "new order of things" is a reference to polygamy that was taught openly by Brigham Young and had been publicly denounced by Joseph Smith.

record shortly after Smith's death. Contrary to the introduction's claim, Smith did not author the *History of the Church*. At the time of his 1844 death, the narrative had been written up to 5 August 1838.[616]

Oliver Cowdery apparently thought that he had the right to alter documents, including revelations.[617] The problem was fairly widespread while Joseph was alive, and became a much greater problem after he died. The texts of scriptures, journals, diaries, and other historical documents do not have the integrity they should. This makes the reconstruction of Mormon history and teachings a daunting task. Many of those involved believed that if the "truth" needed a little embellishment to make it more persuasive, it was appropriate and right to do so. Institutional claims were buttressed by embellishments that are today proving problematic for the LDS church. There is a "faith crisis" for many church members when they realize some historical "facts" are either demonstrably untrue or entirely made up. That, however, should not deter those who are willing to labor at it. Stripped of the falsehoods, what remains is glorious and inspiring, even if it undermines institutional claims. The truth should never have been altered to support anyone's agenda. We should only care to know and understand God's will and work.

The Church Historian's Office is candid about this incident involving Oliver Cowdery. But they are not always equally candid with many other parts of the historical record that were altered by Oliver Cowdery and many others. The test for candor should not be whether it supports or opposes institutional claims. One reason for the third volume of the new scriptures was to painstakingly examine the original documents of the original revelations and to accurately find what came from Joseph Smith. The new third volume will be titled *Teachings and Commandments*. Some of the revelations will be gone altogether because they do not clearly originate with Joseph Smith in a reliable transmission.

The word apostle (Αποστολοσ) literally means, "someone sent away." The word implies they are sent to deliver a message. An English equivalent would be "messenger." There is no such thing as

---

[616] Richard S. Van Wagoner, *Sidney Rigdon: A Portrait of Religious Excess*, (Salt Lake City: Signature Books, 1994), p. 322.

[617] Statements in D&C 9:2; 24:10; 28:1, 4; and in particular 57:13 were apparently enough for Cowdery to feel it his privilege to alter documents.

priesthood called "apostle." It is an office in the church, like relief society president, primary president, or scout leader. It is only an office in the church. This is why Joseph Smith and Oliver Cowdery would hold the office of elder before the restoration of any of the higher priesthood. LDS priesthood lines of authority are particularly vulnerable because for about 22 years during the presidency of Heber J. Grant, ordinations did not confer any priesthood. They ordained to an office in the church. And while the person ordained to the office in the church was authorized to function in the church office, conferral of priesthood is a separate matter. You can (and now do) have apostles without priesthood.

The best source of original material to search the events of the restoration involving Joseph Smith and Oliver Cowdery is the history Joseph Smith began to write in 1838. Oliver Cowdery, David Whitmer and John Whitmer had been excommunicated. John Whitmer had been church historian since 1831.[618] He took the history with him and although asked to return the material,[619] refused to do so. Consequently Joseph began to write a replacement in April 1838.

The first draft of the history Joseph Smith composed in 1838 has been lost. It was copied in 1839 by James Mulholland. In *JSP Histories, Vol. 1*, there are three columns (Draft 1, Draft 2 and Draft 3) of the history side-by-side showing the 1839 copy and later revisions and edits. They begin on page 204. Draft 1 was lost, and therefore column 1 is blank until page 294. There an excerpt, preserved in the *Book of Covenants*, is reprinted. Other parts of Draft 1 are on pages 304, 306-308, 312-314, 316-320, 324-328, 336, 352-354,364-372, then more or less continually beginning on 378. Internal material in Draft 2 suggests it was a faithful copy of Draft 1. It was copied in 1839 but all the dating in it is for 1838. This means Mulholland apparently made a faithful copy and did not alter what Joseph wrote the year earlier.

In the earliest version of Joseph's history there was a revelation in March 1829 at the request of Martin Harris. In the revelation Joseph Smith was told, "Verily I say unto you, that wo shall come unto the inhabitants of the earth, if they shall not hearken to my words; for hereafter you shall be ordained to go forth to deliver my words unto the children of men. Behold if they will not believe my

---

[618] See, D&C 47:1-4.
[619] An insulting letter to John Whitmer on April 9, 1838 from Joseph Smith and Sidney Rigdon asked for the return of his incompetent materials. See, *JSP Documents, Vol. 6*, pp. 78-79.

words, they will not believe you, my servant Joseph, if it were possible that you could show unto them all of these things which I have committed unto you."[620] Joseph was promised that, at some future point, he would be "ordained" to deliver words to the public. Interestingly, if people will not believe the words given him by the Lord, then they would not believe Joseph even if he revealed everything he had received from God. This raises two relevant points: First, Joseph had not yet been ordained. Second, Joseph would not be required to reveal everything, indeed revealing everything would be futile. Only the words given him were to be made public. We should never assume that we are told everything revealed to a man given a dispensation from God. Some things are between him and the Lord.

Two months after the promise of ordination, in May of 1829, Joseph wrote: "[Joseph and Oliver Cowdery] went into the woods to pray and inquire of the Lord respecting baptism for the remission of sins as we found mentioned in the translation of the plates. While we were thus employed praying and calling upon the Lord, a Messenger from heaven descended in a cloud of light, and having laid his hands upon us, he ordained us, saying to us: 'Upon you my fellow servants in the name of the Messiah I confer the priesthood of Aaron, which holds the keys of the ministering of angels and of the gospel of repentance, and baptism by immersion for the remission of sins, and this shall never be taken again from the earth, untill the sons of Levi do offer again an offering unto the Lord in righteousness.' He said this Aaronic priesthood had not the power of laying on of hands for the gift of the Holy Ghost, but that this should be conferred on (us) hereafter and he commanded us to go and be baptized, and gave us direction that I should baptized Oliver Cowdery and afterwards that he should baptize me."[621] Joseph was the first to baptize, but he was the second to be baptized. Oliver Cowdery was baptized by an unbaptized officiator who had been ordained with authority to baptize.

This May 1829 ordination from the angel included the privilege to baptize and to have angels minister, but it lacked something else that involved the power of laying on hands for the gift of the Holy Ghost. They were promised that other authority involving the power

---

[620] *JSP Histories, Vol. 1*, pp. 269-270- Draft 2; also D&C 5:5-7.
[621] *JSP Histories, Vol. 1*, p. 292-Draft 2; see also JS-H 1:68-70.

of laying on hands for the gift of the Holy Ghost would be conferred separately and sometime later.

In Draft 2 (and therefore also in the earlier missing Draft 1) there is no mention of an appearance by Peter, James, and John. It is entirely omitted from Joseph's history. The first reference to Peter, James and John is in an insert into an August 1830 revelation. Briefly here is how the language was originally and how it was altered:

Joseph Smith received a revelation on August 28th, 1830. When it was originally received, here is how it read in the first handwritten version (Revelation Book 1):

A Revelation to the Church given at Harmony sesquehann County State of Pennsylvania given to Joseph the Seer at a time that he went to punch wine Sacrament & he was stopped by an angel & he he spoke to him as follows Saying Listen to the voice of Jesus Christ your Lord your God & your Redeemer whose word is quick & powerful for Behold I say unto you it mattereth not what ye shall eat or what ye shall drink when ye partake of the sacrament if it so be that ye do it with an eye single to my glory Remembering unto the father that my Body which laid down for you & my blood which was shed for you the Remission of y sins Wherefore a commandment I give unto you that ye shall not Purchase Wine neither strong drink of your enemies Wherefore ye shall partake none except it is made new among you yea in this my Fathers Kingdom which shall be built up on the earth Behold this is wisdom in me Wherefore marvel not for the hour cometh that I will drink of the fruit of the Vine with you on the Earth & with those whom my father hath given me out of the world Wherefore life up your hearts & rejoice & Gird up your loins & be faithful until I come even so amen.

The first time it was put into print WW Phelps was the editor in Missouri. The paper was *The Evening and Morning Star*. He edited it and the version he printed read as follows:

225

A COMMANDMENT GIVEN SEPTEMBER 4, 1830 LISTEN to the voice of Jesus Christ, your Lord, your God, and your Redeemer, whose word is quick and powerful.

For behold I say unto you, that it mattereth not what ye shall eat, or what ye shall drink, when ye partake of the sacrament, if it so be that ye do it with an eye single to my glory; remembering unto the Father my body which was laid down for you, and my blood which was shed for the remission of sins:

Wherefore a commandment I give unto you, that you shall not purchase wine, neither strong drink of your enemies:

Wherefore you shall partake of none, except it is made new among you, yea, in this my Father's kingdom which shall be built up on the earth.

Behold this is wisdom in me, wherefore marvel not, for the hour cometh that I will drink of the fruit of the vine with you, on the earth, and with all those whom my Father hath given me out of the world: Wherefore lift up your hearts and rejoice, and gird up your loins.

This printed version was from the Missouri press destroyed by a mob. Some few copies still exist. But the press was destroyed and the effort had to be made again to publish the document. In Kirtland, a new version was printed in the renamed paper. Previously it was THE Evening and Morning Star, in Kirtland the paper was titled: "Evening and Morning Star." This version was edited and updated by Oliver Cowdery. He made additions to many of the revelations "to reflect current organization, doctrine, and practice, which had continued to develop side the revelations were first dictated." (Joseph Smith Papers, Revelations and Transcriptions, Vol 2, p. 199.) Below is the version Oliver Cowdery printed (which subsequently became the source from which the 1835 edition of the D&C was taken):

REVELATION Given September, 1830
Listen to the voice of Jesus Christ, your Lord,
your God, and your Redeemer, whose word is
quick and powerful. For behold I say unto you,
that it mattereth not what ye shall eat, or what
ye shall drink, when ye partake of the sacrament,
if it so be that ye do it with an eye single to my
glory; remembering unto the Father my body
which was laid down for you, and my blood
which was shed for the remission of your sins:
wherefore a commandment I give unto you, that
ye shall not purchase wine, neither strong drink
of your enemies: wherefore you shall partake of
none, except if is made new among you, yea, in
this my Father's kingdom which shall be built
up on the earth. Behold this is wisdom in me:
wherefore marvel not for the hour cometh that
I will drink of the fruit of the vine with you on
the earth, and with Moroni, whom I have sent
unto you to reveal the book of Mormon,
containing the fulness of my everlasting gospel;
to whom I have committed the keys of the
record of the stick of Ephriam; and also with
Elias, to whom I have committed the keys of
bringing to pass the restoration of all things, or
the restorer of all things spoken by the mouth
of all the holy prophets side the world began,
concerning the last days: ale also John the son
of Zacharias, which Zacharias he (Elias) visited
and gav promise that h should have a son, and
his name should be John, and he should be
filled with the spirit of Elias; which John I have
sent unto you, my servants, Joseph Smith, jr.
and Oliver Cowdery, to ordain you unto this
first priesthood which you have received, that
you might be called and ordained even as
Aaron: and also Elijah, unto whom I have
committed the keys of the power of turning the
hearts of the fathers to the children and the
hearts of the children to the fathers, that the

whole earth may not be smitten with a curse: and also, with Joseph, and Jacob, and Isaac, and Abraham your fathers; by whom the promises remain: and also with Michael, or Adam, the father of all, the prince of all, the ancient of days. And also with Peter, and James, and John, whom I have sent unto you, by whom I have ordained you and confirmed you to be apostles and especial witnesses of my name, and bear the keys of your ministry; and of the same things which I revealed unit them, unto whom I have committed the keys of my kingdom, and a dispensation of the gospel for the last time; and for the fulness of times, in the which I will gather together in one all things both which are in heaven and which are on earth: and also with those whom my Father hath given me out of the world: wherefore lift up your hearts and rejoice, and gird up your loins, and take upon you my whole armor, that ye may be able to withstand the evil day, having done all ye may be able to stand. Stand, therefore, having your loins girt about with truth; having on the breastplate of righteousness; and your feet shod with the preparation of the gospel of peace which I have sent mine angels to commit unto you, taking the shield of faith wherewith ye shall be able to quench all the fiery darts of the wicked; and take the helmet of salvation, and the sword of my Spirit, which I will pour out upon you, and my word which I reveal unto you, and be agreed as touching all things whatsoever ye ask of me, and be faithful until I come, and ye shall be caught up that where I am ye shall be also. Amen.[622]

I have not included the version now in the LDS D&C, but it was changed again. It should be apparent that the text revealed originally

[622] Blog entry from http://denversnuffer.blogspot.com/2014/06/history-of-d-section-27.html on June 7, 2014.

and what the editors did with it has been a growing concern. The 1835 D&C used the last version above and edited it. The *Teachings and Commandments* version will return to the original.

When Joseph wrote the history, there was no mention of Peter, James and John. But these revisions added their names and the claim of "ordination" by them. Joseph Smith's 1842 letter contradicts the claim that they performed an "ordination." The only mention Joseph made in the 1842 account was that they "declar[ed] themselves as possessing the keys of the kingdom, and of the dispensation of the fullness of times!" (D&C 128:20.) Oliver Cowdery signed a document during his last illness that supports the claim of "ordination" from Peter, James and John.[623]

> Joseph wanted to obtain the promised greater ordination that would allow him to lay on hands for the gift of the Holy Ghost. He prayed for it from 1829 through 1831. Joseph recorded, "We now became anxious to have that promise ~~which conferred upon~~ (realized to) us, which the angel had that conferred upon us the Aaronick Priesthood ~~upon us~~. had given us, viz, that provided we continued faithful the we should also have the Melchesidec Priesthood, which holds the authority of the laying on of hands for the gift of the Holy

---

[623] Oliver Cowdery died March 3, 1850. During a lengthy illness he signed a document on January 13, 1849 which included this: "While darkness covered the earth and gross darkness the people; long after the authority to administer in holy things had been taken away, the Lord opened the heavens and sent forth His word to the salvation of Israel. In the fulfillment of the sacred Scriptures, the everlasting Gospel was proclaimed by the mighty Angel (Moroni), who, clothed with the authority of his mission, gave glory to God in the highest. John the Baptist, holding the keys of the Aaronic Priesthood; Peter, James, and John, holding the keys of the Melchizedek Priesthood, have also ministered for those who shall be heirs of salvation, and with these administrations ordained men to the same Priesthood. These Priesthoods, with their authority, are now, and must continue to be, in the body of the Church of Jesus Christ of Latter-day Saints. Blessed is the Elder who has received the same, and thrice blessed and holy is he who shall endure to the end. "Accept assurances, dear brother, of the unfeigned prayer of him who, in connection with Joseph the Seer, was blessed with the above ministrations, and who earnestly and devotedly hopes to meet you in the celestial glory." *Deseret Evening News*, December 21, 1901, p. 11.

Ghost we had for some time made this a subject of humble prayer, and at length we got together in the Chamber of Mr Whitmer's house in order more particularly to seek of the Lord information, and if possible obtain what we now so earnestly desired. ~~We had not been long~~ After some time spent in solemn and fervent prayer, the Word of the Lord came unto us, in the Chamber, commanding us, that I should ordain Oliver Cowdery to be an Elder in the Church of Jesus Christ, and the he also should ordain me to the same office, and that after having been thus ordained, we should proceed to ordain others to the same office, according as it should be made known to us.[624]

The office of "Elder" is a position in the association or church not priesthood. However, Joseph's account relates that they were "commanded to proceed... and then attend to the laying on of hands for the Gift of the Holy Ghost."[625] Joseph believed that the "voice of God" gave the authority for laying on hands. This would be the way Melchizedek received the priesthood: By the voice of God.[626] The authority used to ordain others is described in Joseph's history. The authority was the same as in the Book of Mormon. Joseph wrote: "And behold you are they who are ordained of me, to ordain priests and teachers to declare my gospel, according to the power of the Holy Ghost which is in you[.]"[627] The power to ordain in the early days of the Restoration was derived from the power of the Holy Ghost that is within the person who is doing the ordaining. The instruction to ordain "priests and teachers" was enlarged to include elders and deacons also: "Every Elder, priest, teacher, or deacon, is to

---

[624] *JSP Histories, Vol. 1*, p. 326 (Draft 1), all as in original.

[625] *JSP Histories, Vol. 1*, pp. 326-328.

[626] "And thus, having been approved of God, he was ordained an high priest after the order of the covenant which God made with Enoch. It being after the order of the Son of God; which order came, not by man, nor the will of man; neither by father nor mother; neither by beginning of days nor end of years; but of God; and it was delivered unto men by the calling of his own voice, according to his own will, unto as many as believed on his name." JST-Genesis 14:27-29.

[627] *JSP Histories, Vol. 1*,pp. 332-334 (Draft 2); see also D&C 18:32. Compare with Moroni 3:4.

be ordained according to the gifts and calling of God unto him; and he is to be ordained by the power of the Holy Ghost which is in the one that ordains him."[628]

Ordination early in the Restoration was accomplished the same way as ordination was accomplished in the Book of Mormon, that is by the power of the Holy Ghost that is in the person being ordained.

The Joseph Smith 1842 letter was written while he was in hiding in Nauvoo. That letter corresponds with his earlier history, but in it he mentions things that were not in the histories. They are highlighted below:

> Again what do we hear, Glad tidings from Cumorah, Moroni, an angel from Heaven, declaring the fulfilment of the prophets, the book to be revealed, a voice of the Lord in the wilderness of Fayette, Seneca County, declaring the three witnesses to bear record of the book, **a voice of Michael on the banks of the Susquahanah, detecting the devil when he appeared as an angel of light, the voice of Peter, James, and John in the wilderness** between Harmony, Susquahanah County, and Coleville, Broom County on the Susquahanah River declaring themselves as possessing the keys of the kingdom of the dispensation of the fulness of times.
>
> And again, the voice of God in the chamber of old Father Whitmer, in Fayette, Seneca county, and at sundry times, and in divers places through all the travels and tribulations of this Church of Jesus Christ of Latter-day Saints! And the voice of Michael, the archangel; **the voice of Gabriel, and of Raphael, and of divers angels, from Michael or Adam down to the present time, all declaring** their dispensation, their rights, their keys, their honors, their majesty and glory, and the power of their priesthood; giving line upon line, precept upon precept; here a little, and there a little; giving us consolation by holding forth that which is to come, confirming our hope![629]

---

[628] *JSP Histories, Vol. 1*, p. 346 (Draft 2); see also D&C 20:60.

These are carefully worded affirmations by Joseph. The "voice" is not the same thing as the person or even visionary encounter. The "devil" is who "appeared" on the banks of the Sesquahananah, not Michael. It was the "voice of Michael" that detected the deception. The devil appeared, and Michael spoke.

It was "the **voice** of Peter, James, and John" that spoke to Joseph. When they spoke they "declar[ed] themselves as possessing the keys of the kingdom of the dispensation of the fullness of times." Does saying "I have the keys to my Dodge truck" give you the keys to my Dodge truck? The voice of Peter, James and John—not laying on hands or ordination—is what Joseph described took place. Joseph and Oliver left no other account of the "voice of Gabriel, and of Raphael, and of diverse angels" who "declared their" rights, keys, honors, majesty and glory. Recently, there was a new revelation that explains more about this event. The purpose of these visits was not to confer priesthood, but to explain the history of God's dealings with mankind, and to convey essential knowledge about this creation. It was to give Joseph a basis to understand enough so that a temple could be built to house God's revelations. If men are to be taught enough to have "great knowledge" as Abraham had, then the information must be revealed from heaven. These words are like Abraham's words. Joseph affirms he had "great knowledge" and sought for and obtained "greater knowledge." This is all required for the Holy Order to return.

Joseph was called upon by God to lay the foundation for the last days. He did not establish Zion, but he left behind a foundation to move forward. The failure was not Joseph's or Hyrum's. It was the people.

Understanding is brought about by having access to a channel through which all knowledge, doctrine, the plan of salvation, and every important matter is revealed from Heaven. Therefore, Joseph needed to not only be in possession of that channel, but the channel needed to respond to and did respond to Joseph's petitions and inquiries in order for him to be able to function in the position he held.

The January 1841 revelation records,

> And again, verily I say unto you, let my servant William be appointed, ordained, and anointed, as

---

[629] D&C 128:20-21.

counselor unto my servant Joseph, in the room of my servant Hyrum, that my servant Hyrum may take the office of Priesthood and Patriarch, which was appointed unto him by his father, by blessing and also by right; from henceforth he shall hold the keys of the patriarchal blessings upon the heads of all my people, That whoever he blesses shall be blessed, and whoever he curses shall be cursed; that whatsoever he shall bind on earth shall be bound in heaven; and whatsoever he shall loose on earth shall be loosed in heaven. And from this time forth I appoint unto him that he may be a prophet, and a seer, and a revelator unto my church, as well as my servant Joseph; That he may act in concert also with my servant Joseph; and that he shall receive counsel from my servant Joseph, who shall show unto him the keys whereby he may ask and receive, and be crowned with the same blessing, and glory, and honor, and priesthood, and gifts of the priesthood, that once were put upon him that was my servant Oliver Cowdery; That my servant Hyrum may bear record of the things which I shall show unto him, that his name may be had in honorable remembrance from generation to generation, forever and ever. D&C 124:91-96.

Hyrum was put into a position once occupied by Oliver, to act with Joseph, possessing the ability to "ask and receive." Hyrum was given the channel through which you can know and understand what God wants or intends for people. That is one of the most important functions of the Holy Order. The purpose is to save souls.

Hyrum's name was to be had "in honorable remembrance from generation to generation" or his position was to descend through him generation after generation. Descendants of Hyrum occupied the position of Presiding Patriarch of the Church until Eldred G. Smith was made emeritus in 1979. Until his death, he still signed as Patriarch to the Church and he still kept an office in the church office building. The office and the authority of that office ended with the death of Eldred G. Smith on April 4, 2013.[630] Since the Holy Order has a

---

[630] In an interview with Patriarch Smith on February 7, 2012 he was asked if he had or would confer the position on his son, Gary. This is what the transcript of the interview records: "Question: Have you conferred the office on your son Gary, and if not why not? Answer: NO (Based on this, asked a

patriarchal component to it as well, that now will also need to be restored since the institution has rejected and abandoned all right to the office.

Accomplishing what is needed is almost beyond human ability. Even very humble people change when given great blessings. The change from humble to haughty happens so often and so quickly it is astonishing.

Many prophecies foretell the gentiles will reject their invitation. The condemnation in 1832, the expulsion from Missouri, the forced winter exodus from Nauvoo, the suffering during and after the exodus, the afflictions, judgments and wrath of God at the saints all happened in fulfillment of prophecy. The saints' pride, lying, deceit, hypocrisy, murders, priestcrafts, and whoredoms (as Christ foretold would happen), overwhelmed the restoration in Nauvoo. Then after Brigham Young led people into isolation in the wilderness, inquisitorial abuses quickly followed. The awful "Mormon Reformation" led to mass-murders at Mountain Meadows, as well as religious killings based on the idea of "blood atonement." The religion lapsed into contradictions in "fundamental" teachings, adopting a well-paid professional ministerial class of leaders, changes to the ordinances including radical change to the temple endowment in 1990, eliminating washings and anointings in 2005, a quest for popularity and centrally-controlled, tightly correlated rejection of teachings. These unfortunate events are all part of the gentile history of a long, downward path. The gentiles have walked away from the light, and increasingly embraced darkness and foolish trust of men. All Mormon sects are now ruled by traditions contrary to the scriptures and commandments of God. They are asleep and cannot be awakened. God is now doing something new, and left them to find their own way.

---

him if he would then ordain Gary so the office would be passed down?) He emphatically said 'No,' even when I pressed him. He said Gary didn't want it and that Gary wouldn't be accepted. He said that he would need approval of the Q12 and that he probably wouldn't get it. E. said that if one asked individuals in the Quorum there might be a different answer than if one asked the entire Quorum. If you asked the entire Quorum, the answer would be a 'no.'" Portions of the interview can be read at barerecord.blogspot.com/2013/04/162-loss-of-church-patriarch.html, but the above part was not included in that post. A complete transcript of the interview is in my possession.

Emma Smith, Sidney Rigdon and William Marks all said that without Joseph Smith there was no church. They were right. After Joseph died, there was a complete overthrow of the church by the quorum of the twelve. The quorum of the twelve overthrew equality in the church. The twelve substituted themselves in place of an equal distribution of power as mandated by revelation. They pretend to privileges never given to them by God.

The first presidency and quorum of the twelve should be equal in authority. Joseph never moved a single apostle into the first presidency. They were independent, equal bodies. Likewise, the quorum of seventy was equal with the twelve, and therefore should be equal with the first presidency also. The standing high councils of Zion were also equal in authority. All the "keys," to the extent there are any, were held equally by the first presidency, quorum of the twelve, quorum of the seventy, and the high councils. There was no primacy in the twelve, as originally organized.

In the years preceding Joseph's death, as their calling required, the twelve were away from Nauvoo doing missionary work. Joseph spent his last three years in close association with the Nauvoo High Council, as reflected in the Nauvoo High Council Minutes. Following Joseph's and Hyrum's deaths, Emma Smith remarked, "Now as the Twelve have no power with regard to the government of the Church in the Stakes of Zion, but the High Council have all power, so it follows that on removal of the first President, the office would devolve upon the President of the High Council in Zion ...the Twelve... were aware of these facts but acted differently."[631]

None of the equality present in these four different bodies survived Brigham Young. When Brigham Young assumed control, the church became an oligarchy run by the twelve. This is how things are done today. Now the senior apostle automatically becomes the church president, an unscriptural and unwise system for consolidating power. Equality among many has been replaced by the dictatorship of one. "[Emma] bore testimony to [Lucy Messerve] that Mormonism was true as it came forth from the servant of the Lord, Joseph Smith, but ...[said] the Twelve have made Bogus of it."[632] The term "bogus" in those days meant counterfeit.

---

[631] Linda King Newell and Valeen Tippetts Avery, *Mormon Enigma: Emma Hale Smith*, Doubleday, (New York, 1984), pp. 206-207.
[632] *Id.*, p. 211.

One of the last signs indicating the end of the gentiles was the passing of Eldred Smith in 2013, and with him the office of Patriarch to the church. Only one thing now remains. God must send a witness to be the final required "sign" sent to declare God's intention to begin something new.

Joseph Smith cautioned the saints about violating God's trust. Joseph said, "His word will go forth, in these last days, in purity; for if Zion will not purify herself, so as to be approved in all things, in His sight, He will seek another people; for His work will go on until Israel is gathered, and they who will not hear His voice, must expect to feel His wrath."[633] We should expect God's house to be ordered around only one principle: repentance. When the pride of a great organization replaces repentance, the heavens withdraw, and when they do, "Amen" to that portion of God's house. The restoration through Joseph will always remain, even if God chooses to do something different before His return. It is His to do with as He determines best. He has sent me as the witness to declare:

> At the time I was excommunicated, I was in good standing with the Lord. I had nothing amiss in my personal life. There was no sin warranting church discipline. As a former member of the High Council for years, every church disciplinary proceeding I attended that resulted in excommunication, always involved serious moral transgression, betrayal of marriage covenants, and in some cases criminal wrongdoing. In contrast, the reason for my discipline was a book I had

---

[633] *TPJS*, p. 18. To the same effect, during the Mormon Reformation Heber C. Kimball said: "We receive the priesthood and power and authority. If we make a bad use of the priesthood, do you not see that the day will come when God will reckon with us, and he will take it from us and give it to those who will make better use of it? (*JD* 6:125.) George A. Smith said, "God has set his hand at the present time to establish his kingdom. But unless the Saints will so live and so exert themselves that they can preserve the purity of the holy Priesthood among them, the work will be left to other people." (*JD* 6:161.) Even Brigham Young commented on the possibility that only an LDS remnant would remain to carry forward the work. "God will preserve a portion of the meek and the humble of this people to bear off the Kingdom to the inhabitants of the earth, and will defend His Priesthood; for it is the last time, the last gathering time; and He will not suffer the Priesthood to be again driven from the earth." (*JD* 2:184.)

written about church history, in which I attempted to align the events of the Restoration to the prophecies of the Book of Mormon and the Doctrine & Covenants. The stake president admitted to me and my wife before the Council began, that I was then worthy of a temple recommend. By any standard of moral conduct, I was an innocent man, whose only offense was believing the scriptures revealed our condition before God. On the evening of May 1, 2014, the Lord gave me further light and knowledge about His work in His vineyard. The Lord is in control over the church, men, and all things. When He undertakes to accomplish something, "there is nothing that the Lord God shall take in His heart to do, but what He will do it." (Abr. 3:17.) Often the means used by the Lord to accomplish His "strange act," and to perform His "strange work"(D&C 101:95), are very small indeed. "Now ye may suppose that this is foolishness in me; but behold I say unto you, that by small and simple things are great things brought to pass; and small means in many instances doth confound the wise. And the Lord God doth work by means to bring about his great and eternal purposes; and by very small means the Lord doth confound the wise and bringeth about the salvation of many souls." (Alma 37:6-7.)

It is almost always the case that the Lord uses simple things to confound the mighty. I can think of nothing smaller or simpler or less important than myself. Inside the great church to which I once belonged, I was obscure. However, I lived my religion, attended faithfully, served to the best of my ability, upheld church leaders with my prayers, paid tithes, fasted, observed the Word of Wisdom, and helped answer questions for those needing assistance with troubling issues. There was no reason to regard me as a rebel who should be singled out for discipline.

Nevertheless, the Lord chose to use a faithful and believing member to accomplish His design. Only someone who is devoted to His will could accomplish what the Lord had in His heart. Now He has accomplished it.

The Church has Doctrine & Covenants 121, verses 36 to 40, to warn it about abusing His authority. There is an "amen" or end to authority when control, compulsion, and dominion are exercised in any degree of unrighteousness. Therefore, when using authority, great care must be taken. In any case, the church was careless. Therefore, those involved, are now left to kick against the pricks, to persecute the Saints and to fight against God.

Section 121 is a warning to church leaders. It is addressing the powerful, not the powerless. It is addressing those who occupy the seats of authority over others. Only those who claim the right to control, compel, and exercise dominion, are warned against persecuting the saints, who believe the religion and practice it as I did from the time of my conversion. My excommunication was an abuse of authority. Therefore, as soon as the decision was made, the Lord terminated the priesthood authority of the stake presidency and every member of the High Council who sustained this decision, which was unanimous. Thereafter, I appealed to the First Presidency, outlining the involvement of the 12 and the 70. The appeal gave notice to them all. The appeal was summarily denied.

Last general conference, the entire First Presidency, the 12, the 70, and all other general authorities and auxiliaries, voted to sustain those who abused their authority in casting me out of the church. At that moment, the Lord ended all claims of the Church of Jesus Christ of Latter-day Saints, to claim it is led by the priesthood. They have not practiced what He requires. The Lord has brought about His purposes. This has been in His heart all along. He has chosen to use small means to accomplish it, but He always uses the smallest of means to fulfill His purposes.

None of this was my doing. The Lord's strange act, was not, could not, be planned by me. Was not, could not, have been controlled by me. It was not anticipated by me, or even understood by me, until after the Lord had accomplished His will, and made it apparent to me on the evening of May 1, 2014. He alone has done this. He is the author of all of this.[634]

I am not the cause of this, but only a witness it has happened. God gave the signs. I am only to declare what He has done. The Lord has permitted the church to keep its claims without any hindrance from Him through four generations. During that time there were many offenses to the Lord. Now, however, their claims have ended by His voice, so He can continue the restoration without them.

Just because something is true at one moment it does not mean it will remain true forever. Things change because decisions, actions and behaviors matter. The Church of Jesus Christ of Latter-day Saints is not the same as it was in 1973. At this moment it is not even the same church it was in 2012. It is changing rapidly, and will be something different again in a few years. The Lord, knowing the direction the LDS Church is heading, has acted to preserve the restoration. The change obviously does not affect the leadership's legal rights in any way.[635] They are upheld by common consent, and have the right to control the direction of the organization.

This may appear a peculiar event, but God is the same today as yesterday. When Israel refused the fullness offered by God anciently, "he took Moses out of their midst, and the Holy Priesthood also; And the lesser priesthood continued."[636] Israel failed to enter into God's rest, but He commissioned rites through Moses, and then respected them for generations. Israel was not just abandoned by God. He called another servant to end the commission of Israel, so what God began He took responsibility to end. John the Baptist "was ordained by the angel of God at the time he was eight days old unto this power, to overthrow the kingdom of the Jews."[637] What God begins

---

[634] Transcribed from *Journal of Denver Snuffer, Vol. 8*, entry of May 2, 2014, pp. 29-33.

[635] The entire corporate church is organized as a "corporation sole." There is one owner: the LDS Church President. As The Corporation of the President of The Church of Jesus Christ of Latter-day Saints he owns everything from the copyrights to chapels, from temples to business entities, from websites to artwork, the entire "church" belongs to one man. Even if voted out by common consent, he, and not church members, would own all the property. In a very real legal sense, there is only one Mormon in the LDS organization.

[636] D&C 84:25-26.

[637] D&C 84:28.

as an orderly establishment, He will end through an orderly conclusion.

Joseph Smith established The Church of Jesus Christ of Latter-day Saints. Joseph's followers, like ancient Israel with Moses, failed to obtain the fullness.[638] The LDS Church has operated under a commission from the time they rejected the fullness offered through Joseph, with limited authority, just as Israel did after Moses was taken. God decided when and how He would bring an end to the authority of the leaders of the LDS Church, just as He ended the kingdom of the Jews through John. Once God acts, our doubt about it does not change what He has done. God is now free to proceed with another chapter in His "strange act."[639] His house is a house of order, but since the days of Abraham, God's house has included things about which mankind retained very little knowledge.

It is because of the gentile failure that the Lord has begun something new. The Holy Order can give mankind a channel for restoring what was lost. The final work must fully restore what was at the beginning or it will be of no value.

I was asked about children who are kept from access to LDS temples and what can be done to inform them about temple rites. First, although it has been demonstrably corrupted, there is value in the temple. If I had children who could not go to the temple today, I would not personally administer to them the temple ceremony. I made promises in the temple that I have kept. I keep the covenants. Part of that is to not disclose certain things, but rather than do so I would suffer my life to be taken; I was initiated before the changes in 1990. Since I am under an obligation not to disclose certain things, it would be improper to induct anyone into a temple ceremony. However, anyone can go and read the ceremony online. I recommend reading the pre-1990 transcript rather than the post-1990 altered ceremony. If someone learns about the ceremony from reading online, and I did not tell him anything, then discussing it is permissible because it does not include me breaking a covenant to not disclose.

Likewise, if your child goes through the temple today, I would recommend they read the ceremony in the form it was observed before the changes in 1990. I wouldn't be the one to originally

---

[638] D&C 124:28.
[639] D&C 101:94-95.

disclose it to them. I would tell them to read it online. But after they read it I would feel free to discuss what they learn. The ceremony is useful, even though the transmission of it has corrupted it.

Ordinances that are ordained from God cannot be changed. If they are changed, they are broken.[640] If they are broken, they are ineffective. Even a broken ordinance can be informational and if you take it sincerely and honor your covenants, God will work with that. He can dispense every blessing and promise of the temple. It would come from Heaven through the Holy Spirit of Promise. Therefore, there is no down side, but there is a considerable upside if you are true and faithful to the temple rites. The LDS rites make it clear that everything is conditional: "Brothers and Sisters, if you are true and faithful, the time will come when you will be called up and anointed, Kings and Queens, Priests and Priestesses, whereas now you are only anointed to become such. The realization of these blessings depends upon your faithfulness."[641]

Men cannot create covenants with God. In the Answer to Prayer for Covenant the Lord explains the following: "Covenants, promises, rights, vows, associations and expectations that are mine will endure, and those that are not cannot endure. Everything in the world, whether it is established by men, or by Thrones, or by Dominions, or by Principalities, or by Powers, that are not by my word and promise shall be thrown down when men are dead, and shall not remain in my Father's Kingdom. Only those things that are by me shall remain in and after the resurrection." To endure beyond this life anything and everything requires an ordination from God. Men cannot, and those who are in positions of authority in the heavens (including those who occupy thrones, dominions, principalities and powers) cannot. Men can make agreements and call them vows, covenants or promises, and can obligate themselves in this life to perform them, but in the afterlife all such things come to an end if they are not ordained by God. One of the most important opportunities to obtain associations ordained by God occurs when the Holy Order is on earth.

The purpose of the coming last days' temple in Zion is to allow the communication of great knowledge and greater knowledge, and to restore what has been lost since the time of Adam. Important

---

[640] Isa. 24:5.

[641] I recite that from memory. It is close, if not word-for-word what is said at the beginning of the temple rites.

knowledge is required for those who receive the Holy Order. We do not get saved in ignorance.

Peter, James and John did not lay hands on Oliver and Joseph and ordain them to priesthood. But they were on the Holy Mount at the time of the transfiguration, and they were endowed with knowledge there. They saw the history of the world down to the end of time.[642] A brief description is revealed in D&C 45:15-59, copied below:

> Wherefore, hearken and I will reason with you, and I will speak unto you and prophesy, as unto men in days of old. And I will show it plainly as I showed it unto my disciples as I stood before them in the flesh, and spake unto them, saying: As ye have asked of me concerning the signs of my coming, in the day when I shall come in my glory in the clouds of heaven, to fulfil the promises that I have made unto your fathers, For as ye have looked upon the long absence of your spirits from your bodies to be a bondage,[643] I will show unto you how the day of redemption shall come, and also the restoration of the scattered Israel. And now ye behold this temple which is in Jerusalem, which ye call the house of God, and your enemies say that this house shall never fall. But, verily I say unto you, that desolation shall come upon this generation as a thief in the night, and this people shall be destroyed and scattered among all nations. And this temple which ye now see shall be thrown down that there shall not be left one stone upon another. And it shall come to pass, that this generation of Jews shall not pass away until every desolation which I have told you concerning them shall come to pass. Ye say that ye

---

[642] D&C 63:20-21: "Nevertheless, he that endureth in faith and doeth my will, the same shall overcome, and shall receive an inheritance upon the earth when the day of transfiguration shall come; When the earth shall be transfigured, even according to the pattern which was shown unto mine apostles upon the mount; of which account the fulness ye have not yet received."

[643] This motivated Peter and James to ask to come speedily into Christ's kingdom and John to ask to tarry until the Lord's return. (D&C 7:3-5.)

know that the end of the world cometh; ye say also that ye know that the heavens and the earth shall pass away; And in this ye say truly, for so it is; but these things which I have told you shall not pass away until all shall be fulfilled. And this I have told you concerning Jerusalem; and when that day shall come, shall a remnant be scattered among all nations; But they shall be gathered again; but they shall remain until the times of the Gentiles be fulfilled. And in that day shall be heard of wars and rumors of wars, and the whole earth shall be in commotion, and men's hearts shall fail them, and they shall say that Christ delayeth his coming until the end of the earth. And the love of men shall wax cold, and iniquity shall abound. And when the times of the Gentiles is come in, a light shall break forth among them that sit in darkness, and it shall be the fulness of my gospel; But they receive it not; for they perceive not the light, and they turn their hearts from me because of the precepts of men. And in that generation shall the times of the Gentiles be fulfilled. And there shall be men standing in that generation, that shall not pass until they shall see an overflowing scourge; for a desolating sickness shall cover the land. But my disciples shall stand in holy places, and shall not be moved; but among the wicked, men shall lift up their voices and curse God and die. And there shall be earthquakes also in divers places, and many desolations; yet men will harden their hearts against me, and they will take up the sword, one against another, and they will kill one another. And now, when I the Lord had spoken these words unto my disciples, they were troubled. And I said unto them: Be not troubled, for, when all these things shall come to pass, ye may know that the promises which have been made unto you shall be fulfilled. And when the light shall begin to break forth, it shall be with them like unto a parable which I will show you— Ye look and behold the fig trees, and ye see them with your eyes, and ye say when they begin to shoot forth, and their leaves are yet tender, that summer is now nigh at hand; Even so it shall be in that day when they shall see all these things, then shall they know that the hour is nigh. And it shall come to pass that he that feareth me shall be looking forth for the great day of the Lord to come, even for the signs of the coming of the Son of Man. And they shall see signs and wonders, for they shall be shown forth in the heavens above, and in the earth beneath. And they shall behold blood, and fire, and vapors of smoke. And before the day of the Lord shall come, the sun shall be darkened, and the moon be turned into blood, and the stars fall from heaven. And the remnant shall be gathered unto this place; And then they shall look for me, and, behold, I will come; and they shall see me in the clouds of heaven, clothed with power and great glory; with all the holy angels; and he that watches not for me shall be cut off. But before the arm of the Lord shall fall, an angel shall sound his trump, and the saints that have slept shall come forth to meet me in the cloud. Wherefore, if ye have slept in peace blessed are you; for as you now behold me and know that I am, even so shall ye come unto me and your souls shall live, and your redemption shall be perfected; and the saints shall come forth from the four quarters of the earth. Then shall the arm of the Lord fall upon the nations. And then shall the Lord set his foot upon this mount, and it shall cleave in twain, and the earth shall tremble, and reel to and fro, and the heavens also shall shake. And the Lord shall utter his voice, and all the ends of the earth shall hear it; and the nations of the earth shall mourn, and they that have laughed shall see their folly. And calamity shall cover the mocker, and the scorner shall be consumed; and they that have watched for iniquity shall be hewn down and cast into the fire. And then shall the Jews look upon me and say: What are these wounds in thine hands and in thy feet? Then shall they know that I am the Lord; for I will say unto them: These wounds are the wounds with which I was wounded in the house of my friends. I am he who was lifted up. I am Jesus that was crucified. I am the Son of God. And then shall they weep because of their iniquities; then shall they lament because they persecuted their king. And then shall the heathen nations be redeemed, and they that knew no law shall have part in the first resurrection; and it shall be tolerable for them. And Satan shall be bound, that he shall have no place in the hearts of the children of men. And at that day, when I shall come in my glory, shall the parable be fulfilled which I spake concerning the ten virgins. For they that are wise and have received the truth, and have taken the Holy Spirit for their guide, and have not been deceived—verily I say unto you, they shall not be hewn down and cast into the fire, but shall abide the day. And the earth shall be given unto them for an inheritance; and they shall multiply and wax strong, and their children shall grow up without sin unto salvation. For the Lord shall be in their midst, and his glory shall be upon them, and he will be their king and their lawgiver.

Like others who are initiated into the Holy Order, they were endowed with greater knowledge. It fortified them for their ministry. It qualified them to be among those who would declare their dispensation to Joseph Smith. Peter, James and John are symbols of Abraham, Isaac and Jacob. Like the earlier grandfather, father, and son, Peter, James and John were adopted into the line of the Holy Order.

It was the last in the line, Jacob, through whom the nations or tribes of Israel would descend. And it was Jacob through whom the nations, the twelve tribes and the twelve nations of Israel were established. He was the one through whom the righteous progeny and birthright descended. Likewise, John is the last one in the line who chose to remain behind to create, as a ministering angel, a great "posterity" among mortals, to serve as a ministering angel to those who would be heirs of salvation.[644] I do not believe the reason Peter,

James and John came was to ordain Joseph and Oliver. That was accomplished in either the chamber of Old Father Whitmer or at the conference in June of 1831, or both. Below is an excerpt beginning on page 19 of *A Man Without Doubt* discussing the moment Joseph identified the "Melchizedek" priesthood or "high priesthood" first appeared:

> Joseph's history explains his hope to receive this other, greater priesthood ordination as the angel had promised: "We now became anxious to have that promise which conferred upon (realized to) us, which the angel had that conferred upon us the Aaronick Priesthood upon us, had given us, viz, that provided we continued faithful, the we should also have the Melchesidec Priesthood, which holds the authority of the laying on of hands for the gift of the Holy Ghost." (*JS Papers, Histories, Vol. 1*, 1832-1844, (Church Historian's Press: Salt Lake City, 2013), p. 326, all as in original.)
>
> In anticipation of getting the promise fulfilled and priesthood conferred, a conference was scheduled for June 1831. Joseph promised there would be a great endowment of power given in the conference. At the conference, on June 3, 1831, a revelation to Joseph directed that twenty-three attendees were to be ordained to this heavenly priesthood. (At the time of the conference it was called "high priesthood" but later would be called "Melchizedek Priesthood.") (See "Melchizedek Priesthood" in Glossary.)
>
> Today, the LDS church tells a different story to support their claim to have "Melchizedek Priesthood." Every LDS priesthood holder tracks his authority back to "Peter, James and John" who purportedly ordained Joseph and Oliver Cowdery on an unknown day in 1829, prior to Joseph even founding a church. The records kept contemporaneous to the events contradict the claims of the LDS church. Below are accounts written at the

---

[644] D&C 7:6.

time of the June 1831 conference where the "high priesthood" was first given to Joseph Smith and others:

Jared Carter's journal records "Friday" (3 June) as the "memorable day when God first gave the fullness of the high priesthood to the elders of the Church of Christ." (*JS Papers, Documents Vol. 1: July 1828-June 1831*, p. 318, footnote 412, spellings as in original.)

"JS's history uses very similar language, further suggesting that Melchizedek was first publicly used in ordinations at the June 1831 conference: 'The authority of the Melchisedec priesthood was manifested and conferred for the first time, upon several of the elders.'" (*Id.*, p. 320, spellings and italics as in original.)

John Corrill confirms: "In John Corrill's 1839 history, he used the term Melchizedek priesthood instead of high priesthood as though the two were synonymous. He explained that 'the Malchisedec priesthood was then for the first time introduced, and conferred on several of the elders.'" (*Id.*, spellings and italics as in original.)

Parley P. Pratt confirmed the same thing. "Parley P. Pratt later explained the ordination to the high priesthood in this way: 'Several were then selected by revelation, through President Smith, and ordained to the High Priesthood after the order of the Son of God; which is after the order of Melchisedec. This was the first occasion in which this priesthood had been revealed and conferred upon the Elders in this dispensation, although the office of an Elder is the same in a certain degree, but not in the fullness. On this occasion I was ordained to this holy ordinance and calling by President Smith.' (Pratt, *Autobiography of Parley P. Pratt*, p. 72.)" (*JS Papers, Documents Vol. 1: July 1828-June 1831*, p. 318, footnote 422, spellings and cited source as in original.)

The official History of the Church ("*DHC*") published by the LDS Church states: "On the 3rd of

June, the Elders from the various parts of the country where they were laboring, came in; and the conference before appointed, convened in Kirtland; and the Lord displayed His power to the most perfect satisfaction of the Saints. The man of sin was revealed, and the authority of the Melchizedek Priesthood was manifested and conferred for the first time upon several of the Elders." (*DHC, Vol. 1*, pp. 175-176.)

Joseph wanted power in the priesthood so Zion could be established in a New Jerusalem on earth. This was the priesthood Enoch used to move mountains and control rivers. As the revised version of Genesis reported, Melchizedek and "every one being ordained after this order and calling should have power, by faith, to break mountains, to divide the seas, to dry up waters, to turn them out of their course; To put at defiance the armies of nations, to divide the earth, to break every band, to stand in the presence of God; to do all things according to his will, according to his command, subdue principalities and powers; and this by the will of the Son of God which was from before the foundation of the world." This authority was necessary for Zion to be protected from destruction by the world.

In the June 1831 conference, Joseph Smith ordained five, and Lyman Wight ordained eighteen, for the total of twenty-three. For a moment they rejoiced. The heavenly priesthood returned! But the results that followed were anything but satisfactory. The authority did not "take" and the power did not come. Most of the men involved fell away and rejected Joseph shortly after their ordination. The more receptive of the men were left confused. The great blessing Joseph had waited years to receive turned into the first great crisis Joseph would confront.

"Levi Hancock, who was present at the June conference, later recalled a conversation he had in January 1832 with Lyman Wight, who ordained

248

several individuals to the high priesthood at the June conference. Speaking about the priesthood, Hancock remarked that 'neither of us understood what it was.' 'I did not understand it,' wrote Hancock, 'and he [Wight] could give me no light.'" (*JS Papers, Documents Vol. 2: July 1831-January 1833*, p. 79.)

Not only was the ordination confusing, subsequent performance by those ordained did not mirror Melchizedek or Enoch. Of the five Joseph ordained,

-Lyman Wight was excommunicated in 1848

-Harvey Whitlock was excommunicated in 1835

-Thomas Marsh left the church in 1838, signed an affidavit against Joseph which contributed to his imprisonment in Missouri, and was excommunicated in 1839

-Parley Pratt apostatized and was excommunicated in 1842, reinstated in 1843.

Of the eighteen Lyman Wight ordained,

-John Whitmer was excommunicated in March 1838

-Sidney Rigdon was excommunicated in September 1844

-Edward Partridge died in 1840

-Ezra Thayer refused to follow the Twelve after Joseph and Hyrum were martyred

-Joseph Wakefield was excommunicated in January 1834 -Ezra Booth apostatized within months, and went on to write anti-Mormon and anti- Joseph Smith publications

-John Corrill was excommunicated in 1839

-Jacob Scott denied the faith

-Wheeler Baldwin joined the RLDS Church in 1859

-Martin Harris left the LDS Church, later followed James Strang, but returned to the LDS Church and was rebaptized in 1870.

None of those ordained turned rivers out of their course, divided the earth or held armies in defiance. Instead of breaking bands, they broke fellowship away from Joseph. It became apparent that ordination to this high priesthood did not confer the hoped for great endowment of power. Instead of producing power like Enoch and Melchizedek held, it produced disappointment, quickly followed by open dissent. Ezra Booth, one of those ordained by Wight, was not content to leave quietly. He wrote a series of nine letters published in the Ohio Star newspaper in 1831. These were later collected by E.D. Howe and included in the 1834 anti-Mormon book Mormonism Unvailed. Booth was disappointed with Mormonism in general. He criticized Joseph, and pointed at the 1831 priesthood ordination as evidence of Joseph's false, grandiose pretentions. It does not appear Booth's damning letters exaggerate or misstate the events. He told his understanding of the events. He apparently thought the truth was bad enough. The Booth letters said, in relevant part:

> ...Great promises are made to such as embrace it, signs and wonders are to attend them, such as healing the sick, the blind made to see, the lame to walk, &c,; and they are to receive an everlasting inheritance in "the land of Missouri," where the Savior will make his second appearance; at which place the foundation of the temple of God, and the City of Zion, have been laid, and are soon to be built. It is also to be a city of Refuge, and a safe asylum when the storms of vengeance shall pour upon the earth, and those who reject the Book of Mormon, shall be swept off as with the besom of destruction. ... Many of them have been ordained to the High Priesthood, or the order of Melchisedec; and profess to be endowed with the same power as the ancient apostles were. But they have been hitherto unsuccessful in finding the lame, the halt, and the blind, who had faith

sufficient to become the subjects of their miracles... (*Ezra Booth, Letter 2*, September 1831.) ...As the 4th of June last was appointed for the sessions of the conference [referring to the June 1831 conference where the ordinations occurred], it was ascertained, that that was the time specified, when the great and mighty work was to be commenced, and such was the confidence of some, that knowledge superceded their faith, and they did not hesitate to declare themselves perfectly assured that the work of miracles would commence at the ensuing conference. With such strong assurances, and with the most elevated expectations, the conference assembled at the time appointed. To give, if possible, energy to expectation, Smith, the day before the conference, professing to be filled with the spirit of prophecy, declared, that "not three days should pass away, before some should see their Savior, face to face." Soon after the session commenced, Smith arose to harangue the conference. He reminded those present of the prophecy, which he said "was given by the spirit yesterday." He wished them not to be overcome with surprise, when that event ushered in. He continued, until by long speaking, himself and some others became much excited. He then laid his hands on the head of Elder Wight, who had participated largely in the warm feeling of his leader, and ordained him to the High Priesthood. He was set apart for the service of the Indians, and was ordained to the gift of tongues, healing the sick, casting out devils, and discerning spirits; and in like manner he ordained several others; and then called upon Wight to take the floor. Wight arose, and presented a pale countenance, a fierce look, with arms extended, and his hands cramped back, the whole system agitated, and a very unpleasant object to look upon. He exhibited himself as an instance of the great power of God, and called upon those around him "if you want to see a sign, look at me." He then stepped upon a bench, and declared with a loud voice, he saw the Savior: and thereby, for the time being, rescued Smith's prophecy from merited contempt. –It, however, procured Wight the authority to ordain the rest. So said the spirit, and so said Smith. The spirit in Smith selected those to be ordained, and the spirit in Wight ordained them. But the spirit in Wight proved an erring dictator; so much so, that some of the candidates felt the weight of hands thrice, before the work was rightly done. Another Elder, who had been ordained to the same office as Wight, at the bidding of Smith, stepped upon the floor. Then ensued a scene, of which you can form no adequate conception; and which, I would forbear relating, did not the truth require it. The Elder moved upon the floor, his legs inclining to a bend; one shoulder elevated above the other, upon which the head seemed disposed to recline, his arms partly extended; his hands partly clenched; his mouth partly open, and contracted in the shape of an italic O; his eyes assumed a wild ferocious cast, and his whole appearance presented a frightful object to the view of the beholder. –

252

"Speak, Brother Harvey" said Smith. But Harvey intimated by signs, that his power of articulation was in a state of suspense, and that he was unable to speak. Some conjectured that Harvey was possessed of the devil, but Smith said, "the Lord binds in order to set at liberty." After different opinions had been given, and there had been much confusion, Smith learnt by the spirit, that Harvey was under a diabolical influence, and that Satan had bound him; and he commanded the unclean spirit to come out of him. It now became clearly manifest, that "the man of sin was revealed," for the express purpose that the elders should become acquainted with the devices of Satan; and after that they would possess knowledge sufficient to manage him. This, Smith declared to be a miracle, and his success in this case, encouraged him to work other and different miracles. Taking the hand of one of the Elders in his own, a hand which by accident had been rendered defective, he said, "Brother Murdock, I command you in the name of Jesus Christ to straighten your hand;" in the mean while endeavoring to accomplish the work by using his own hand to open the hand of the other. The effort proved unsuccessful; but he again articulated the same commandment, in a more authoritative and louder tone of voice; and while uttering with his tongue, his hands were at work; but after all the exertion of his power, both natural and supernatural, the deficient hand returned to its former position, where it still remains. But ill success in this case, did not discourage him from undertaking another. One of the Elders who was decrepit in one of his legs, was set upon the floor, and commanded, in the name of Jesus Christ to walk. He walked a step or two, his faith failed, and he was again compelled to have recourse to his former assistant, and he has had occasion to use it ever since. A dead body. Which had been retained above ground two or three days, under the expectation that the dead would be raised, was insensible to the voice of those who commanded it to awake into life, and is destined to sleep in the grave till the last trump shall sound, and the power of God easily accomplishes the work, which frustrated the attempts, and bid defiance to the puny efforts of the Mormonite.** That an attempt was made to raise the child, is denied, of course, as every other attempt has been, after the entire failure was obvious to all. The parents of the deceased child, however, state, that they were prevented from procuring medical aid for the child, by the representations of the elders, that there was no danger -- that it would certainly be restored. The father had no other idea but that the child was to be raised; neither did his faith fail him till preparations were made for its interment. He then awoke from his dream of delusion, and dissolved his connection with the impostors. Under these discouraging circumstances, the horizon of Mormonism gathered darkness, and a storm seemed to hang impending over the church. The gloom of disappointed expectation, overspread the countenances of many, while they labored to investigate the cause of this failure. To add, if possible, to their mortification, a larger assembly collected on the Sabbath, in order to hear preaching. In the midst of the meeting the congregation was dismissed by Rigdon, and the people sent to their homes. He was directed to do this, he said, by the spirit. But it was generally believed, that he was directed solely by fear; and that he had mistaken the spirit of cowardice, for the spirit of the Lord. Several of the Elders said they "felt the spirit to preach" to the congregation: and Rigdon felt the spirit to send the people home: such was the unity which then prevailed among them. You will doubtless say, can it be possible that the minds of men, and men who possess the appearance of honesty, can be so strangely infatuated, as still to adhere to a system, after it had occasioned so much agitation, and so much disappointment. One reason which can be assigned for this, is, the adherents are generally inclined to consider the system so perfect, as to admit of no suspicion; and the confusion and disappointment, are attributed to some other cause. Another, and principal reason is, delusion always effects the mind with a species of delirium, and this delirium arises in a degree proportionate to the magnitude of the delusion. These men, upon other subjects, will converse like other men; but when their favorite system is brought into view, its inconsistencies and contradictions are resolved into inexplicable mystery; and this will not only apply to the delusions now under consideration, but in my view, to every delusion, from the highest to the lowest; and it matters not whether it carries the stamp of popularity or its opposite. (*Ezra Booth, Letter 3*, September 1831.)

These harsh but candid words were printed in the local newspaper immediately before a second conference in October 1831. Joseph again conferred the high priesthood on a second group during that conference. It is noteworthy, that despite his failure in June, Joseph tried again in October.

In addition to the discouraged participants, there were others who reflected on the ordinations for years before concluding Joseph made a mistake. David Whitmer (one of the Three Witnesses to the Book of Mormon) was not present when the first ordinations took place. He heard of them, and read the account written by his brother John, the church historian. David Whitmer remained faithful for seven more years. However, later he would claim that he never believed these ordinations were proper, and would dissent and reject Joseph's leadership altogether. Eventually he published a stinging criticism of the ordinations performed in June 1831 as improper and unscriptural. He retold early Mormon history in his pamphlet, *Address to All Believers in Christ*, published in 1887. It included these reflections regarding the June 1831 conference:

> This matter of priesthood, since the days of Sydney Rigdon, has been the great hobby and stumbling block of the Latter Day Saints. Priesthood means authority; and authority is the word we should use. I do not think the word priesthood is mentioned in the New Covenant of the Book of Mormon. Authority is the word we used for the first two years in the church—until Sydney Rigdon's days in Ohio. This matter of the two orders of priesthood in the Church of Christ, and lineal priesthood of the old law being in the church, all originated in the mind of Sydney Rigdon. ...In Kirtland, Ohio, in

June, 1831, at a conference of the church, the first High Priests were ordained into the church. Brother Joseph ordained Lyman Wight, John Murdock, Harvey Whitlock, Hyrum Smith, Reynolds Cahoon and others to the office of a High Priest. When they were ordained, right there at the time, the devil caught and bound Harvey Whitlock so he could not speak, his face being twisted into demon-like shape. Also John Murdock and others were caught by the devil in a similar manner. How brethren, do you not see that the displeasure of the Lord was upon their proceedings in ordaining High Priests? Of course it was. These facts are recorded in the History of the Church— written by my brother, John Whitmer, who was the regularly appointed church historian. I was not at that conference, being then in Hiram, which is near Kirtland, Ohio. I also have the testimony of Harvey Whitlock whom the devil caught and bound; also John Whitmer, who was present, and others who were present at the time, so I know it is true. (*An Address to All Believers in Christ*, Chapter 9: High Priests.)

Joseph's followers may have been confused and discouraged by the priesthood ordination, but he was not. They did not share his vision, but that did not discourage Joseph. He proceeded with confidence and conviction to help others see that something great could be gained from heavenly priesthood. He never showed any sign of doubt about his own experience with God and angels. He described his certainty: "I had seen a vision; I knew it, and I knew that God knew it, and I could not deny it, neither dared I do it; at least I knew that by so doing I would offend God, and come under condemnation." (JS-H

1:25.) Because Joseph was certain God appeared to and spoke with him, there was nothing in the priesthood failure to cause him doubt. Despite the mess created by Ezra Booth's nine letters, Joseph proceeded confidently to address his followers' lack of faith.

At the next round of ordinations in October 1831, Joseph tried to address the problem directly. This time, Joseph instructed, admonished and encouraged, while Rigdon warned about God's rejection of them if they failed to faithfully measure up. The minutes of the conference report that Joseph Smith told the new priests, "It is the privilege of every Elder to speak of the things of God &c, And could we all come together with one heart and one mind in perfect faith the vail [sic] might as well be rent to day as next week or any other time and if we will but cleanse ourselves and covenant before God, to serve him, it is our privilege to have an assurance [sic] that God will protect us at all times." (*JS Papers, Documents, Vol. 2*: July 1831-January 1833, p. 81.) He continued, "the order of the High priesthood is that they have power given them to seal up the Saints unto eternal life. And said it was the privilege of every Elder present to be ordained to the Highpriesthood [sic]." (*Id.* at p. 82.)

Sidney Rigdon was far less encouraging. He warned the newly ordained, "it was the privilege of those Elders present to be ordained to the High Priesthood, telling them that if they then should doubt God would withdraw his Spirit from them." (*Id.* p. 83.) Thereafter Joseph interviewed the candidates. He concluded, "he had a testimony that each had one talent and if after being ordained they should hide it God would take it from them." (*Id.* p. 86.)

As the conference concluded, Rigdon was apparently unimpressed with some of the new priests. His closing comments included this frank assessment, "the Lord was not well pleased with some of them because of their indifference to be ordained to that office, exhortation to faith and obedience setting forth the power of that office." (*Id.*) These conference minutes reveal the low expectations of both Joseph and Sidney Rigdon. Low expectations were justified. No mountains moved, no rivers turned out of their course, and Zion did not appear.

Still Joseph was not shaken in his belief that God would allow mankind to receive the same miraculous priesthood the ancients held. The power, visions, control over elements, and outpouring of gifts would be given again. He likewise believed God had authorized it to be conferred. But nothing positive happened. Ordinations had been most noteworthy in what they did NOT accomplish. Those ordained did not even remain faithful. The dilemma was how to fix the failure. Joseph did not view the meager results as evidence of his or God's inability, but man's. Joseph often explained that a man was saved no faster than he gains knowledge. (See, e.g., *TPJS*, p. 217; D&C 130: 18-19.) Therefore, the failure could be cured if only those ordained learned enough to become adept priests.

In this first, great crisis, Joseph Smith's response reveals more about him than all that happened before in his life. He composed a series of lectures designed to teach others how to have faith. These lectures were delivered first orally, and later published. When printed in 1835 as part of a volume of new scripture titled Doctrine and Covenants, Joseph edited the lectures and vouched for them as true doctrine.

The lectures were the first portion of the book, and constituted the "Doctrine" of the volume. The Lectures were part of the Mormon scripture from 1835 until they were later dropped. The various Mormon churches discarded them, until only the LDS church retained them as scripture. In 1921, a committee of LDS church leaders thought the lectures had errors. Mormonism's founder prepared the lectures to encourage faith. Later Mormon leaders discarded them because they did not have any faith in their reliability.

In 2010, Boyd K. Packer, the President of the Twelve Apostles for the LDS Church, lamented in general conference that their church lacked priesthood power. As he put it, "We have done very well at distributing the authority of the priesthood. We have priesthood authority planted nearly everywhere. We have quorums of elders and high priests worldwide. But distributing the authority of the priesthood has raced, I think, ahead of distributing the power of the priesthood. The priesthood does not have the strength that it should have and will not have until the power of the priesthood is firmly fixed in the families as it should be." (Boyd K. Packer, *The Power of the Priesthood*, April 2010 LDS General Conference, emphasis in original.) Joseph Smith provided the cure for the lack of priesthood power in Lectures on Faith. But the LDS Church discarded Lectures only to find they are now just like the confused and powerless 1831 priests.[645]

The disarray following the ordinations in June 1831 illustrates how difficult it is to restore any great portion of priesthood. The Holy Order is much greater than what was attempted in 1831. The Kirtland Temple was built 5 years later. There, additional light and truth was given, but that also stopped short of restoring what Adam and the first patriarchs held.

More was to be given in the Nauvoo Temple. The Nauvoo Temple was not finished before Hyrum and Joseph died, and nothing further was given to the institutional churches that claim Joseph as founder.

What was given in the Kirtland Temple in 1836 has been recently clarified by additional revelation. What has been Section 110 was replaced by a more accurate revelation of the event included below:

On the third day of April 1836 Joseph and Oliver were in the temple in Kirtland, Ohio, The veil was taken from their minds, and the eyes of their

---

[645] *A Man Without Doubt*, pp. 19-34.

understanding were opened. They saw the Lord in his glory standing above them and the breastwork of the pulpit; and under his feet appeared as it were a paved work of pure gold, in color like amber. His eyes were as a flame of fire; the hair of his head was white like the pure snow; his countenance shone above the brightness of the sun; and his voice was as the sound of the rushing of great waters, even the voice of Jehovah, saying:

I am the Alpha and the Omega; I am he who was slain, I am he who lives; I am your advocate with the Father.

Behold, your sins are forgiven you; you are clean before me; therefore, lift up your heads and rejoice. Let the hearts of your brethren also rejoice, and let the hearts of all my people rejoice, who have, with their might, built this house to my name. For behold, I have accepted this house, and my name shall be here; and I will manifest myself to my people in mercy in this house. Yea, I will appear unto my servants, and speak unto them with mine own voice, if my people will keep my commandments, and do not pollute this holy house.

Behold and see: the hearts of thousands and tens of thousands shall greatly rejoice in consequence of the blessings that shall be poured out, and the endowment with which my servants will be endowed in this house. Behold: the fame of this house shall spread to foreign lands; and this is the beginning of the blessings I shall pour out upon my people. Even so. Amen. As this vision closed, the heavens were again opened to their view, and they saw and beheld, and were endowed with knowledge from the beginning of this creation to the ends thereof. And they were shown unspeakable things from the sealed record of Heaven which man is not capable of making known but must be revealed by the Powers of Heaven.

They beheld Michael, the archangel; Gabriel and Raphael, and divers angels, from Michael or Adam down to the end of time, showing in turns their dispensations, their rights, their keys, their honors, their majesty and glory, and the Powers of their Priesthood; giving line upon line, precept upon precept; endowing them with knowledge, even here a little, and there a little; holding forth hope for the work God was yet to perform, even the revelation of all things which are to come upon the earth until the return of the Lord in glory with His holy angels—to pour out judgment upon the world, and to reward the righteous.

And they were unable to take it in; therefore they were commanded to pray and ask to comprehend by the power of the Spirit, to bring all things to their remembrance, even the Record of Heaven which would abide in them.

Amen and Amen.

This clarifies that Joseph and Oliver were "unable to take it in" at the time this event took place. Oliver Cowdery would not mention anything about it, even in his final testimony recounting the visions and visitations he and Joseph witnessed. Six years later Joseph was able to write a letter shedding further light on what happened.[646] The visitations in the Kirtland Temple laid a foundation that could have led to the recovery of the original Holy Order, had enough time been granted Joseph and Hyrum. Michael the Archangel, or Adam, as the head of the human family, provided this outpouring as proof that the dispensation given Joseph was a legitimate opportunity for mankind to recover the original Holy Order. The failure was not because of unwillingness in heaven. It was because of apostasy on earth.

The Holy Order is familial. It does not involve establishing a church, but instead connecting together the Family of God, or in other words the Government of God. This can only be done in a temple prepared for that purpose. The Nauvoo Temple was intended to be the place where God could come to restore again that which has been lost, even the fullness of the Holy Order.[647] Before they died, Hyrum was given "the office of Priesthood and Patriarch."[648] Joseph

---

[646] See, D&C 128.
[647] See, D&C 124:28.
[648] Id., v. 91.

began to construct a ceremony for the planned temple to portray in ritual form some of the information held by the Holy Order. That incipient effort was never completed. Joseph also initiated a ritual ordination of himself and Emma as a "king and queen" as well as "priest and priestess." On September 28, 1843 in the upper room of the Mansion House they were initiated into the Quorum of the Anointed together.[649] Emma was the first woman to be initiated into this ritual. Joseph was "anointed and ord[ained] to the highest and holiest order of the priesthood (and companion [Emma Hale Smith])."[650] This new 1843 highest and holiest order did not include plural wives.[651]

The first mention I can find by Joseph of "adoption" in a discussion about the Kingdom of God was in October 1843, eight months before his death.[652] He began the actual practice of adopting men, but it did not get well enough defined for the rite to continue following his death. As I explained about adoption earlier in *Passing the Heavenly Gift*:

> Joseph's original instruction... connected the living faithful to the 'fathers' Abraham, Isaac and Jacob. The connection was through Priesthood, not genealogy... Joseph was connected by his priesthood, becoming the 'father' of all who would live after

---

[649] See Anderson, Devery S., *Joseph Smith's Quorum of the Anointed 1842-1845*, pp. 25-26 (Salt Lake: Signature Books, 2005); citing both *Joseph Smith Diary* and *Meetings of Anointed Quorum*, also referring to the February 26, 1867 retrospective account in Wilford Woodruff's *Historian's Private Journal*.

[650] *Joseph Smith's Quorum of the Anointed 1842-1845*, p. 25, supra.

[651] "On September 28, 1843, Emma received the highest ordinance of the church, that of the second anointing. This ordinance, also referred to as the 'fullness of the priesthood,' assured the recipient exaltation if he or she did not shed innocent blood or blaspheme against the Holy Ghost. In order to participate, Emma would have been endowed sometime between her sealing to Joseph on May 28 and the latter date. Joseph did not teach plural marriage in the Endowment Council; only first wives of male members and widows were admitted." Linda King Newell and Valeen Tippetts Avery, *Mormon Enigma: Emma Hale Smith*, (Garden City: Doubleday, 1984), p 161.

[652] The first time Joseph tied the word "adoption" to the Kingdom of God that I have been able to find was on October 15, 1843: "one thing to see the kingdom. & another to be in it. must have a change of heart. to see the kingdome of Good [God]. & subs[c]ribe the articles of adoption to enter therein." *JSP Journals, Vol. 3: May 1843-June 1844*, p. 114.

him. Families would be organized under Joseph, as the father of the righteous in this dispensation. Accordingly, men were sealed to Joseph Smith as their father, and they as his sons. This was referred to as 'adoption' because the family organization was priestly, according to the law of God, not biological. As soon as Joseph died, the doctrine began to erode, ultimately replaced by the substitute practice of sealing genealogical lines together. In between the original adoptive sealing to Joseph Smith, and the current practice of tracking genealogical/biological lines, there was an intermediate step when families were tracked back as far as research permitted, then the line was sealed to Joseph Smith. That practice is now forgotten, and certainly no longer practiced.[653]

When Joseph died, all understanding of the practice of "adoption" was quickly lost. As Jonathan Stapley has explained:

The period after Taylor's death in July 1887 appears to have been one of continued confusion regarding the law of adoption. Two months later in September 1887, John M. Whitaker, John Taylor's son-in-law wrote: "I went back to the office where I found [Apostle] Brother Lorenzo Snow and [First Council of the Seventy member] Jacob Gates. They conversed a long time. He finally entered into a deep subject on 'The Law of Adoption.' Brother Gates said he didn't believe in it as did also bother Snow. He reference back to the time that Brigham Young was in Kirtland[;] he had a person asked him about it and he said 'I don't know nothing about it.' President Taylor on one different occasion had a letter written to him for the following reason: it was [two undecipherable words] of Prophet J Smith or rather sister Eliza R. Snow Smith (Brother Gates didn't know which[;] a bout [sic] 70 persons were adopted into President J Smith's [family;] Sister Snow Smith said 'she didn't understand the law' but had no objections to them being sealed to her

---

[653] See, *Passing the Heavenly Gift*, pp. 481-482.

husband. And this led Brother Gates to write to President Taylor asking him if he knew anything about it. He never answered the letter. But on another occasion Brother Gates saw him and asked him plainly. President Taylor said he knew nothing about it. And also just lately when asked by Brother Snow, President Wilford Woodruff knew nothing about it. [']It hadn't been revealed to him.' I know this at this time to say [or show] a prevailing feeling among the Twelve that they don't understand it. George [undecipherable] Cannon also said he didn't understand it.[654]

Joseph Smith regarded adoption to be important for salvation. It was lost when he died. Before the Lord's return, this will need to be clarified by the Lord returning to a place on the earth, in which He can "come and restore again what has been lost, even a fullness of the priesthood" and its attendant rites.[655] This is an orderly process ordained in heaven before the creation and implemented at the time of Adam, and it must be followed in every generation. Until we receive the "kingdom" or Family of God, and the fathers in heaven, in strict order, we will remain unprepared for the Lord's return. The hearts of the fathers and hearts of the children must be sealed together. Pretenders cannot accomplish it, because they will neither know how nor have the authority.

Like almost all the late developments introduced by Joseph Smith, there was no fixed ordinance well enough defined to be perpetuated once he died. But these steps taken by Joseph certainly pointed the direction the restoration would take if Joseph and Hyrum had been allowed to live on. They are also what God intends to have practiced in the temple He has commanded must always be built by His people.[656]

---

[654] Jonathan Stapley, *Adoptive Sealing Ritual in Mormonism, The Journal of Mormon History*, pp. 53-117; citing to *John M. Whitaker, Diary, Book No. 4, September 16, 1887 to September 20, 1888*, November 16, 1887, MS 0002, Marriott Special Collection; transcription from Pitman shorthand by LaJean Purcell Carruth.

[655] See D&C 124:28.

[656] In the *Answer to Prayer for Covenant* the Lord explained: "Whenever I have people who are mine, I command them to build a house, a holy habitation, a sacred place where my presence can dwell, or where the Holy Spirit of Promise can minister, because it is in such a place that it has been ordained

The way to understand the role of Peter, James and John is that they came, not for the purposes of conferring priesthood, but for reconnecting the genealogical line to link the living with the fathers who are in heaven. Some have argued that meant Joseph Smith was **the** birthright holder in the line from Ephraim. Given the way genealogical lines run, and given all of the intermarriages in history, there are probably many who could qualify as potential holders of the birthright. Because of disruptive events in history like the Black Plague, Thirty Years War, World War I, and World War II, there is no way for man to determine who God has designated to possess the birthright.

Even if the living heir can be identified, he may not qualify because of a lack of righteousness. Esau was older than Jacob, but Jacob was more righteous. Seth had older brothers who were grandfathers by the time he was born. But the birthright went to Seth because he was true and faithful. It may be possible there are many people living who could qualify.

The heir must receive the same gospel as Abraham. That requires a dispensation from heaven to restore what has been lost. Correct information must be restored. It is either amusing or depressing for people in their arrogance to assume that they know enough to understand what God is doing or has done. The things of God are of deep import and careful and solemn and ponderous and prayerful thought can only find them out. Understanding has to reach into Heaven itself and search into and contemplate the darkest abyss to save any soul including your own.[657] That will not be accomplished casually. Nor is it accomplished without sacrifice. The Lord, whose own heart was broken, ultimately requires us to give a broken heart and a contrite spirit. It requires trials, tests and temptations to prove us. The Holy Order will return before the Lord comes again in glory. It will be necessary before the return of the Lord for the original Holy Order to exist in all of its ramifications. It must be established on the

---

to recover you, establish by my word and my oath your marriages, and endow my people with knowledge from on high that will unfold to you the mysteries of godliness, instruct you in my ways, that you may walk in my path. And all the outcasts of Israel will I gather to my house, and the jealousy of Ephraim and Judah will end. Ephraim will not envy Judah and Judah will not provoke Ephraim."

[657] See *TPJS*, p. 137.

earth and include all of the rights that originally belonged to Adam. It must be accounted for and returned back to Adam and then to Christ.

Christ will return to exercise dominion over the earth. Therefore everyone who has held dominion must recognize His right to claim the earth. If dominion belonged to someone other than Him, He would not be able to interfere with that right. His word cannot be broken.

The Holy Order, including the right to dominion, must return to the earth. It will be fully restored. It will be in the possession of those who will not covet it. Those who will not, like Cain, attempt to influence the conditions of salvation for souls of men. The right candidates are those who look upon it merely as a burden to be held under the authority of God, belonging to Him, to be returned to Him, so that He can come and fix this broken world and bring wickedness to an end. If an aspiring, ambitious, vain person were to hold such a position, all of the Lord's plans can be frustrated. Therefore, we need to be like our Lord, the greatest of all,[658] the most intelligent of all,[659] who came here to serve, who knelt and washed the feet of others. He gave His life as a sacrifice. Despite His reluctance He partook of the bitter cup, to the dregs.[660] He was slain, and He gave all glory and all majesty to the Father.[661] That is the kind of person who will be trusted to hold the Holy Order.

The restoration of all things literally means the restoration of ALL things, including the Holy Order. It will not and cannot stop with organizing a New Testament church. The restoration must reach back to the beginning, to the days of Adam.

This generation does not seem to value the truth enough for the Lord to reveal what will save them. God truly does have things that the eyes of man have not seen, nor have the ears heard; nor has yet entered into the hearts of man.[662] God sends knowledge into the world for the meek and humble, and He perpetually keeps great things hidden from the strident, vulgar, proud, haughty and foolish. Whether the Lord completes His work and fulfills His promises in this generation, or in a future generation, will be decided by us. We

---

[658] D&C 19:18.
[659] Abr. 3:19.
[660] D&C 19:18-19.
[661] 3 Ne. 11:11.
[662] D&C 76:10.

must repent and offer a broken heart and a contrite spirit if we hope to please God.

There is a great deal more that needs to be restored. There is so much resistance to restoring truths from the worldly that this journey may not be possible until man has been humbled by God's hand. The Lord really is trying to restore the original fullness and Holy Order. But there is a sobering prophecy of a coming moment when the Lord will lament to the living and the dead over the way in which the world has responded to His messages:

> And again, the Lord shall utter his voice out of heaven, saying: Hearken, O ye nations of the earth, and hear the words of that God who made you. O, ye nations of the earth, how often would I have gathered you together as a hen gathereth her chickens under her wings, but ye would not! How oft have I called upon you by the mouth of my servants, and by the ministering of angels, and by mine own voice, and by the voice of thunderings, and by the voice of lightnings, and by the voice of tempests, and by the voice of earthquakes, and great hailstorms, and by the voice of famines and pestilences of every kind, and by the great sound of a trump, and by the voice of judgment, and by the voice of mercy all the day long, and by the voice of glory and honor and the riches of eternal life, and would have saved you with an everlasting salvation, but ye would not![663]

---

[663] D&C 43:23-25. Many of those sent by the Lord have labored in their ministries without hope of seeing Zion. Mormon explained: "But behold, I was without hope, for I knew the judgments of the Lord which should come upon them; for they repented not of their iniquities, but did struggle for their lives without calling upon that Being who created them." (Mormon 5:2.) Joseph Smith said, "There has been a great difficulty in getting anything into the heads of this generation. It has been like splitting hemlock knots with a corn-dodger for a wedge, and a pumpkin for a beetle. Even the Saints are slow to understand. I have tried for a number of years to get the minds of the Saints prepared to receive the things of God; but we frequently see some of them, after suffering all they have for the work of God, will fly to pieces like glass as soon as anything comes that is contrary to their traditions: they cannot stand the fire at all. How many will be able to abide a celestial law,

## Chapter 7: Our Divine Parents:
© Denver C. Snuffer, Jr. 2018

This discussion of our Divine Parents fits very comfortably inside the Father's Great Plan of Happiness.[664] Unfortunately, we have so little understanding of that Plan that this subject is left to assumptions and innuendos rather than forthright declarations. In this essay I will make forthright declarations.

If discussing this subject confuses you, set it aside for now and spend some time studying the scriptures; increase your understanding of the Father's Great Plan of Happiness, including *Lectures on Faith*. Those who welcome more truth eventually understand God's plan more fully and, in turn, comprehend more of the God's vast work.[665] Please do not offend God by rejecting any truth coming from Him.[666]

The only reason I have the audacity to address this topic candidly is because Those of whom I speak in this talk have permitted me to do so. Without Their approval, I would not presume to address this topic publicly.

This topic may seem foreign to traditional Protestants. Despite that, Christ's gospel includes things you may not yet understand. The Apostle Paul referred to hidden truths as "unspeakable" because they are not yet understood.[667] They are true, but remain "mysteries" for those who are not shown them by God.[668] One servant of God may

---

and go through and receive their exaltation, I am unable to say, as many are called, but few are chosen." (*DHC* 6:184-185.) We are very late in history, and have greater reason to humble ourselves and obey God than any previous generation. Yet most of us also seem far too disinterested to spare ourselves from the coming tribulations by establishing Zion and dwelling in peace with one another.

[664] This is a term used twice by Alma the Younger in his instruction to his son Corianton, recorded in New Covenants Alma 19:13 (hereafter "NC"); Alma 42:8, 16. Joseph Smith referred to this plan as "eternal progression."

[665] Some people have denounced a subject because they claim it is "not consistent with the gospel of Christ." It would be more correct and meek to say a subject is "not consistent with their present, limited understanding of the gospel of Christ" rather than to reject something outright.

[666] "The moment we revolt at anything that comes from God, the devil takes power." (*TPJS*, p. 181.)

[667] NC 2 Cor. 1:41; KJV 2 Cor. 12:4.

know but be forbidden from revealing a matter, while another is later commanded to reveal it.[669] Therefore, because you have a Bible you should not assume it contains all of God's words or that He has not revealed more or will not reveal more.[670] An infinite and eternal God has spoken many things, and will yet reveal more things.[671]

Some truths are already in scripture, but hidden from view by God's decree. Christian scriptures declare "It is the glory of God to conceal a thing: but the honour of kings is to search out a matter."[672] So we search out matters God has concealed to see more of His glory:

Our scriptures speak carefully about the existence and importance of a Heavenly Mother: a Divine Female whose greatest attribute is to bestow wisdom upon the whole of this creation. It is possible to miss Her presence. That cultural and theological blindness is not because of Her absence from the scriptures. It is not hard to detect Her, if you know what to look for. WE just don't yet understand how to look.

The Old Testament (now retitled The Old Covenants) was preserved and transmitted in the Hebrew language for generations. Some characteristics[673] of that language are important to understand as part of this discussion. First, Hebrew has no neuter, only masculine and feminine. Furthermore, when there are multiple persons involved, even if only one member of a group is male, Hebrew uses **only** the masculine to refer to the group. Women and men collectively are referred to using a masculine noun or pronoun.

When a masculine noun or pronoun from the Hebrew language is translated into English, English language readers assume it means

---

[668] Paul referred to those in possession of hidden knowledge as "stewards of the mysteries of God." NC 1 Cor. 1:14; KJV 1 Cor. 4:1.

[669] For example Nephi was "forbidden that [he] should write the remainder of the things which [he] saw." But was told God had "ordained the apostle of the Lamb of God [John] that he should write them." NC 1 Ne. 3:30-31; 1 Ne. 14:25, 28.

[670] See NC 2 Ne. 12:10; 2 Ne. 9:9-10.

[671] See 9th Article of Faith, PofGP.

[672] KJV Proverbs 25:2; Old Covenants Proverbs 4:1: "It is the glory of God to conceal a thing, but the honor of kings to search out a matter." (Hereafter "OC".)

[673] These are not necessarily impediments, as long as you understand a handful of basic Hebrew language rules.

"man" or "men" and excludes "women." In English we can use neuter pronouns like "they" or "them" to refer to a group of both men and women. Hebrew would use "men" or "he" if the group included even a single male in the group.

We all know that the Hebrew word "Elohim" is used to refer to God and that it is plural.[674] In English it should be translated as "Gods," but because we allow theology to control translating the text, the term "Elohim" in Hebrew is therefore rendered in English as a singular "God." It should be plural; and if plural, rendered masculine in English. But that is Hebrew to English, and does not mean, as we shall see, there is no female among the Elohim.

The story of creation starts by identifying Heavenly Parents, a couple clearly described as the true and living "God." In the King James Version, the creation of mankind is told in these words: "*So God created man in his own image, in the image of God created he him; male and female created he them.*"[675]

The context of the words "created he (God) **him** (man)" is immediately clarified to refer to both the male and female and not a just the male: "created he him; **male** and **female** created he them." The English translation follows the masculine pronoun implied in Hebrew. Therefore, looking at it in the Hebrew language, there were two persons described and only one of them was male. It could be translated: "created they (Gods) them (man and woman); male and female." In the King James Version the Gods are described using a masculine pronoun taken from the Hebrew. Moving from Hebrew into English, the translation stayed true to the Hebrew and the human couple is likewise described using a masculine pronoun. They are called "him" in English because of this.

The words "So God created man in his (God's) own image," affirm two points:

First, the plurality of God.

Second, that plurality are a couple that includes both a male and a female.[676] Man is created in God's image, and that image is a couple: a man and a woman. This is not figurative language. It is literally

---

[674] The number of those who were included in the original "Elohim" is not the focus of this paper. In this the focus is on the inescapable conclusion that both male and female companions were essential for the members of the Elohim.

[675] KJV Gen. 1:27.

[676] Or a council that includes any number of couples.

describing mankind having two sexes and that is godlike, or what God's own "image" is.

I was recently listening to a podcast with my wife. Philip McLemore was being interviewed by Dan Wotherspoon. They were discussing attributes of the Divine male and female.[677] In their discussion the dual nature of God was incorrectly regarded as figurative, not literal. It was suggested that this dual nature was intended to be part of every individual, with all men and women having both masculine and feminine attributes Dan Wotherspoon thought individuals would develop through successive stages of growth.[678] This idea may bring comfort to some, but the scriptural account is not ambiguous. It refers to a literal male and a literal female created by the Elohim. The male is named Adam and the female is named Eve. They are made in the image of the Elohim, or the Gods of creation, whose image is a male and a female.

There is even more meaning added to the scriptures describing the creation of man in the Joseph Smith Translation. The JST renders the account in Genesis this way: "And I, God, created man in mine own image, **in the image of mine Only Begotten** created I him; male and female created I them."[679] Here, not only is the Father male and female, but so is the image of the Only Begotten, who is therefore also two separate beings (male and female). Joseph's clarification helps us understand who the Son was and is. The Son has a female counterpart, or, like His Father, a spouse.

There are instances in which Hebrew uses the feminine directly to describe God. For example, the spirit of God (*Ruach Elohim*)[680] is a feminine noun. Likewise when referring to the "presence of God" Hebrew uses the feminine.[681] God's presence includes the feminine.

---

[677] Mormon Matters podcast 328: *Explorations in Depth: The Two Lost Sons and Growing in God.*

[678] The idea is reminiscent of Aristotle's faulty notions of biology resulting in the erroneous conclusion that women were incomplete men, whose development made them inferior to men.

[679] OC Gen. 2:7. The King James Version differs materially by omitting any reference to "mine Only Begotten" as the prototype image: "So God created man in his own image, in the image of God created he him; male and female created he them." (Gen. 1:27.)

[680] KJV Genesis 1:2.

[681] The word *Shekhinah* was coined as a proper noun to replace a phrase

If you begin with these truths, then throughout the scriptures you can find both the Father and Mother, even when English translations speak only of a male God. Keep this in mind as you read either English or Hebrew language scriptures.

Another Hebrew language characteristic involves verb tenses. Although Elohim is plural, when speaking of the God of Israel, it is almost always combined with a singular verb. In English we say "they are" and not "they is." But when it comes to Hebrew and the plural "Gods," the verbs are almost always singular. Even though Israel's God is plural, the singular form of the verb has been used to support theological arguments for "monotheism" or a single being for God.

Hebrew combines the plural Elohim or Gods with a singular verb, as in this example from Genesis: "thou mayest inherit the land wherein thou art a stranger, which God [Elohim] gave [singular verb] unto Abraham."[682]

The Old Testament and Christ proclaimed that the God of Israel is "one."[683] But then Christ explained that "one" is not singular in person, but in harmony of heart.[684] Accordingly, using a singular verb was meant to convey that all action undertaken by the Gods is done with a singular, harmonious purpose. They act as one. They are one.[685]

---

literally meaning "he caused to dwell." That phrase is better understood to convey "the Presence of God" and therefore the word *Shekhinah* was adopted. Old Testament examples are found in Exodus 13:21-22; 24:16-18; 25:22; 40:34-38; Leviticus 16:2; Numbers 9:15-23; 10:11-36; Psalm 18:7-15; 80:1; 2 Samuel 6:2; Isaiah 37:16; Ezekiel 9:3; 10:18; Haggai 2:9; and Zechariah 2:5—all KJV cites.

[682] OC Gen. 7:77; see also KJV Gen. 28:4.

[683] In OC Deuteronomy 2:14; also KJV Deuteronomy 6:4 it states: "Hear, O Israel: The Lord our God is one Lord[.]" Which Christ quotes in NC Mark 5:44; also KJV Mark 6:29: "And Jesus answered him, The first of all the commandments is, Hear, O Israel; The Lord our God is one Lord[.]"

[684] KJV John 17: 20-23: "Neither pray I for these alone, but for them also which shall believe on me through their word; That they all may be one; as thou, Father, art in me, and I in thee, that they also may be one in us: that the world may believe that thou hast sent me. And the glory which thou gavest me I have given them; that they may be one, even as we are one. I in them, and thou in me, that they may be made perfect in one; and that the world may know that thou hast sent me, and hast loved them, as thou hast loved me.

When the Gods speak to Moses on the Mount, English recounts the story in these words: "And God [Elohim-plural] spake [singular] unto Moses and said unto him, I am the Lord [Yhwh]."[686] In Hebrew this account is very helpful. It reiterates the clarification Joseph Smith made to the Genesis account of the creation of man: The Elohim are plural. And the voice is identified as Jehovah's [Yhwh]. Given the plurality of this God and His name is "Jehovah" [Yhwh], it means that Jehovah, like the Father, is plural and has a female companion, or wife. The Gods are never single. This is why man was made male and female, in the image of the Gods. If the Egyptians' quest to imitate the order that came down from the beginning failed,[687] they nevertheless preserved the idea of a male/father and female/mother in their pantheon of their gods.[688] Taking the language of this passage literally, Jehovah spoke with Moses as a duo, a dyad or a couple, necessarily comprised of both a male and a female—for that is God's image.

Another example is provided by Elijah: "And call ye on the name of your **gods** [Elohim], and I will call on the name of the **Lord** [Yhwh]: and the **God** [Elohim] that answereth by fire, let him be **God** [Elohim]. And all the people answered and said, It is well spoken."[689] Here again Jehovah is identified as a plural.

To reflect the image of God, there are two sexes, male and female. Man was organized in this way to help us to understand who and what the Gods are. The importance of this is illustrated in a passage of the *Lectures on Faith*:

> Let us here observe, that three things are necessary, in order that any rational and intelligent being may exercise faith in God unto life and salvation. First, The idea that he actually exists.

---

[685] Throughout the Nag Hammadi text, *Apocryphon of John*, the references to God are to the "Mother-Father" as a single exalted identity.

[686] OC Exo. 2:12; see also KJV Exo. 6:2: "And God [Elohim] spake [singular] unto Moses, and said unto him, I am the Lord [Yhwh]."

[687] Abr. 1:26.

[688] In the earliest (and most reflective of the original imitation) version of their theology, Amun (male) had a female companion Hathor (female). Their son Horus (male) had a wife Isis (female). God's son Horus became the mortal Osiris and was slain by his usurping brother Set. But even in death Osiris was able to produce a posterity.

[689] OC 1 Kings 4:8; KJV 1Kings 18:24.

Secondly, A correct idea of his *character, perfections, and attributes*. Thirdly, An actual knowledge that the course of life which he is pursuing, is according to his will. —For without an acquaintance with these three important facts, the faith of every rational being must be imperfect and unproductive; but with this understanding, it can become perfect and fruitful, abounding in righteousness unto the praise and glory of God the Father, and the Lord Jesus Christ.[690]

Eventually every man—and I use that word in the Hebrew sense, meaning every male and female—will be brought to stand before the Throne of God.[691] Then all questions about the image of the Gods will be answered by what is apparent to anyone standing in Their presence.[692]

These truths are in the scriptures accepted by every Christian denomination. They are in the scriptures believed by the Jews. Yet the Heavenly Mother's existence is not acknowledged.

While a great deal more could be said to demonstrate that God the Father necessarily includes God the Mother, we want to know more than merely She exists. We want to understand her character, perfections and attributes also.

The Father and the Son are masculine and therefore personified by the word "knowledge." The Mother as well as the Son's companion are feminine, and personified by the word "wisdom." These personifications reflect an eternal truth about these two parts of the One True God.

Knowledge (masculine) initiates, Wisdom (feminine) receives, guides and tempers. Knowledge can be dangerous unless it is informed by wisdom. Wisdom provides guidance and counsel to channel what comes from knowledge. The Mother maintains cosmic

---

[690] *Lecture Third*:3-5.

[691] New Covenants Revelation 2:12 (hereafter "NC Rev."): "After this I beheld, and, lo, a great multitude, which no man could number, of all nations, and kindreds, and people, and tongues, stood before the throne and before the Lamb, clothed with white robes and palms in their hands and cried with a loud voice saying, Salvation to our God which sitteth upon the throne and unto the Lamb."

[692] For example, heavenly visions refer to "concourses" (NC 1 Ne. 1:3; Alma 17:5; T&C 160:1), or "hosts" (OC Isaiah 2:1; T&C 122:13; 2 Chron. 7:13).

harmony, assisted by all divine women who attain the status of "wisdom" in their progression. These are eternal attributes, part of what it means to be a male or a female. Creation begins with the active initiative of knowledge, but order and harmony for the creation requires wisdom. Balance between them is required for an orderly creation to exist.

A great deal can be learned about Heavenly Mother by searching for the word "wisdom" in scripture. Very often the reference to "wisdom" is to Her distinctly, and not merely an abstract attribute.[693] If we are blind to Her existence, we cannot see the reference to Her in those passages. Although many scriptures have the Divine Mother's words, Her presence is veiled by our ignorance and refusal to acknowledge Her. There is one extensive passage in scripture in Her voice that we look at today. It teaches us a great deal about Her.

This was once a temple text and has become somewhat corrupted. I will not make any corrections or clarifications. This is from Proverbs 8. The version we have has additional passages about the foolish woman at the beginning and again at the end. I discard those so the words attributed to the Heavenly Mother can be considered. She states:

> *Hear, for I will speak of excellent things and the opening of my lips shall be right things. For my mouth shall speak truth and wickedness is an abomination to my lips. All the words of my mouth are in righteousness, there is nothing froward or perverse in them.*

She proclaims Herself as the reliable source of truth, righteousness and plain—meaning clear—understanding. She is opposed to wickedness, frowardness—meaning stubbornness or contrariness—and perversity.

If we are "froward" we are stubborn or contrary with one another. We dispute. We find it difficult to agree. How much debate and anger are produced by frowardness!

Jacob (called James in the King James Bible) mentioned "wisdom" in his letter. In contemplating Her, Jacob suggested we should be "easy to be entreated."

---

[693] See, e.g., KJV Proverbs 8:1; 9:1; Psalms 136:5; Jer. 10:12; Luke 7:35; 1 Cor. 12:8; 2 Ne. 21:2; Mosiah 8:20, among many others. Joseph Smith was searching for "wisdom" when he read KJV James 1:5. His prayer for the wisdom to distinguish between true and false religions was the attempt to access Heavenly Wisdom.

Who is a wise man, and endowed with knowledge among you? Let him show out of good conduct his works with meekness of wisdom. But if you have bitter envying and strife in your hearts, glory not and lie not against the truth. This wisdom descends not from above, but is earthly, sensual, devilish; for where envying and strife are, there is confusion and every evil work. But the wisdom that is from above is *first pure, then peaceable, gentle and easy to be entreated, full of mercy and good fruits, without partiality and without hypocrisy. And the fruit of righteousness is sown in peace of them that make peace.*[694]

Wisdom from above can endow us with the kindly demeanor of brothers and sisters who seek what is good for one another. How often are the words of our mouths froward and "perverse?" The Divine Mother refuses to speak wickedness and abominations, and Her influence brings others to depart from such failures.

Continuing:

*They are all plain to him that understandeth and right to them that find knowledge. Receive my instruction and not silver, and knowledge rather than choice gold. For wisdom is better than rubies and all the things that may be desired are not to be compared to it.*

Proclaiming, "wisdom is better than rubies," she asks us to receive Her instruction rather than seek silver and gold. Nothing else is to be compared with Her wisdom. She instructs in virtues that would make any person better. But Her instruction will also make living in peace with others possible. Nothing in this world is more desirable than acquiring wisdom: understanding and putting knowledge to wise use. Zion will require the wisdom to use pure

---

[694] NC Jacob 1:14, emphasis added. In KJV James 3:13-17 this same passage reads: "Who is a wise man and endued with knowledge among you? let him shew out of a good conversation his works with meekness of wisdom. But if ye have bitter envying and strife in your hearts, glory not, and lie not against the truth. This wisdom descendeth not from above, but is earthly, sensual, devilish. For where envying and strife is, there is confusion and every evil work. But the wisdom that is from above is first pure, then peaceable, gentle, and easy to be entreated, full of mercy and good fruits, without partiality, and without hypocrisy."

knowledge in meekness, humility and charity. Zion will require Her influence.

Continuing:

> *I, wisdom, dwell with prudence and find out knowledge of witty inventions. The fear of the Lord is to hate evil, pride, and arrogancy, and the evil way and the froward mouth do I hate.*

Wisdom and prudence go together as companions. "Prudence" means good judgment or common sense. It is the quality of assessing things correctly and making a sound decision in light of the circumstances and persons involved. Prudent judgment is not hasty or unfair. Arrogance is destroyed and pride overtaken by "fear of the Lord"—meaning that we do not want to disappoint our Lord by our low, vulgar and mean conduct.[695]

She mentions a second time Her opposition to the froward. This time She declares She hates the froward mouth. We repel Her by being argumentative and contrary with one another.

Continuing:

> *Counsel is mine and sound wisdom, I am understanding, I have strength.*

The Mother must possess great strength because She hates the forward—the contentious. She does not welcome that spirit in Herself or any of Her offspring.

Christ taught this to the Nephites, which seems to be clearly taken from the Mother's wisdom:

> And there shall be no disputations among you as there hath hitherto been, neither shall there be disputations among you concerning the points of my doctrine as there hath hitherto been. For verily, verily I say unto you, He that hath the spirit of contention is not of me, but is of the Devil, who is the father of contention, and he stirreth up the hearts of men to contend with anger one with another. Behold, this is not my doctrine, to stir up the hearts of men with anger one against another,

---

[695] As Joseph Smith cautioned: "How vain and trifling have been our spirits, our conferences, our councils, our meetings, our private as well as public conversations; too low, too mean, too vulgar, too condescending for the dignified characters of the called and chosen of God, according to the purposes of His will from before the foundation of the world!" T&C 47:18.

but this is my doctrine, that such things should be done away.[696]

It requires strength to refrain from contention and disputes with froward and arrogant people. When we feel strongly that we are right, or are firmly convinced someone else is wrong, it is difficult to bridle our tongue and meekly persuade without contention. But the Heavenly Mother possesses the strength required to look with compassion on our failings. She deals with Her offspring using good judgment and common sense. She is opposed to arrogance, and when we are arrogant we offend Her.

How many religious arguments, even religious wars have been caused because mankind is too weak to patiently reason together? The history of this world is a bold testimony of what weak and deceived men do when they reject wisdom.

Mankind cannot have Zion without wisdom to guide us. Zion must be a community. Developing wisdom requires us to patiently interact with one another. This counsel from the Heavenly Mother is a gift to help us understand what we lack.

Continuing with Her words:

*By me kings reign and princes decree justice. By me princes rule and nobles, even all the judges of the earth.*

Never doubt this claim by the Divine Mother. She knows best the strengths and weaknesses of Her sons. She decides who will be made kings. The earliest generations knew this about Her. In the beginning it was the mothers who decided between sons. Consider a few examples from early history and how the mothers acted on this matriarchal right:

In the case of Mother Eve, it was she and not Adam who weighed and decided that Cain would be Adam's first successor to the Holy Order. She did not do this in haste, but after many years of observing how Cain was unlike his many, rebellious, older siblings. He hearkened to his parents and had interest in knowing and following God. She decided that this son was indeed from the Lord and would not be yet another one to reject His words:

And Adam knew Eve his wife, and she conceived and bare Cain, and said, I have gotten a man from the Lord, wherefore he may not reject his words. But, behold, also Cain[697] hearkened not saying, Who

---

[696] NC 3 Ne. 5:8.

is the Lord, that I should know him? And she again conceived, and bare his brother Abel. And Abel hearkened unto the voice of the Lord.

To the sorrow of both Adam and Eve, Cain changed. After his initial faithfulness, he no longer continued to follow the Lord's words.

When he felt his right to stand second only to Adam in the Holy Order was threatened, he resorted to murder to keep that position. That right cannot be handled with any degree of unrighteousness. Therefore, his ambition undid his mother's choosing, and he fell from grace.[698] But note in the account that it was Eve, being deceived by Lucifer, who chose Cain. That was her right. That right came down from the Mother in Heaven as one of the roles occupied by all mothers over their offspring.

While Rebekah was pregnant with twins, her unborn sons struggled within her. She prayed to know the cause of her difficulties and learned that the younger would rule over the elder.[699] This answer stayed with her, and when the time came she acted consistent with God's voice to her.[700] Even though it required her to supplant Isaac's

---

[697] The language, "but behold, also Cain" means that time passed, and the course Cain followed changed. He, like the many children of Adam and Eve before him, "also" chose to rebel and reject his parent's teaching.

[698] Like so many others have done, Cain was called but ultimately not chosen. His heart was so set upon honors that he failed to grasp that the rights belonging to his father could not be controlled by unrighteousness in the least degree.

[699] See Genesis 7:61: "And Isaac entreated the Lord for his wife, that she might bare children, because she was barren. And the Lord was entreated of him, and Rebekah his wife conceived. And the children struggled together within her womb, and she said, If I am with child, why is it thus with me? And she went to inquire of the Lord. And the Lord said unto her, Two nations are in thy womb, and two manner of people shall be separated from thy bowels, and the one people shall be stronger than the other people, and **the elder shall serve the younger**. And when her days to be delivered were fulfilled, behold, there were twins in her womb. And the first came out red, all over like a hairy garment, and they called his name Esau. And after that came his brother out, and his hand took hold on Esau's heel, and his name was called Jacob, and Isaac was threescore years old when she bare them." (Emphasis added.) See also KJV Gen. 25:21-26.

[700] Josephus claimed God's answer was given to Isaac, not Rebecca. See, *Antiquities of the Jews*, 1:18:1. However both the JST and the KJV declare God's answer came to her, and if Joseph Smith did not correct it we should

intention to set Esau ahead of Jacob, it was Rebekah's right as the mother. Rebekah preferred Jacob because of revelation. Her preference for him is mentioned **before** Esau sold his birthright. We do not know if Esau sold his birthright because Rebekah put that idea in Jacob's mind beforehand, or if Jacob wanted the birthright separate from his mother's influence. But Rebekah's decision is mentioned before Jacob obtained it. Her involvement directly resulted in her unwary husband conferring the blessing on Jacob:

> And the boys grew. And Esau was a skillful hunter, a man of the field, and Jacob was a plain man, dwelling in tents. And Isaac loved Esau, because he did eat of his venison, but Rebekah loved Jacob. And Jacob cooked stew, and Esau came from the field and he was faint. And Esau said to Jacob, Feed me, I pray you, with that same red stew for I am faint. Therefore was his name called Edom. And Jacob said, Sell me this day your birthright. And Esau said, Behold, I am at the point of dying and what shall this birthright profit me? And Jacob said, Swear to me this day. And he swore unto him and he sold his birthright unto Jacob. Then Jacob gave Esau bread and stew of lentils. And he did eat and drink, and rose up and went his way; thus Esau despised his birthright.[701]

Rebekah's choice was honored by this turn of events. Jacob obtained the legal right to hold the birthright under the Holy Order because Esau abandoned it—conveyed it to Jacob. Some time later the time arrived to appoint Isaac's successor and heir.

> And it came to pass that when Isaac was old, and his eyes were dim so that he could not see, he called Esau his eldest son and said unto him, My son. And he said unto him, Behold, here am I. And he said, Behold, now I am old, I know not the day of my death. Now therefore, take, I pray you, your weapons, your quiver and your bow, and go out to the field and take me some venison. And make me savory food, such as I love, and bring it to me that I

---

be confident it was given to her.
[701] OC Genesis 9:3.

may eat, that my soul may bless you before I die. And Rebekah heard when Isaac spoke to Esau his son. And Esau went to the field to hunt for venison and to bring it. And Rebekah spoke unto Jacob her son, saying, Behold, I heard your father speak unto Esau your brother, saying, Bring me venison and make me savory food, that I may eat and bless you before the Lord before my death. Now therefore, my son, obey my voice according to that which I command you. Go now to the flock and fetch me from there two good kids of the goats, and I will make them savory food for your father such as he loves. And you shall bring it to your father that he may eat and that he may bless you before his death.[702]

While Isaac intended to bless his older son, Esau, Rebekah, as their mother, knew the younger brother Jacob was the chosen one. Rebekah proceeded with the confidence of knowing that decision was hers to make. She took appropriate steps, as was her right, to appoint the heir. She managed her ailing husband wisely and subtly. At that time Isaac's "eyes were dim" –a symbolic description of his condition— and he was unable to see the correct choice.

Jacob realized his mother's plan involved risks. He raised his concerns with his mother:

And Jacob said to Rebekah his mother, Behold, Esau my brother is a hairy man and I am a smooth man. My father perhaps will feel me, and I shall seem to him as a deceiver, and I shall bring a curse upon me and not a blessing. And his mother said unto him, Upon me be your curse my son, only obey my voice and go fetch me them.

And he went and fetched and brought them to his mother. And his mother made savory food such as his father loved. And Rebekah took handsome raiment of her eldest son Esau, which was with her in the house, and put them upon Jacob her younger son. And she put the skins of the kids of the goats upon his hands, and upon the smooth of his neck[703]

---

[702] OC Genesis 9:12-13.
[703] OC Genesis 9:13-14.

When Jacob worried about being cursed for deceiving his father, his mother reassured him and, if there was to be one, offered to take the curse. Jacob did not want to deceive his father, but his mother said it was she, not her son, who would be responsible.

Mother Rebekah then prepared the meal for Isaac. Rebekah also clothed her son with the "handsome raiment of her eldest son"—a description filled with symbolism. Then she used the skins of slain lambs to cover the hands and neck of Jacob—another description filled with symbolism and foreshadowing. Thus outfitted in the eldest son's raiment and a slain lamb covering his skin, Jacob was presented as the heir.

If you interpret this account as a type of Christ, it helps us to appreciate the unacknowledged role of Christ's Mother in preparing Him as an acceptable Son and heir to His Father.

Following his mother's guidance Jacob proceeded:

> And she gave the savory food and the bread, which she had prepared, into the hand of her son Jacob. And he came unto his father and said, My father. And he said, Here am I. Who are you my son? And Jacob said unto his father, I am Esau your firstborn,[704] I have done according as you bade me. Arise, I pray you, sit and eat of my venison, that your soul, may bless me. And Isaac said unto his son, How is it that you have found it so quickly my son? And he said, Because the Lord your God brought it to me. And Isaac said unto Jacob, Come near, I pray you, that I may feel you my son, whether you be my very son Esau or not. And Jacob went near unto Isaac his father. And he felt him and said, The voice is Jacob's voice, but the hands are the hands of Esau. And he discerned him not, because his hands were hairy as his brother Esau's hands, so he blessed him.[705]

On choosing the lawful heir, Isaac was blind to the correct choice. But Rebekah was not, and it was her right to choose. To accomplish the foreordained result, Isaac's eyes were dimmed. Rebekah used that to prevent him from making the wrong choice. And so the heir chosen by Rebekah was given the blessing.

---

[704] He had previously acquired this right and therefore could answer this way.
[705] OC Genesis 9:14-15.

> And he said, Are you my very son Esau? And he
> said, I am.

This answer from Jacob is not as wrong as some have claimed. Jacob purchased the birthright, and therefore on the issue Isaac raised (if he was the rightful heir), Jacob had Esau's right and could answer truthfully as to the blessing that he WAS lawfully standing in Esau's place.

> And he said, Bring it near to me, and I will eat of my
> son's venison that my soul may bless you. And he
> brought it near to him and he did eat. And he
> brought him wine and he drank. And his father Isaac
> said unto him, Come near now and kiss me my son.
> And he came near and kissed him. And he smelled
> the smell of his raiment and blessed him, and said,
> See, the smell of my son is as the smell of a field
> which the Lord has blessed. Therefore, God give
> you of the dew of heaven, and the fatness of the
> earth, and plenty of grain and wine. Let people serve
> you and nations bow down to you. Be lord over your
> brethren and let your mother's sons bow down to
> you. Cursed be everyone that curses you and blessed
> be he that blesses you.[706]

As a result of his mother's guidance, counsel and labors, Jacob inherited the birthright belonging to the Holy Order. Whatever else this may reflect on the relationship between these family members, it was through appropriate guidance and direction of his mother that Jacob was blessed to become the appointed heir, the prince and patriarch through whom the promised Messiah would descend.[707]

---

[706] OC Genesis 9:15. These words signify a position in the Holy Order in which others will be obligated to respect the government of God. Therefore we will "bow down" to Jacob, because he will be a father over us. The "cursing" of those who curse him, and "blessing" of those who bless him are the inevitable result of Jacob occupying a position in the Holy Order.

[707] In Wilford Woodruff's notes of a talk given by Joseph Smith just prior to the twelve's mission to England in 1839, Joseph explained this: "An Evangelist Is a patriarch, even the oldest man of the Blood of Joseph or the seed of Abram whare ever the Church of Christ is established in the Earth there should be a Patriarch for the benefit of the posterity of the Saints, as it was with Jacob in given his patriarchal bles[s]ing unto his Sons &c." (*JSP Documents Vol. 6*, p. 526.) This is a good explanation as far as it goes, but this

This pattern of the mother choosing the heir is not just an allegory or an event in family history. It is an eternal right belonging to the mothers. It can also be seen in the New Testament.

The mother of James and John approached Christ to request a princely position for her sons. The incident makes more sense when you realize the mother's request was consistent with her role. Her sons' position in the future kingdom was within the lawful concerns for her to seek on their behalf:

> Then to him came the mother of Zebedee's children, with her sons, worshipping Jesus and desiring a certain thing of him. And he said unto her, What do you will that I should do? And she said unto him, Grant that these my two sons may sit, the one on your right hand, and the other on your left, in your kingdom. But Jesus answered and said, you know not what you ask. Are you able to drink of the cup that I shall drink of, and to be baptized with the baptism that I am baptized with? They said unto him, We are able. And he said unto them, You shall drink indeed of my cup and be baptized with the baptism that I am baptized with. But to sit on my right hand, and on my left is for whom it is prepared of my Father, but not mine to give.[708]

It was altogether appropriate for this request to come from their mother. It was squarely within the traditional role and right of the righteous matriarch. Christ's answer to the disciples' mother mentions His "Father" –which necessarily included His Mother.

---

original order was frequently disrupted by the death or unworthiness of the oldest heir. It would be more correct to say the "oldest worthy man"— because often, as with Esau and Jacob, a younger displaces an older brother. Identifying this as a singular position held by only one man at a time is correct, although there may be others in a line of descent upon whom the same authority has been conferred. They become the single Patriarch once they are the oldest one upon whom the right has been conferred. Although Jacob was given the birthright, he would not ascend to the Patriarch's position until after the death of his father Isaac.

[708] NC Matt. 10:2; see also KJV Matt. 20:20-23. Christ's reference to His Father must be understood to include both His Parents, and His Mother's rights as well.

In the Answer to the Prayer for Covenant,[709] it is explained that establishing any throne is done through a covenant requiring a mother-companion and female counterpart to elevate a father to a throne. It is also clear that once elevated, these two sit together upon a throne. Every throne and every kingdom in eternity requires these two separate parties, the man and the woman, to be one.[710]

> And again, I say to you, Abraham and Sarah sit upon a Throne, for he could not be there if not for Sarah's covenant with him. Isaac and Rebecca sit upon a Throne, and Isaac likewise could not be there if not for Rebecca's covenant with him. And Jacob and Rachel sit upon a Throne, and Jacob could not be there if not for Rachel's covenant with him. And all these have ascended above Dominions and Principalities and Powers, to abide in my Kingdom. Therefore the marriage covenant is needed for all those who would likewise seek to obtain from me the right to continue their seed into eternity, for only through marriage can Thrones and Kingdoms be established.[711]

Given this, any mention of the Heavenly Father is also mention of both Divine Parents, for there is neither man nor woman alone in the Divine state.[712] When first created, man and woman were joined together by God. This union happened before death entered the world. Therefore their companionship was eternal when first established, and when rescued from death would return. As Christ put it,

> Have you not read that he who made man at the beginning made him male and female, and said, For this cause shall a man leave father and mother, and shall cleave to his wife, and they two shall be one flesh? Wherefore they are no more two, but one flesh. What therefore God has joined together, let not man put asunder.[713]

---

[709] T&C 157.

[710] "Nevertheless, neither is the man without the woman, neither the woman without the man, in the Lord." (NC 1 Cor. 1:44; see also KJV 1 Cor. 11:11-12.)

[711] T&C 157:42-43.

[712] Id.

This union of Adam and Eve, and this plan of God for all who would thereafter be married, was to make the man and wife "one flesh." What God has joined together and made into "one" no one should "put asunder" by rejecting the eternal nature of marriage. It was always intended to last through the resurrection.[714]

Continuing with the Heavenly Mother's declaration in Proverbs 8:

> *I love them that love me and those that seek me early shall find me. Riches and honor are with me, yea, durable riches and righteousness. My fruit is better than gold, yea, than fine gold and my revenue than choice silver.*

Of all the Mother's "fruit" the most valuable to fallen man is without doubt the Redeemer, Christ Jesus. The account of how Jesus Christ came into the world begins with a virgin and an angel. There is more to this than Christians have noticed. The prophecy relied on to identify the birthplace of Christ in Bethlehem continues with a description of His Mother. It was prophesied that only when "she which travaileth hath brought forth; then the remnant of his brethren shall return unto the children of Israel."[715] Because of the labor and travail of His Mother, the prophesy of Israel returning to God was fulfilled. She made His entry into this world possible. The redemption of the remnant is as much the consequence of Her as of Her Son.

What was Mary's role? Who was she? Is it possible she was "the mother of God"[716] before she came into mortality? These are

---

[713] NC Matt. 9:19.

[714] In the same discussion Christ condemned Jewish divorce practice: "Moses, because of the hardness of your hearts, suffered you to divorce your wives; but from the beginning it was not so." *Id.* There is no difference between accepting and teaching divorce and accepting and teaching marriage is intended to end at death and not survive into the resurrection.

[715] "But thou, Bethlehem Ephratah, though thou be little among the thousands of Judah, yet out of thee shall he come forth unto me that is to be ruler in Irael; whose goings forth have been from of old, from everlasting. Therefore will he give them up, unto the time that she which travaileth hath brought forth; then the remnant of his brethren shall return unto the children of Israel. And he shall stand and feed in the strength of the Lord, in the majesty of the name of the Lord his God; and they shall abide: for now shall he be great unto the ends of the earth." Micha 5:2-4.

[716] In the Original Translation text, the Printer's Manuscript, and First Edition of the Book of Mormon the phrase describing Mary was "the Mother of God after the manner of the flesh." (Sometimes "Mother" was

important questions that ought to be asked. If we can learn the answers they would indeed be glorious.

The Greek title "Mother of God" (Θεοτοκοσ[717]) has been used in Eastern Christianity since the Third (perhaps as early as the Second) Century. The title was exclusively associated with Mary. By the Fifth Century the title became controversial and a replacement term "Mother of Christ" (Κριστοτοκοσ[718]) was substituted.

Since the pre-earth existence of man is not universally accepted in Christianity, most Christians have never considered even the possibility of a pre-earth identity for Mary. Despite this, she, like all mankind, existed before this world.[719]

If God the Father obeys the same commandments He imposes upon His children, then for Him to father a child with any woman other than His Wife would violate His decrees about adultery[720] and chastity.[721] Marian theology is largely absent from Mormonism other than to suggest that because the Father impregnated her[722] she is

---

capitalized and sometimes "God" was capitalized.) Joseph Smith changed the 1837 edition to say, "the mother of the Son of God, after the manner of the flesh." (1 Ne. 11:18.)

[717] The title in English is "Theotokos." It can be also be interpreted "bearer of God."

[718] The title in English is "Christotokos." It can also be interpreted "bearer of Christ."

[719] "[T]he first shall be last and that the last shall be first, in all things whatever I have created by the Word of my Power, which is the Power of my Spirit. For by the Power of my Spirit created I them, yea, all things both spiritual and temporal, firstly spiritual, secondly temporal, which is the beginning of my work. And again, firstly temporal and secondly spiritual, which is the last of my work[.]" D&C 29:30-31. "And now, behold, I say unto you, that these are the generations of the heaven and of the earth, when they were created, in the day that I, the Lord God, made the heaven and the earth, And every plant of the field before it was in the earth, and every herb of the field before it grew. For I, the Lord God, created all things, of which I have spoken, spiritually, before they were naturally upon the face of the earth. For I, the Lord God, had not caused it to rain upon the face of the earth. And I, the Lord God, had created all the children of men; and not yet a man to till the ground; for in heaven created I them; and there was not yet flesh upon the earth, neither in the water, neither in the air[.]" Moses 3:4-5. See also, Abraham 3:22-26.

[720] OC Exo. 20:14; NC Matt. 3:21; KJV Matt. 5:27.

[721] NC Jacob 2:11.

destined to be added to His eternal harem as an additional spouse.[723] Traditional Mormon teachings have been crudely fixated on the mechanics of Mary's conception. There is almost no interest in whether she has any pre-earth role with the Father, or whether she

---

[722] Mormonism consistently claimed this was a literal "fathering" through conjugal relations: "President Ezra Taft Benson stated, 'The Church of Jesus Christ of Latter-day Saints proclaims that Jesus Christ is the Son of God in the most literal sense. The body in which He performed His mission in the flesh was fathered by that same Holy Being we worship as God, our Eternal Father. Jesus was not the son of Joseph, nor was He begotten by the Holy Ghost. He is the Son of the Eternal Father!' ([*Teachings of Ezra Taft*] *Benson*, p. 4). From Mary, a mortal woman, Jesus inherited mortality, including the capacity to die. From his exalted Father he inherited immortality, the capacity to live forever. The Savior's dual nature—man and God—enabled him to make an infinite Atonement, an accomplishment that no other person, no matter how capable or gifted, could do (cf. Alma 34:9-12)." (*Encyclopedia of Mormonism, Vol.2*, "Jesus Christ, Mortal Jesus," p. 725.) Currently Mormonism appears to be walking away from, if not altogether abandoning, this teaching. See, *Did God have sex with Mary*, fairmormon.org/archive/publications/did-god-have-sex-with-mary

[723] "The fleshly body of Jesus required a Mother as well as a Father. Therefore, the Father and Mother of Jesus, according to the flesh, must have been associated in the capacity of husband and wife; hence the Virgin Mary must have been, for the time being, the *lawful* wife of God the Father: we use the term *lawful* wife, because it would be blasphemous in the highest degree to say that He overshadowed her or begat the Saviour unlawfully. ...He had a lawful right to overshadow the Virgin Mary in the capacity of a husband, and beget a Son.. Whether God the Father gave Mary to Joseph for time only, or for time and eternity, we are not informed. Inasmuch as God was the first husband to her, it may be that He only gave her to be the wife of Joseph while in this mortal state, and that *He intended after the resurrection to again take her as one of his own wives* to raise up immortal spirits in eternity." (Orson Pratt, *The Seer*, Vol. 1, No. 10, October, 1853, p. 158, emphasis added). "[T]he Only Begotten of the Father. (Moses 5:9) These name-titles all signify that our Lord is the only Son of the Father in the flesh. Each of these words is to be understood literally. Only means *only*; Begotten means *begotten*; and Son means *son*. Christ was begotten by an Immortal Father in the same way that mortal men are begotten by mortal fathers." (Bruce McConkie, *Mormon Doctrine*, (Salt Lake: Bookcraft, 1966; 12th printing 1973), p. 546-547.) There is an accompanying false idea that Mary bore children from Joseph. The "brothers and sisters" mentioned in the Gospels of Matthew and Mark were begotten by Joseph, but were not the children of Mary.

was the Mother in Heaven, the Divine Spouse of the Father, who condescended to come to earth to bear Their Only Begotten in the flesh. If She were to be acknowledged in that role, it would require a complete re-envisioning of Her. It would raise the issues of why or how She, an immortal and exalted God, could return from that exalted state back to mortality to bring our Redeemer and Savior into this world. Only She could accomplish the work of bearing the Father's Only Begotten. It would draw a contrast between the Father's involvement with this creation[724] and the Mother's.

> The Father can, and does, acknowledge others as His.[725] But, unlike the Son who has repeatedly visited this earth, walked upon it,[726] been handled by people,[727] and eaten here,[728] the Father does not come into contact with this earth in its fallen state.[729]

---

[724] As I have previously explained, in His glorified condition, man has ascended to Him, but He has not descended to contact with this creation.

[725] Ps. 2: 7: "I will declare the decree: the Lord hath said unto me, Thou art my Son; this day have I begotten thee."

[726] Luke 24:15-16: "And it came to pass, that, while they communed together and reasoned, Jesus himself drew near, and went with them. But their eyes were holden that they should not know him."

[727] Luke 24:36-39: "And as they thus spake, Jesus himself stood in the midst of them, and saith unto them, Peace be unto you. But they were terrified and affrighted, and supposed that they had seen a spirit. And he said unto them, Why are ye troubled? and why do thoughts arise in your hearts? Behold my hands and my feet, that it is I myself: handle me, and see; for a spirit hath not flesh and bones, as ye see me have." 3 Ne. 11: 14-15: "Arise and come forth unto me, that ye may thrust your hands into my side, and also that ye may feel the prints of the nails in my hands and in my feet, that ye may know that I am the God of Israel, and the God of the whole earth, and have been slain for the sins of the world. And it came to pass that the multitude went forth, and thrust their hands into his side, and did feel the prints of the nails in his hands and in his feet; and this they did do, going forth one by one until they had all gone forth, and did see with their eyes and did feel with their hands, and did know of a surety and did bear record, that it was he, of whom it was written by the prophets, that should come."

[728] John 21: 13: "Jesus then cometh, and taketh bread, and giveth them, and fish likewise."

[729] Matt. 17: 5: "While he yet spake, behold, a bright cloud overshadowed them: and behold a voice out of the cloud, which said, This is my beloved Son, in whom I am well pleased; hear ye him."

The only time the Father had contact with this earth was before the Fall, in the Paradisiacal setting of Eden—which was a Temple at the time.[730] Whenever there has been contact with the Father thereafter, He has been at a distance from this earth.[731]

There is a formality with the Father that does not exist with the Son. For example, the Son has eaten with mortal man while He was immortal, both before His ministry in the flesh[732] and after.[733] As our Redeemer, He is directly responsible for us and has contact with us to perform His redemptive service. The Father, on the other hand, is different in status, responsibility, glory and dominion. The Son

---

JS-H 1: 17: "It no sooner appeared than I found myself delivered from the enemy which held me bound. When the light rested upon me I saw two Personages, whose brightness and glory defy all description, standing above me in the air. One of them spake unto me, calling me by name and said, pointing to the other—*This is My Beloved Son. Hear Him!*"

[730] Gen. 3: 8: "And they heard the voice of the Lord God walking in the garden in the cool of the day: and Adam and his wife hid themselves from the presence of the Lord God amongst the trees of the garden." Following the fall of Adam, the Father has appeared to man, but has been above the earth, not standing upon it.

[731] See, e.g., Moses 7: 24: "And there came generation upon generation; and Enoch was high and lifted up, even in the bosom of the Father, and of the Son of Man; and behold, the power of Satan was upon all the face of the earth." 1 Ne. 1: 8: "And being thus overcome with the Spirit, he was carried away in a vision, even that he saw the heavens open, and he thought he saw God sitting upon his throne, surrounded with numberless concourses of angels in the attitude of singing and praising their God." Alma 36: 22: "Yea, methought I saw, even as our father Lehi saw, God sitting upon his throne, surrounded with numberless concourses of angels, in the attitude of singing and praising their God; yea, and my soul did long to be there."

[732] Ex. 24: 9-11: "Then went up Moses, and Aaron, Nadab, and Abihu, and seventy of the elders of Israel: And they saw the God of Israel: and there was under his feet as it were a paved work of a sapphire stone, and as it were the body of heaven in his clearness. And upon the nobles of the children of Israel he laid not his hand: also they saw God, and did eat and drink."

[733] Luke 24: 41-43: "And while they yet believed not for joy, and wondered, he said unto them, Have ye here any meat? And they gave him a piece of a broiled fish, and of an honeycomb. And he took it, and did eat before them."

can appear to mortal man without showing His glory or requiring any alteration of the mortal who beholds Him.[734] To behold the Father, to endure His presence, one must be transfigured.[735] Mortal man cannot behold the Father's works while mortal, for if you comprehend them you cannot afterward remain mortal in the flesh.[736]

That is taken from pages 383-387 of *Removing the Condemnation*, and includes the footnotes. Like this description of the Son, the same description should apply to His Mother.

The Father is the source of glory and likened to the sun. The Mother reflects and shares this glory, and is likened to the moon. She reflects God's glory, endures within it and is empowered by it. She can participate with Him in all that is done wielding that glory. "Knowledge" is the initiator or force, and "wisdom" is the regulator, guide, apportioner and weaver of that power. If not tempered and guided by wisdom, knowledge can be destructive. Wisdom makes the prudent adaptations required for order. The Father and Mother are One. But the Mother bridges the gulf between the Throne of the Father and fallen man. She made it possible for the Son of God to enter this fallen world for the salvation of everything in it.

A great deal of reflection and study is needed to understand all this implies.[737] This is an introduction of some basic information

---

[734] John 20: 15-17: "Jesus saith unto her, Woman, why weepest thou? whom seekest thou? She, supposing him to be the gardener, saith unto him, Sir, if thou have borne him hence, tell me where thou hast laid him, and I will take him away. Jesus saith unto her, Mary. She turned herself, and saith unto him, Rabboni; which is to say, Master. Jesus saith unto her, Touch me not; for I am not yet ascended to my Father: but go to my brethren, and say unto them, I ascend unto my Father, and your Father; and *to* my God, and your God."

[735] Moses 1: 2: "And he saw God face to face, and he talked with him, and the glory of God was upon Moses; therefore Moses could endure his presence."

[736] Moses 1: 5: "Wherefore, no man can behold all my works, except he behold all my glory; and no man can behold all my glory, and afterwards remain in the flesh on the earth."

[737] For example, the term "inseparably connected" as used in D&C 93:33 ("For man is spirit. The elements are eternal, and spirit and element, inseparably connected, receive a fullness of joy") does not prohibit such a being from voluntarily condescending. It does assure all who are resurrected

about the Mother of God, or "the Mother of the Son of God after the manner of the flesh." More will be given in a temple where mankind's understanding of things kept hidden from the world[738] will be greatly increased. When God directs one be built to His name.

There was a time when Christians recognized that the stars of heaven bore witness of the significance of Mary, Christ's earthly mother. Few Christians now look at the constellations as "signs" set in the firmament by God as His testimony.[739] The "light" that was meant to shine on earth[740] was to illuminate both the eyes and mind of man. Man in the first generations understood this. Abraham received that same understanding, and "a knowledge of the beginning of the creation, and also of the planets,[741] and of the stars, as they were made known unto the fathers"[742] was written by him.

At the time of Christ's birth, there were those who understood the testimony written in the lights of the firmament. They reported that they "saw his star in the east[743] and have come to worship him."[744] These "wise men" watched and waited for the heavenly alignment to testify of the birth of a promised "king." The Matthew text makes

---

that they can safely endure the presence of glorified beings without being destroyed. Likewise, Alma's teaching that the immortal body uniting spirit and body "never to be divided" (NC Alma 8:17, also Alma 11:45) does not prohibit voluntary condescension, by choosing, as did Christ and the Mother, to enter the mortal state. For a further discussion of this see *Essays: Three Degrees*, pp. 21-52.

[738] See, e.g., NC 1 Ne. 3:31, also 1 Ne. 14:28; NC 3 Ne. 12:2, also 3 Ne. 26:16-18; NC Ether 1:15-16, also Ether 3:25-27.

[739] KJV Gen. 1:14.

[740] KJV Gen. 1:15.

[741] The word "planets" has been a stumbling block for many critics of Joseph Smith and the Book of Abraham. That word is considered too modern to have been known at the time of Abraham. Anciently the planets were termed "wandering stars"—the word "planet" means "wanderer." Joseph therefore used a term commonly understood in our language. But the ancients would also have accepted "wanderer" as the appropriate name for these heavenly lights.

[742] Abr. 1:31.

[743] Because they saw it "in the east" they necessarily traveled from the west. They were, therefore, far more likely to have traveled from the Iberian Peninsula or British Isles than from Persia. But this is a topic for another day.

[744] JST Matt. 1:6; KJV Matt. 2:2.

such casual mention of this that we give it little notice. Today, Christians and Mormons alike have little understanding of the lights in the firmament, and so give little heed to the signs set by God in the heaven above. Our ignorance does mean these signs are meaningless. It only means we are poorly informed of God's full message.[745]

John's Revelation mentions two of the heavenly signs that testify of Mary. One of these is on the ecliptic and since earliest times has been identified as a virgin woman, called by us the constellation "Virgo." The circle of heaven is divided into the north and south at the ecliptic. On the ecliptic, from the north to the south poles, there are twelve constellations that can be seen everywhere on earth. Some constellations cannot be seen from one of the hemispheres, but those twelve on the ecliptic are ever-present overhead. These move in the same plane as the sun, moon and wandering planets. Most of those who discuss these twelve constellations allocate the 360 degrees of the heavenly circle into 12 equal, 30-degree segments, allocating for each constellation on the ecliptic the same distance. Today, these twelve constellations are called the Zodiac.

Unlike the equal division between the twelve constellations of the Zodiac (or Mazzaroth[746] in the old Hebrew of the Book of Job), the star fields of these twelve constellations are unequal in sizes. The two largest star fields belong to Virgo (46.79°) and Aquarius (50.86°). These two largest of the Zodiac constellations are heavenly witnesses testifying of Christ's mother Mary and the returning Christ. For Christ's first coming, the heavenly testimony focuses the greatest part of the starfield on His Mother. We should reflect on what that may

---

[745] The heavenly signs in the lights of the firmament are testifying and confirming many of the events currently happening on the earth. Very few today are giving that any notice.

[746] That passage in Job refers to other constellations when mentioning the Zodiak, or "Mazzaroth": "Canst thou bind the sweet influences of Pleiades, or loose the bands of Orion? Canst thou bring forth Mazzaroth in his season? or canst thou guide Arcturus with his sons? Knowest thou the ordinances of heaven? canst thou set the dominion thereof in the earth?" (Job 38:31-33.) The Pleiades was also called "the seven sisters" anciently and is a star cluster riding atop the shoulder of Tarus. Orion is a constellation just below the ecliptic and located beneath the bull, Tarus and the twins, Gemini. Arcturus is one of the brightest stars in the heavens, is located northward from the brightest star in Virgo, Spica. The name Arcturus means "a gathering together."

mean. We ought to contemplate why Christ's first coming was symbolized on the heavenly ecliptic by the Virgin Mother. Why was She the focus?

Christ's Second Coming is the largest starfield on the ecliptic.[747] He will return to pour out judgment, blessing those who follow Him and destroying those who rebel. The destruction of the wicked is what Christ identified as "the end of the world."[748] Aquarius has two outflows from the "Waterbearer's urn." One represents water (giving life) and the other represents fire (purging).[749]

It is a mistake to divide the Zodiac into twelve equal parts of 30° apiece. These divisions mark and testify to different stages of this creation, and movement from one stage to another corresponds to the timing of the movement of the actual starfields, not the artificial division into 30° segments. The Age of Pisces, corresponding to Christ making men "fishers" of men, overlaps with the Age of Aquarius, corresponding to Christ's return to pour out judgment and blessing. While Pisces remains in the east during the Vernal Equinox, Aquarius began when its first star entered the Vernal Equinox while Joseph Smith was still living.

Traditionally we interpret the constellation Virgo as a woman holding a sheaf of wheat in her left hand. The sheaf represents her seed. The brightest star in the constellation, a magnitude 1 star, is "spica"[750]-- "the seed of the woman." That star is placed on the

---

[747] There are other constellations testifying of Christ, but that is not the subject of this paper.

[748] "The harvest is the end of the world or the destruction of the wicked[.]" NC Matt. 7:9. "So shall it be at the end of the world, and the world is the children of the wicked." NC Matt. 7:12. His disciples understood this as evidenced by the question they posed to the Lord in NC Matt. 11:2: "And what is the sign of your coming and of the end of the world? Or the destruction of the wicked, which is the end of the world?"

[749] Hence "the great and dreadful day of the Lord" (Mal. 4:1-5; NC 3 Ne. 11:4-5; 3 Ne. 25:1-5)—in which it will be "great" for those who are the Lord's and "dreadful" for the wicked, or the world.

[750] The "signs" in the lights of heaven are meant to be seen and understood by the unaided human eye from the surface of the earth. However, an interesting discovery made using telescopic magnification reveals that the "seed of the woman" is not a single star, but binary stars so closely orbiting one another that they are reaching toward one another at their equators because of their gravitational attraction. These two are seen as one from the surface of the earth.

ecliptic.[751] Most other stars in Virgo are located above the ecliptic. "The seed of the woman" represents Christ. His star on the ecliptic represents that everything in the firmament is divided in relation to Him. All of heaven is either above or below the ecliptic. The position of His star, like His role as judge, divides the heavens.

Traditionally Virgo is drawn looking down at the earth, facing us. This view places the seed of the woman in her left hand. The left hand is usually a symbol of cursing.[752] The right hand symbolizes blessing.[753] If the seed of the woman is meant to be in her right hand, then she would be drawn looking up heavenward, and her back would be facing us. Reorienting Virgo to face upward —with the seed of the woman in her right hand —is more fitting.

John described Virgo and the movement of other lights on the ecliptic as follows, "And there appeared a great wonder in heaven; a woman clothed with the sun, and the moon under her feet, and upon her head a crown of twelve stars[.]"[754] The sun and moon move on the ecliptic through the constellation Virgo and at times "clothe" her and at other times appear "under her feet." This "wonder" John described is overhead in the starry firmament of "heaven" as one of the "signs" put there to testify of heavenly things.

Christ's Mother Mary is a figure of such preeminence that testimony of Her is emblazoned upon the ecliptic in an enduring, towering figure outlined in the stars. This is not happenstance. It is God's witness to us. We should accept it as meaningful and ponder on the meaning.

Another of the constellations John mentions is a "woman" who brought forth a son, who is then caught up to the throne of God.[755] This is also depicted in another constellation. One of the constellations immediately associated with Virgo,[756] located next to

---

[751] The placement of the lights in the firmament is to be interpreted by the unaided human eye from the surface of the earth. Therefore, although this star is approximately 2° below, to the unaided eye it appears to be on the ecliptic.

[752] See, NC Matt. 11:24; NC Mosiah 3:3.

[753] See, NC Matt. 11:22; NC Mosiah 3:2.

[754] NC Rev. 4:1; KJV Rev. 12:1.

[755] "And she brought forth a male child, who was to rule all nations with a rod of iron; and her child was caught up unto God and his throne."

[756] The earliest traditions associated three "decan" constellations for each of the twelve Zodiacal constellations, for a total of 48 constellations. The

her in the northern sky, is a constellation anciently depicted as a mother seated on a throne holding a son in her hands.[757] This image of a woman seated on a throne with her son is located just to the north, above Virgo. It suggests both the mother and her son descended from a throne they once occupied in heaven, and is destined to return again there. If you can accept the witness written of them in the stars of the firmament, then She came to earth, with Her Son. And She will return again to a Throne in the north. Contemplate what this witness of Mary could mean. Taken at full value, Mary, like Her Son, condescended to come here.

The Book of Mormon gives an extended description of Mary, the Mother of God. In the original translation text the words "mother of God" were used, but was changed by Joseph Smith in 1837 to "mother of the Son of God." Here is how it reads following that change:

> And it came to pass that I looked and beheld the great city of Jerusalem, and also other cities. And I beheld the city of Nazareth; and in the city of Nazareth I beheld a virgin, and she was exceedingly fair and white. And it came to pass that I saw the heavens open; and an angel came down and stood before me; and he said unto me: Nephi, what beholdest thou? And I said unto him: A virgin, most beautiful and fair above all other virgins. And he said unto me: Knowest thou the condescension of God? And I said unto him: I know that he loveth his children; nevertheless, I do not know the meaning of all things. And he said unto me: Behold, the virgin whom thou seest is the mother of the Son of God, after the manner of the flesh. And it came to pass that I beheld that she was carried away in the Spirit; and after she had been carried away in the Spirit for the space of a time the angel spake unto me, saying: Look! And I looked and beheld the virgin again,

---

original have been forgotten, and modern interpretations have 88 constellations and figures.

[757] This constellation is named Coma, and was reinterpreted later as "Coma Bernieces" and the depiction changed to a woman's hair. This false reinterpretation was based on Ptolemy's wife, Bernice, who sacrificed her hair to the gods once her husband returned alive from a battle.

bearing a child in her arms. And the angel said unto me: Behold the Lamb of God, yea, even the Son of the Eternal Father! Knowest thou the meaning of the tree which thy father saw? And I answered him, saying: Yea, it is the love of God, which sheddeth itself abroad in the hearts of the children of men; wherefore, it is the most desirable above all things. And he spake unto me, saying: Yea, and the most joyous to the soul.[758]

Most who read this passage interpret the "condescension" reference solely as Christ's. They view it as Christ alone who condescended by being borne of Mary here in mortality. However, when leading up to the angel's question, "Knowest thou the condescension of God," the text focuses exclusively on Mary. When the angel clarified the "condescension," he again focused primarily on Mary and secondarily on Her Son. The angel explained, "Behold, **the virgin** whom thou seest is **the mother of the Son of God**, after the manner of the flesh. And it came to pass that I beheld that **she** was carried away in the Spirit; and after **she** had been carried away in the Spirit for the space of a time the angel spake unto me, saying: Look! And I looked and **beheld the virgin again**, bearing a child **in her arms**. And the angel said unto me: Behold the Lamb of God, yea, even the Son of the Eternal Father!"

Who would you reasonably expect to be the woman chosen before this world was organized to become the mortal Mother of the Lord? Who would you expect Heavenly Father would want to bear His child, if not His Spouse? Together God the Father and Mary can be acknowledged as the Parents of Christ.[759] The scriptures shift the focus of the "condescension" from Christ, to His Mother, and then back to Her Son, "the seed of the woman."[760]

*Lectures on Faith* identifies Christ as "the prototype of the saved man."[761] Lecture 7 focuses attention on Christ as the Savior and

---

[758] NC 1 Ne. 3:8-9; 1 Ne. 11:13-23.

[759] Mary indeed "had a little lamb whose fleece was white as snow." And in the great condescension of God, "everywhere that Mary went the lamb was sure to go."

[760] The text of the New Covenants does this better by the layout dividing ¶¶8 and 9. Paragraph 8 includes the angel's question about "condescension" and Mary's role. Paragraph 9 then continues with Mary and adds the birth of Christ.

Redeemer. But the lecture extends the requirements met by Jesus Christ to also apply for every saved man. In other words, for any man to be saved they must "attain to the resurrection,"[762] like Christ. Shifting attention for a moment from Jesus Christ as our Redeemer and Savior to His Mother, we could acknowledge Her as "the prototype of the saved woman." In other words, could we consider what She did a Divine pattern to be followed by women?

"Attaining to the resurrection" does not mean merely being resurrected from the grave. We must conquer death:

> But even when we rise from the grave, we will still not have "attained to the resurrection of the dead" nor hold the keys of resurrection. No one will until they, like Christ, have gone from exaltation to exaltation, until they can obtain the power to resurrect all that depends upon them. For us *to attain to the resurrection of the dead* requires us to have the power to resurrect, not only ourselves, but also those who are dependent on us. This is what the prototype of the saved man did. This is Who we worship. This is who and what we must precisely and exactly become.
>
> Remember Christ said, "The Son can do nothing of himself, but what he sees the Father do. For whatever things he does, these also does the Son likewise."[763] The Father went before, and the Son follows after.[764] To be like Him, sit on His throne,[765]

---

[761] Christ "is the prototype or standard of salvation, or in other words, that he is a saved being." *Lecture 7*, ¶10.

[762] "Here, then, is eternal life--to know the only wise and true God; and you have got to learn how to be Gods yourselves, and to be kings and priests to God, the same as all Gods have done before you, namely, by going from one small degree to another, and from a small capacity to a great one; from grace to grace, from exaltation to exaltation, until you attain to the resurrection of the dead..." (*TPJS* p. 348.) This is where people attain the resurrection: through development from exaltation to exaltation.

[763] NC John 5:4; see also KJV John 5:19.

[764] I have previously explained how Christ, as well as the "noble and great" were all embodied and therefore resurrected beings before this world. They were "souls." (Abraham 3:23.) The definition of "soul" given through Joseph years prior to his translation of the Book of Abraham was the "spirit and the body" together. (D&C 88:15-17.) For more on this see *The First Three Words*

and attain to their same status, we must do precisely what the Gods have done.

For us to understand Christ we must understand the challenging path Joseph Smith explained in his final church conference in April 1844. All must progress, *"Until you attain to the resurrection of the dead and are able to dwell in everlasting burnings, and to sit in glory, as do those who sit enthroned in everlasting power."*

Even that which we envision as the highest heaven requires those who sit enthroned in everlasting burnings to condescend to be there. D&C 130:26 reveals that a white stone is given to heirs of the celestial kingdom to reveal to them things pertaining to "a higher order of kingdoms."[766] We must go from "exaltation to exaltation" because there is a great deal not yet revealed to man about the eternities. There are places where, in everlasting glory, the personages are embodied in "spirit, glory, and power" like The Father.[767]

Did Mary also "attain to the resurrection?" Protestants dismiss the Catholic veneration of Mary. But it may just be that Catholics have preserved something of value about her that ought not be ignored.

The Catechism of the Catholic Church states: "The Most Blessed Virgin Mary, when the course of her earthly life was completed, was taken up body and soul into the glory of heaven, where she already shares in the glory of her Son's Resurrection, anticipating the resurrection of all members of His Body."

Karl Keating of *Catholic Answers* explains:

We know that after the crucifixion Mary was cared for by the apostle John. (John. 19:26-27.) Early Christian writings say John went to live at Ephesus

---

in the book *Essays: Three Degrees*.

[765] NC Rev. 1:20; see also KJV Rev. 3:21.

[766] D&C 130:9-11 makes clear that the celestial kingdom, while much higher than this telestial world, is inferior to other, still higher exaltations called "higher order of kingdoms."

[767] See *Lecture Fifth*, ¶2.

and that Mary accompanied him. There is some dispute about where she ended her life, perhaps there, perhaps back at Jerusalem. Neither of these cities nor any other claimed her remains, although there are claims about possessing her (temporary) tomb. Why did no city claim the bones of Mary? Apparently because there were no bones to claim, and people knew it.

Remember, in the early Christian centuries, relics of saints were jealously guarded and highly prized. The bones of those martyred in the Colosseum, for instance, were quickly gathered up and preserved; there are many accounts of this in the biographies of those who gave up their lives for the Faith [for example, the bones of St. Peter and St. Paul were widely known to be preserved in Rome, and the sepulcher of David and the tomb of St. John the Baptist are both mentioned in Scripture]. Yet here was Mary, certainly the most privileged of all the saints ... but we have no record of her bodily remains being venerated anywhere.

A 5th Century letter from the Patriarch of Jerusalem responding to the Byzantine Empress Pulcheria's request for relics of the Holy Virgin Mary states[768] there was a centuries old tradition that Mary was taken into heaven when she died and therefore there were no relics. He expressed surprise that the Empress was not acquainted with this well-known tradition. This was apparently common knowledge among the early Christians.

According to the tradition the apostles assembled to bury her, but burial was unnecessary because she had already been assumed into heaven, body and spirit.[769] This teaching was an extension of

---

[768] St. John Damascene preserved a copy of the letter written by a 5th century Patriarch of Jerusalem named Juvenalius to the Empress.

[769] St. Gregory of Tours wrote an account in the 6th Century in *Book of Miracles*, 1:4. Pope Pius XII fixed the Catholic teaching in his *Munificentissimus Deus* on November 1, 1950 in which he declared both the Immaculate Conception of Mary and her Assumption into heaven. The declaration states in ¶3: "Actually God, who from all eternity regards Mary with a most favorable and unique affection, has "when the fullness of time came" put the plan of his providence into effect in such a way that all the privileges and

another Catholic belief regarding Mary called "Immaculate Conception." The teaching was propounded by Pope Pius IX and declared that Mary was free from the weaknesses of the Fall of Adam, and born without the sinful nature of fallen man.[770] Although an estimated 1.2 billion Catholics accept these teachings about Mary today, Protestants and Mormons have not. The angel's words in 1st Nephi seem more akin to Catholic veneration of Mary than the crude, incidental and dismissive way Mormon traditions have discussed the Virgin Mary.

The Heavenly Mother was also there with the Father in the Garden when the first man was born.[771] She was with the Father when He said, "Let **us** make man"—for no man ever fathered a child without a mother to bear his seed. She was with the Father when man fell and was cast out of the Garden and made vulnerable to death. These Heavenly Parents were jointly committed to saving their offspring from death and hell.

If "the condescension of God" included the Mother of God as well as Her Son, then She was also a critical participant for providing the sacrificial lamb required for our redemption.[772] Since the Fall of Adam, every one who enters mortality must die to exit mortality. But unlike Adam and the rest of his posterity, Christ lived so as to be able to defy death. The wages of sin are death, but Christ did not earn those wages. Therefore, Christ could return from death because He attained to the resurrection. Joseph Smith explained,

---

prerogatives he had granted to her in his sovereign generosity were to shine forth in her in a kind of perfect harmony."

[770] His 1854 Papal Bull *Ineffibilis* stated: "We declare, pronounce and define that the doctrine which asserts that the Blessed Virgin Mary, from the first moment of her conception, by a singular grace and privilege of almighty God, and in view of the merits of Jesus Christ, Saviour of the human race, was preserved free from every stain of original sin is a doctrine revealed by God and, for this reason, must be firmly and constantly believed by all the faithful[.]"

[771] At the end of this paper I will return to this subject and further clarify Her role and the wife of Christ's role there.

[772] The hymn *I Stand All Amazed* focuses on Jesus Christ as Redeemer and Savior, and rightly so. But some of the language in that hymn might be applied equally to His Mother, who condescended to bear Him into mortality: "I marvel that [they] would descend from [their] throne[s] divine, To rescue a soul so rebellious and proud as mine."

The Scriptures inform us that Jesus said, As the Father hath power in Himself, even so hath the Son power--to do what? Why, what the Father did. The answer is obvious--in a manner to lay down His body and take it up again. Jesus, what are you going to do? To lay down my life as my Father did, and take it up again. Do we believe it? If you do not believe it, you do not believe the Bible. The Scriptures say it, and I defy all the learning and wisdom and all the combined powers of earth and hell together to refute it. Here, then, is eternal life--to know the only wise and true God; and you have got to learn how to be Gods yourselves, and to be kings and priests to God, the same as all Gods have done before you, namely, by going from one small degree to another, and from a small capacity to a great one; from grace to grace, from exaltation to exaltation, until you attain to the resurrection of the dead..."[773]

Since Christ attained to the resurrection through His progression from one small capacity to a great one, going from grace to grace and from exaltation to exaltation,[774] did His Mother do anything less? Was

---

[773] *TPJS* p. 348.

[774] In Chapter V of the Gnostic text, *Vision of Isaiah*, Christ's descent from the seventh heaven is described as follows: "And I heard the Great Glory commanding my Lord. And then the Lord went out from the seventh heaven and descended into the sixth heaven. And the angel who guided me said to me, 'Understand and see the manner of His transfiguration and descent.' When the angels saw Him, they praised and glorified Him, for He was not transfigured into their image, and I sang with them. When He had descended into the fifth heaven, there at once He was transfigured into the form of those angels and they did not sing to Him or adore Him, for He was of a form like theirs. And He descended into the fourth heaven and appeared to them in their form. And they did not sing to Him for He was of a form like theirs. Moreover, He came into the third heaven, and into the second and the first, transfiguring Himself in each of them. Consequently, they did not sing to Him or adore Him, for He appeared to them in [a form] like theirs. And He showed them a sign. Moreover, He descended into the firmament and there gave the signs, and His form was like unto theirs, and they did not glorify Him and they did not sing to Him. And He descended to the angels who were in this air as though He were one of them. And He gave them no sign, nor did they sing to Him."

Her coming into this world any less a condescension? Reflect on the Mother of God and consider this passage of *Lecture 7* which describes Christ,

> And if we should continue our interrogation, and ask how it is that he is saved, the answer would be, because he is a just and holy being. And if he were anything different from what he is he would not be saved, for his salvation depends on his being precisely what he is and nothing else. For if it were possible for Him to change in the least degree, so sure he would fail of salvation and lose all his dominion, power, authority and glory, which constitutes salvation. For salvation consists in the glory, authority, majesty, power and dominion which Jehovah possesses, and in nothing else, and no being can possess it but himself or one like him.[775]

It requires as much to save a woman as a man. No person, male or female, can dwell where God dwells without possessing the same attributes as all those who have gone before. The pattern is unchangeable. We cannot claim to be like Them without possessing the same holiness these holy beings possess.[776]

We have more quotes of Mary in the New Covenants book of Luke. When She was visited by the angel Gabriel and told of Her ministry to bear the Messiah, She responded: "Behold the handmaid of the Lord; be it unto me according to your word."[777] The term "handmaid" includes the possible meanings wife, female partner or consort. Mary was all of these to God the Father.

The account continues with Mary going to visit her cousin Elizabeth, who was at that time six-months pregnant with John the Baptist. When Mary arrived, Elizabeth addressed her with this inspired utterance, "Elisabeth was filled with the Holy Ghost: And she spoke out with a loud voice, and said, Blessed are you among women, and blessed is the fruit of your womb. And why is it that this blessing is upon me, that the mother of my Lord should come to

---

[775] *Lecture 7*, ¶10.

[776] "The sacrifice required of Abraham in the offering up of Isaac, shows that if a man would attain to the keys of the kingdom of an endless life; he must sacrifice all things. When God offers a blessing or knowledge to a man, and he refuses to receive it, he will be damned." *TPJS* p. 325.

[777] NC Luke 1:6; see also, KJV Luke 1:38.

me?"[778] Consider what it may mean to be "blessed among women?" Elizabeth addressed Her as "the mother of my Lord"—which should not be interpreted narrowly or construed merely to mean a biological vessel to accomplish a pregnancy. When read in combination with the Book of Mormon description, it can mean so much more.

Mary responded with a psalm, giving us a glimpse into Her heart. What we find there is wondrous.

> And Mary said, My soul does magnify the Lord, and my spirit rejoices in God my Savior. For he has regarded the low estate of his handmaiden. For, behold, from henceforth all generations shall call me Blessed. For he who is mighty has done to me great things; and I will magnify his holy name, for his mercy on them that fear him from generation to generation. He has shown strength with his arm. He has scattered the proud in the imagination of their hearts. He has put down the mighty from their high seats and exalted them of low degree. He has filled the hungry with good things, but the rich he has sent away empty. He has helped his servant Israel in remembrance of mercy, as he spoke to our fathers, to Abraham and to his seed for ever.[779]

These words are worthy of the Mother of God. She clearly "magnifies" or increases Her Lord, or Her Husband.[780] Christ did the same thing, glorifying the Father.[781]

When Mary said the words, "he has regarded the low estate of his handmaiden" the "condescension of God" seems to apply particularly for Her. She laid aside glory to be here, and the Father still held "regard" for His "handmaiden" in this "low estate." What a great work our Heavenly Parents have undertaken for their children!

Mary declared, "from henceforth all generations shall call me Blessed." All generations include the living, the unborn and the dead. Eventually every soul who has come to this world will recognize Her

---

[778] NC Luke 1:7; see also, KJV Luke 1:41-43.

[779] NC Luke 1:8; see also, KJV Luke 1:46-55.

[780] The "God, my Savior" belonging to Her was the Father. Likewise, He belonged to Her. They are one.

[781] KJV John 17:4 "I have glorified thee on the earth: I have finished the work which thou gavest me to do."

as "Blessed"—not only for what She is, but for what She did to magnify the work of our Father in Heaven.

Her description of the Heavenly Father includes these words of admiration and praise:

> [H]is mercy on them that fear him from generation to generation. He has shown strength with his arm. He has scattered the proud in the imagination of their hearts. He has put down the mighty from their high seats and exalted them of low degree. He has filled the hungry with good things, but the rich he has sent away empty.

Clearly both the Father and Mary despise the "proud" whose overestimation of themselves is informed by "the imagination of their hearts" and not God's regard. Both the Father and Mary want those who are "mighty" to be dispossessed from "their high seats" of power. The Parents of Christ prefer "them of low degree" whose humility and selflessness make them suitable to be exalted. The hungry are fed and the rich are sent away empty—which may not be fully realized until after this world.[782] But the Parents of Christ will be the final judges of all people and will judge mankind based exactly upon the criteria They have revealed.

Based on several verses in Matthew,[783] Protestants claim that Joseph fathered other children with Mary. Catholic theology venerates Mary and teaches Her perpetual virginity.[784] Catholics believe the brothers mentioned in the scriptures are sons of Joseph from a prior marriage and not other children born to Mary. The Catholic view on this point is strengthened by Christ assigning John to be Mary's son as one of His dying acts.[785] If Mary had other sons to care for Her,

---

[782] See, e.g., KJV Luke 16:19-31.

[783] NC Matt. 6:18: "And while he yet talked to the people, behold, his mother and brethren stood outside, desiring to speak with him. Then one said unto him, Behold, your mother and your brethren stand outside[.]" Matt. NC Matt. 7:14; also KJV Matt. 13:55-56: "Is not this the carpenter's son? is not his mother called Mary? and his brethren, James, and Joses, and Simon, and Judas? And his sisters, are they not all with us? Whence then hath this man all these things?"

[784] See, *Catholic Encyclopedia,* discussion of the topics: Immaculate Conception; Mary in the Gospels; Devotion to the Blessed Virgin Mary. The four Marian Catholic dogmas are: Divine motherhood, Perpetual Virginity, Immaculate Conception, and The Assumption.

that assignment of John would not have been necessary. The Catholics are much closer to the truth about Mary, but they still have an incomplete theology.

Returning to the words of the Divine Mother in Proverbs 8:

> *I lead in the way of righteousness, in the midst of the paths of judgment. That I may cause those that love me to inherit substance and I will fill their treasures.*

These treasures are not earthly, but "durable" and incapable of depreciation. What the Mother offers cannot be harmed by moth or rust, nor lost to thieves. They are in heaven.[786] But obtaining them requires us to walk as She guides "in the way or righteousness, in the midst of the paths of judgment." The great white throne is not occupied by the Father alone. Nor will that great judgment be made without the Mother's involvement, for She lives in "the paths of judgment" and wisely counsels Her children to obtain durable "riches and honor".

The Mother explains how She was present from the beginning as part of the God we call the Father, or in Hebrew the Elohim:

> *The Lord possessed me in the beginning of his way before his works of old. I was set up from everlasting, from the beginning, or ever the Earth was. When there were no depths I was brought forth, when there were no fountains abounding with water. Before the mountains were settled, before the hills was I brought forth, while as yet he had not made the Earth, nor the fields, nor the highest part of the dust of the world. When he prepared the heavens I was there, when he set a compass upon the face of the depth, when he established the clouds above, when he strengthened the fountains of the deep, when he gave to the sea his decree that the waters should not pass his commandment, when he appointed the foundations of the Earth, then I was by him, as one brought up with him, and I was daily his delight, rejoicing always before him, rejoicing in*

---

[785] John 19:25-27: "Now there stood by the cross of Jesus his mother, and his mother's sister, Mary the wife of Cleophas, and Mary Magdalene. When Jesus therefore saw his mother, and the disciple standing by, whom he loved, he saith unto his mother, Woman, behold thy son! Then saith he to the disciple, Behold thy mother! And from that hour that disciple took her unto his own home." See also NC John 10:13.

[786] NC 3 Ne. 6:15.

*the habitable part of his Earth and my delights were with the sons of men.*

Before this creation, the Mother in Heaven was with the Father. She was beside Him when His work began. She was there when the plan was laid, the boundaries established, and the compass applied to establish order for the creation. All the Father knows, the Mother knows. All the Father established and ordered, the Mother established and ordered. They are One. She is the Father's "delight" and the potential of Her sons to be like Her Husband brings Her delight.

To be like their Father, Her sons must become one with Her daughters, for it is not good for man to be alone.[787] The Father and Mother are "one" and Her sons and daughters must likewise become "one." Only when the man and woman were together was the creation "good." When men rebel, disobey, act cruelly or mistreat Her daughters, we are anything but a "delight" to the Heavenly Mother. When we offend Her we also offend Her Husband.

Before any of us will plan, measure, set a compass, and apportion the foundations of another earth, we must grow together and become like Them. Their work is glorious. They possess love – the power that creates and organizes. Love is what generates the power of light to create all Their works. We cannot be like them without a loving relationship that mirrors Theirs.

The account continues:

> *Now therefore hearken unto me, O ye children, for blessed are they that keep my ways. Hear instruction, and be wise, and refuse it not. Blessed is the man that heareth me, watching daily at my gates, waiting at the posts of my doors. For whoso findeth me findeth life and shall obtain favor of the Lord. But he that sinneth against me wrongeth his own soul, all they that hate me love death.*

These interesting words do not mean just discovering the abstract presence of "wisdom" as a characteristic attributable to the Mother in Heaven. Instead they require us to discover Her existence and acknowledge Her—otherwise we have not "found" Her. When She declares "whoso findeth me findeth life and shall obtain favor of the Lord," it should be taken literally. This does not mean we now pray to Her, for we are commanded to pray to the Father.[788] But it

---

[787] Abraham 5:14; KJV Gen. 2:18.
[788] NC 3 Ne. 6:14.

308

does mean when we use the word "Father" to describe God we finally regard God to be both "male and female"—the original "image of God."[789]

There are seven stages of development through which God's children must pass. It is not all to be done in this life.[790] Christ is the "prototype of the saved man,"[791] and He qualified by passing through these stages of development. We should not be surprised that the Heavenly Mother was responsible for planning and creating these developmental opportunities for Her children.

*Wisdom hath builded her house, she hath hewn out her seven pillars, she hath killed her beasts, she hath mingled her wine, she hath also furnished her table...*

When any of us arrive at the end of the journey through the seven rungs of Jacob's ladder, we will discover that the Mother was present throughout that journey. She declared: "I lead in the way of righteousness, in the midst of the paths of judgment." She is present all along the way through the seven pillars. This recognition of the Heavenly Mother requires wisdom.

When a female deity has been worshiped in past cultures, more often than not the result is a gradual degeneration into fertility cults and sexual excesses. Ritual prostitution was often practiced by ancients who believed in a divine mother. Even Israel fell into sexual deviancy as part of their worship of the female god.

At a pivotal time for ancient Israel,[792] Jeremiah condemned worship of "the queen of heaven." Because some scholars want a divine female to be authentic, Jeremiah's condemnation is considered problematic. His words can be interpreted to denounce altogether a

---

[789] KJV Gen. 1:27.

[790] "When you climb up a ladder, you must begin at the bottom, and ascend step by step, until you arrive at the top; and so it is with the principles of the gospel—you must begin with the first, and go on until you learn all the principles of exaltation. But it will be a great while after you have passed through the veil before you will have learned them. It is not all to be comprehended in this world; it will be a great work to learn our salvation and exaltation even beyond the grave." (*DHC* 6:306-307.)

[791] *Lecture Seventh*, ¶9.

[792] He prophesied beginning just prior to the Babylonian captivity. He was there when the reforms marking the end of the First Temple Period of Israel's history began. That was when those called the "Deuteronomists" began to alter the scriptures.

female god. In part because of this, in current scholarship Jeremiah has become a controversial figure. Even his existence is now questioned. Margaret Barker recently wrote the following:

> This assumes that a person of that name existed, since scholars cannot begin to agree if Jeremiah even existed, nor on the process by which the present texts of Jeremiah were formed. Many have resorted to other ways of dealing with the text. A recent volume on the latest trends in Jeremiah studies was introduced thus: "Jeremiah is an intractable riddle." "Taken together, the essays in this volume press for an end to 'innocent' readings of Jeremiah... And the turn to Jeremiah as a social semiotic discourse presses for an end to "innocent biblical theology readings that have companioned historical-critical orthodoxy in one fashion or another." No help there in our quest for reconstructing what happened in the time of Josiah! (Quoting A.R.P. Diamond, Introduction, pp. 15, 32, in A.R.P. Diamond, K.M. O'Connor and L Stulman, eds, *Troubling Jeremiah*, Sheffield: Sheffield Academic Press, 1999.)[793]

But we know Jeremiah was real and that he was a prophet because Nephi mentions him in his description of what had been preserved on the brass plates of Laban. The description includes the following:

> And also a record of the Jews from the beginning, even down to the commencement of the reign of Zedekiah, king of Judah. And also the prophecies of the holy prophets, from the beginning, even down to the commencement of the reign of Zedekiah; and

---

[793] *The Mother of the Lord, Volume 1: The Lady in the Temple*, (London: Bloomsbury Publishing, 2012.) That volume attempts to partially reconstruct the earliest religion of the patriarchs, but is unable to do more than raise doubts about the subject. Joseph Smith provided a great deal more, and the scholar who took Joseph as a guide, Hugh Nibley, has been able to make a far better attempt to explain antiquity. In the end, however, it will require God to restore by revelation more of what remains missing before we will have complete answers to our questions.

also many prophecies which have been spoken by the mouth of Jeremiah.[794]

The Book of Mormon confirms Jeremiah's existence and status as a prophet. We can accept him even if today's scholars doubt.[795] Revelation remains more reliable than mere scholarship and opinion.[796]

Jeremiah denounced the form of veneration taken by ancient Israel. He rebuked those in his day, preaching among other things this:

> Seest thou not what they do in the cities of Judah and in the streets of Jerusalem? The children gather wood, and the fathers kindle the fire, and the women knead their dough, to make cakes to the queen of heaven, and to pour out drink offerings unto other gods, that they may provoke me to anger. Do they provoke me to anger? saith the Lord: do they not provoke themselves to the confusion of their own faces?[797]

These words have been incorrectly used to denounce and deny the very existence of a Heavenly Mother. However, Jeremiah was not denying or denouncing Her existence, only the improper form of worshipping Her to the exclusion of Heavenly Father.

It requires wisdom to deal with the Mother. Rejection of Her has resulted in religious and social errors. Ignoring Her has produced celibacy, religious eunuchs, and a collapsing birth rate. On one end, fixation on Her has produced fertility cults, sacred prostitution and religious orgies. At the other end, the Shakers (or The United Society of Believers in Christ's Second Appearing) were celibate and procreation was prohibited. This resulted in the gradual death of their community and as of 2017 only two surviving members. Either end

---

[794] NC 1 Ne. 2:22; 1 Ne. 5:12-13.

[795] Paul's description of the last days includes mention of those who will be "[E]ver learning and never able to come to the knowledge of the truth." NC 2 Tim. 1:8; 2 Tim. 3:7.

[796] "Salvation cannot come without revelation; it is in vain for anyone to minister without it. No man is a minister of Jesus Christ without being a prophet. No man can be a minister of Jesus Christ except he has the testimony of Jesus; and this is the spirit of prophecy. Whenever salvation has been administered, it has been by testimony." *TPJS*, p. 160.

[797] KJV Jeremiah 7:17-19.

of the religious-sexual spectrum that misapprehends the Divine Feminine has been plagued with degrading or calamitous imbalances.

The Sun and Moon are symbols of the Father and Mother planted overhead as a testimony from Them to Their children. From the surface of the earth[798] they occupy equal space in the firmament. Although the circumference of the sun is approximately 400 times larger than the moon, the moon is approximately 400 times closer to the earth. As a result they are visibly equal in size and occupy the same path on the ecliptic. This is why the moon is able to eclipse the sun.

The Father, represented by the Sun, is stable, unchangeable, reliable and predictable. The Sun rises every day on the horizon in the east and sets every evening on the horizon in the west. He is unvarying in His course from day-to-day and year-to-year. The Mother, represented by the Moon, changes each day. She waxes and wanes. She does not just move from east to west, but the moonrise also constantly moves in the opposite direction from west to east. Every day She reappears further to the east before beginning Her movement to the west. She moves approximately 50 minutes eastward each day.

Her complex movements overhead were part of the reason She was known anciently as "the Great Dancer." Her movements display constantly changing motions, contrasting with Her Companion Sun. This contrast between the movements of the sun and the moon reminds me of the quip by cartoonist Bob Thaves about Ginger Rogers, the dancing partner of acclaimed Fred Astair, "Sure he was great, but don't forget that Ginger Rogers did everything he did...backwards and in high heels."

We are often told that life on earth depends on the Sun. But life here is equally dependent on the Moon. Without the moon slowing the earth's rotation, we would only have 6 to 10 hour days. The shorter days would result in the earth being much colder, as the sun would have less time to warm the earth's surface. This would cause a dramatic decrease in plant and animal life. Tides would be eliminated, and weather would be more violent. The stable rotation of the earth would change, and we would no longer rotate on a constant axis. The poles and equator would no longer exist or would be constantly

---

[798] All the lights of the firmament are to be interpreted from the surface of the earth using the unaided human eye.

changing. The earth's tectonic plates, continents and mountain ranges are all formed by the effect of the moon on the earth. Without the moon, there would be less variety in the earth's habitats. Many life forms could not exist. Richard Lathe, a molecular biologist at Pieta Research in Edinburgh, UK,[799] advanced a theory in 2003 explaining that life on earth could not have happened without the moon. A number of astronomers believes that life on any planet throughout the universe requires a nearby moon and, without this nighttime companion for the sun, life cannot exist.[800]

While acknowledging a Divine Mother is appropriate, singling Her out for worship is not. The words of the Divine Mother's Proverb and Mary's psalm both venerate and praise the Father. The role of God the Father is critical to acknowledge and understand for our salvation. Jesus Christ is the essential Savior and Redeemer whose atoning sacrifice is the means ordained by God to now rescue us from sin and death. Our salvation depends on knowing, confessing and worshiping Christ. Anything that distracts us from that can become an impediment to salvation.

For us the Mother's greatest accomplishment has been to take the seed of God the Father and magnify it. She controls and weaves His seed into Their organized spirit offspring. From Their glory, or intelligence,[801] She produces organized intelligences, or spirits.[802] One of the titles for the Heavenly Mother is "The Great Weaver" because She formed unorganized intelligence[803] into organized spirits[804]

---

[799] Lathe was the primary inventor of a vaccine to eradicate rabies, which has resulted in extensions of vaccines for cervical and breast cancers. His research led him to postulate a theory that evolutionary life on earth was dependent upon the moon's influence on tides, which he published in 2004 in the journal Icarus. (*Fast tidal cycling and the origin of life*, Vol. 168, Issue 1, March 2004, pp. 18-22.) While scripture affirms that God, not chance, established life in this creation, there is no scriptural explanation of the means employed by God to plant life here during the creation. Nor, for that matter, is any explanation given for the length of time involved in each "day" of creation. The work accomplished is called a "day" without any attempt to otherwise set out a reliable fixed length of time.

[800] See, e.g., Peter Ward and Donald Brownlee, *Rare Earth: Why Complex Life Is Uncommon in the Universe*, (Copernicus, 2000); John Gribbin, *The Reason Why: The Miracle of Life on Earth*, (Allen Lane, 2011).

[801] "The glory of God is intelligence, or, in other words, light and truth." D&C 93:36.

[802] Abraham 3:22-23.

becoming the Mother of All Living. All of us are intimately connected to Her, for we came from Her, often through Her daughters.

Mortal women have inherited a similar power from Her. This inheritance empowers them to become mothers here. The capacity to fashion matter into another human being belongs only to Her daughters. All human life begins inside the womb of the woman where the work of The Great Weaver is replicated for each one of us who has ever lived in this world.

There is a natural and inevitable affection children hold for their mothers. That affection is close to the hearts of all dying men. There are many battlefield accounts of how dying men call out in their last breath for their mother. Roland Bartetzko, former German Army soldier, when under fire in his first combat experience uttered "Mother" when fire struck others beside him. As he reflected on why he spoke that out loud he concluded, "Our lives begin with our mothers giving birth to us and on the day when I thought that my life was over, my mind circled back to where it all had begun." For Mother's Day 2015, Lt. Col. Zumwalt[805] wrote the following regarding soldiers crying for their mothers on the battlefield.

> Typically, and understandably, the bond between mother and son is very close.
>
> The gift of life and nurturing comfort given to a child by a loving mother is never forgotten by a grateful son—especially one still lucid as he takes his last breath on a battlefield.
>
> This bond is not necessarily a product of nationality or culture. Battlefield witnesses have

---

[803] D&C 93:29: "Intelligence, or the light of truth, was not created nor made, neither indeed can be[.]"

[804] Abraham 3:22: "Now the Lord had shown unto me, Abraham, the intelligences that were organized before the world was[.]" For a further discussion of this topic see *Beloved Enos* and the essay The *First Three Words*.

[805] 10 May 2015; Lt. Colonel James G. Zumwalt, USMC (Ret.), is a retired Marine infantry officer who served in the Vietnam war, the U.S. invasion of Panama and the first Gulf war. He is the author of *Bare Feet, Iron Will–Stories from the Other Side of Vietnam's Battlefields, Living the Juche Lie: North Korea's Kim Dynasty* and *Doomsday: Iran–The Clock is Ticking.* He frequently writes on foreign policy and defense issues.

attested to its existence in various conflicts as the last cogent thought uttered by a young dying warrior.

Mother's Day is perhaps an appropriate time to recognize this bond. While sad to do so, it is a most telling tribute to a son's love for a mother.

In her book *Year of the Comets*, Jan Deblieu shares a conversation she had with her husband, Jeff, depressed as his mother lay dying of cancer:

> 'I heard somewhere,' Jeff said, 'that soldiers dying on the battlefield cry out for their mothers. People walking through the carnage at Normandy heard grown men calling out 'Mommy!' He shook his head. 'Calling not for their girlfriends or wives, but for their mothers.'

Decades later, Normandy survivors attest to still hearing such cries. As emotional D-Day veteran Frank Devito noted in a 2014 interview with Tom Brokaw commemorating the 70th anniversary of the Normandy invasion, "You know there's a fallacy people think that when a man is dying. They don't ask for God. The last word they say before they die is 'Momma.'"

There is a tendency by those who have never known combat to dismiss stories of this bond as fantasy. But numerous battlefield testimonials from wars past and present tell us otherwise.

The last survivor of World War I, Harry Patch, who died in 2009 at the age of 111, bore witness to the bond.

A website dedicated to the British soldier notes:

> [Patch] recalled, with a sense of guilt, crawling across no-man's land with the wounded crying out in agony all around him and just passing them by...He remembered coming across a still-living shattered bleeding wreck of a man who begged Patch to shoot him, but in the time of Patch's indecision the man uttered the cry 'Mother!' and died.

Robert Serafin—a U.S. Army corpsman assigned to a mobile field hospital—landed in France in February 1945. He supported the U.S. 1st Army's advance deep into Germany.

Serafin had vivid memories of the pain and suffering the wounded endured. He recalled one young soldier, for whom little more could be done than offering morphine, who cried out for his mother.

Serving in Vietnam as well, Serafin found there, too, "as soon as a guy would be in bad shape, he'd always ask for his mother. Whenever I heard that, it killed me inside."

A young warrior's dying battlefield cry for a mother he will never again see knows no cultural boundaries.

In 2014, Ukrainian surgeon Oleksandr Zeleniuk tended to the wounded on a Crimean battlefield. Twelve soldiers died on his operating table. "We struggled for their lives," he said, "but death won. When soldiers are dying, they all say the same thing: they call for their mother…"

An amazing testimonial to the strength of the mother-son bond is forged into the steel of the U.S. Marine Corps' Iwo Jima Memorial outside of Washington, D.C.

The inspiration for this memorial came from Joseph Rosenthal's famous photograph of six Marines raising the American flag atop Mount Suribachi on the island of Iwo Jima during World War II.

A heartfelt story about one of those Marines and his mother is told by James Bradley in Flags of Our Fathers.

His book shares the individual stories of each of the six Marines—of which Bradley's father was one.

When the photograph first appeared in U.S. newspapers, Bradley tells us, the six were not identified.

The mother, Belle, of one Marine, Harlon Block, took a look at the photograph and exclaimed, "That's Harlon." Harlon's younger brother chided his mother as the photograph was taken from behind the flag-raisers so faces were not visible.

A few days later the photograph was re-published, this time with names. But Harlon's was not among them. Belle remained adamant—the Marine on the far right was most definitely her son.

Only days after the photograph was taken, three of the six—including Harlon—were dead.

After the war, one of the three remaining survivors, Ira Hayes, visited Belle to inform her an identification error had been made—it was her son in the photograph. The official record was corrected to reflect what a loving mother knew all along.

When asked how she was so confident it was her son in the photograph since his face was not visible, Belle commented she had changed his backside as a baby so many times she knew Harlon's when she saw it!

With such stories attesting to the bond between mother and son and with all the battlefields of all the wars humanity has fought, one wonders how many cries of a dying warrior son for his mother have gone unheard.

While sad, it is a beautiful tribute to the mother-son bond that the last thought of the latter is for the former. In the throes of death, the son cries out for the mother who not only gave him life but nurtured and comforted him before he answered his country's call to arms.

It is beautiful, but also merciful the mother is not there to witness it.

There is something primal, unavoidable and universal in the connection between children and mothers. Life begins in her arms and at her breast. Approaching death always brings the beginning of life, and therefore motherhood, back into focus. This primal connection is one reason why acknowledging the Heavenly Mother has proven overwhelming, even a burden for some societies. As soon as they are aware of Her, they focus veneration and worship on Her alone.

The presence of the female counterpart to God the Father does not include a scriptural command or permission to single Her out and worship Her apart from the Father. Indeed, the psalm of Mary in the book of Luke and the words of the Mother in Proverbs direct our attention to the Father. She may be part of a Divine Couple, but it is clear She wants honor and worship to be on Her Husband and Her Son.

Mary's psalm focused on God the Father and His Son. Look carefully at Her adoration of God:

> My soul doth *magnify the Lord*, And my spirit hath rejoiced in *God my Saviour*. ... *holy is his name*. And *his mercy is on them that fear him* from generation to generation. *He hath shewed strength with his arm; he hath scattered the proud* in the imagination of their hearts. *He hath put down the mighty* from their seats, and exalted them of low degree. *He hath filled the hungry* with good things; and the rich he hath sent empty away. *He hath holpen his servant Israel*, in remembrance of *his mercy*; As *he spake to our fathers*, to Abraham, and to his seed for ever.[806]

She pointed us to the Father. Remember also that the brightest star in Her constellation is in her hand – the "seed of the woman." The stars testify of Her, but point to Her "seed" as the greatest light for us here and now.

The moon reflects the light of her sun. Just as Mary did in Her psalm, this physical example testifies to the glory of the Father and the faithful reflection of the Mother. It is the sun that provides the light, heat and gravity governing the planets of this creation under its influence. It is the moon that stabilizes and makes life possible.

As mentioned already, Jeremiah witnessed some of the corrupt practices of ancient Israel when they singled out the "queen of heaven" for uninvited, uninspired primacy in their worship. God prompted him to condemn what he saw. His condemnation has been wrongly interpreted as an outright rejection of Her existence.[807] But

---

[806] Luke 1:46-55.

[807] See, e.g., Jeremiah 44: 44:16-28: "As for the word that thou hast spoken unto us in the name of the Lord, we will not hearken unto thee. But we will certainly do whatsoever thing goeth forth out of our own mouth, to burn

Jeremiah has preserved for us the fact that ancient Israel once burned incense to the "queen of heaven." This happened in their temple. Israel incorrectly attributed prosperity to their worship and appeasement of the "queen of heaven." They turned the "queen of heaven" into a magic talisman to be placated by incense, drink offerings and cakes. It was idolatry, incapable of changing the inner-

---

incense unto the queen of heaven, and to pour out drink offerings unto her, as we have done, we, and our fathers, our kings, and our princes, in the cities of Judah, and in the streets of Jerusalem: for then had we plenty of victuals, and were well, and saw no evil. But since we left off to burn incense to the queen of heaven, and to pour out drink offerings unto her, we have wanted all things, and have been consumed by the sword and by the famine. And when we burned incense to the queen of heaven, and poured out drink offerings unto her, did we make her cakes to worship her, and pour out drink offerings unto her, without our men? Then Jeremiah said unto all the people, to the men, and to the women, and to all the people which had given him that answer, saying, The incense that ye burned in the cities of Judah, and in the streets of Jerusalem, ye, and your fathers, your kings, and your princes, and the people of the land, did not the Lord remember them, and came it not into his mind? So that the Lord could no longer bear, because of the evil of your doings, and because of the abominations which ye have committed; therefore is your land a desolation, and an astonishment, and a curse, without an inhabitant, as at this day. Because ye have burned incense, and because ye have sinned against the Lord, and have not obeyed the voice of the Lord, nor walked in his law, nor in his statutes, nor in his testimonies; therefore this evil is happened unto you, as at this day. Moreover Jeremiah said unto all the people, and to all the women, Hear the word of the Lord, all Judah that are in the land of Egypt: Thus saith the Lord of hosts, the God of Israel, saying; Ye and your wives have both spoken with your mouths, and fulfilled with your hand, saying, We will surely perform our vows that we have vowed, to burn incense to the queen of heaven, and to pour out drink offerings unto her: ye will surely accomplish your vows, and surely perform your vows. Therefore hear ye the word of the Lord, all Judah that dwell in the land of Egypt; Behold, I have sworn by my great name, saith the Lord, that my name shall no more be named in the mouth of any man of Judah in all the land of Egypt, saying, The Lord God liveth. Behold, I will watch over them for evil, and not for good: and all the men of Judah that are in the land of Egypt shall be consumed by the sword and by the famine, until there be an end of them. Yet a small number that escape the sword shall return out of the land of Egypt into the land of Judah, and all the remnant of Judah, that are gone into the land of Egypt to sojourn there, shall know whose words shall stand, mine, or theirs."

man. Acknowledgment of Her devolved to degrading appeasement of a female sky-god, who could be manipulated into blessing worshipers by the offering of presents. But to put this into prospective, that condemnation by Jeremiah was comparable to Jesus Christ's denunciation of the scribes and Pharisees. Christ did not reject God the Father. He vindicated Him. But Christ denounced their foolish, superficial idolatry associated with God the Father. Jeremiah was condemning worship of the "queen of heaven" that had strayed outside the bounds authorized by God.

History has proven that it is less problematic to ignore Heavenly Mother than to acknowledge Her. Historically speaking mankind has shown there is less of a downside to ignoring Heavenly Mother than the downside of acknowledging Her. "Faith" in God is not dependent on fully realizing the things disclosed in this talk.

*Lecture Third* in *Lectures on Faith* clarifies what is essential to enable us to have saving faith in God:

> 2 Let us here observe that three things are necessary in order that any rational and intelligent being may exercise faith in God unto life and salvation.
>
> 3 First, the idea that he actually *exists*.
>
> 4 Secondly, a correct idea of his *character, perfections, and attributes*.
>
> 5 Thirdly, an actual knowledge that *the course of life* which he is pursuing *is according to His will*. For without an acquaintance with these three important facts, the faith of every rational being must be imperfect and unproductive, but with this understanding it can become perfect and fruitful, abounding in righteousness unto the praise and glory of God the Father and the Lord Jesus Christ.

The idea that a Heavenly Mother exists is implicit in the scriptures. But because it is not explicit, a person can believe that God exists without understanding the duality of the Heavenly Parents. Likewise, the character, perfections and attributes do not require anybody to understand what is explained in this talk.

Their character, perfections and attributes are mercy, righteousness, love, compassion and truthfulness. They are without partiality, no respecter of persons, regarding all alike. They make the sun to shine and the rain to fall on both the righteous and the wicked.

They regard wickedness as an abomination. They prize truth, meekness and peacemakers. They abhor the froward, prideful, evil and arrogant. They are full of grace and truth, and are more intelligent than us all. They are the Creators and will be the final judges of this cycle of existence and no one will be permitted to progress further without Their permission. There is nothing vile or perverse about Them. They are repelled by contention and seek for us all to associate with one another equally, as brothers and sisters. They are "perfect" in the sense of having completed the journey to the end of the path and entered into Eternal Lives and Exaltation. They now seek to guide Their children along that same path. If you understand and accept these things about God, that is enough. You may imagine Them as a male and female, or a Great Spirit, a bearded old man, or an incorporeal but difficult to envision being of pure glory. Whatever young Joseph Smith imagined God to be when he asked God for wisdom was unimportant because he believed God to be just, pure, holy and no respecter of persons. The answer he received cleared up a great many mysteries for Joseph, but those clarifications went beyond God's character, perfections and attributes.

The keystone of our religion gives examples of how faith in God does not require any comprehension of the corporeal existence, or physical dimensions of God. The understanding the Brother of Jared had before he saw God was decidedly limited. Despite this he was redeemed from the fall by returning to God's presence where he gained greater knowledge of God. Beforehand he did not understand Christ had a tangible finger, nor did he understand he would one day take upon Himself a mortal body:

> And the veil was taken from off the eyes of the brother of Jared, and he saw the finger of the Lord. And it was as the finger of a man, like unto flesh and blood; and the brother of Jared fell down before the Lord for he was struck with fear. And the Lord saw that the brother of Jared had fallen to the earth and the Lord said unto him, Arise. Why hast thou fallen? And he saith unto the Lord, I saw the finger of the Lord and I feared lest he should smite me, for I knew not that the Lord had flesh and blood. And the Lord said unto him, Because of thy faith thou hast seen that I shall take upon me flesh and blood. And none of those now living have come before me with

such exceeding faith as thou hast, for were it not so, ye could not have seen my finger.[808]

When Ammon was teaching king Lamoni, the instruction began by only acknowledging that God was "a Great Spirit."

Believest thou that there is a God? And he answered unto him, I do not know what that meaneth. And then Ammon said, Believest thou that there is a Great Spirit? And he said, Yea. And Ammon said, This is God. And Ammon said unto him again, Believest thou that this Great Spirit who is God created all things which are in Heaven and in the Earth? And he said, Yea, I believe that he created all things which are in the earth, but I do not know the heavens. And Ammon said unto him, The heavens are a place where God dwells and all his holy angels.[809]

When Aaron taught king Lamoni's father, he likewise described God vaguely as "that great Spirit,"

Behold, assuredly as thou livest O king there is a God. And the king said, Is God that great Spirit that brought our fathers out of the land of Jerusalem? And Aaron said unto him, Yea, he is that great Spirit, and he created all things both in Heaven and in earth; believest thou this? And he said, Yea, I believe that the great Spirit created all things, and I desire that ye should tell me concerning all these things and I will believe thy words.[810]

These examples demonstrate that understanding there is both a Father and a Mother who jointly comprise a single "Heavenly Father" is not essential for mankind to be able to have saving faith in God. Knowing the "character, perfections and attributes" does not extend to these particulars. To be like them is to be patient, faithful, obedient, loving, charitable and pure. These are the important "character, perfections and attributes" of godliness. Their appearance, even that they are two separate beings, "male and female," and yet they are "one," is not required for faith.

---

[808] NC Ether 1:12.
[809] Alma 12:15.
[810] Alma 13:8.

First and foremost, for fallen man in this creation, salvation is dependent upon Jesus Christ. We have a revealed account that explains who we worship and how to worship:

> And I, John, saw that he received not of the fulness at the first, but received grace for grace; And he received not of the fulness at first, but continued from grace to grace, until he received a fulness; And thus he was called the Son of God, because he received not of the fulness at the first. And I, John, bear record, and lo, the heavens were opened, and the Holy Ghost descended upon him in the form of a dove, and sat upon him, and there came a voice out of heaven saying: This is my beloved Son. And I, John, bear record that he received a fulness of the glory of the Father; And he received all power, both in heaven and on earth, and the glory of the Father was with him, for he dwelt in him. And it shall come to pass, that if you are faithful you shall receive the fulness of the record of John. I give unto you these sayings that you may understand and know how to worship, and know what you worship, that you may come unto the Father in my name, and in due time receive of his fulness. For if you keep my commandments you shall receive of his fulness, and be glorified in me as I am in the Father; therefore, I say unto you, you shall receive grace for grace. And now, verily I say unto you, I was in the beginning with the Father, and am the Firstborn; And all those who are begotten through me are partakers of the glory of the same, and are the church of the Firstborn. Ye were also in the beginning with the Father; that which is Spirit, even the Spirit of truth; And truth is knowledge of things as they are, and as they were, and as they are to come. And whatsoever is more or less than this is the spirit of that wicked one who was a liar from the beginning.[811]

---

[811] D&C 93:12-25. This is John the Beloved's testimony of Christ and is clarified in T&C 171: *The Testimony of St. John* 10:9: "In the journey through my Father's realms are many stages with temporary abodes. If it were not so, I would have told you. I go to prepare an abode for your upward journey."

Like Christ, we are expected to grow from grace to grace. Those words are in a revelation that begins with this promise: "Verily, thus saith the Lord: It shall come to pass that every soul who forsaketh his sins and cometh unto me, and calleth on my name, and obeyeth my voice, and keepeth my commandments, shall see my face and know that I am[.]"[812] This is how we are to grow from grace to grace. This is how we can receive of His fullness. There is no mention of redirecting our obedience to another. Nor is there any name provided to us to call upon other than Christ's. Nor is there any voice we are to hearken unto other than Christ's.

We are in a fallen state and need to be saved. Like Mary acknowledged to Elizabeth when they met, we need to be rescued by a Savior. That Savior is Jesus Christ. She pointed us to Him and if we will heed Her wise counsel, we will rely on the merits of Christ, who is mighty to save.[813]

There are other revelations that clarify how our attention and adoration must center in Christ. It is Jesus Christ who we are to acknowledge as the great Creator and Redeemer of this creation:

> God, the holiest of all, through Jesus Christ his Son—He that ascended up on high, as also he descended below all things, in that he comprehended all things, that he might be in all and through all things, the light of truth; Which truth shineth. This is the light of Christ. As also he is in the sun, and the light of the sun, and the power thereof by which it was made. As also he is in the moon, and is the light of the moon, and the power thereof by which it was made; As also the light of the stars, and the power thereof by which they were made; And the earth also, and the power thereof, even the earth upon which you stand. And the light which shineth, which giveth you light, is through him who enlighteneth your eyes, which is the same light that quickeneth your understandings; Which light proceedeth forth from the presence of God to fill the immensity of space— The light which is in all things, which giveth

---

Christ passed through those stages as He ascended "from grace to grace."
[812] D&C 93:1.
[813] Alma 7:14; 2 Ne. 31:19; D&C 133:47; Isa. 63:1.

life to all things, which is the law by which all things are governed, even the power of God who sitteth upon his throne, who is in the bosom of eternity, who is in the midst of all things.[814]

There are Heavenly Parents, to be sure. They are two separate beings: a Father and a Mother. She exists and Her role is acknowledged in scripture. We are supposed to "find" Her. And in the last-days temple (should it be finally built by a humble and and obedient people), Her open presence will be there.

In the temple ceremonies women veil their faces. Among other things, this symbolizes the hidden Heavenly Mother. Her presence is veiled because She is sacred and not to be regarded as accessible apart from Heavenly Father. That which is most holy is veiled from the vulgar and profane. Women should be regarded as daughters of the Divine Mother. Like Her, they carry the power to produce new life. Mothers are the physical veil between pre-earth spirits and physical bodied inhabited in mortality. They clothe children in the veil of flesh. This power is honored in the temple veiling of women. This power to give life has been regarded in almost all societies as something sacred and holy. In our coarse and vulgar society we have rejected as a matter of law the idea that women engage in a sacred and holy labor when bearing children.[815]

The Great Weaver organizes intelligence into life itself through motherhood. It is in the womb that disorganized intelligence is organized into spirits resembling the Heavenly Parents in eternity. Mothers in this creation do likewise. That power, endowed by the Divine pattern, is present in this creation to testify of She who wove our spirits before this world. She is ever providing wisdom to guide the energy of Her Divine counterpart so balance and order are maintained.

For the present, it is enough to know She is there and that She urges us to be faithful and obedient to Her Son, our Redeemer and Savior. We need to be rescued from our fallen state. Jesus Christ is our rescuer.

---

[814] D&C 88:5-13.

[815] Since 1973, the United States has killed 60,147,378 children. Since 1980, worldwide, there have been 1,483,069,000 abortions, many funded by US aid. These numbers are published by the Guttmacher Institute, a division of Planned Parenthood of America, the worldwide numbers are tracked and funded by the World Health Organization.

Finally, there is one last clarification about the Heavenly Mother that needs to be made. Brigham Young taught a confusing doctrine that has been labeled "Adam-God." Although he gave some illuminating and true sermons during Joseph Smith's lifetime, following Joseph's death Brigham Young seemed to be doctrinally adrift. He made little claim to revelation.[816] But his guesses about what happened in the Garden of Eden[817] have marred all of the

---

[816] "I am not going to interpret dreams; for I don't profess to be such a Prophet as were Joseph Smith and Daniel; but I am a Yankee guesser[.]" *JD* 5:77.

[817] "Adam was an immortal being when he came on this earth; He had lived on an earth similiar [sic] to ours; he had received the Priesthood and the keys thereof, And had been faithful in all things and gained his resurrection and his exaltation, and was crowned with glory, immortality and eternal lives, and was numbered with the Gods for such he became through his faithfulness. And had begotten all the spirits that was to come to this earth. (*Unpublished Revelations of the Prophets and Presidents of the Church of Jesus Christ of Latter-day Saints*, complied by Fred C. Collier, Vol 1, pp. 116-117, (Salt Lake: Collier's Publishing Co., 2nd edition 1981) "Now hear it, O inhabitants of the earth, Jew and Gentile, Saint and sinner! When our father Adam came into the garden of Eden, he came into it with a celestial body and brought Eve, one of his wives, with him. He helped to make and organize this world. He is MICHAEL, the Archangel, the ANCIENT OF DAYS! about whom holy men have written and spoken--HE is our FATHER and our GOD, and the only God with whom WE have to do. Every man upon the earth, professing Christians or non-professing, must hear it, and will know it sooner or later... Now, let all who may hear these doctrines, pause before they make light of them, or treat them with indifference, for they will prove their salvation or damnation." (*JD* 1:50-51, Brigham Young, April 9, 1852). "How much unbelief exists in the minds of Latter-day Saints in regard to one particular doctrine which I revealed to them, and which God revealed to me - namely that Adam is our father and God ..Then he said, 'I want my children who are in the spirit world to come and live here. I once dwelt upon an earth something like this, in a mortal state. I was faithful. I received my crown and exaltation...I want my children that were born to me in the spirit world to come here and take tabernacles of flesh that their spirits may have a house, a tabernacle...'" (Brigham Young, *Deseret Weekly News*, June 18, 1873, page 308; *Deseret Evening News*, June 14, 1873) "Who was the Savior begotten by?....Who did beget him? His Father, and his father is our God, and the Father of our spirits, and he is the framer of the body, the God and Father of our Lord Jesus Christ. Who is he? He is Father Adam; Michael; the Ancient of Days." (President Brigham Young, Feb. 19, 1854, *Complete*

largest branches of Mormonism. To be fair, he said he "guessed" and "reckoned" about the subject. But he also called it a "revealment" to him, which led others to regard his incorrect ideas as reliable. Brigham Young's false ideas have produced a library of material defending or disputing his teaching. There are today both fervent defenders and convicted detractors. Because of this strong partisan divide, it might be more prudent to leave what happened in Eden unexplained. Nevertheless, what follows will either help clarify events or add to the confusion and debate:

Our Heavenly Mother, the companion of Heavenly Father, was in the garden when man was created. But so were others. In addition to the man Adam and the woman Eve, the plural Elohim who were in Eden included two Divine couples who were parents of Adam and Eve. One Divine couple were the parents of Adam. The other were the parents of Eve.

The account of the creation from Moses in Genesis is a parable. The account veils identities of the role players unless the parable is explained. Christ did this when He taught publicly.[818] The parable written by Moses relates:

---

*Discourses of Brigham Young*, Vol. 2, p. 763.) "Some have grumbled because I believe our God to be so near to us as Father Adam. There are many who know that doctrine to be true." (Brigham Young, October 7, 1857, *JD* 5:331). "Some years ago I advanced a doctrine with regard to Adam being our Father and God...It is one of the most glorious revealments of the economy of heaven..." (Brigham Young, October 8, 1861, *Complete Discourses of Brigham Young*, Vol. 3, pp. 1913-1914.) "I tell you more: Adam is the father of our spirits. He lived upon an earth, he did abide his creation and did honor to his calling and priesthood and obeyed his master or lord, and probably many of his wives did the same, and they lived and died upon an earth and then were resurrected again to immortality and eternal life. I reckon, and as the Yankees say I guess; but I will tell you what I reckon. I reckon that Father Adam was a resurrected being, with his wives and posterity, and in the Celestial Kingdom were crowned with Glory, Immortality and Eternal Lives, with Thrones, Principalities and Powers: and it was said to him, 'It is your right to organize the elements; and to your Creations and Posterity there shall be no end, but you shall add Kingdom to Kingdom, and Throne to Throne; and still behold the vast eternity of unorganized matter.'" (Brigham Young, October 8, 1854, *Complete Discourses of Brigham Young*, Vol. 2, p. 851.)

[818] "Then the disciples came and said unto him, Why do you speak unto them in parables? He answered and said unto them, Because it is given unto

And I, God, said unto my Only Begotten, who was with me from the beginning, Let us make man in our image, after our likeness. And it was so. And I, God, said, Let them have dominion over the fish of the sea, and over the fowl of the air, and over the cattle, and over all the earth, and over every creeping thing that creeps upon the Earth. And I, God, created man in my own image. *In the image of my Only Begotten created I him.* Male and female created I them. And I, God, blessed them.[819]

The creation of the man Adam was secondarily in the image of God the Father, but was primarily and specifically "in the image of my Only Begotten"—meaning Jesus Christ. The reason Adam was born "in the image of" God the Father's "Only Begotten" was because the Only Begotten was the one who begat Adam. God the Father was the father of Jesus Christ in the spirit, and the biological father of Jesus Christ in the flesh. God the Father was also the Father of the spirit of the man Adam. But the biological Father of Adam in the garden was "in the image of the Only Begotten," or Jesus Christ. Christ and His companion were the physical Parents of the man Adam.

Jesus Christ was among the "souls" who were "noble and great" before this cycle of creation.[820] The word "soul" as used in the 1842 publication of the Book of Abraham[821] had been defined in a revelation received in 1832: "Now verily I say unto you, that through the redemption which is made for you is brought to pass the

---

you to know the mysteries of the kingdom of heaven, but to them it is not given; for whoever receives, to him shall be given, and he shall have more abundance. But whoever continues not to receive, from him shall be taken away even that he has. Therefore I speak to them in parables because they seeing, see not, and hearing, they hear not, neither do they understand. And in them is fulfilled the prophecy of Isaiah concerning them, which says, By hearing you shall hear and shall not understand, and seeing you shall see and shall not perceive. For this people's heart is waxed gross, and their ears are dull of hearing, and their eyes they have closed, lest at any time they should see with their eyes, and hear with their ears, and should understand with their hearts, and should be converted, and I should heal them." NC Matt. 7:2.

[819] OC Gen. 2:7, emphasis added.

[820] Abraham 3:22-24.

[821] The first publication of the Book of Abraham was in the *Times and Seasons* during March to May 1842.

resurrection from the dead, and **the spirit and the body is the soul of man**, and the resurrection from the dead is the redemption of the soul, and the redemption of the soul is through him who quickeneth all things, in whose bosom it is decreed that the poor and the meek of the Earth shall inherit it."[822] Christ is identified in scripture as a "soul" before this world was created. Therefore, before this world was created Christ had both a "spirit and a body"—having gone through the necessary progression required for all who ascend to be "like unto God."[823] Christ had the physical capacity to be the biological father of offspring. He did this with Adam.

The account continues and describes the creation of the woman. Here the parable distinguishes between the process of creating the man Adam and creating his spouse, the woman Eve:

And I, the Lord God, said unto mine Only Begotten, that it was not good that the man should be alone, Wherefore, *I will make an help meet* for him.[824]

God the Father said to the Only Begotten and that He (God the Father), will be the one to make Adam's "help meet." It was not good for Adam to be alone because he was not complete without a suitable companion to help him progress and develop. The creation parable continues:

And I, the Lord God, caused a deep sleep to fall upon Adam, and he slept, and I took one of his ribs, and closed up the flesh in the stead thereof, and the rib, which I, the Lord God had taken from man, made I a woman, and brought her unto the man. And Adam said, This I know now is bone of my bones, and flesh of my flesh. She shall be called woman, because she was taken out of man.[825]

---

[822] Teachings and Commandments (hereafter "T&C") 30:4; see also D&C 88:14-17, emphasis added.

[823] "[T]here stood one among them that was like unto God, and he said unto those who were with him: We will go down, for there is space there, and we will take of these materials, and we will make an earth[.]" Abr. 3:24. This is explained in greater detail in the essay *The First Three Words* in the book *Essays: Three Degrees* and in the chapter *Christ: The Prototype of the Saved Man* in the book *Preserving the Restoration*.

[824] OC Gen. 2:11.

[825] OC Gen. 2:12.

The parable of the creation of the woman therefore differs from the creation of the man. She was not formed from the dust of the ground. She was formed from a "rib" –from an already existing part of the man. She was born from something equal to him and able to stand beside him in all things.

But the parable about the woman Eve means a great deal more. She was at Adam's side before the creation of this world. They were united as "one" in a prior estate when they progressed to become living "souls" with both bodies and spirits. They were sealed before this world by the Holy Spirit of Promise and proved true and faithful. They once sat upon a throne in God the Father's Kingdom. In that state they were equal and joined eternally together. She sat beside him and was a necessary part of his enthronement. Her introduction into this world to join her companion was needed to complete Adam. It was not good for him to be alone. They were "one" and therefore Adam without Eve was not complete—or in the words of the parable "not good to be alone."

Like the man Adam, the woman Eve was the spirit offspring of Heavenly Father and Heavenly Mother. But unlike the man Adam, who was the physical offspring of Christ, the woman Eve needed to be the physical offspring of God the Father and God the Mother. Eve was Adam's sister in spirit. Eve was also his physical aunt. She had to be the direct descendant of the Heavenly Mother in order to endow her with her Mother's creative abilities. That power belongs to the Mother. The fertility of Eve, and thereafter of all the daughters of Eve, came because of the power given from direct descent from the Heavenly Mother.[826]

Men descend from Christ. Christ founded the family of men and is accountable for them. He was placed in that position to enable Him to atone for any failure on their part. Through Adam "sin entered the world" and death was imposed upon all mankind.[827] Jesus Christ, one greater than Adam, made Himself responsible for all mankind's

---

[826] At birth, women possess an endowment of eggs that enable them to bear children: "During fetal life, there are about 6 million to 7 million eggs. From this time, no new eggs are produced. At birth, there are approximately 1 million eggs; and by the time of puberty, only about 300,000 remain. Of these, only 300 to 400 will be ovulated during a woman's reproductive lifetime." *The Cleveland Clinic Foundation*, 2018; using information provided in part by Planned Parenthood.

[827] NC Romans 1:23; see also, Romans 5:12.

failures and transgressions. Through the obedience of Jesus Christ all mankind were justified and "made righteous."[828] The Father made mankind Christ's posterity. This was necessary to qualify Christ as "the last Adam."[829] Christ was the rightful "heir of all things" because He always stood at the head.[830] When "all things were made by Him" it included the man Adam.[831] Death came upon all mankind through Adam. Before Adam there was one greater who has made it possible for mankind to inherit life through Him. Christ has the standing to answer for man's disobedience. He could and did take upon Him the sins of all His posterity.[832]

Women descend from mother Eve, who was born the biological daughter of Heavenly Mother. Women descend from Heavenly Mother to endow them with Her creative power of fertility to bear the souls of men. Eve was not beneath Adam, nor subject to his rule when first created. Eve was put beside him to complete him and be his helpmeet.

There was another condition required to enable Christ to lawfully redeem the daughters of Eve as well as the sons of Adam. The parable of the creation includes this step to put Eve under Adam's responsibility. The account explains that Eve (and by extension her daughters) was put under Adam's rule. Adam was handed responsibility and accountability for Eve. These are the words in the parable:

> [T]hy desire shall be to thy husband, and he shall *rule over thee*.[833]

Adam was made accountable to "rule" in the fallen world.[834] All the mistakes, mismanagements, failings, wars, and difficulties of mortality are the responsibility of the appointed "ruler."[835] Adam would not have been accountable for Eve unless she was made subject to his "rule." Once under Adam's rule, the redemption of Adam became also the redemption of Eve. Therefore Adam and the

---

[828] NC Romans 1:24; see also, Romans 5:18-19.

[829] NC I Cor. 1:66; see also, I Cor. 15:45.

[830] NC Hebrews 1:1; see also, Heb. 1:2.

[831] NC John 1:1; see also, John 1:3.

[832] Isa. 53:4-8.

[833] OC Gen. 2:15, emphasis added.

[834] A "ruler" is a teacher responsible for instructing others. See, e.g., NC 1 Ne. 1:9.

[835] See NC Jacob 1:4; see also, Jacob 1:19.

sons of Adam, and Eve and the daughters of Eve, were all rescued through Christ's atonement for mankind.

The parable continues with another allusion to Heavenly Mother:

> And Adam called his wife's name Eve, because *she*
> was the mother of all living, for thus have I, the Lord
> God, called the first of all women, which are many.[836]

One of the names of Heavenly Mother is "Eve."[837] She was the "mother of all living" because She was the one who mothered the spirits of Adam and Eve and was therefore parent of them both. Out of respect for Her, Adam called his companion by the same name as the Heavenly Mother.

Redemption of all mankind, male and female, required Adam to descend from Jesus Christ. It also required Adam to "rule," or be responsible to teach all those in his dominion. That role assigned to Adam was in order to extend the legal effect of Christ's redemption to Adam, Eve and their posterity.

However, for women to bear the souls of men, Eve had to be a direct descendant of Heavenly Mother. Although veiled for present, women's direct descent from the Heavenly Mother is also required for men to be placed on a throne in the hereafter. The Answer to Prayer for Covenant states:

> And again, I say to you, Abraham and Sarah sit
> upon a Throne, for *he could not be there if not for Sarah's
> covenant with him.* Isaac and Rebecca sit upon a
> Throne, and Isaac likewise *could not be there if not for
> Rebecca's covenant with him.* And Jacob and Rachel sit
> upon a Throne, and Jacob *could not be there if not for
> Rachel's covenant with him.* And all these have ascended
> above Dominions and Principalities and Powers, to
> abide in my Kingdom. Therefore the marriage
> covenant is needed for all those who would likewise
> seek to obtain from me the right to continue their

---

[836] OC Gen. 2:15, emphasis added. The "she" is the Heavenly Mother, who bore the spirits of all the souls who descend from Adam and Eve.

[837] She holds many names and titles. In this paper a few have been mentioned: The Great Weaver, The Great Dancer, Heavenly Mother and Eve. She has many others, having acquired those names by the works She has accomplished through eons of experience.

seed into eternity, for only through marriage can Thrones and Kingdoms be established.[838]

The creation of woman was designed to fulfill the work and the covenants of the Father in this world and will be critical in eternity. Families come through the union of the man and woman. Women bear the souls of mankind and bring all of us into this world through childbirth. That power was inherited from the Heavenly Mother. But there are other rights belonging to women that will only be apparent in either a completed temple or the afterlife. They have been endowed with an everlasting authority required for any man to occupy a throne in the Father's Kingdom.[839]

A fuller explanation of woman's role will require worthy people willing to be taught, and to build an acceptable house for the Elohim to return.-

Let me briefly mention the Word of Wisdom. This was a revelation inspired by a woman, Emma Smith, and given to her husband. It declares it is a "greeting" and "not a commandment or constraint." But it is a "revelation and the word of Wisdom" given to show "forth the order and will of God in the temporal salvation of all saints in the last days." The revelation is charged with kindly, motherly advice. "Wine or strong drink" is "not good" apart from the sacrament. For the sacrament it should be "pure wine of the grape of the vine" that we make. We are warned that "strong drinks" are not "for the belly" because many avoidable foolish physical and emotional errors are made when under the influence of "strong

---

[838] In Facsimile 3 of the Book of Abraham, the "Figure 2" standing behind the throne of Pharaoh is clearly female (although identified in this instance as King Pharaoh himself). Hathor, the great female god who personified motherhood and joy, was often depicted with the horned sun disc, carrying the ankh symbol, as in "Figure 2." Amun was the Egyptian equivalent to God the Father. Hathor was his female companion. Their son was called Horus in his immortal state and Osiris when he became mortal. Osiris' wife was Isis. As the mortal Horus, Osiris was slain by his usurping brother Set. In depicting male figures on thrones, there is usually a female (Hathor or Isis) standing behind and supporting the male on the throne.

[839] For example, prior to His death Christ had to be anointed by a woman. He said, "she has wrought a good work upon me." (NC Matt. 12:1.) This had to be done by a woman, and needed to be done before Christ's death. "She has poured this ointment on my body for my burial." (*Id.*) Whenever that original version of the religion Christ restored is preached, it must include the same rite as a memorial to her. (*Id.*)

drink."[840] Wine and strong drink tempt us into errors.[841] The Mother urges us to find wisdom, prudence, counsel, understanding, truth, excellent things, and nothing that is froward or perverse. "Wine is a mocker, strong drink is raging and whosoever is deceived thereby is not wise."[842] Wine and strong drink remove us out from the correct pathway, cause us to err in vision, and make us stumble in judgment.[843] We must do better.

Any kindly advice from a caring Mother ought to be followed. Particularly when we are promised that by following it we will "receive health in their navel and marrow to their bones; and shall find wisdom and great treasures of knowledge, even hidden treasures; and shall run and not be weary, and shall walk and not faint."[844]

If you think of yourself as a Christian and this essay offends you, or confuses your imagined picture of God's Great Plan of Happiness, then I would recommend you leave this topic alone for the present. Do not reject truth only because you find it challenging. Just leave it alone. If you think of yourself as a Mormon and this talk introduces ideas you have not heard before, look at the scriptures with this talk in mind and see if these teachings have not been in your scriptures all along. You just haven't noticed it. Truth deserves patient and careful consideration.

If you welcome this information, then take care that you do not, as ancient Israel did, "burn incense, pour out drink offerings and bake cakes" to a Being who has never invited you to do so. She has invited you to worship God the Father and His Son, Jesus Christ. If you would like to honor Her, then accept Her testimony and look to Jesus Christ alone for redemption and salvation from the fall of Adam. That is where we presently find ourselves, and Christ is the way our Divine Parents have provided to deliver us from our fallen plight.

---

[840] D&C 89.

[841] Christ listed drinking with the "drunk" as one of the signs of those who would be unprepared at his return. See NC Matt. 11:14

[842] OC Proverbs 4:298; see also KJV Prov. 20:1. In the New International Version this verse reads: "Wine is a mocker and beer a brawler; whoever is led astray by them is not wise."

[843] "But they also have erred through wine, and through strong drink are out of the way; the priest and the prophet have erred through strong drink, they are swallowed up of wine, they are out of the way through strong drink; they err in vision, they stumble in judgment." KJV Isa. 28:7.

[844] D&C 89:18-20.

## Chapter 8: Problems in Restoration History

Reconstructing a complete and accurate history for the restoration using available records is challenging if not outright impossible. Although there have been many histories written attempting to provide an accurate account, serious problems remain in understanding the restoration. There are two separate challenges. First, it is difficult to describe an accurate record of events. That is followed by the greater difficulty to decide how to interpret the events. History requires understanding how and why events are to be understood in an overall pattern. Determining that pattern is more challenging than sorting out the record.[845]

Restoration history begins with Joseph Smith. He was a controversial figure and people who met him became noteworthy because of their association with him. Assuming they had something to say regarding their relationship with him, their opinions about him became important to historians. Opinions based on personal experience with someone noteworthy are considered important: even if their contact was passing and colored by their prejudices, limitations or ignorance. Hence, there are many contemporaneous opinions about Joseph Smith used by historians to reconstruct events.

Those unkindly disposed toward him, took the opportunity to speak poorly about him. Any event that reflected badly, or any negative embellishment of an event, became part of the record. The earliest adverse account was by Doctor Philastus Hulbut, who made it his mission to gather impugning affidavits about Joseph Smith. Eber D. Howe published that collection in the anti-Mormon book *Mormonism Unvailed*[846] There were also four derisive pamphlets

---

[845] An Appendix follows this essay to illustrate these challenges. It has an introduction followed by three documents. They allow the reader to evaluate whether they should be used to understand events in Nauvoo, and, if so, how they should be used.

antagonistic to Joseph Smith and the religion he was founding published in 1838.[847] A flood of other unfavorable histories soon followed. Historians who want to portray Joseph in a negative light have a wealth of information from such sources with which to compose a contrary interpretation.

Followers and believers in Joseph's claims were disposed to tell, and oftentimes embellish, anything that held him in a positive light.[848] Doting admirers wrote a great deal of laudatory material.[849] Historians who want to portray Joseph in a heroic light also have a wealth of information from these sources with which to compose a positive interpretation.

Should the history of the restoration be composed relying only on Joseph's critics? Should it be written relying only on Joseph's admirers? Until recently, most of the histories written of the restoration chose one or the other. Recent histories attempt to walk a middle path and allow both sides to contribute to the story. However, both sides are prone to exaggeration and overstatement. Mixing them together is not much better than leaving them apart. Sorting through the contradictions has made for interesting storytelling, but it does not give an accurate history.

After the first challenge is addressed by deciding what facts to trust, the second problem is how to interpret the facts. Is there a theme? Is there an overall narrative that accounts for the facts, smoothing them into a consistent tale that makes sense?

Assembling events into a sensible story is influenced by what kind of historian tells the tale. For example, the Annales School of historical materialism[850] categorizes events into major trends over

---

[846] The book was published in 1834. Its full title is, *Mormonism Unvailed: Or, A Faithful Account of That Singular Imposition and Delusion from Its Rise to the Present Time. With Sketches of the Characters of Its Propagators, and a Full Detail of the Manner in Which the Famous Golden Bible Was Brought Before the World. To Which Are Added, Inquiries into the Probability That the Historical Part of the Said Bible Was Written by One Solomon Spalding, More Than Twenty Years Ago, and by Him Intended to Have Been Published As a Romance.*

[847] *Mormonism Exposed* by Sunderland, *Mormonism Exposed* by Bacheler, *Antidote to Mormonism* by M'Chesney, and *Exposure of Mormonism* by Livesey.

[848] For example, *The Autobiography of Parley P. Pratt.*

[849] For example, John Taylor's announcement of Joseph Smith's death was canonized in scripture. Orson Pratt's *An Interesting Account of Several Remarkable Visions* was published in 1842.

long periods of time. Demographic changes, economic crises, even geography are used to explain why events happened. Cultural historians look at anthropological and linguistic themes[851] to develop their account of history. Psychohistorians attempt to uncover the inner motivations of individuals to explain why things happened.[852] They attempt to use social sciences to determine the emotional origin behind events.[853] There are dozens of different schools of historical thought. How each retells these events is based on framing the experiences to fit their view of how history should be told. Writing history is explaining how to interpret events.

People do not live interpreted lives. They pass through a sequence of adventures, sometimes wildly disconnected from any overall theme, day-by-day, inside common experiences. Even if you are in the place at the time something happens because all the world is at war with one another, and you have been brought to the battlefield by one of the great opposing powers, your day will begin by waking up and eating breakfast. President Roosevelt and Adolph Hitler are not part of your daily experience. Even Eisenhower, as Supreme Commander of the Allied Forces, is so distant from an infantryman as to hardly be noticed in daily life. If you ask the infantryman to tell his story about what happened on June 6, 1944, he will tell you of the violence, noise, injuries, and death he witnessed on 175 yards of a 3.6 mile-long beach code-named "Omaha." Life is experienced in a microcosm. History is told as if each microcosm fit into a narrative having sweep and breadth and height to give meaning and message for the microcosm.

During the leading edge of the attack, one Navy sailor who piloted a landing craft filled with Army Infantrymen to Omaha Beach was so frightened by the conflagration he sailed toward that he dropped the ramp too soon, exposing the troops aboard to incoming fire. The Infantrymen on his boat, including my father, jumped into

---

[850] Fernand Braudel and Marc Bloch founded the *Annales d'Histoire Economique et. Sociale* in 1929 as the written voice for their approach.

[851] They try to bring the past to life by including beliefs, ritual, and everyday objects to recreate the world as it was experienced in the past.

[852] Psychohistorians believed conventional historians ignored important psychological and sociological influences on events and wanted these influences to be used to explain events.

[853] Fawn Brodie used this approach in writing her biography of Joseph Smith, *No Man Knows My History*.

the English Channel weighed down by approximately 80 pounds of gear and munitions. Because they had not yet reached the beach, my father and his companions faced drowning as the first threat in the battle. Years later he reflected, "if I had known the Navy pilot was a coward I would have shot him, commandeered the boat, and drove it ashore to save my friends. Everyone shorter than me drowned before they had a chance to fight."

What my father saw, heard and felt that day was deeply personal and extremely local. His life that day, and every day thereafter, was experienced moment-to-moment with no overarching theme or school of interpretation guiding it. He lived it. It was his; and when he died after 86 years of those experiences he took them all with him.

How should his story be told? Hiding behind tank traps on the shoreline was necessary to survive the incoming machinegun and mortar fire. It was common sense. But after these men had been surrounded for a time by deafening death and dismemberment, pitiful cries from the dead and dying, paralyzing desperation turned to outrage and anger. That supreme moral indignation propelled first a few, and then a wave of men from behind the safety of the tank traps, mortar divots, and fallen comrades to charge their protected enemy above. These men hazarded their lives to end this outrage. The value of lives of their slaughtered friends deserved respect. It was because of their losses that they charged forward to stop this unmerciful hail of death.

Were there geopolitical issues involved? Not for my father and his companions on that morning. Was military history being written? Of course, but that was nothing to those men. They gave it no thought. A violent and merciless enemy, behind concrete and atop a bluff overlooking the beach, needed to be destroyed. Every instant these predators remained capable of inflicting death was an insult to the memory of slain friends. More friends would die in coming moments if those in the bunkers overhead were not destroyed.

Great moments, even the greatest of moments, are experienced only by individuals inside a very small sphere. This is true of the restoration. The great narratives that have been written about the restoration tell us nothing about what happened. Historians always interpret and massage an account no one experienced, no one lived, no one understood as it happened. Historians provide interpretations. They cannot tell us what individuals understood when they were writing letters or diaries. They cannot explain how personal conversations were interpreted, or how difficult events were framed in the lives of those who experienced them. Historians of the restoration can never explain what individuals understood and experienced who wrote the letters and diaries, who had the personal conversations, who lived through the difficult events. We are all denied access to the daily thoughts of those now long deceased. We do not know and those involved cannot tell us.

Perhaps it does not matter which school of history is used in retelling the story of the restoration. Maybe all of them will invariably be wrong. That seems to be what Nephi predicted. Nephi condemns using our carefully studied historical techniques, rather than inspiration from God:

> [T]hey shall contend one with another, and their priests shall contend one with another, and they shall teach with their learning, and deny the holy ghost which giveth utterance. And they deny the power of God, the Holy One of Israel. And they say unto the people, Hearken unto us and hear ye our precept, ...there shall be many which shall teach after this manner false, and vain, and foolish doctrines, and shall be puffed up in their hearts, and shall seek deep to hide their counsels from the Lord. And their works shall be in the dark, and the blood of the saints shall cry from the ground against them.[854]

Restoration history has been more or less composed using the 'learning of men', or recognized historical interpretive forms. If teaching with man's learning will cause us to accept false, vain and foolish ideas, then it is a mistake. True history should be informed by God's viewpoint. Do people believe the scriptures? I could not find a history written by someone who trusted scripture to provide the interpretation.

I wrote a history of the restoration.[855] In it, instead of interpreting events from existing records, I used the scriptures to give the interpretation. The book assumes the prophecies found in the Book of Mormon and the revelations of Joseph Smith give to us the correct interpretation. Using the prophecies as the framework, I

---

[854] NC 2 Nephi 12:1.
[855] *Passing the Heavenly Gift*, (Salt Lake: Mill Creek Press, 2011).

looked for support in the known events to see if the events met the predicted narrative. There is abundant proof. It is sobering.

For example, Christ prophesied the gentiles would reject the fullness of the gospel. He attributed the prophecy to His Father. The prophecy is unequivocal, and does not speak about gentile rejection as merely possible or uncertain, but declares it as an inevitable event to certainly occur:

> At that day when the gentiles shall sin against my gospel, and shall reject the fullness of my gospel, and shall be lifted up in the pride of their hearts above all nations and above all the people of the whole earth, and shall be filled with all manner of lyings, and of deceits, and of mischiefs, and all manner of hypocrisy, and murders, and priestcrafts, and whoredoms, and of secret abominations, and if they shall do all these things, and shall reject the fullness of my gospel, Behold, saith the Father, I will bring the fullness of my gospel from among them.[856]

The question then is what would that have looked like? Was there anything in the events from 1820 to 1844 to suggest the gentiles did reject the fullness of Christ's gospel? Joseph Smith was driven out of Kirtland. In Missouri, the betrayal by church leaders, including the three witnesses and several apostles, resulted in his imprisonment. There is a detailed account of this treachery by the Mormons in a book about Joseph.[857]

If Christ's prophecy is true, gentiles must at some point reject the fullness of the gospel. They must become extraordinarily lifted up in the pride of their hearts. How might this have already been accomplished? Does the claim they are the "only true church" and only they will be saved, while all others will be damned, fit the charge? The Lord foretold of gentile pride that will be "above all nations and above all the people of the whole earth." There is evidence to suggest this has happened, and is happening.

As for lying and deceiving, the LDS church appears to have adopted dishonesty as a policy to deal with troubling historical issues.[858]

---

[856] NC 3 Nephi 7:5.

[857] *A Man Without Doubt*, (Salt Lake: Mill Creek Press, 2016).

[858] See, e.g., Boyd Kirkland, Building the Kingdom with Total Honesty, in *Dialogue: A Journal of Mormon Thought* Volume 31, Number 3, Fall 1998, "Letters to the Editor." He tells his experience with leaders' deception about

The institution's history of deceit is not difficult to uncover. Because of this historic lack of honesty, the LDS Historian's Office is now publishing essays on church history to address this lack of candor. The essays attempt to explain First Vision Accounts,[859] Plural Marriage in Kirtland and Nauvoo,[860] Race and the Priesthood,[861] Book of Mormon Translation,[862] Translation and Historicity of the Book of Abraham,[863] Joseph Smith's Teachings about Priesthood, Temple and Women,[864] and others.[865] The LDS church recently published a new version of the restoration history using heterodox sources for the first time.[866]

---

the Adam-God doctrine during Spencer W. Kimball's presidency. Lying was used to keep from losing its members. He learned from first presidency secretary Michael Watson that his inquiry was channeled through apostle Mark E. Peterson. They acknowledged they were deliberately deceiving church members about the issue. He inquired, "Wasn't there concern that some might be dismayed and disillusioned by their church leaders' lack of candor?...they said, in essence, 'If a few people lose their testimonies over this, so be it; it's better than letting the true facts be known, and dealing with the probable wider negative consequences to the mission of the church.'" See also, D. Michael Quinn, LDS Church Authority and New Plural Marriages: 1890-1904, Dialogue: A Journal of Mormon Thought, Vol. 18, No. 1, Spring 1985, pp. 9-105, in which he documents lying about discontinuing plural marriages during a 14 year period between the dishonest and misleading public abandonment and actual policy change. See also, Boyd K. Packer, The Mantle is Far, Far Greater Than the Intellect, 1981 BYU Studies, Vol. 21, No. 3, pp. 259-271, in which he advised Church Education Employees to suppress historical truths if they were "not very useful." Dallin Oaks declared that criticizing church leaders was never appropriate, "It does not matter that the criticism is true." Reading Church History, CES Doctrine and Covenants Symposium, BYU, 16 August 1985, p. 25; which he repeated in Criticism, Ensign, February 1987, p. 68. Among many other examples.

[859] https://www.lds.org/topics/first-vision-accounts?lang=eng
[860] https://www.lds.org/topics/plural-marriage-in-kirtland-and-nauvoo?lang=eng
[861] https://www.lds.org/topics/race-and-the-priesthood?lang=eng
[862] https://www.lds.org/topics/book-of-mormon-translation?lang=eng
[863] https://www.lds.org/topics/translation-and-historicity-of-the-book-of-abraham?lang=eng
[864] https://www.lds.org/topics/joseph-smiths-teachings-about-priesthood-temple-and-women?lang=eng
[865] https://www.lds.org/topics/essays?lang=eng
[866] *Saints: Vol. 1, 1815-1846: The Standard of Truth*, (Salt Lake: Deseret Book,

An example of some historical hypocrisy is evident in looking at the part the Mormons played in alienating their neighbors in Missouri and Illinois. The Missourians were rough, but Mormons were equally terrible neighbors. It was the July 4th "Salt Sermon" given by Sidney Rigdon that first threatened to "exterminate" the Missourians. However, when Mormons retell the events, they express outrage and contempt over Governor Lilbern Boggs' *Extermination Order*, as if he originated the idea of "extermination." Even when Mormons were the aggressors they portray themselves as victims and all others as their unjust persecutors. Sometimes Missourians were scared by threats from the Mormons. Sometimes Mormons shot first. Sometimes Mormons raided and burned farms first.

These are not happy things. There is no celebrating the gentile rejection of the fullness. But it is more harmful to ignore that rejection than to acknowledge it. There can be no attempt to fix the failure until there is an admission that it has happened. The fullness was rejected. Mormonism lapsed into apostasy.

Mormon warned the gentiles about polluting the holy church of God by loving wealth more than the suffering and needy:

> O ye wicked, and perverse, and stiffnecked people, why have you built up churches unto yourselves to get gain? Why have ye transfigured the holy word of God that ye might bring damnation upon your souls? Behold, look ye unto the revelations of God, for behold, the time cometh at that day when all these things must be fulfilled. Behold, the Lord hath shewn unto me great and marvelous things concerning that which must shortly come at that day when these things shall come forth among you. Behold, I speak unto you as if ye were present, and yet ye are not. But behold, Jesus Christ hath shewn you unto me, and I know your doing, and I know that ye do walk in the pride of your hearts. And there are none, save a few only, who do not lift themselves up in the pride of their hearts, unto the wearing of very fine apparel, unto envying, and strifes, and malice, and persecutions, and all manner of iniquity. And your churches, yea, even every one,

---

2018).

have become polluted because of the pride of your hearts. For behold, ye do love money, and your substance, and your fine apparel, and the adorning of your churches, more than ye love the poor and the needy, the sick and the afflicted. O ye pollutions, ye hypocrites, ye teachers who sell yourselves for that which will canker, why have ye polluted the holy church of God? Why are ye ashamed to take upon you the name of Christ? Why do ye not think that greater is the value of an endless happiness than that misery which never dies? Because of the praise of the world? Why do ye adorn yourselves with that which hath no life, and yet suffer the hungry, and the needy, and the naked, and the sick, and the afflicted to pass by you and notice them not?[867]

There is proof this has happened among the gentiles who believe the Book of Mormon. The LDS church-owned Deseret News helped advance a program to discourage the public from noticing and contributing to beggars. Billboards in Salt Lake proclaimed: "Support panhandlers, and you support drug trafficking." "Support panhandlers, and you support crime." "Support panhandlers, and you support alcoholism."[868] LDS church owned KSL did an expose titled, *Business of Begging: The real stories behind Utah panhandling*, in which every story they reported showed the panhandlers were engaged in fraud and criminality.[869] There is compelling evidence, or at least some reason, to conclude the gentiles, in their pride, suffer the needy and hungry to pass by unnoticed.

In addition to advocating that people suffer the hungry and needy to pass by unnoticed, the LDS church has also accumulated great wealth. The Salt Lake television station, KUTV, reported that at the end of 2017 the LDS church had stock investments totaling $32,769,914,000.00.[870] The LDS church invested in excess of $2

---

[867] NC Mormon 4:5

[868] Officials: Begging 'abets lawlessness,' don't give panhandlers cash, *Deseret News*, July 13, 2017.

[869] See Mike Headrick, KSL.com, November 25, 2013.

[870] The report was based on documents made public by MormonLeaks. The investments included: Ashmore Wealth Management LLT, valued at $1,918,532,000.00; Argyll Research LLC, valued at $446,327,000.00; Clifton Park Capital Management, LLC, valued at $880,518,000.00; Cortland

billion in a shopping mall across from Temple Square in Salt Lake City.[871] In November 2013, the LDS church purchased 382,834 acres in the Florida panhandle for $565,000,000.[872] The *Christian Science Monitor* reported this purchase, added to the previous holdings, which include Deseret Ranches, near Orlando, Florida, made the LDS church the largest landowner in Florida.[873]

The LDS church does not make its financial information public. The total value of its land, banking, printing, radio, television, universities, and other non-religious holdings likely dwarf the total value of its extensive chapel, temple and church administration properties. Consider for a moment the present value of the LDS church against the words of Mormon that "ye do love money, and your substance, and your fine apparel, and the adorning of your churches, more than ye love the poor and the needy, the sick and the afflicted." There is compelling proof, or at least some reason to conclude, that "the holy church of God" has been polluted by the gentiles. Why not at least consider the possibility that prophecy has been fulfilled?

If Mormon has given us the correct interpretation, the gentiles have lifted themselves up in pride, and love money and substance in a way that pollutes their church and offends God. This should awaken people. It is time to face an awful situation. Nothing can be done to improve this bleak outlook until the failures are acknowledged.

In a January 1841 revelation, the gentiles were commanded to build a temple. God offered to visit that temple and restore again the

---

Advisers LLC, valued at 2,177,742,000.00; Elkfork Partners LLC, valued at $3,687,774,000.00; Flinton Capital Management LLC, valued at $2,943,847,000.00; Glen Harbor Capital Management LLC, valued at $4,407,275,000.00; Green Valley Investors LLC, valued at $2,098,464,000.00; Meadow Creek Investment Management LLC, valued at $4,603,236,000.00; Neuburgh Advisers LLC, valued at $2,791,122,000.00; Riverhead Capital Management LLC, valued at $2,361,388,000.00; Tiverton Asset Management LLC, valued at $1,598,252,000.00; Tyers Asset Management, valued at $2,855,436,000.00. The companies have a combined value of $32,769,914,000.00.

[871] See, The money behind the message, *Salt Lake Tribune*, October 5, 2012.

[872] See, LDS Church makes large timberland purchase in Florida Panhandle, *Deseret News*, November 10, 2013.

[873] Gary Fineout, Associated Press, Mormon church: Florida's biggest private landowner? November 9, 2013.

fullness.[874] However, God's offer was conditional, and the required temple was to be built within "sufficient time" to meet His command:

> But I command you, all you my saints, to build a house unto me, and I grant unto you a sufficient time to build a house unto me, and during this time your baptisms shall be acceptable unto me. But behold, at the end of this appointment, your baptisms for your dead shall not be acceptable unto me. And if you do not these things, at the end of the appointment, you shall be rejected as a church, with your dead, says the Lord your God. For verily I say unto you that after you have had sufficient time to build a house unto me, wherein the ordinance of baptizing for the dead belongs, and for which the same was instituted from before the foundation of the world, your baptisms for your dead cannot be acceptable unto me, for therein are the keys of the Holy Priesthood ordained that you may receive honor and glory.[875]

The revelation does not explain how long the "appointment" would last. It did not set a limit on "sufficient time" for the command to be accomplished. But the Lord does make it very clear that if the commandment was not obeyed, the gentiles faced the risk of being rejected as a church with their kindred dead. Accordingly, this revelation set a requirement that put the gentiles in peril.

Although there was no set time, there was a sign given. The sign would make it possible to determine whether the time expired and the gentiles were rejected. Here is the sign:

> If you labor with all your mights, I will consecrate that spot that it shall be made holy. And if my people will hearken unto my voice and unto the voice of my servants whom I have appointed to lead my people, behold, verily I say unto you, They shall not be moved out of their place. And it shall come to pass that if you build a house unto my name and do not do the things that I say, I will not

---

[874] See T&C 141:10: " For there is not place found on earth that he may come and restore again that which was lost unto you, or which he has taken away, even the fullness of the Priesthood."

[875] T&C 141:11

perform the oath which I make unto you, neither fulfill the promises which you expect at my hands, says the Lord. For instead of blessings, you, by your own works, bring cursings, wrath, indignation, and judgments upon your own heads, by your follies and by all your abominations which you practice before me, says the Lord.[876]

The "appointment" that granted "sufficient time" would either be accomplished or the gentiles would be rejected. The sign of accomplishing the commandment would be, "They shall not be moved out of their place." This could either mean the servants "appointed to lead" (Joseph and Hyrum) would not be moved out of their place. Or, it could refer to the gentiles that would not be moved out of Nauvoo. Either meaning was fulfilled by the sign of gentile rejection. Joseph and Hyrum were slain three-and-a-half years later on June 27, 1844. At that time the Nauvoo Temple had only been completed up to the second floor. So the servants were removed. Then in the winter of 1846 the gentiles were forcibly evicted from Nauvoo under threat of attack. Both the Lord's chosen servants and the proud Nauvoo gentiles themselves were moved out of their place. Either way, the events comport with the promised sign and testify that God rejected the gentiles.

The second part of the sign foretold what would happen thereafter. Instead of securing the blessings God offered them, the gentiles would inherit "cursings, wrath, indignation, and judgments upon [their] own heads, by [their] follies and by all [their] abominations." The history of the gentile suffering in their westward exile to live on a salt flat is well documented. Nauvoo was located beside the largest river in North America. The gentiles relocated to a desert where they struggled for generations to survive.

Like Mormon, Nephi also foretold of the gentile failure to receive and obey when given the opportunity. He identified it as a problem caused by gentile leadership:

> Yea, they have all gone out of the way, they have become corrupted; because of pride, and because of false teachers, and false doctrine, their churches have become corrupted, and their churches are lifted up; because of pride, they are

---

[876] T&C 141:13-14.

puffed up. They rob the poor because of their fine sanctuaries; they rob the poor because of their fine clothing, and they persecute the meek and the poor in heart because in their pride they are puffed up. They wear stiff necks and high heads, yea, and because of pride, and wickedness, and abominations, and whoredoms, they have all gone astray, save it be a few who are the humble followers of Christ. Nevertheless, they are led, that in many instances they do err because they are taught by the precepts of men.[877]

This description by Nephi, though slightly different, contains the same message as Mormon's. Corrupt leaders who teach false doctrine would lead the gentiles. As though they already had all truth that would save them, they would urge and condone pride in their religion. Again the theme of robbing the poor by aggregating religious wealth describes the gentile rejection of the truth. Nephi states bluntly, "They have all gone astray." There is no "true church" but only prideful false ones that proclaim corrupt and false doctrine. "All" have "gone astray"—except only some "few who are the humble followers of Christ." It was to those I dedicated the first book I wrote.[878]

Although the gentiles were destined to reject the fullness, they nevertheless kept the Book of Mormon in print for over a century-and-a-half. The Book of Mormon contains the guidance necessary to recover the fullness. And the Book of Mormon also predicts that, despite their failure, some few gentiles could yet become covenant people.

Christ gave a sign to watch for as evidence the covenants made with the Father were about to be fulfilled. At some point following the gentile rejection of the fullness, some few gentiles would accept a covenant. When they accept the covenant they become numbered with the remnant. These covenant gentiles, numbered with the remnant, will build the last days Zion.

> [T]he gentiles, if they will not harden their hearts, that they may repent, and come unto me, and

---

[877] NC 2 Nephi 12:2.

[878] The dedication in *The Second Comforter: Conversing With the Lord Through the Veil* states: "Dedicated to the 'few, who are the humble followers of Christ.' (2 Ne. 28:14)"

be baptized in my name, and know of the true points of my doctrine, that they may be numbered among my people, O house of Israel — and when these things come to pass, that thy seed shall begin to know these things, it shall be a sign unto them that they may know that the work of the Father hath already commenced unto the fulfilling of the covenant which he hath made unto the people who are of the house of Israel. And when that day shall come, it shall come to pass that kings shall shut their mouths, for that which had not been told them shall they see, and that which they had not heard shall they consider.[879]

This happened on September 3, 2017 in Boise, Idaho when the Lord renewed a covenant with the gentiles. Some of the gentiles are now numbered among the Lord's people as part of the House of Israel. They have the right, if they continue faithfully, to establish Zion. To do so, the lusts, strife and contentions that doomed the gentiles in Joseph Smith's day must be avoided.

No single individual ever experienced the history of the restoration. After the church historian left the faith and absconded with the records he had maintained, Joseph Smith wrote down his recollection of events in 1838. Joseph could only tell what he knew. Thereafter, histories have been written by weaving together excerpts from here and there, never attempting to see if the results mirrored the story scripture foretold. Even excerpts from here and there are not the full pictures. Mark Twain observed:

What a wee little part of a person's life are his acts and his words! His real life is led in his head and is known to none but himself. All day long, and every day, the mill of his brain is grinding, and his thoughts, not those other things, are his history. His acts and his words are merely the visible, thin crust of his world, with its scattered snow summits and its vacant wastes of water—and they are so trifling a part of his bulk! A mere skin enveloping it. The mass of him is hidden—it and its volcanic fires that toss and boil, and never rest, night nor day. These

---

[879] NC 3 Nephi 9:11.

are his life, and they are not written, and cannot be written. Every day would make a whole book of eighty thousand words—three hundred and sixty-five books a year. Biographies are but the clothes and buttons of the man—the biography of the man himself cannot be written.[880]

There are many histories of D-Day. The code name for that invasion was "Operation Overlord." The plan was intended to spread soldiers across sites on the shores of Normandy codenamed Utah, Sword, Gold, Juno and Omaha beaches. The hope was for some or all to break through the shoreline defenses and establish an Allied base of operations to invade Europe.

My father rarely spoke of Omaha Beach. He never used his role in D-Day as a credential. For him it was just an experience, not something to boast about. Most of those who met him after WWII were unaware of his experience. He did not want it to define him.

My mother said for a long time after the war he would have a recurring nightmare. He dreamt he was in a foxhole that was overrun by Nazis. When he tried to shoot the soldier in front of him his gun fell apart. His enemy took advantage of his defenselessness and bayonetted my father, at which point he would awaken in a jump, sometimes letting out a yell. After some years the nightmares ended.

My father was reluctant to talk about the war. When we could coax something from him it would be a sentence, not a paragraph. He mentioned on one occasion the English Channel looked that morning as if it "was made of GI[881] blood."

I was with him the night before he died. It was the first time he raised the subject of that battle. He said it puzzled him why his life had been spared when so many of his friends had died that morning. I gave him no answer, but know that without his survival I would not have been born. He was as healthy and well on the morning of June 7th as he had been before wading ashore on June 6th. Although his mind was perplexed by the kindness of providence watching over him, and heaven allowing others to be injured or slaughtered that day, he lived gratefully and fully for nearly a half-century. His history was not written. In all the accounts that have explained D-Day, none of

---

[880] *Mark Twain's Autobiography*, with an introduction by Albert Bigelow Paine, 2 vols. (New York: Harper and Brothers, 1924), 1:[xviii].
[881] The letters "GI" stood for "government issued" and was the shorthand way of referring to a soldier.

them can be complete if they do not address why providence spared some and took others. Of course, that is an answer only God can provide.

God has not written histories for most of this world's events. But God did give an account of the restoration in scripture.[882] That account was composed as prophecy, foretelling how the gentiles would first fail, and later some few would covenant with Him and be numbered with Israel.

The history of the restoration is incomplete and still being written. Its conclusion will be years in the future, and there is tremendous work left to complete. Until everything returns and God has gathered again in one all of His revelations, restored the religion taught to Adam in the beginning, established Zion, and opened the veil between heaven and earth so that God, men and angels again mingle with one another, the restoration is not finished.

When the earth is full of the knowledge of God as the seas are filled with water, the restoration will be completed. At that future time no one will need to say to another, "know the Lord" because everyone will know Him.[883]

Until then there is a great task remaining. If you do not realize the work remains undone, then you do not believe the Book of Mormon.

There is no reason to think us specially favored by God. But there is good reason to think us challenged by God to do much more than has been done by the gentiles. There is every reason to fear failure because of the prior gentile failures. Even while a great and wealthy gentile church proclaims that it is the Lord's, and it is the only true church, and it cannot lead any astray, all need to awaken and arise from the deep slumber that has overtaken the restoration. We have been misled. We have fallen from the truth. We have rejected the fullness. And we must repent and return, or as the Book of Mormon warns, "awake and arise" from this awful situation.[884]

There have been many casualties. We may miss those who are taken in by the many false claims exploding all around us. But the objective is clear: Rise up to occupy that raised bluff where Zion is to

---

[882] In addition to the Book of Mormon and prophecies of Joseph Smith, the *Prayer for Covenant*, T&C 156, was written under the inspiration of God and also provides an account of events during the restoration.

[883] OC Jeremiah 12:9.

[884] See, e.g., NC 2 Ne. 1:3; Mosiah 1:12; 3 Ne. 9:9; Ether 3:18; Moro. 10:6.

be built. The battle rages all around. All must charge forward to engage the battle, and hasten to the sound of that conflict. There must be success where others have failed.

# APPENDIX

The most often discussed issue in Mormon history is polygamy. It is in the center of on-going controversy, and continues to be publicly debated. A library of conflicting material has been written to imagine how it started. Therefore, polygamy is a useful topic to illustrate the challenge of reconstructing accurate history.

Mormons who followed Brigham Young were told that Joseph Smith introduced polygamy and intended to have it continue. Splinter groups from followers of Young likewise attribute its introduction and necessity to Joseph Smith. The RLDS rejected this idea. They trusted Smith's widow, Emma Smith, who denied that Joseph ever practiced polygamy. The renamed Community of Christ has, in recent years, begun to concede the point polygamy was Joseph Smith's creation.

Three documents are in this Appendix. They involve determining what events should be used for retelling history. These were written by eye witnesses who lived through the events described in the letters, and were composed in 1853, 1859 and 1879. The first two were written by William Marks, the stake president of Nauvoo at the time Joseph and Hyrum were killed. Both of his letters address polygamy. Both show Joseph Smith was opposed to the practice and intended to eliminate it in Nauvoo. These two letters raise as many questions as they answer, but clearly show Joseph Smith was intent on eliminating polygamy or plural wives.

The third letter is by William B. Smith, one of the church's twelve apostles and the brother of Joseph and Hyrum. He explains in his letter to Joseph's son what William understood caused the death of his father and uncle. William Smith believed there was a conspiracy among leaders in Nauvoo to kill Joseph and Hyrum. He also accuses Brigham Young, John Taylor, and Willard Richards of teaching secretly abominable doctrines involving the "plural wives system."

Even though the Nauvoo events and Carthage killings happened in the 1840s, we do not yet have an undisputed truth to tell. There are too many economic and ecclesiastical interests threatened by one story or the other. These three documents allow readers to reflect on how they should influence understanding events.

Should these sources be trusted? Did the stake president have a good opportunity to observe and report? Did he have any motivation to lie about the events? Did the brother and church apostle have a good opportunity to observe and report? Did he have any motivation to lie about the events? Should his suspicions be trusted? Does his description of those leading the LDS church as "reveling in the spoils of the Church robbed from the innocent and unsuspecting saints" betray any jealousy or envy of their wealth and power? Or does it instead justify his conclusion that ambitious men benefitted by killing his brothers?

As a thought experiment, consider these three letters as reliable and ask yourself: Do they change the way you understand the restoration? If so, in what way do they change your understanding? Then consider them as unreliable and ask yourself: Why should they be ignored? Are there any parts that should be considered, even if their overall message is unreliable? Does that change your understanding of the restoration? If so, in what way do they change your understanding? Are they consistent with scripture and prophecy?

Every document, letter, newspaper article, journal entry and note that has been written by any of the eye-witnesses need to go through that same sifting. Almost all of the restoration histories were written by advocates without disclosing how they sifted their sources. They may not even have a criteria to test reliability. If they start with a premise in mind, they may cull through material to support their premise, ignoring and dismissing all contrary proof. This is how I wrote *Passing the Heavenly Gift*: I started with the premise that prophecy foretold what would happen. Then I looked to see if there was proof consistent with prophecy. That may not be what an impartial historian would do, but I believe it is the only likely way to find the truth.

—o0o—

Epistle of Wm. Marks, Chief Evangelical Teacher in the School of Faith, to all the Traveling Teachers, Quorums and Classes of said School, in Jehovah's Presbytery of Zion, Greeting:[885]

Beloved Brethren:

Having been chosen and ordained chief Evangelical Teacher of the Schools of Faith in Jehovah's Presbytery of Zion, it becomes my

---

[885] William Marks, "Epistle", *Zions Harbinger and Baneemy's Organ* 3 (July 1853): 52-54 (published in St. Louis, by C.B. Thompson).

duty, to say something by way of encouragement, and also by way of instruction to those who are placed under my care, and supervision, and first, by way of encouragement let me state what I know in reference to the work in which we are engaged, in order to do this I must of necessity refer to my experience in the church. I was a member of the church some ten years before the death of Joseph and Hyrum Smith. I was appointed President of the Stake in Kirtland, Ohio in 1837, and continued in that office at Kirtland until the fall of 1838, when I was called by Revelation to Far West, Mo.; but before I arrived there, the Saints were ordered to leave the State; and when the Stake was organized at Nauvoo in the fall of 1839, I was appointed President thereof and continued in that office up to the death of Joseph the prophet. I always believed the work was of Divine origin, and that Joseph Smith was called of God to establish the church among the Gentiles.

During my administration in the church I saw and heard of many things that was practiced and taught that I did not believe to be of God; but I continued to do and teach such principles as were plainly revealed, as the law of the church, for I thought that pure and holy principles only would have a tendency to benefit mankind. Therefore, when the doctrine of polygamy was introduced into the church as a principle of exaltation, I took a decided stand against it; which stand rendered me quite unpopular with many of the leading ones of the church. I was also witness of the introduction (secretly) of a kingly form of government in which Joseph suffered himself to be ordained a king, to reign over the house of Israel forever; which I could not conceive to be in accordance with the laws of the church, but I did not oppose this move, thinking it none of my business.

Joseph, however, became convinced before his death that he had done wrong; for about three weeks before his death, I met him one morning in the street, and he said to me, "Brother Marks, I have something to communicate to you, we retired to a by-place, and set down together, when he said: "We are a ruined people." I asked, how so? He said: "This doctrine of polygamy, or Spiritual-wife system, that has been taught and practiced among us, will prove our destruction and overthrow. I have been deceived,"[886] said he, "in reference to its

---

[886] This report by Marks does not identify how Joseph was deceived. For example, should this be interpreted to mean Joseph was deceived when he taught it, or that he was deceived by others who taught it without his approval or consent? Who was the deceiver(s)?

practice; it is wrong; it is a curse to mankind, and we shall have to leave the United States soon, unless it can be put down and its practice stopped in the church. Now," said he, "Brother Marks, you have not received this doctrine, and how glad I am. I want you to go into the high council and I will have charges preferred against all who practice this doctrine, and I want you to try them by the laws of the church, and cut them off, if they will not repent and cease the practice of this doctrine; and" said he, "I will go into the stand and preach against it, with all my might, and in this way we may rid the church of this damnable heresy."

But before this plan could be put into execution, the mob began to gather and our attention necessarily, was directed to them.

I again met Joseph when he was about to start for Carthage. He said to me, "Bro. Marks, I have become convinced since I last saw you, that it is my duty to go to Carthage, and deliver myself up as a lamb to the slaughter."

I mentioned the circumstances of these conversations with Joseph to many of the brethren, immediately after his death, but the only effect it had was to raise a report that Brother Marks was about to apostatize; and my statement of the conversation in reference to the practice of polygamy was pronounced false by the Twelve and disbelieved; but I now testify that the above statements are verily true and correct.

When I found that there was no chance to rid the church of that abominable sin, as I viewed it, I made my arrangements to leave Nauvoo, and I did so firmly believing that the plans and designs of the great Jehovah in inspiring Joseph to bring forth the book of Mormon would yet be carried out in his own time, and in his own way. Well brethren I have lived to see the foundation, and the platform laid, the principles revealed, and the order given whereby the great work of the Father, can, and will be accomplished. There is no doubt resting on my mind in reference to this work of Baneemy being the work of God, for I am fully convinced that it is the work it purports to be, the work of the Father, spoken of in the book of Mormon to prepare the way for the restoration of his covenants to the house of Israel. Now all who are convinced of this fact ought to move forward and take a decided stand to labor for Jehovah and the benefit of mankind.

I intend from this time henceforth to labor in the cause, and give my influence and substance to speed the work. Now, I call upon you my brethren, one and all, who have been ordained and set apart to teach, and gather up the remnant seed of the church, to use all diligence and perseverance to gather them up to the place of preparation, (which place will be made known through the Harbinger and Organ, in the sub-committee's report) that we may be prepared, and receive the necessary instructions, to bear the kingdom to Israel.

It is necessary that all should bear in mind that the school of works in its first department will be opened at the next Solemn Assembly; and all should be prepared to send up an offering of sufficient magnitude to entitle them to receive a large blessing. The present impoverished condition of the Lord's treasury and the urgent necessity of obtaining a printing Press, and the removing of the Chief teacher to the place of gathering, and other contingent expenses, appeal forcibly to us to bring a large offering to the next Solemn Assembly to meet the present requirements of the work. A printing Press, we must have, and Brother Thompson must be removed, which will require means to accomplish and all should have the privilege of contributing their gift oblations, for the accomplishment of so desirable an object.

The gathering should be taught and all who have means to remove and to sustain themselves through the winter should be to the place of gathering this fall, so as to get the necessary instructions, for the work hereafter to be assigned to them. I expect to be at the Solemn Assembly in August and to go from thence to the place of gathering, there to remain during the winter, and I want the Chiefs of the different Quorums of Traveling Teachers to report to me as often as once in a month, that I may know of their whereabouts and what they are doing that I may communicate to them such information as they need in reference to their mission, and that of their Quorums.

Signed, Wm. MARKS

St. Louis, June 15, 1853.


—oOo—


OPPOSITION TO POLYGAMY,[887]

---

[887] WILLIAM MARKS. Shabbonas, Co., Ill., Oct. 23rd, 1859. (*The True Latter Day Saints' Herald*, published by the New Organization of The Church of Jesus Christ of Latter Day Saints, No. 1, Vol. 1, January 1860, pp.25 -26.)

BY THE PROPHET JOSEPH.

BROTHER Sheen-

I feel desirous to communicate through your periodical, a few suggestions made manifest to me by the Spirit of God, in relation to the Church of Jesus Christ of Latter Day Saints. About the first of June, 1844, (situated as I was at that time, being the Presiding Elder of the Stake at Nauvoo, and by appointment the Presiding Officer of the High Council) I had a very good opportunity to know the affairs of the Church, and my convictions at that time were, that the Church in a great measure had departed from the pure principles and doctrines of Jesus Christ. I felt much troubled in mind about the condition of the Church. I prayed earnestly to my Heavenly Father to show me something in regard to it, when I was wrapt in vision, and it was shown me by the Spirit, that the top or branches had overcome the root, in sin and wickedness, and the only way to cleanse and purify it was, to disorganize it, and in due time, the Lord would reorganize it again. There were many other things suggested to my mind, but the lapse of time has erased them from my memory. A few days after this occurrence I met with Brother Joseph. He said that he wanted to converse with me on the affairs of the Church, and we retired by ourselves. I will give his words verbatim, for they are indelibly stamped upon my mind. He said he had desired for a long time to have a talk with me on the subject. of polygamy. He said it eventually would prove the overthrow of the Church, and we should soon he obliged lie leave the United States, unless it could be speedily put down. He was satisfied that it was a cursed doctrine, and that there must be every exertion made to put it down. He said that he would go before the congregation and proclaim against it, and I must go the High Council, and he would prefer charges against those in transgression, and I must sever them from the Church, unless they made ample satisfaction. There was much more said, but this was the substance. The mob commenced to gather about Carthage in a few days after, therefore there was nothing done concerning it. After the Prophet's death I made mention of this conversation to several hoping and believing that it would have a good effect, but to my great disappointment, it was soon rumored about that Brother Marks was about to apostatize, and that all that he said about the conversation with the Prophet was a tissue of lies. From that time I was satisfied that the Church would be disorganized, and the death of the Prophet and Patriarch tended to confirm me in that opinion. From that time I was looking for a re-organization of the Church and Kingdom of God. I feel thankful that I have lived to again behold the day, when the basis of the Church is the revelations of Jesus Christ, which is the only sure foundation to build upon. I feel to invite all my brethren to become identified with us, for the Lord is truly in our midst.

—o0o—

## THE DEATH OF THE TWO MARTYRS.[888]

Joseph; Dear Nephew: -- Several times I have taken pen to write you on the subject of this caption, the death of the two Martyrs, and the principal causes that led to their death. But the causes have been so misunderstood and I have felt so diffident about writing the facts in the case as I understand them, that I have refrained from the task, for fear that the circumstances I have to name might throw a [black] influence upon the character of the man whom we all esteem as the prophet of God; and the longer I have put this matter off the more and more I have felt it impressed upon my mind that I should write. The history and the circumstances connected with the death of your father, and your Uncle Hyrum, are events that transpired, for the greater part while I was residing in Philadelphia in 1842-3-4, having charge of the Church in the east. But the links in the chain of circumstances that I am about to relate were occurrences that took place while I was on a visit to Nauvoo, for the purpose of attending the April Conference in 1844.

After attending the Conference held by the Church at that time, and also several of the political caucuses to nominate candidates for President of the United States, and business matters of this sort having been disposed of, (in which Lyman Wight, Brigham Young, John Taylor, Willard Richards, and H. C. Kimball were the principal speakers), I began to arrange matters to return to my family who were, as I have before stated, residing in the City of Philadelphia; and on the morning previous to my leaving Nauvoo, I called on your father and took breakfast with him. While seated at the table a conversation was had participated in by your mother, concerning some things that she had learned in the discharge of her mission

---

[888] *The Saints Herald, Official publication of the Reorganized Church of Jesus Christ of Latter Day Saints*, Vol. 26., No. 8, Plano, Ill., April 15, 1879.

among the Saints as one of a committee appointed by the Female Relief Society, to visit the Saints and look after the interest of the poor of Church; to enquire after their occupation and financial prospect for food and means of support. In relating her report she said that some complaint had been made to her by females whom she had visited, that John Taylor, Willard Richards, and Brigham Young had been teaching some doctrines among the Saints privately that was going to ruin the Church, unless there was a stop put to it, as it was contrary to the law and rules governing the Church. Your father remarked that he would attend to the matter as soon as he got through with his troubles with the Laws and Fosters. But mark you their conversation took place only a few days previous to your father's death. What that private teaching might have been, that those persons whom your mother named, were circulating in a clandestine manner, (since there has been so much said about a doctrine called the plural wife doctrine on this subject), I leave the reader to judge.

One other point I wish to notice in the conversation that took place while I was eating at your father's table, and that was, as the conversation turned upon Brigham Young, your father remarked that with regard to the charge brought against these brethren, that he expected that he would have trouble with Brigham Young, especially, and added that "should the time ever come that this man B. Young should lead the Church that he would lead it to hell." And these words I remember as plainly as though they were spoken but yesterday; as at this time I had not known that there could have been a charge of fault brought against the man. My association with this man Brigham Young for near three years previous, had been very limited, in consequence of our different localities and fields of labor.

These matters that I have thus named do not comprise the whole ground of the causes that led to your father's death; although in part it did, as this secret evil that had crept into the Church, by means of this private teaching, gave food and material for the Expositor press to pour out its vials of wrath upon the head of the prophet, making him responsible for the conduct and teachings of these secret and clandestine teachers. What fixes the stain of guilt upon these parties named in this letter making them more criminally murderous, is the part that the City Council at Nauvoo took in getting up the ordinance which resulted in the destruction of the Expositor press. And I wish here to name the fact that the principal instigators in getting up that ordinance were men who feared the revelations that this organ (Expositor) was about to make of their secret and ungodly doings to the world. The persons who were most conspicuous in the work, and were the means of bringing on the scenes that finally resulted in the bloody tragedy which took place at Carthage Jail were no other than John Taylor and Willard Richards, who by constant importunities prevailed upon your father to sign his own death warrant by placing his name to that accursed ordinance which resulted in his death and the death of your Uncle Hyrum.

To these importunities of Richards and Taylor I was a witness, and was present when Richards brought in the book containing the ordinance and asked for your father's signature to make it a law in the City of Nauvoo. I remonstrated with Richards at the time, against my brother Joseph putting his name down in such a place, as it would most certainly result in his death. Richards, failing to secure your father's name at this time, both he and Taylor called on your father the next morning, with feigned tears of desperation, expatiating upon the great necessity of having that Expositor removed, as a means to the further growth and prosperity not only of the City of Nauvoo, but of the cause of the Church abroad. Thus these men, with the sophistry of their lying tongues, like wolves in sheep's clothing, ensnared the prophet from off his watch tower, and led him as a lamb to the slaughter, they promising, also, to be his assistants in case he should fall into trouble, as a result of his name being placed to that ordinance. This accounts for the whys and the wherefores, that Taylor and Richards were both in the jail at the time your father and your uncle Hyrum were murdered. The principal reasons why these conspirators against your father's life did not suffer the same fate that your father and your uncle Hyrum did, are because, like cowards they hid themselves away -- Taylor under a bed that was in the room where the prisoners were confined and Richards behind the door. Thus you see, by the secret workings and secret doings of these men for years gone by, the Church was robbed of her prophet and patriarch, by a most hellish plot that had been in vogue for not only months, but years previous to the time of their deaths. When I see men whose finger stains show positive signs of their guilt in the death of the martyrs, now reveling in the spoils of the Church robbed from the innocent and unsuspecting saints, I cannot restrain my pen from writing the facts and incidents that I do know before God and man were the means of your father and uncle Hyrum's death.

There is one more fact I will notice and that is, that however strange or great the testimony that might be brought against these men, John Taylor and others, in this murderous affair, the Utah Mormons would not credit it though one rose from the dead to bear witness of it, and as for the redemption of any from their blindness, who have willingly given their names in support of this great apostasy, I am in much doubt that there are many who will be saved or forsake the great error they have fallen into.

And especially do I believe this in regard to the remnants of the Smith family in Utah, whose chances for knowing the erroneous position they are in, and with ample proof from the Word of God that their whole system of church organization is founded in corruption and fraud; and still they persist in their unholy alliance with that apostate and God-forsaken people. "There are none so blind as those who will not see."

This then, is the end of this epistle, and I conclude with many good wishes to you and to all good saints.

Your brother in bonds of love.      Wm. B. Smith.

Kingston, Caldwell Co., Mo., March 25th, 1879.